MW00838156

The Legendary
MODEL A FORD

---

*The ultimate history of one of
America's great automobiles*

PETER WINNEWISSER

© 1999 by
Peter Winnewisser

All rights reserved.
No portion of this publication may be reproduced or transmitted in any form or by any means,
electronic or mechanical, including photocopy, recording, or any information storage and retrieval
system, without permission in writing from the publisher, except by a reviewer who may quote brief
passages in a critical article or review to be printed in a magazine or newspaper,
or electronically transmitted on radio or television.

Published by

**krause
publications**

700 E. State Street • Iola, WI 54990-0001
Telephone: 715/445-2214

Please call or write for our free catalog.
Our toll-free number to place an order or obtain a free catalog is 800-258-0929
or please use our regular business telephone 715-445-2214
for editorial comment and further information.

Library of Congress Catalog Number: 99-61148
ISBN: 0-87341-615-5

Printed in the United States of America

Contents

Front cover Model A photos	**Rear cover Model A photos**
The author's 1930 Standard Fordor - Peter Winnewisser photo	1931 Town Sedan, 20 millionth Ford - *Old Cars Weekly* photo
Indiana dealership with 1930 Tudor and 1931 Coupe - Henry Ford Museum & Greenfield Village photo	1928 Speedster - Joe Tedesco photo
1929 Roadster - Long Island Auto Museum photo	1931 A-400 and 1930 Station Wagon with F101 military planes - U. S. Air Force photo
1931 Pickup - Florence Williams photo	

Introduction

To fully grasp the significance of the Model A Ford and its place in history, it is necessary to look beyond the sheet metal to the people whose lives it has touched. That is the story that I have tried to tell. This book is a social history of the car; its development, the workers who made it, the dealers who sold it, and the people who bought and drove it in the days when it was truly "The New Ford." Beyond that, it is the story of men and women who are keeping the Model A alive today. To all these people, past and present, I dedicate this book.

During the past two years, which I have devoted happily to the Model A Ford, there have been many people, too numerous to mention by name, who have contributed to this effort. I thank each and every one for their contributions that have helped make this book a reality.

In particular, I would like to thank my wife, Claire, and daughter, Amy, who have been unfailing in their enthusiasm and support these many months; Wally Towne of Rome, New York, who graciously shared material from his collection along with advice and insights on the Model A Ford; Dr. David Lewis of the University of Michigan whose encouragement and support has been unwavering these many years; Linda Skolarus and the staff of the Henry Ford Research Center for their most generous and courteous help with my research. I would also like to thank my book editor Ron Kowalke and John Gunnell, editor of *Old Cars Weekly*, who have been so willing to guide and assist me.

This book is the culmination of two years of research and writing, and forty years of gathering information and experiencing the thrill of owning, driving and enjoying my own Model A Ford. Although I have made every effort to be accurate, I realize only too well my fallibility, and take full responsibility for any errors that may have, regrettably, crept in. I also realize that what I have written is only the tip of the iceberg, so to speak, in recording how the Model A Ford has been involved in the lives of people around the globe.

In their ground-breaking book, *The Ford Model "A"* George DeAngelis, Edward P. Francis and Leslie R. Henry write: "Model A's popularity stems partly from its sentimental value to many who came to know and use it before World War II. Its popularity is as enduring as the car itself and this very durability, which makes the car still available, also inspires confidence and continues it in use despite its advanced age." Those words, written originally in 1971, still ring true almost thirty years later.

For a brief time, Model A met every expectation—it had power, speed, comfort, safety and appearance. It became a best seller and then departed rather abruptly. Yet, it has endured to this day, as no other car ever made. And so, I give you the legendary Model A Fords. May they live forever!

Peter Winnewisser

Foreword

"The 1996 Taurus is the most important vehicle Ford has ever launched," Ford Division's national advertising manager grandly proclaimed in 1995. On the contrary, that vehicle is the Model A. The '96 Taurus, like the A's predecessor, the Model T, was introduced at a time when the company had other successful models. But the A was all Ford had to sell, or could hope to sell, except for a few thousand Lincolns. Henry Ford bet his company on the Model A.

Fortunately, the A's launch and success exceeded the highest of expectations. Its introductory publicity and advertising campaigns remain a benchmark against which all new-car and other product launches are measured and found wanting. The number of people who flocked to public showrooms, convention halls, assembly plants, and dealers to see the new car has never been equaled. In addition, the vehicle, contrary to claims for the Ford Fairmont, still holds the industry-wide record for first-year sales. Also, the A, along with the T, remains the only vehicle to have outsold all General Motors lines combined.

Although the A was produced for only four years, it is generally rated by auto historians, publications, and others as one of the greatest cars of all time. In 1973, it was rated the seventh best American car by a *Life* panel of historians, designers, and collectors. In 1986, "Henry's Lady" was ranked by the *Detroit News* as "one of the ten most important and influential cars of all time." It also has been named to *Motor Trend*'s Hall of Fame and appears on lists of the ten most economical and dependable cars.

The Model A continues to be well publicized. Indeed, it often receives more annual press than many vehicles now in production.

Many news stories describe novel ways in which the Model A is used. One serves as Georgia Tech's official mascot, the "Ramblin' Wreck of Georgia Tech"; another ran drugs in Detroit until confiscated by the police in 1993. An A was driven cross-country by a blindfolded magician; a pink A shuttled guests between a Detroit hotel and the city's convention center; and another A provided transportation for residents of a suburban Detroit retirement home.

Other news stories, as this book notes, cite the car's ruggedness, durability, and long-distance trips. In 1937, a Model A plunged through the ice of Idaho's Lake Couer d'Alene. Forty-seven years later, two hours after the car was raised and equipped with a new battery, its engine, horn, and headlights performed perfectly. In 1972, a national news story reported that a 1931 South Carolina Model A was in its thirty-second year as a postal delivery vehicle. In 1986, a 1931 pickup, bought new, still served a Wisconsin farm family. A bemused 85-year-old Illinoisian wondered whether he or his Model A would outlive the other.

Abroad, two New Zealanders made news as they drove their Model A through Southern Asia and Europe to Great Britain's National Motor Museum; and New Zealand honeymooners delighted romantics by shipping their A to America's West Coast, then driving it 10,500 miles through the United States and Canada. Three Argentinians made headlines by motoring

from Buenos Aires to New York, and in 1988, a Michigan couple drove their Model A around Australia's 13,000-mile shoreline.

Thus, the Model A continues to make history and delight A lovers, old-car enthusiasts, and the general public alike.

I met Peter Winnewisser at a Franklin meet in his hometown, Cazenovia, New York, in the early-1970s, by which time he had been driving and researching the A for fifteen years or so. We continued to meet through the years, mostly at Hershey, and I increasingly came to appreciate him as a dedicated old-car enthusiast, a meticulous researcher, a man most willing to share his knowledge and treasures, and a gentleman of the first rank. Impressed by Peter's superb qualifications, I reinforced his desire to write a book on his favorite car. His dream is now fulfilled, and all admirers of the A—and that includes everyone who has seen one—are forever in his debt.

David L. Lewis
Ann Arbor, Michigan
April 1999

Chapter One

1927: The Beginning

On May 26, 1927, each of the 10,000 Ford dealers in the United States received the following telegram printed here exactly as it was received by Cazenovia, New York, dealer D.D. Norton, Inc.:

"Starting early production entirely new Ford car announcing Thursday new model superior design and performance to any now in low price light car field - stop - Mr. Henry Ford states new model recognizes that present conditions make further refinements in motor car construction desirable - stop - new model has speed style flexibility and control in traffic more costly to manufacture but more economical to operate - stop - Model T will continue important part of factory production for ten million owners requiring replacements and service - stop - give no information about details until you receive plan for your part in supplying public description.

Edsel B. Ford

The telegram was followed by a letter dated May 25, from W.A. Ryan, manager of sales for Ford, who sent dealers a copy of the complete new car announcement released to morning newspapers on May 26 and a warning that "under no circumstances are details of the new Ford car to be given out to anyone."

Clearly, this announcement was not a surprise. The demand for more style, greater comfort, more power and mechanical refinements had been weaning buyers away from the Model T for some time. As Ford's grip on the market weakened, competitors were getting stronger. In 1926, Ford's worldwide sales were down almost 450,000 units from the peak year of 1923. At the same time Chevrolet production increased by over twenty-nine percent. Ford's portion of total sales fell from forty-eight percent in 1924 to thirty percent in 1926.

The great debate that had raged for months in Ford executive offices as to whether or not it was time for the venerable Model T to go, and public speculation about what Ford would do, were now ended. These would be replaced by six months of intense interest across the country, and throughout the world, about the new model. But the reality is that, in May 1926, no one in the Ford Motor Co., not even Henry Ford himself, knew for cer-

tain exactly what the new car would be like or when it would be ready.

Now that the die had been cast and Model T's reign had come to an end, there were three tasks to be accomplished as soon as possible. These were to design the new car, retool the factory and assembly plants and reorganize the sales force to market it.

In *My Forty Years With Ford*, production boss Charles Sorensen says that "clearing the design and getting into production took only 90 days" after the May announcement. This was possible only because some preliminary work had already been done. Although the exact chronol-

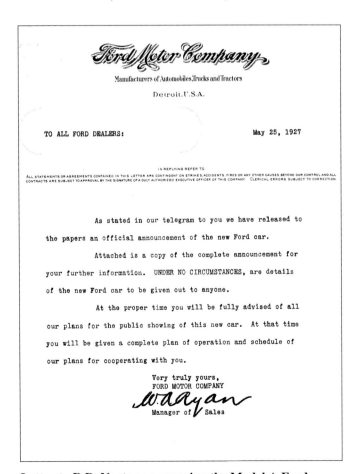

Letter to D.D. Norton announcing the Model A Ford.

For Release in the Morning Papers of May 26, 1927

Detroit, May 25—Early production of a new Ford car superior in design and performance to any now available in the low-priced, light-car field, was announced today by the Ford Motor Company.

Henry Ford, designer of the car, and Edsel Ford, president of the Company, both stated that within the next few weeks they will give a complete description of the new model.

The famous Model T Ford, which still leads the automobile industry after twenty years of manufacture, will continue to be a substantial factor in Ford production, in view of the fact that about ten million cars of this model are still in use and will require replacement parts and service.

"The Model T Ford car was a pioneer," said Henry Ford today. "There was no conscious public need of motor cars when we first made it. There were few good roads. This car blazed the way for the motor industry and started the movement for good roads everywhere. It is still the pioneer car in many parts of the world which are just beginning to be motorized. But conditions in this country have so greatly changed that further refinement in motor car construction is now desirable and our new model is a recognition of this.

"Besides the Model T itself, another revolutionary element which the Ford Motor Company introduced twenty years ago was the idea of service. Some of the early manufacturers proceeded on the theory that once they had induced a man to buy a car they had him at their mercy; they charged him the highest possible price for necessary replacements. Our company adopted the opposite theory. We believed that when a man bought one of our cars we should keep it running for him as long as we could and at the lowest upkeep cost. That was the origin of Ford service.

"The Model T was one of the largest factors in creating the conditions which now make the new model Ford possible. The world-wide influence of the Ford car in the building of good roads and in teaching the people the use and value of mechanical power is conceded. Nowadays everybody runs some kind of motor power but twenty years ago only the adventurous few could be induced to try an automobile. It had a harder time winning public confidence than the airplane has now. The Model T was a great educator in this respect. It had stamina and power. It was the car that ran before there were good roads to run on. It broke down the barriers of distance in rural sections, brought people of these sections closer together and placed education within the reach of everyone. We are all still proud of the Model T Ford car. If we were not we could not have continued to manufacture it so long.

"With the new Ford we propose to continue in the light-car field which we created on the same basis of quantity production we have always worked, giving high quality, low price and constant service. We began work on this new model several years ago. In fact, the idea of a new car has been in my mind much longer than that. But the sale of the Model T continued at such a pace that there never seemed to be an opportunity to get the new car started. Even now the business is so brisk that we are up against the proposition of keeping the factory going on one model while we tool up for another. I am glad of this because it will not necessitate a total shut-down. Only a comparatively few men will be out at a time while their departments are being tooled up for the new product. At one time it looked as if 70,000 men might be laid off temporarily, but we have now scaled that down to less than 25,000 at a time. The lay-off will be brief, because we need the men and we have no time to waste.

"At present I can only say this about the new model—it has speed, style, flexibility and control in traffic. There is nothing quite like it in quality and price. The new car will cost more to manufacture, *but it will be more economical to operate.*"

News release sent to Ford dealers, May 26, 1927.

An early, possibly pre-production engine (no number). Note the powerhouse generator with cadmium-plated back cover and generator on top. (Photo courtesy of Henry Ford Museum and Greenfield Village)

ogy is "hazy," as Allan Nevins and Frank Ernest Hill put it in *Ford Expansion and Challenge 1915-1933*, it appears that Ford issued an oral order to proceed with design of a new four-cylinder car about August 1926, although some work may have been done before that. Lawrence Sheldrick, one of the key men involved in bringing the Model A to life, notes in his oral "Reminiscences" that there was an existing drawing showing some special work being done, which was dated May 3, 1926.

In December, drawings for the body-layout were begun and the first blueprints were available sometime in January 1927. Sheldrick says that there is a sketch in the Ford Archives, dated December 20, 1926, of a body layout on the Model A that shows the gas tank in the cowl. "That was one of Mr. Ford's insistences at the time," he says. By March a chassis with a bucket seat was being driven about, but there was still much to be accomplished.

The new model's basic dimensions were determined by the Fords. "Edsel and I," stated Henry Ford, "decided on the wheelbase and size right away. . . after that it was a matter of working things out on the drawing board until

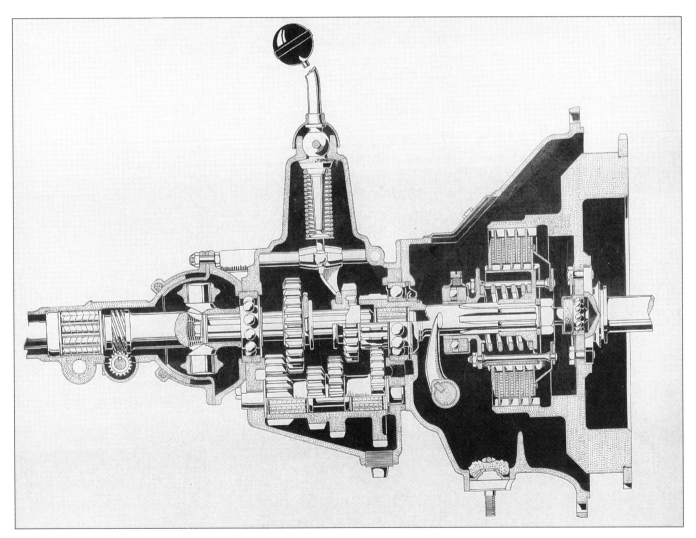

Model A clutch and transmission. Shows multiple disc clutch, installed until November 1928. (Photo courtesy of Henry Ford Museum and Greenfield Village)

Early Model A chassis. (Photo courtesy of Henry Ford Museum and Greenfield Village)

we got them right." The overall length of the chassis was set at 113-7/16 inches and the wheelbase at 103-1/2 inches. At the insistence of Edsel the car-height with a clearance of 9-1/2 inches would be three-quarters of an inch lower than that of a Model T.

To design and develop the new car, Henry Ford relied on the Ford engineering department (thirty-four engineers at that time), his son, and a key group of seven employees: Joseph Galamb who worked on the body and frame in close harmony with Edsel Ford; Eugene Farkas who moved from overall design coordination to special tasks such as the dash, axles, brakes, shocks and other mechanical details; Frank Johnson, clutch and transmission; Lawrence Sheldrick, engine, chassis and, eventually, project director; Harold Hicks, engine and exhaust system; Rouge production bosses Peter Martin and Charles Sorensen.

Also contributing, although in lesser capacities, were J.L. McCloud who was in charge of chemical and metallurgical research and William Klann who helped solve production problems on the assembly lines. These men, controlled and guided by Henry Ford, were largely responsible for the Model A Ford.

Edsel Ford was heavily involved in styling the car both inside and out. It was Edsel who devised the various color settings and he is credited with the idea of placing a grille on the front end. His contributions were significant enough to cause his father to comment favorably, "We've got a pretty good man in my son. He knows style—how a car ought to look. And he has mechanical horse sense, too."

There are a number of fascinating stories about the development of the Model A. In April 1927, Harold Hicks was called from his work in aircraft engineering to a meeting with Edsel Ford and Rouge production bosses Charles Sorensen and Peter Martin. They showed Hicks a 203 cubic inch displacement engine that was only developing twenty-two horsepower and asked him how much he could get out of the engine. After a few calculations Hicks told them that he could get forty horsepower and that it would take about three weeks to do the job.

Given the assignment, Hicks, working closely with Carl Schultz, concentrated on changing the manifold and carburetor. He also opened up the passages around the exhaust valve and changed the shape of the gasket. Within three weeks the engine was developing the promised forty horsepower. After exhaustive dynamometer testing even Henry Ford was convinced that Hicks had kept his promise.

According to Hicks, the Model A engine had a quick take off. "Up to thirty miles an hour," he says in his "Reminiscences," "the Model A could skin the pants off anything that was on the road." He recalls the chief engineer at Packard calling him and saying, "Hicks, what are you fellows out there trying to do? You really have just made us look silly below thirty miles an hour because we can't catch these Model As."

Hicks was also involved in the use of the Zenith carburetor. While working on the development of the engines on the stand he would needle Charles Sorensen,

"Of course, we are developing 40 horsepower, but you'll never use the Zenith carburetor." After a week, this got under Sorensen's skin and he said to Hicks, "Why in hell do you keep telling me we won't use the Zenith carburetor? By God, we are going to use the Zenith carburetors. You get the Zenith Company in."

On instructions from Henry Ford to reduce the number of bolts holding the carburetor together, Hicks had the Zenith Company design a carburetor with only two bolts rather than fourteen little screws. When he proudly took the design to Ford he was sent back with, "Two is too many. Make just one bolt!" And that's why the famous Model A carburetor has only a single bolt down through it.

While running economy, speed and acceleration tests on the four carburetors under consideration for the Model A (Holley, Zenith, Stromberg, and Kingston), Hicks was seated in the front seat of a car being driven at about fifty mph. He had a little gas tank in front of him, which they were using for the economy test. About an eighth of a mile ahead they saw a Model T car waiting to make a left turn. Hicks describes what happened next.

"Just as we were getting ready to pass this fellow, he turned directly in front of us. The cars hit; we head on, and he at an angle. That was a terrific crash. When I finally woke up, we were in the ditch. The engine had been driven back under my feet because we had 750 pounds of lead in the back seat in addition to the three men to run the complete tests for the thing. That was quite a crash.

"I had gone through the windshield. My arm was bleeding. It was all cut open in the forearm. I came to

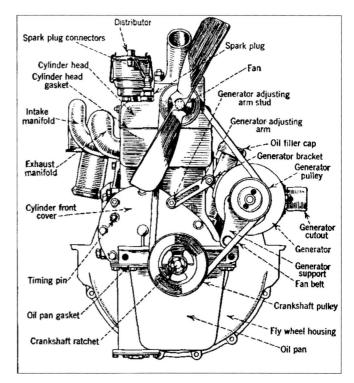

Front view of engine (October 1928 or earlier).

before the other fellows did. The door of the car was open, and I crawled out of that car. I was a terrible looking mess."

Later, the two Fords, looking at the wreck of the car, decided that laminated (safety) glass would be used in the Model A windshield. "My crash and going through the windshield," Hicks says, "probably saved the lives of a good many people."

As can be seen, Hicks' contributions to Model A were considerable but that did not guarantee recognition at Ford. In his "Reminiscences," Al Esper, an associate of Hicks, writes, "this man was never given much credit for what he had done. . .they just said 'thank you' for the job, and he went back on the aircraft job. It wasn't too long before the Aircraft folded up, and they let him go along with it. I could never figure out why he got such a deal."

Hicks himself believed that Henry Ford did not like him because Ford "resented the fact that I had done something that had helped him out. All along from that time on, Ford and men working on the car would take trips out into the country, and he would never invite me to go along although I had charge of the development of the engine and ran the tests in the car and so forth." At the time Hicks worked on the engine he was being paid $600 a month, but received no raise that year. Lawrence Sheldrick, working on a less important job, was raised from $400 to $1,000 a month.

Although Edsel's work on the Model A brought an admission from his father that he was talented, there were clashes between the two men over the car's development. For example, the two Fords did not see eye to eye on the transmission and brakes for the new car. Henry wanted to stick with the Model T planetary trans-mission and Model T brakes while Edsel wanted a different transmission and new-style brakes. Eventually, Edsel's thinking won out. The Model A was equipped with a sliding-gear transmission and brakes with balanced pressure on all four wheels, but the battle was not won easily.

Charles Sorensen writes that at one time there was so much tension between the two men, that Henry told Sorensen to tell his son to go to California and stay there until ordered to come back. Sorensen delayed relaying the message and in a few days the situation eased and father and son were back on speaking terms, at least for

Cartoon "The Suspense is Awful." (Photo courtesy of *The Ford Dealer News*, September 10, 1927)

Cartoon "Propaganda." (Photo courtesy of *The Ford Dealer News*, June 4, 1927)

a while. "It was this struggle between father and son," writes Sorensen, "that was the chief reason for the delay in bringing out Model A."

As reported by Nevins and Hill, the addition of hydraulic shock absorbers to the Model A was the result of a test run by Henry Ford through a rough field bumping over stones and fallen timbers. At the end of the run Ford got out of the car and commented, "Rides too hard. Put on hydraulic shock absorbers."

In his "Reminiscences," Eugene Farkas says that Ford asked him about shock absorbers and he recommended Houdaille shock absorbers as the best and also most expensive on the market. With that Ford said, "That's what we want." The Model A was the first low-priced car equipped with shock absorbers as standard equipment and this feature was a key factor in providing for passenger comfort. Farkas says that the Houdaille shock absorbers cost the company one dollar apiece.

Typically, for Ford, the development of the new car's components was largely a system of trial and error. "For the men who designed the car," say Nevins and Hill, "the work was a long nightmare of nerve-racking absorption in design, experiment, rejection, and fresh experiment."

In the *New York Times*, Waldemar Kaempffert writes "As parts of the new car were fashioned, they were turned over to the testing staff with hardly a word. The testers proceeded to crush, twist, bend, and pound. They

Cartoon "When Rumor Gets Through With It." (Photo courtesy of Henry Ford Museum and Greenfield Village)

sent back transmission gears out of which they had succeeded in tearing teeth, and rear axles which they had reduced to junk. No suggestion of a possible method of making a part stronger or shaping it more nicely to suit its purpose, nothing but the battered part and the baldest statement of what happened in the testing machine. The designers made their own deductions and began anew. Thus engines, transmissions, axles, steering gears were tossed back and forth."

The car that emerged from this intense, relatively brief period was different and better than Model T. There were a number of innovations incorporated into it. Among these Sheldrick singles out the use of stainless steel, shatterproof glass, the fuel tank as part of the cowl and Houdaille hydraulic shock absorbers.

Using stainless steel for the bright parts was initially opposed by Sheldrick because of the cost. Thinking that the pressure for stainless was coming from Sorensen and Martin, Sheldrick argued about it heatedly until one day Henry Ford said to him, "Don't argue with those fellows about that. That's my idea and I want it." End of discussion.

Making the fuel tank part of the body, the upper half of the cowl, required the development of new techniques in electric seam welding and new equipment for its manufacture. Sheldrick says that it was criticized by everyone in the industry as a fire hazard. Several state regulating boards objected to it and he recalls trips made to those states to try to reassure their regulating bodies that danger didn't exist, although, he says, "we knew in our hearts that it did."

The Model A prototype was put together by hand using sixteen-gauge black iron, according to Thomas Alexander, who worked on the car. His comments are quoted in "Ford Country" by David L. Lewis. The work was done in the "white room" at the Highland Park Plant, so-called because it was a top security project surrounded by white curtains.

Prior to the May 26 announcement of the new Ford, there were rumors about the end of Model T but little in the way of hard information from the company either to Ford dealers or the general public. A February 9 letter to Buffalo Branch dealers appeals to them to have "faith and confidence" as they wonder what the ultimate plans of the company will be.

The letter urges dealers to read an article by Samuel Crowther in the *Review of Reviews*, which discusses the rumors circulating about Ford's plans. A reading of the article leaves the impression that while some changes are being contemplated, an all-new car is not being considered. But, shortly after, in mid-February, Ford admitted publicly for the first time that he was considering a new car.

On April 1, 1927, the car distributor from the Green Island, New York, Ford branch sent a letter to D.D. Norton of Cazenovia, New York, acknowledging Norton's request to cancel cars previously requested for April. The letter also addresses the issue of rumors and

states that "we have no definite knowledge concerning change in our products." Regarding the rumors, the letter quotes from an *Automotive Daily News* editorial of March 18th that mentions rumors as wild as Ford giving away his cars and making a profit on selling replacement parts and says that there is "no end to these sporadic outbursts, and, no matter how obviously foolish the rumor, each one obtains brief credence in some quarters. Meanwhile, Henry Ford seems to accept all the uproar philosophically and goes about his very considerable business undisturbed."

From May 26 into early December an eager world waited, wondered and speculated about what the new Ford would be like. The "complete description of the new car" promised in a few weeks after the May announcement did not materialize. Rumors were even more fanciful than before the announcement and ran the gamut from Ford was producing a twelve-cylinder car, an electric or a diesel, to the car had wooden pistons, to Ford was in despair because the car was a disappointment.

Amateur and press photographers vied with each other for photos but, despite their best efforts only two authentic photos were published. One by the *Automotive Daily News* when a representative found a sales promotion folder containing a picture of the Model A, and the other by the *Brighton* (Michigan) *Argus* whose reporter stumbled by chance on a new Ford parked in his town.

During this time there were experimental cars out and about, although few people who saw them, if any, realized what they were. Sheldrick says that one of Henry Ford's favorite trips to test the new Ford was from Detroit to Clair, Michigan, and back, a distance of about three hundred miles. Before the official announcement, before anyone had a picture, Sheldrick recalls Henry Ford telling him to take his family on a weekend trip in one of the experimental cars. "We ought to see what womenfolk think about it," Ford said.

On a Saturday morning, Sheldrick loaded his family into the Model A and drove to visit a friend in Three Rivers, Michigan. The car got little attention on the way up and it wasn't until Sunday, about an hour before they were ready to leave, that word got out that one of the new Fords was in town. People started gathering around the garage where Sheldrick had hidden the car so he got out of there as quickly as possible.

On the way home, one of the front wheel bearings started to squeal and smoke probably because it had been adjusted too tight. Praying that he could make it back to Dearborn, Sheldrick eased down on the speed and was finally able to get home. However, this time the car was noticed. "I haven't figured out to this day why he (Ford) specifically told me to make that pre-announcement exposure," Sheldrick says. "This was about three weeks before the formal announcement. No one got photographs, but there were a lot of people who tried to run along the side and look at it on the way into Detroit."

In the meantime, Ford's "Golden Silence," as historian David Lewis in *The Public Image of Henry Ford* has characterized the lack of information from Ford, only served to elevate the suspense and mystery to fever pitch and keep the coming of the new Ford, as well as speculation about its success or failure, very much in the news. The Sunday, June 26, *New York Times* featured a lengthy article about Ford's reversal from first place in 1924 with forty-eight percent of the total to second place and a steadily dwindling production in 1927, and headlined it, "Ford's New Car Keeps Motor World Guessing." In its August 1927 issue, *Reader's Digest* condensed a *Review*

Cartoon "In The Higher Brackets of Publicity." (Photo courtesy of Henry Ford Museum and Greenfield Village)

of Reviews article that states that "the new Ford will be either an ineffective gesture or the beginning of a new era in automobile manufacturing."

Finally, on August 10, the company ended its silence with a simple, but only slightly informative announcement from Edsel Ford: "The new Ford automobile is an accomplished fact. The engineering problems affecting its design and equipment and affecting also its manufacture have all been solved. The tests already made show it is faster, smoother, more rugged and more flexible than we had hoped for in the early stages of designing." *Time* magazine reported that Edsel claimed the car had run 27 miles the first half-hour, 56.1 miles the first hour, 110 miles in two hours. Top speed was 65 mph. Gas and oil consumption were "less. . .than any of our previous models."

Two weeks later a letter to Ford dealers from their branches informed them they would shortly receive a folder containing advertising to cover the interim leading up to the arrival of the new car. The keynote of this advertising would be, "Wait For The New Ford." Dealers were advised that getting this slogan before the public in every conceivable way would "greatly increase the curiosity and interest which is now being manifested throughout the country and strengthen your position when the new car does arrive."

During the months of waiting after the end of the Model T, the Ford Motor Co. was faced with the formidable task of converting its production facilities for the new model. It was, said the company in-house organ *Ford News*, "an industrial task which in magnitude and complexity surpasses any similar task the world has yet known." The *New York Times* credited the changeover as "probably the biggest replacement of plants in the history of American industry."

Converting to the Model A involved developing the River Rouge (Fordson) plant into the primary factory for Model A car and truck production and overhauling thirty-four assembly plants in the United States and Canada, twelve overseas factories and numerous shops of the independent suppliers. Eventually there would be thirty-six domestic (including Canada) and seventeen overseas plants assembling the Model A or parts of it.

At a cost of $250,000,000, the Ford Motor Co., in five months, made changes more sweeping than had taken place in nineteen years of Model T production. Factory space amounting to 1-1/2 million square feet was added. The new car and its 5,580 parts called for changes all

Assembly line.

along the line: in design, in materials, in construction, in production methods and machines. That meant moving, eliminating, changing or replacing better than 40,000 machines, forcing the company, Henry Ford said, "to get rid of or materially alter seventy percent of our machinery." At the same time the company had to bring back thousands of workers laid off when Model T production ended and give new training to about 200,000 workmen. It was indeed a formidable task.

One example of a new unit was a group of six huge power presses used to shape frames for the new Ford chassis. The largest of these were more than thirty feet high and weighed 480,000 pounds each. Others were taller but weighed less. With its die in place one of the largest pair weighed 536,000 pounds. These new presses stood in pits from ten to fifteen feet deep. Even more amazing were the more than sixty miles of conveyors, an ever increasing maze that gradually and efficiently moved their flow of parts from machine to machine and from department to department until they reached their common destination—the final assembly line.

Among the more radical advances was the body department, which allowed bodies to be handled by conveyors, hoists, elevators and transfer tables and did not require the use of body trucks as in Model T production. This meant that loading, unloading, switching and moving 2,500 freight cars a year would be eliminated. Additionally, the new body system with its more than twenty-seven miles of conveyors, allowed for the assembly of all

types of Model A bodies on a single line rather than separate body lines for the different types as at the Highland Park plant.

In human terms, the workers paid a steep price for the Model A. In a 1955 pamphlet, *We Work At Fords*, the UAW-CIO describes what happened. "When the plant started up again after the big Model T shutdown, most of the 60,000 workers Ford had laid off six months to a year earlier asked for their jobs back. Foremen and superintendents were hired back in, if they were hired, as production workers. Many of the older men were not taken back at all. Men who had worked up to seven or eight dollar a day scales were taken back on at five or six dollars a day. Office workers were given their choice between production jobs and nothing.

"When the workers got back in the plant they found, according to a report in *Forbes* magazine, 'It is nothing but a continual speedup and driving from Monday morning to Wednesday or Thursday night. . .the men and women on the way home from work slump down in the buses and street cars so near dead that they often go a half mile beyond their destination.'"

At the beginning of October, *Ford News* said that the final assembly line had been transferred to the Rouge and was "now practically ready to begin assembly operations." The space used for this line was about one-half that at Highland Park, but the capacity remained the same. Shortly after, on October 11, Edsel Ford announced that the new vehicle would begin production within a few days

One of the first 200 Model A Fords, a Tudor. Note the open end bumpers. Dated November 12, 1927. (Photo courtesy of John Conde)

One of the earliest 1928 models with open end bumpers. (Photo courtesy of AACA Library and Research Center)

An early 1928 Phaeton. Note absence of door handles. Dated November 23, 1927.

and that 125,000 down payments had already been received. By mid-October, the Rouge was producing parts and about one hundred-fifty hand-made experimental cars (most without bodies) had been road-tested.

Finally, late in the afternoon of October 20, 1927, the first Model A engine was numbered by Henry Ford with a hand stamp and machine hammer. The next day this engine was incorporated into a Tudor sedan and driven to the Dearborn laboratories and put through ten days of testing and inspection. In the meantime the assembly lines were silent. On November 1, the word was given to resume production and new Fords crept off the lines at about twenty a day.

The first Model A chassis and engine number one was eventually given to Thomas Edison by Henry Ford. Writing in *Model "A" News* (January-February 1974), Randy Mason of the Henry Ford Museum, says that at Edison's request a touring car body was installed and the car delivered to Edison in June 1928. This car is now in the collection of the Henry Ford Museum. Edison was involved with at least one other Model A. On December 19, 1927, he drove off the line the first Model A turned out of the Kearny, New Jersey, assembly plant. A photo of the car and Edison can be found in *The American Ford*, by Lorin Sorensen.

Not everyone agrees that the first Model A went to Edison. For example, an article in *Ford Dealer & Service Field* (March 1931) about movie stars and Ford cars, claims that Beverly Hills Motors Inc., of Beverly Hills, California, delivered the first Model A in the United States to world-famous comedian, Will Rogers.

Henry Ford numbers the first Model A engine, October 20, 1927. (Photo courtesy of Henry Ford Museum and Greenfield Village)

THOSE DOUBTFUL MODEL T OWNERS

Tell 'Em You Will Always Carry Parts for Their Service

Reassure some of your doubtful car owners as to the service they will get on their model T in a letter something like that we reprint below and which was written by L. W. Shanesy and Co., dealers at Chicago. It will help: Many owners of the present model and now discontinued Ford cars have been wondering what service facilities would be available to them during the next few years. It is our intention to maintain our repair and parts departments for these cars on exactly the same basis in the future as in the past, taking care of all Model T passenger cars and Model TT trucks just as long as our customers need this service. The new model Ford cars will be on display almost immediately—fast, powerful, beautiful, more economical to operate and mechanically redesigned throughout. On the day they arrive we will notify you of the fact, in order that you may lose no time in examining this result of Mr. Ford's indisputable superiority in the greatest of automobile production.

Column regarding sales of Model T parts: "Those Doubtful Model T Owners" from *The Ford Dealer News*, September 10, 1927.

THE NEW FORD CAR

An announcement of unusual importance to every automobile owner

by HENRY FORD

"NINETEEN years ago we made and sold the first Model T Ford car. In announcing it to the public we said:

"'We will build a motor car for the great multitude. It will be large enough for the family, but small enough for the individual to run and care for. It will be constructed of the best materials, by the best men to be hired, after the simplest designs modern engineering can devise. But it will be so low in price that no man making a good salary will be unable to own one.'

"If I were starting in business today, or asked to restate my policy, I would not change one sentence or one word of that original announcement. In plain, simple language it gives the reason for the very existence of the Ford Motor Company and explains its growth.

"IN THE last nineteen years we have made 15,000,000 Ford cars and added to the world nearly 300,000,000 mobile horse-power. Yet I do not consider the machines which bear my name simply as machines. I take them as concrete evidence of the working out of a theory of business which I hope is something more than a theory of business—a theory that looks toward making this world a better place in which to live.

"The Model T Ford car was a pioneer. There was no conscious public need of motor cars when we first conceived it. There were few good roads and only the adventurous few could be induced to buy an automobile.

"The Ford car blazed the way for the motor industry and started the movement for good roads. It broke down the barriers of time and distance and helped to place education within the reach of all. It gave people more leisure. It helped people everywhere to do more and better work in less time and enjoy doing it. It did a great deal, I am sure, to promote the growth and progress of this country.

"We are still proud of the record of the Model T Ford car. If we were not, we would not have continued to manufacture it so long. But 1927 is not 1908. It is not 1915. It is not even 1926.

We have built a new car to meet modern conditions

"We realize that conditions in this country have so greatly changed in the last few years that further refinement in motor car construction is desirable. So we have built a new car. To put it simply—we have built a new and different Ford to meet new and different conditions.

"We believe the new Ford car, which will be officially announced on Friday of this week, is as great an improvement in motor car building as the Model T Ford was in 1908.

Smart new low lines and beautiful colors

"The new Ford is more than a car for the requirements of today. It goes farther than that. It anticipates the needs of 1928, of 1929, of 1930.

"The new Ford car is radically different from Model T. Yet the basic Ford principles of economy of production and quality of product have been retained. There is nothing quite like the new Ford anywhere in quality and price.

"The new Ford has exceptional beauty of line and color because beauty of line and color has come to be considered, and I think rightly, a necessity in a motor car today. Equally important is the mechanical beauty of the engine. Let us not forget this mechanical beauty when we consider the beauty of the new Ford.

"The new Ford has unusual speed for a low-price car because present-day conditions require unusual speed.

"The world moves more quickly than it used to. There are only so many hours in the day and there is much to be done.

"Fifty and sixty miles an hour are desired today where thirty and forty would have satisfied in 1908. So we are giving you this new speed.

Quiet and smooth-running at all speeds

"The new Ford will ride comfortably at fifty and sixty miles an hour. It has actually done sixty-five miles an hour in road tests.

"Since modern conditions demand more speed, they also demand better brakes to balance this speed. So we are giving you four-wheel brakes in the new Ford.

"The new Ford will be quiet and smooth-running at all speeds and you will find it even easier to handle in traffic than the old Model T Ford.

"The new Ford has durability because durability is the very heart of motor car value. The Ford car has always been known as a car that will take you there and bring you back. The new Ford will not only do that, but it will do it in good style. You will be proud of the new Ford.

"THIS new Ford car has not been planned and made in a day. Our engineers began work on it several years ago and it has been in my mind much longer than that. We make automobiles quickly when we get in production. But we take a long time planning them. Nothing can hurry us in that. We spent twelve years in perfecting our former Model T Ford car before we offered it to the public. It is not conceivable that we should have put this new Ford car on the market until we were sure that it was mechanically correct in every detail.

"Every part of it has been tested and retested. There is no guessing as to whether it will be a successful model. It has to be. There is no way it can escape being so, for it represents the sum total of all we have learned about motor car building in the making of 15,000,000 automobiles.

The new Ford will sell at a low price

"The price of the new Ford is low in accordance with the established Ford policy. I hold that it is better to sell a large number of cars at a reasonably small margin of profit than to sell a few cars at a large margin of profit.

"We never forget that people who buy Ford cars are the people who helped to make this business big. It has always been our policy to share our profits with our customers. In one year our profits were so much larger than we expected that we voluntarily returned $50 to each purchaser of a car. We could never have done that if this business had been conducted for the sole benefit of stockholders rather than to render service to the public.

"No other automobile can duplicate the new Ford car at the Ford price because no other manufacturer does business the way we do.

"We make our own steel—we make our own glass—we mine our own coal—we make virtually every part used in the Ford car. But we do not charge a profit on any of these items or from these operations. We would not be playing fair with the public if we did so. Our only business is the automobile business. Our only profit is on the automobile we sell.

"WE ARE able to sell this new Ford car at a low price because we have found new ways to give you greater value without a great increase in our own costs.

"We did not set out to make a new car to sell at such-and-such a figure. We decided on the kind of car we wanted to make and then found ways to produce it at a low price.

"The new Ford car, as I have said, will be officially announced on Friday of this week. In appearance, in performance, in comfort, in safety, in all that goes to make a good car, it will bear out everything I have said here. We consider it our most important contribution thus far to the progress of the motor industry, to the prosperity of the country, and to the daily welfare of millions of people."

© 1927, Ford Motor Company

From the ad campaign by N.W. Ayer & Son just prior to the Model A Ford's introduction day, December 2, 1927.

Henry Ford

FORD MOTOR COMPANY
Detroit, Michigan

"The New Ford Car" advertisement. (Photo courtesy of Henry Ford Museum and Greenfield Village)

World Startled By False Rumor of Mussolini's Death

Springfield Daily News

The Weather
CLOUDY TONIGHT AND FRIDAY

LARGEST EVENING CIRCULATION 2c

48th YEAR, NO. 170   Established in 1880 By CHARLES T. BELLAMY   SPRINGFIELD, MASS.; THURSDAY EVENING, DECEMBER 1, 1927   TWENTY-EIGHT PAGES

FORD AUTO WAR HITS STOCK MARKET

HERE AT LAST --- HENRY FORD'S NEW CARS WHICH HAVE STARTLED THE AUTOMOTIVE WORLD

Clarence Chamberlin Here for Conference on Airplane Motor Factory

Man Who Flew to Germany "To Get a Glass of Beer" Discusses Project With Vice-President Hillman of Chamber of Commerce; May Return Again to Meet City's Financial Leaders

May Locate Airplane Plant in Springfield

DRIVES CAR UP ONE MILE CLIMB TO THE SUMMIT OF MOUNT TOM

Ralph Mulford, Noted Racer and Hill Climber, Is First to Make Trip

FAVORS RED PEPPER IN FIGHTING YEGGS

UKRANIANS IN SHARP REVOLT, LATEST REPORT

More Than 5000 People Killed Word Heard in Bucharest

TWO FIREMEN INJURED AS TRUCK HITS TREE

FEMALE "HUSBAND" GOES TO JAIL

MARRIAGE BAR TO THE WOMEN AS TEACHERS IN CHICOPEE

School Committee Will Appoint No More of Them in the Day School

Beach Confessed Murder To Him, Witness Says as State Plays Trump Card

Samuel Bark Declares on Stand That Poultry Fancier, Accused With Mrs Lilliendahl, Asked for Money to Help His Defense; Plea for Cash Came During Talk in Baltimore

MUSSOLINI AT HIS DESK AFTER DEATH RUMOR

World Aroused by Report That Originates on Berlin Market

AGED VETERAN DROPS DEAD AT RELIEF BUREAU

Sylvester Pendleton, 84, Civil War Soldier, Dies at City Hall

FOUR KILLED WHEN ERIE TRAIN HITS CAR

Automobile Was Carrying Employes of General Electric Coll's Decatur Plant

FORMER YALE STAR HELD FOR GRAND JURY IN SHOOTING CASE

Gilbert Stanley's Bail Raised to $20,000 and Furnished at Great Barrington

General Motors Issues Slump as New Car Appears

Hand of Auto Magnate Felt in Wall Street on Eve of Public Demonstration of Late Ford Models; Cities Throughout Nation Will be Scene of Displays Tomorrow; Action Comes as Ford's Reply to His Competitors

New York, Dec. 1—The hand of Henry Ford was felt in Wall street today.

Prices Regarded as Lower Than Those On the Old Model

DAWES OUT OF WHITE HOUSE RACE, HE SAYS

Disavows Candidacy in Formal Statement

Continued on Page Twenty-four

Front page of *Springfield Daily News*, December 1, 1927.

First Pictures of the New Ford Car

Get complete details TODAY at Ford salesrooms

FOR several years we have been working on the new Ford car. For weeks and months you have been hearing rumors about it. For the past few days you have been reading some of the details of it in the newspapers.

Whatever you do today, take at least fifteen minutes to get the full story of this new automobile.

You will realize then that it is an entirely new and different Ford car, designed and created to meet modern conditions—a car that brings you more beauty, speed, quiet, comfort, safety, economy and stamina than you ever thought possible in a low-price car.

Automobile history will be made today, for the new Ford is not only new in appearance and performance . . . it is new in mechanical design. Many features of it are exclusive Ford developments. Some are wholly new in automobile practice. Its low price is a reflection of manufacturing improvements and economies that are as epoch-making as the car itself.

Nineteen years of experience in building 15,000,000 automobiles are behind the new Ford car and have counted in its making. Resources unmatched in the motor car industry are its heritage and its birthright.

The Ford policy of owning the source of raw materials, of making virtually every part, of doing business at a small profit per car, has cut many dollars off the price you would ordinarily have to pay for a car like this.

So we say to you—learn about this new Ford car today. Compare it with any other car in the light-car field, for beauty of line—for comfort—for speed—for quick acceleration—for flexibility in traffic . . . for steadiness at all speeds . . . for power on the hills . .

for economy and low cost of up-keep . . . for its sturdy ability to stand up under countless thousands of miles of service.

Then you will know why today will be remembered as one of the greatest days in the entire history of the automobile industry. . . . Then you will know why the new Ford car will be *your* car.

NOTE THESE FEATURES

Beautiful new low body lines

Choice of four colors

55 to 65 miles an hour

Remarkable acceleration

40 horse-power

Four-wheel brakes

Standard, selective gear shift

Hydraulic shock absorbers

20 to 30 miles per gallon of gasoline

Theft-proof coincidental lock

Typical Ford economy and reliability

STANDARD EQUIPMENT ON ALL NEW FORD CARS

Starter	Dashlight
Five steel-spoke wheels	Mirror
Windshield wiper	Rear and stop light
Speedometer	Oil gauge
Gasoline gauge	Tools
Pressure grease gun lubrication	

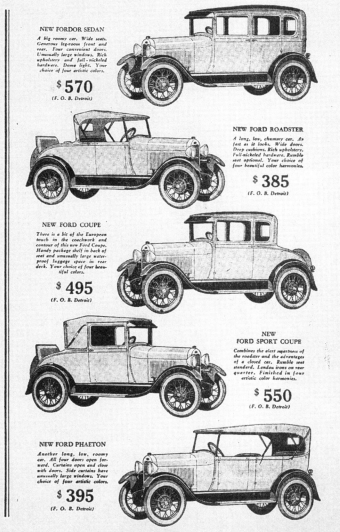

NEW FORD TUDOR SEDAN
An example of the fine coachwork of the new Ford cars. New military-type sun visor, and crown roof. Narrow pillars and new door construction give unusual vision. Both front seats fold forward, giving easy access to rear seats. Ample space between seats. Your choice of four artistic color harmonies—an unusual feature in a low-price car.
$495
(F. O. B. Detroit)

NEW FORDOR SEDAN
A big roomy car. Wide seats. Generous leg-room front and rear. Four convenient doors. Unusually large windows. Rich upholstery and full-nickeled hardware. Dome light. Your choice of four artistic colors.
$570
(F. O. B. Detroit)

NEW FORD ROADSTER
A long, low, chummy car. As fast as it looks. Wide doors. Deep cushions. Rich upholstery. Full-nickeled hardware. Rumble seat optional. Your choice of four beautiful color harmonies.
$385
(F. O. B. Detroit)

NEW FORD COUPE
There is a bit of the European touch in the coachwork and contour of this new Ford Coupe. Handy package shelf in back of seat and unusually large waterproof luggage space in rear deck. Your choice of four beautiful colors.
$495
(F. O. B. Detroit)

NEW FORD SPORT COUPE
Combines the alert smartness of the roadster and the advantages of a closed car. Rumble seat standard. Landau irons on rear quarter. Finished in four artistic color harmonies.
$550
(F. O. B. Detroit)

NEW FORD PHAETON
Another long, low, roomy car. All four doors open forward. Curtains open and close with doors. Side curtains have unusually large windows. Your choice of four artistic colors.
$395
(F. O. B. Detroit)

FORD MOTOR COMPANY
Detroit, Michigan

© 1927, Ford Motor Company

"First Pictures of the New Ford Car" advertisement. (Photo courtesy of Henry Ford Museum and Greenfield Village)

This statement is backed by a telegram, dated December 22, 1927, from Will Rogers to Edsel Ford, quoted by David Lewis in his column in *Cars & Parts* magazine (October 1981). "Got the car and the first time I have stopped is to write this telegram. Tell your dad it's my first bribe. But it runs so good it eases my conscience. Proud to have delivery on the first of the second fifteenth million. Next to an airplane, it's the best thing made."

During the interim period from May 25 to December 2, Ford dealers were limited to selling their remaining stock of Model Ts, providing service, parts and accessories, selling tractors, used cars, ammonium sulfate fertilizer and, eventually, advertising the new model in their showrooms through posters, pictures and displays rather than the real thing. Rumors, lack of specific information and production delays combined to keep them almost as much in the dark as the public. Many of them lost money and about fifteen percent of the 10,000 dealers quit during the year. The normal yearly dealer loss average was ten percent.

John Henry Eagal, Sr., Ford dealer in Stockton, California, did not find the interim period difficult because he listened to the advice of the Ford Motor Co. and built up his service and parts departments. When the shutdown came, he solicited all kinds of insurance business and bought wrecks from insurance companies and used car dealers. In his "Reminiscences," Eagal recalls the time he surveyed the stock of a used car dealer, made him an offer, and bought thirty-eight cars and trucks. He put them in his shop to be refurbished and made a nice sales profit on each piece.

Branch managers also had to cope with the down time. In his "Reminiscences," H.C. Doss, manager of the Kansas City Branch, says that he visited every one of his five hundred-twenty-one dealers, covering 30,000 miles in about six months. He kept the dealers sold on Ford and what Ford had and would have. He talked to bankers about loans, helped dealers build up their service departments and found ways to encourage them to get rid of non-productive relatives on their payrolls. The result was that he did not lose one dealer because there were no cars to sell.

Another manager, Arthur S. "Hard Rock" Hatch, who was the acting plant manager of the Chicago Branch, had to shut down his plant briefly because the Model As being produced early on were stalling. The problem turned out to be the regulator that controlled the cutout between the battery and the engine. Henry Ford had all the assembly plants ship the faulty regulators (costing about $4.50 each) back to Detroit. Later, Hatch went to Detroit and was shown a pile of regulators higher than the roof of the engineering building. "Look at those things!" Henry Ford said to him, "Look at all the dummies I have got around here!" (Hatch's story is featured in *Ford Life* November-December 1973.)

Frustrated by the lack of information, three Chicago area dealers drove to Detroit in October 1927 in hopes of getting some tangible information. As luck would have it, they were driving on Woodward Avenue toward the Highland Park plant when a nameless car came toward them and they spotted Henry and Edsel Ford in the car. "We turned around right in the middle of Woodward," related dealer John Murphy, and chased the car down the street to the plant gates. We stopped in back of it and sat tight."

When Edsel Ford found out that they were dealers from Chicago he invited them into the plant where Henry Ford personally described the Model A from one end to the other. They were also given a ride around the plant by Edsel. Returning home the three were met with skepticism from other dealers and it was not until the new car became available that, Murphy says, "the dealers in town realized we had not exaggerated a bit."

Motivated by this and probably other attempts, an October 31 letter asked dealers not to visit the Detroit factories because the company was still completing its production facilities and was not able to entertain dealers as it would like. Dealers were advised to concentrate on selling tractors and await developments at the Detroit factories.

A few weeks later each dealer received a portfolio with general instructions on the procedure they were to follow in presenting cars to the public when they became available. They also received a large box containing window posters, banners, showroom display cards, car illustrations and color pictures of the cars. Towards the end of November branches notified dealers of the locations of new car exhibits.

The Green Island Branch in Troy, New York, informed dealers of three locations, in addition to the Branch, where there would be exhibits of the new car. They were urged to get as many people as possible to see an exhibit and told that some dealers had already arranged to run buses into the Branch or one of the other locations to assure that as many prospects as possible saw the car on the first day.

Following up on these instructions, some dealers, such as Koelle-Greenwood of Germantown, Pennsylvania, sent letters personally inviting prospective buyers to showings. "Think of it!", urged Clifford Koelle in his November 29, 1927, letter, "This car—a car that promises to revolutionize the whole light-car industry—at a price in keeping with Ford standards."

Now, finally, it was time for the great unveiling. As cars were being shipped to showrooms zipped in canvas bags, a series of five full-page ads produced by N.W. Ayer & Son at a cost of $1,300,000 and carried in 2,000 daily newspapers introduced the new car to a world that was ready for the real thing in every sense of the term. Over a period of five years, from 1927 to 1931, Ford would spend $5,199,798 on magazine advertising. (See "The Passenger Car Industry," a 1931 survey commissioned by the Curtis Publishing Co.)

These ads and subsequent Ford illustrations in newspapers and magazines from 1927 to 1937 were the work of James W. Williamson, one of the great magazine

illustrators of the 1930s and 1940s. In the Winter 1979 issue of *Automotive History Review* (Society of Automotive Historians), editor John M. Peckham salutes Williamson as deserving a high rating for his artistic talents and an even higher rating for overcoming a major obstacle for any artist. Williamson was color blind.

On December 1, the eve of the showing, the fourth ad for the first time whetted the public's appetite with actual pictures and prices of the Model A. Unprecedented at the time and still noteworthy even today, the series was, in the opinion of the president of the Advertising Club of New York, "the most soundly coordinated advertising campaign in America's advertising history." On November 30, the press was invited to a special preview in Dearborn and on December 1, a private display for 7,000 invited New Yorkers was held at the Waldorf-Astoria.

December 2, 1927, the first day introduction of the new Model A Ford, was marked by tremendous enthusiasm throughout the United States, Canada and foreign countries despite rain, sleet, snow and sub-zero temperatures in many areas. *Ford News* claimed an accurate count of attendance at all the places where the car was displayed in the United States, gave a total of 10,534,992 or nearly ten percent of the total population. About one quarter of the people in the United States saw the car in the first few days.

In Detroit, where forty cars were on display in Convention Hall, 114,849 people visited the exhibit during the first day's showing. Cars were shown at eleven places in the New York metropolitan area on Friday, December 2,

and drew heavy crowds that, by noon of the following Wednesday, numbered more than 1,250,000 people. In the Charlotte, North Carolina, territory 308,890 people saw the car on the first day despite heavy rain.

Crowds were so heavy in Cincinnati that many were turned away, yet total attendance for the day was 296,475. These figures were easily exceeded by Chicago, which checked through 514,096 people the first day and the Kansas City territory where 651,000 people saw the new car. In the St. Paul territory, cars arrived at the branch the night before the first showing. Some of these then had to be driven as much as two hundred miles to their destinations in spite of a raging blizzard and a temperature of eighteen below zero. All the cars arrived on time and showed remarkable performance in traveling over snow-drifted roads.

With all this interest orders for the new car poured in. At Convention Hall in Detroit, dealers reported sales at the rate of one every five minutes. Within the first two weeks about 400,000 orders were placed for the new vehicle and thousands more had already been placed by willing buyers sight unseen in the previous months. *Time*

Placards announcing the new Ford cars as the headline feature of the day's edition were carried by the newsboys in Milwaukee, Wisconsin.

Newsboy, *Ford News*, December 22, 1927.

New ~Ford~ Prices
THE UNIVERSAL CAR

Effective Dec. 2, 1927
PRICES ON ALL FORD CARS

Phaeton	**$395.00**
Roadster	**$385.00**
Chassis	**$325.00**
Coupe	**$495.00**
Sport Coupe	**$550.00**
Tudor Sedan	**$495.00**
Fordor Sedan	**$570.00**
Roadster Pick up	**$395.00**
Truck Chassis	**$460.00**

F. O. B. Detroit — Federal Tax Extra

PLACE YOUR ORDER NOW

RAY T. PARFET

450 W. Main St.   Dial 7107

Dealer card with December 2, 1927, prices, f.o.b. Detroit.

KOELLE-GREENWOOD CO.

161 WEST CHELTEN AVENUE

GERMANTOWN

BELL PHONE, GER. 1025-1026-1027

SALES SERVICE
AND
PARTS DEPARTMENT

PHILADELPHIA, PA.,

November 29, 1927.

Mr. C. Betts,
6811 Quincy St.,
Phila. Pa.

Dear Mr. Betts:

Though you will no doubt see the announcement of the new
Ford car in the newspapers, we want to add this personal word
of invitation to you to visit the Commercial Museum at 34th &
Spruce Streets on Friday or Saturday. The doors will be open
at ten o'clock in the morning and will remain open until late
in the evening.

For nineteen years there has been no vital change in the
Ford motor — few in the body. Yet the famous Model "T" has
led the world through all that time.

But the new Ford car is as far in advance of present-day
requirements as the old one was in 1908!

Good looking — low — trim — rakish — smooth — roadcling-
ing speed — flexibility — pickup! Economy — greater economy,
even, than the old models! Durability — better materials
than have ever before been put into any motor-car of the same
price class!

Think of it! This car — a car that promises to revolutionize the whole light-car industry — at a price in keeping
with Ford standards!

Come in Friday or Saturday and let us give you the full
story of the new Ford car!

Most cordially yours,

KOELLE-GREENWOOD COMPANY

Clifford R. Koelle

Letter from Koelle-Greenwood Co. inviting a customer to view the new Ford.

Volume VIII.   F   Dearborn, Mich., December 22, 1927   Number 10

TEN PER CENT OF U. S. POPULATION SEES NEW FORD FIRST DAY OF SHOW

New Iron Mine Is Fine Plant

Surface Structure Is Standard Ford Building

Named by Henry Ford, Planned and Constructed for Maximum of Safety and Efficiency

The new iron mine of the Ford Motor Company owes its name to Henry Ford. Mr. Ford visited the property on his trip to the Upper Peninsula in 1926. The mine lies in a rich blueberry-producing district, and at the time of Mr. Ford's visit the crop was at its peak. As Mr. Ford gathered a handful of the berries near the site of the present shaft, he remarked: "I have a name for this mine; we will call it the 'Blueberry'." And the Blueberry it has been called ever since.

That was in the fall. The work of clearing the ground for the shaft and buildings had begun only in September. Today, fifteen months later, the surface plant stands practically com-

Concluded on page 6

3,281-Mile Trip in Ninety Hours New Car Record

Leaving Dearborn at 10:05 a. m. December 2 in a new Model A Ford car, Ray Dahlinger, manager of Henry Ford Farms at Dearborn, arrived in Los Angeles, California, at 1:02 a. m., Tuesday, December 6, completing the run in 89 hours and 57 minutes. This constitutes the longest cross-country run made by one of the new cars up to the present time, proving its ability to stand up under trying conditions. No difficulty was experienced en route, although the car was driven at high speed most of the way.

The car used by Mr. Dahlinger was a standard stock model Tudor sedan taken directly from the assembly line at Fordson. No additional testing or inspection was given it other than that which all cars receive during their construction.

Henry Ford accompanied Mr. Dahlinger for the first thirty-three miles, to Saline, Michigan.

Eager Crowds Block Traffic in Effort to Gain First Look at New Model; Newspapers Feature Event

Rain, Sleet, Snow and Sub-Zero Temperatures Fail to Dampen Enthusiasm of Millions; Record Unequaled in History

Tremendous enthusiasm marked the first day's showing, on December 2, of the new Model A Ford car throughout the United States, Canada, and foreign countries. Traffic was blocked in many cities by the crowds. Wherever people met, it was the chief topic of discussion. It was featured on the front page of all leading newspapers, and in Dallas, Texas, extra editions proclaimed the event the "greatest since the signing of the Armistice."

An accurate check of the first day's attendance at all places where the car was displayed and at dealers' establishments throughout the United States gave a total of 10,534,992, or nearly 10 per cent of the total population of the country. The crowds on the following days nearly equaled those of the first, making a total which included approximately one-quarter of the country's population. In Pittsburgh, 12½ per cent of the city's population saw the car during the first day.

Despite torrents of rain in the South and the East, snow and driving sleet farther north, and below-zero temperatures in the north-central section, the attendance everywhere surpassed all expectations. At most display points extra police were required to keep traffic moving.

At Convention Hall in Detroit, where forty cars were on display, 114,849 people visited the exhibit during the first day's showing. Seventy-five policemen were necessary to handle the crowds and prevent traffic jams.

Within a few minutes after the doors were opened, spectators were grouped eight and ten deep around all the exhibits, and by the end of the first hour it was difficult to approach any of them.

The new models were also on display at the sales showroom at the Highland Park plant, 31,368 people visiting this exhibition the first day.

In Milwaukee, Wisconsin, a hastily constructed fence was necessary to prevent the packed masses of humanity from breaking the showroom windows. In Los Angeles, California, a crowd began to assemble at 7 a. m. and grew until it blocked traffic.

Concluded on page 8

Schedule of prices new CAR and TRUCK	
Phaeton	$395
Roadster	385
Sedan—Two Door	495
Sedan—Four Door	570
Coupe	495
Sport Coupe	550
Chassis	325
AA Truck chassis	460
Express Body and Cab	140
Platform Body and Cab	135
Stake Body and Cab	150
All Prices F.O.B. Detroit.	

J. W. Capek, manager Los Angeles branch, Ford Motor Company, congratulating Mr. Dahlinger upon his arrival in Los Angeles with the first transcontinental Model A Ford. At right, Arthur H. Vultee, sales manager for Hamlin W. Nerney, Inc., Los Angeles Ford dealer and Duke Kahanamoku, Hawaiian Olympic and world champion swimmer.

Front page of *Ford News*, December 22, 1927.

magazine reported that in Manhattan one enterprising rascal took advantage of the opportunity and wandered through the showroom crowds with an "order book" in hand and took orders from those willing to give him the twenty-five dollar deposit. When detectives approached him he ran away, *Time* said, "with many a $25 stuffed in his coat pockets."

"It's history what a tremendous reception the Model A had," says C.W. Doss. "In Kansas City they literally broke the doors down to get in before it was time to open to the public. They pushed them right through. You couldn't control that mob. There will never be another introduction like that; never was before. That was the story all over the country. It was tremendous, fabulous. The advance orders on that car were tremendous. They just ran over you to get one."

Production, however, lagged far behind demand and was only up to one hundred a day at the time of the car's introduction and one hundred-twenty-five to one hundred-forty a day by the New Year. According to the Ford Motor Co. Assembly Record Types, just 4,186 Model A Fords were actually produced during 1927. Of this total, 3,998 were built at the Rouge and 188 at the Kearny (New Jersey) Branch.

The list of Ford Model A engine numbers, indicates that numbers 1 through 5275 were produced in 1927 at the Fordson Plant, although that does not mean they were all installed in cars in 1927. Hans Kalinka, whose area of expertise is the early 1928 cars, believes that many of the first engines did not work and had to be sent back. Therefore, the number actually installed in cars was 3,500 to 4,000, possibly less.

There was no single reason for the delay in getting the assembly lines up to speed. It was a combination of factors including lack of adequate preparation for the new model change, readjustment of machinery, the necessity of retraining workers and inevitable factory delays and adjustments as reports came back about problems experienced in actual use by the public. For example, both the new starter and the single brake system on the early cars had to be replaced and the engine tended to be rough and caused too much vibration. These and other changes often involved the rearranging of machines and men and slowed down the production process.

As might be expected, there was no lack of editorial comment on the new Ford and the publicity coup that accompanied its introduction. Most reviewers heaped praise on Henry Ford for the manner of the car's introduction and viewed it as a car of its times and a much needed replacement for the Model T. To the *Kansas City Star* Henry Ford was "the world's greatest salesman."

The *Ohio State Journal* acknowledged surprise at the remarkably low prices of the new car, while a writer for the Raton, New Mexico, *Reporter* wrote that a demonstration ride in the new car convinced him that the Model A is "the most automobile ever assembled for service within one thousand pounds of the weight or within one thousand dollars of the price." Confessing to shock at

what he experienced, a reviewer for the Youngstown, Ohio, *Vindicator* said, "I drove the new Ford. And you are not going to believe a thing I write about the car, for it is unbelievable unless you experience the sensation yourself."

Taking a different tack, likely with tongue-in-cheek, a *New York Evening Post* editorial writer lamented the new Ford because it wasn't a Ford. "It is a remarkable piece of machinery," he wrote, "but still it isn't a Ford, because the Ford was an educational institution as well as a machine. The old Ford, the old, black, rusty, cantankerous, obstinate, sputtering Ford brought wisdom to many fools and made many wise men go raving, tearing mad. This new lily of the valley isn't going to teach us anything. It looks as if it would run indefinitely without complaint, which is all wrong. It is made for serenity and comfort, which is also all wrong.

"Where is the gas tank? Out in front where it can be reached. Where is the timer? Up on top where it can no longer bark your knuckles. Where are the brake-bands? In a ridiculously exposed position where their value as trainers of character and refined language is completely lost. . .the new Ford is a garage car. Back to the pioneer days when we threw sand under the fan belt and tightened the horn with a dime—the days when the Ford was a boy!"

With all the hullabaloo about the new Ford where did the average dealer fit into the picture? The fact is that most of them did not have a car in early December, many would wait until January, some even into February. Despite this they managed to display an amazing amount of enthusiasm and ingenuity in keeping their customers interested, if not actually ordering cars.

One of the ways this was done was by arranging showings of the "New Car Film" about the Model A prepared by Ford. Each branch was assigned two copies of this sales film and requests for them shattered all records as dealers competed for the opportunity to show them to their customers. The films, in sixteen millimeter size, were soon available for dealer's to buy at a price of fifty-two dollars per copy.

Imaginative dealers found innovative ways to retain customer interest. Most arranged attractive displays featuring, if possible, the car itself. If one was not available, they organized displays of pictures, posters, ads and signboards. One dealer surrounded views of the new car, displayed on easels and walls, with ropes and flower arrangements. Several dealers held Model A days at their luncheon clubs. Another offered a prize to the child from the local public school who wrote the best three hundred word essay on the new car.

H.O. Melone, Ford dealer at Long Branch, California, was not deterred by the fact that he did not have a new car. With the aid of pictures of the different types and placards enumerating the Model A's most striking features, he lectured every half-hour to capacity crowds from early morning until midnight of the date of the premier showing, and for several days following.

What the Editors Are Saying

The advent of the Model A caused news-paper editors throughout the United States, cartoonists and special writers, to make special reference to the car and its significance. The advertisements that appeared in the press were just as eagerly read as the news stories. The following editorials have been selected at random from a large collection and illustrate varied styles of comment as made in New York City, Columbus, Indianapolis and Kansas City:

IT'S A GIRL

The old Ford has joined the procession of ancient history along with Barnum and the buffalo. The new Ford enters our lives with flowers and soft music and a pink ribbon across its dove-gray hood. The old Ford dripped oil into our upturned faces as we lay under it on country roads at midnight. The new Ford is shown off like a modiste's manikin to a generation which has lost the joy of getting its hands dirty. The old Ford ruined ten million pairs of overalls. The new Ford is unveiled in hotel ballrooms by salesmen in dinner jackets.

The new Ford is new; but it isn't a Ford. It is swung low (sweet chariot); it is the color of fog at sunrise or of trees at dawn; it has theft-proof coincidental locks, pressure grease-gun lubrication and five steel-spoke wheels; it is as silky as a debutante and as neat as a watch; it will go sixty-five miles an hour and thirty miles on a gallon; it has a gas tank behind the engine and a switch for all lights on the steering post; it was made with Johansson precision gauges, accurate to the incalculable fraction of an inch, and it wipes its own windshield; it is masculine in reliability and feminine in grace; it is, in other words, the heart's desire of America.

But it isn't a Ford. It is a remarkable piece of machinery, but still it isn't a Ford, because the Ford was an educational institution as well as a machine. The old Ford, the old, black, rusty, cantankerous, obstinate, sputtering Ford, brought wisdom to many fools and made many wise men go raving, tearing mad. This new lily of the valley isn't going to teach us anything. It looks as if it would run indefinitely without complaint, which is all wrong. It is made for serenity and comfort, which is also all wrong. Where is the gas tank? Out in front where it can be reached. Where is the timer? Up on top where it can no longer bark your knuckles. Where are the brake-bands? In a ridiculously exposed position where their value as trainers of character and refined language is completely lost.

We are degenerating. We are entering a period of Roman luxury. The new Ford is a garage car. Back to the pioneer days when we threw sand under the fan belt and tightened the horn with a dime—the days when the Ford was a boy!
—*New York Evening Post, 12-5-27.*

NEW FORD PRICES

The biggest surprise in all the revelations concerning the new Ford is the price list. When the cars are placed on the market, probably next month, you can buy a roadster for $385, a phaeton for $395, a coupe for $495, a two-door sedan for $495 or a four-door sedan for $570. These prices are remarkably low, in view of the appearance and, no doubt, the workmanship of the cars. They are very little higher than the prices of the old models.

Evidently Mr. Ford means to stick to his original idea of production in huge quantities relying for himself on the volume of sales rather than on the percentage of profit per car. He must face strong competition but that any of his competitors can meet his prices for a long period of time is doubtful. We imagine he will sell some cars.
—*Ohio State Journal, 12-2-27.*

FORD KEPT A NATION ON TIPTOE

It is probably not overstating the case to say that we have witnessed this week a thing that could have happened only in America and that could have been brought about only by Henry Ford.

Irrespective of the public's final attitude toward the new Ford motor car and also irrespective of its merits, the obvious facts entitle Mr. Ford to another shining star in his crown of personal achievement.

The financial and economic factors entering into his latest coup are stupendous. About a year ago he began to curtail production and a few months later virtually stopped building cars. He ceased to make shipments of cars to the largest sales organization in the world. His many branch assembly plants stopped building cars. His dealers stressed service rather than sales.

Today this vast manufacturing and distributing structure is about to function again. Workmen, mechanics, clerks and salesmen by the hundred thousand are ready to take up new tasks. Even Wall Street is reacting to the advent of the new car.

And the public seems ready to give the Ford car its place in the limelight. Dinner talk and street gossip will sparkle as of old. Vaudeville repartee and the best sellers will be enriched with Ford references. The whole body of our social and industrial life will be affected by the announcement of the new Ford car.

Where else but in America! Who else but Henry Ford!
—*Kansas City Star, 12-5-27.*

THE NEW FORD CAR

For months there has been speculation about what Henry Ford planned to do in the matter of manufacturing automobiles. Now he has given an answer to all questioners. Indeed, he has given several answers. Throughout the United States he has been using newspaper advertisements to tell of his plans, to describe his new car and to explain not only how it is made, but what he expects it to do.

There is an old story, told in the schools of engineering, that it was easy enough to prove that the old Model T Ford would not run. The difference between theory and practice was evident, as Ford manufactured 15,000,000 of them and all ran and continued to run even when there was no visible reason why they should. He was a pioneer.

The public is told that it will find the biggest difference between the old Model T and the new Model A in the gear shift. Ever since the original Fords were offered there has been argument about methods of gear shifting.

Anything that Ford does is news. He has planned the announcement of his new car in such manner that public curiosity has been aroused to the highest pitch.
—*Indianapolis News, 12-1-27.*

—Reynolds, *Portland Oregonian.*

THE JOYS OF ANTICIPATION.

"What The Editors Are Saying" from *Ford News* Dealer's Supplement, January 1, 1928.

In 1968, in an article in *Model "A" News*, Bill Hage recounts his impressions as a fifteen year old when he and his Dad attended the first showing of the Model A in their hometown. The high point of the sales demonstration was when the salesman removed the gas cap, lit a match and held it near the filler opening. The crowd gasped and Hage headed for the door until he realized that only a flickering blue flame appeared at the opening and that there was no explosion. The salesman then cupped his palm over the opening and the flame went out. He explained to the suitably impressed crowd that the screen located inside the tank was a safety feature. Hage never forgot this part of the demonstration.

For the real thing many dealers waited until a Ford traveler brought through a Model A for a few hours or possibly a day at their dealerships. One of these travelers battled a raging blizzard, sub-zero temperatures and snow-blocked highways on December 7 to bring a Model A Tudor into the Ford Agency at Black River Falls, Wisconsin, the night before the scheduled showing. The next day, despite impossible roads and streets, a large portion of the 7,243 people living in the town availed themselves of the opportunity to see the much-talked-of car and 187 of them placed an order.

These flying visits occasioned tremendous enthusiasm. For example, 17,000 people pushed into the Flint, Michigan, showroom of Otto P. Graff, and bodily moved the car on display up against a wall. In Seattle, Washington, William O. McKay drove his first car there from Dearborn and exhibited it on a theater stage with the mayor making a speech of welcome.

John Henry Eagal displayed his first Model A on December 5, and counted 9,284 people in the sales room that day. His salesmen took sixty orders the first day and, by the end of the first week, had approximately five hundred orders on file with twenty-five dollar deposits. Unfortunately, since people had to wait five, six or seven months for a car, about half bought something else and got their deposits back. "In fact," Eagal says, "it went so long that we could not even locate some of the buyers to give back the deposit."

Determined to prove the speed and exceptional riding qualities of the Model A Ford as well as its ability to stand up under grueling punishment, Ray Dahlinger and Henry Ford left Dearborn on December 2 in a stock Model A Tudor chosen at random off the assembly line. Ford accompanied Dahlinger for the first thirty-three miles of an 8,328-mile trek that crisscrossed the country. Dahlinger was at the wheel for the entire time except for five hundred-thirty-two miles when his relief driver drove while he rested.

Alerted by Ford publicists, throngs of curious well-wishers greeted Dahlinger as he drove the new Ford over roads ranging from concrete to rutted dirt and sandy trails. He arrived in Los Angeles after a run of eighty-nine hours and fifty-seven minutes (actual running time was seventy-three hours and seventeen minutes), in which he encountered extremes of desert heat, icy cold, snow, rain and floods as well as pleasant driving conditions. An average speed of 40.9 mph was maintained on this leg of the trip and gasoline consumption was recorded at 20.1 mpg.

From Los Angeles, Dahlinger drove to San Francisco, then returned across the country to New York City and eventually to Dearborn on December 23. The Model A did all it was expected to do. Only minor difficulties (horn, tie rod, a burned out headlamp and a flat tire) were encountered.

Great demand and few cars meant that there was intense competition and pressure from people, especially prominent ones, to get a Model A sooner rather than later. "To be the first owner of a new Ford in Hartford or Topeka," writes Charles Merz in his book, *And Then Came Ford* (1929), became an honor as distinct as being elected member of an exclusive club." Some people did get preference early on, but, Nevins and Hill say, "The granting of priorities even to a few individuals created such problems that in the spring of 1928 it was discontinued."

Among those who were accorded preference were Senator James Couzens, former Ford official, who was presented with Model A No. 35, a Sport Coupe, on December 13. This was the first Model A delivered in the nation's capital. Douglas Fairbanks ordered a Model A for Mary Pickford for Christmas and wired Edsel Ford requesting special delivery. The car arrived in Beverly Hills Christmas eve.

Cazenovia, New York, dealer D.D. Norton received a telegram at 10 a.m. on December 2, listing the new Ford models available and the prices, f.o.b. Detroit. The telegram was signed "Ford Walrath" (G.E. Walrath, manager of the Green Island Branch). A confirming letter arrived the next day. The models and their prices as listed in the telegram were: Phaeton - $395; Roadster - $385; Chassis - $325; Coupe - $495; Sport Coupe with rumble seat as standard - $550; Tudor sedan - $495; Fordor sedan - $570; Pickup - $395; Truck chassis - $460; Truck cab - $85; Express body - $55; Stake body - $65; Platform body - $50.

Norton was also told in the telegram that starters were now standard equipment on trucks that would have a ton-and-one-half rating. Tires on all trucks, regardless of body type, would be 32 x 6.00 rear and 30 x 5.00 front. Bumpers on all cars front and rear were extra at fifteen dollars for the pair. Discount to dealers would remain the same at twenty percent.

On December 6, still without a car, Norton was assured by the Branch manager that every effort was being made to provide a car for inspection by the public as soon as possible and, after that, a demonstrator for use by the agency so that prospective buyers could actually ride in the new car. Around the same time he received a six-page packet titled "The New Ford Car" for use in preparing dealer presentations and general letter No. 41, which provided information on the new Ford truck.

A December 8 letter informed dealers that cars on hand at the Green Island Branch would not be sold to dealers but retained for exhibition purposes. On December 13, Norton received word that a Tudor sedan was being placed in service at the Green Island Branch as a demonstrator. He was urged to come with his salesmen, mechanics and other employees as well as any prospects to receive a demonstration ride in the new car.

The next day Norton was informed that a car would be exhibited at his place the following Saturday and that he should be prepared to move the car from the Clark Mills agency on Friday evening. "This will give you a splendid opportunity to test its performance," wrote the Branch manager.

A complete listing of "drive out prices" for the Model A was sent to dealers by the Green Island Branch on December 20, 1927. It lists the f.o.b. Detroit price, dealer price, miscellaneous costs and the final cost to the dealer when he drove the car from the Branch. For example, the Tudor sedan was listed at $495 f.o.b. Detroit, and $396 to the dealer with his twenty percent discount. Freight charges of $46.80, tax of $13.28 and $1.98 for gas and oil meant a total cost to the dealer of $458.06. This price did not include spare tire, tube and bumpers, which were extra equipment. Each car was filled with nine gallons of gas costing fifteen cents a gallon and five quarts of oil costing fifty cents per gallon. The total drive out price from Green Island, including the dealer discount, was $557.06.

During the rest of December, Norton, still without a car, received numerous notices from the Branch including a warning that a minimum twenty-five dollar deposit was required for each car ordered, information on how to display Model A parts at the dealership, a sample of follow-up letters to visitors to the showroom, a suggestion to demonstrate the Model A to prominent citizens when the new car was finally received, and an invitation to send a shop foreman to the Branch for a Model A service school.

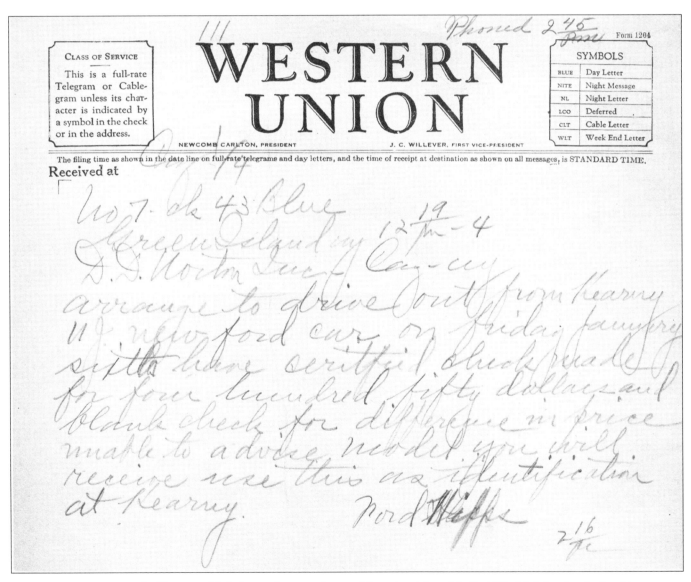

Telegram received by D.D. Norton with information on when and how to pick up his first Model A for the dealership.

GREEN ISLAND
DRIVE OUT PRICES
MODEL "A" AND "AA" FORD CARS
DECEMBER 20th, 1927.

MODEL	LIST FOB DETROIT	NET DEALER PRICE	FREIGHT	ADV FRT ON BODY EQUIPT.	TAX	GAS & OIL	TOTAL COST TO DEALER	GREEN IS. DEL. PRICE.
Phaeton	395	316	46.80		10.88	1.98	375.66	454.66
Roadster	385	308	46.80		10.64	1.98	367.42	445.42
Roadster with Rumble Seat	420	336·	46.80		11.48	1.98	396.26	480.26
Coupe	495	396	46.80		13.28	1.98	458.06	557.06
Coupe with Rumble Seat	530	424	46.80		14.12	1.98	486.90	592.90
Sport Coupe (Rumble Seat Standard)	550	440	46.80		14.60	1.98	503.38	613.38
Tudor Sedan	495	396	46.80		13.28	1.98	458.06	557.06
Fordor Sedan	570	456	46.80		15.08	1.98	519.86	633.86
Chassis	325	260	46.80		9.20	1.98	317.98	382.98
Pickup	395	316	46.80			1.98	364.78	442.78

NOTE: The above prices do not include spare tire and tube and bumpers which are extra equipment. Each car contains 9 gals of gasoline @ 15¢ per gal and 5 qts. of oil @ 50¢ per gal.

	LIST FOB DETROIT	NET DEALER PRICE	FREIGHT	ADV FRT ON BODY EQUIPT.	TAX	GAS & OIL	TOTAL COST TO DEALER	GREEN IS. DEL. PRICE.
Tractors	495	396	27.00				423.00	522.00
Tractors with Fenders	530	422.25	27.00				449.25	557.00

1-1/2 Ton Truck

	LIST FOB DETROIT	NET DEALER PRICE	FREIGHT	ADV FRT ON BODY EQUIPT.	TAX	GAS & OIL	TOTAL COST TO DEALER	GREEN IS. DEL. PRICE.
Chassis	460	358.80				1.98		
Chassis with Cab	545	425.10				1.98		
Chassis with Cab and Express Body	600	468.00				1.98		
Chassis with Cab and Stake Body	610	475.80				1.98		
Chassis with Cab and Platform Body	595	464.10				1.98		

1-1/2 Ton Truck - Dual High Transmission

	LIST FOB DETROIT	NET DEALER PRICE	FREIGHT	ADV FRT ON BODY EQUIPT.	TAX	GAS & OIL	TOTAL COST TO DEALER	GREEN IS. DEL. PRICE.
Chassis	510	397.80				1.98		
Chassis with Cab	595	464.10				1.98		
Chassis with Cab and Express Body	650	507.00				1.98		
Chassis with Cab and Stake Body	660	514.80				1.98		
Chassis with Cab and Platform Body	645	503.10				1.98		

NOTE: 20% discount on passenger cars including "Pick Up".
22% discount on Trucks and Truck Body Equipment.
Freight charges on Truck Chassis and Equipment will be announced later.

Green Island Drive Out Price List sent to D.D. Norton, December 20, 1927.

Finally, on December 29, after enduring almost a month of agonized waiting, Norton was informed that he could expect a delivery date of shortly after January 1, 1928, for a car to be used for demonstration purposes only. On January 4, 1928, a brief telegram delivered the happy news to Norton that on January 6 he should arrange to drive out from Kearny, New Jersey, a new Ford car, body style unknown. He was instructed to bring a certified check for four hundred-fifty dollars and a blank check for the difference in price.

What about the car itself? What was it like? Descriptions of the Model A Ford can be found in numerous books and articles written over the past seventy-two years. But, for our purpose, let's quote the words of contemporary writers to enlighten us as to how the car was presented and viewed at the time when it was introduced.

Charles Merz writes that the Model A "was as abruptly unlike the old Model T as the new America of traffic lights and parking rules and modern styles was unlike the old frontier. The angularity of its line had disappeared. Its rakish hood had gone over to the modern cult of beauty. . . . Style had come to River Rouge. Model T went down in a riot of new colors."

Pointing out that the new Model A constitutes a complete surrender of the utilitarian austerity of Model T, an editorial writer for the *New Republic* continues, "It makes every concession to taste and convenience—real or fancied—which is embodied in cars selling for three or four times the price. The most common comment—that it looks like a baby Lincoln—is the crux of the matter. Four choices of color combinations. Stream-line form. High radiator and hood. Illuminated instrument board on the dash. Nickeled radiator and headlights. Four-wheel brakes. Even such improvements as the speed of sixty mph, standard gearshift, twenty to thirty miles on a gallon of gas, and hydraulic shock absorbers are valuable in their sales appeal more because they make the Ford like other cars than because they are intrinsically useful. . . .

"We predict that the chief handicap of Model A will be the points at which it retains something of the old Ford individuality—the four-cylinder engine, the transverse springs and the gasoline tank in front of the driver rather than hidden at the rear. . . at only one point has Ford boldly stuck to his guns—the low price. The irresistible pressure of public preference has so molded and trimmed him that he has now gone to the point of offering a car as much like others as possible—only for less money."

Features of the new Ford included fifty-five to sixty-five miles per hour, forty horsepower engine and quick get-away. Tests showed that a Tudor sedan with two passengers was capable of accelerating from five to twenty-five miles per hour in eight-and-one-half seconds. Other features were gasoline economy from twenty to thirty miles per gallon, unique new oiling system, centrifugal water pump and large radiator, ignition system of new design, selective sliding gear transmission with standard shift, easy steering, four-wheel brakes, multiple dry-disc clutch, transverse, semi-elliptic springs, hydraulic shock absorbers, three-quarter floating rear axle and Ford-designed steel-spoke wheels.

The initial offering, as explained in a 1927 Ford showroom booklet, included six body types: Sport Coupe, Coupe, Roadster, Phaeton, Tudor sedan, Fordor sedan and a truck. One of these, the Fordor, was not available until well into 1928. Bodies were made of steel with full crown-type fenders and nickeled headlamps and radiator shell. Four color choices were offered: Niagara Blue, Arabian Sand, Dawn Gray and Gun Metal Blue. The finish was pyroxylin lacquer.

Standard equipment on all new Ford cars included: starter, five steel-spoke wheels, windshield wiper, speedometer, gasoline gauge, ammeter, dash light, mirror, rear and stop light, oil measuring rod (bayonet or, more commonly, the dipstick), ignition lock, complete tool set and shatterproof glass in the windshield.

Henry Ford had an extraordinary vision for his new Ford, found printed on an original poster used in a dealer's showroom when the Model A Ford was being introduced: "The New Ford Car embodies the best results of our experience in making 15,000,000 automobiles. We consider it our most important contribution thus far to the progress of the motor industry, to the prosperity of the country, and to the daily welfare of millions of people."

Chapter Two

1928: Ford Comes Back

The year 1928 was one of the most active in the history of the Ford Motor Co. Production of Model A Fords increased from 195 a day in January to 1,000 on February 13. By September, production reached 4,788 units per day and, at the end of the year, 6,435 Model A Fords were coming off Ford assembly lines each day.

At the one-year anniversary, December 1, 1928, *Ford News* reported that 733,044 Model A Fords had been built. By the end of the year, the total was 818,734 units worldwide, still considerably less than the 1,193,212 Chevrolets built, but a much improved showing over 1927 when the company's production lines were largely silent for five months.

Nevins and Hill argue that a considerable help in the increase of production was the company's new policy of using outside parts manufacturers much more than before. By the second half of 1928, Kelsey-Hayes was making one-third of the wheels, Briggs was supplying 2,500 bodies daily and the Murray Corp. had also begun to fill orders. Ford was buying 8,000 shock absorbers a day from the National Acme Co. and others from Houdaille and Spicer. Also bought outside were batteries, starting and lighting systems and piston rings. "Indeed," comment Nevins and Hill, "it would not be long before 2,200 firms would be supplying the Ford Motor Co., some of them devoting all their facilities to its needs."

As production increased, more assembly lines were opened and the hiring and training of workers picked up. At the end of the year, 186,313 men were employed by Ford and assembly plants on line increased from just two at the turn of the year (the Fordson plant in the Detroit area and Kearny, New Jersey) to more than forty worldwide. By December, there were thirty-five Branches handling more than 8,000 dealers in the United States.

The Fordson plant was now the main factory for Model A. It would be renamed the Rouge in 1929. To Highland Park was assigned the manufacture of parts for the Model T, of which hundreds of thousands would remain on the roads for years to come. In April 1928, the *New York Times* reported that during the inactive period while construction and renovation were in process, "orders amounting to $10,000,000 a month for Model T parts were filled, and even now about one-eighth of the plant capacity in Detroit is being used for making parts for this older model."

Before the end of August, 275,000 Model As were in the hands of buyers as the company worked hard to fill the 727,000 orders that Edsel Ford announced were on hand in January 1928, seventy-four percent of these with cash deposits of twenty-five dollars or more. By November, Model A sales led those of all other makes in forty-five out of forty-eight states as well as in the District of Columbia.

Increasing production and sales meant more jobs. What was it like at Ford for the workers behind the sheet metal? And for those who toiled in the pits and on the

Ad from *Ford News* Dealers' Supplement for Gimbels.

Sir Harry Lauder shows off his new Model A Tudor. (Photo courtesy of Henry Ford Museum and Greenfield Village)

assembly lines at Fordson and other Ford plants? As mentioned previously, their lot was far from ideal. If they were lucky enough to be rehired after the shutdown, they often worked for less than before. (Average labor rates at Fordson for October 1928 were $.8856 per hour. The average for U.S. Branches was $.7896.) They had to contend with the speed-up, insecurity about their job tenure and a hundred petty regulations.

In *Henry Ford The Wayward Capitalist*, Carol Gelderman argues that "The humanitarianism that Henry Ford had shown so dramatically in his early days no longer existed." Workers could be and were fired for things as simple as talking to another worker, staying too long in the men's room, not displaying the plant badge on the left pocket, eating lunch on a conveyor or on the floor or of not obeying any of the other regulations of the plant.

In April 1928, a disgruntled worker sent a letter to Henry Ford about the conditions at the Kansas City Assembly Branch. The man worked there for eight days and then, he writes, "I became so disgusted I walked out." Portions of his letter follow:

"A man, regardless of how hard he works and how hard he tries to please and put out the work is never sure of a job the day ahead. The men in that prison work like

Testing a new Model A. (Photo courtesy of AACA Library and Research Center)

slaves and are given more work than is hardly humanly possible to do (sic), yet if they get behind they are cursed out and talked to like dogs." The worker also noted that the factory often required workers to work some hours without pay.

"This treatment and working conditions are making many enemies for you," the letter writer continued, "and from first-hand knowledge I know it has hurt your business. For myself, I would rather work ten hours a day and receive thirty cents an hour and be treated like a man, than work there and receive seventy-five cents an hour and the treatment that is given."

This letter, from the files of the Henry Ford Research Center, is attached to a letter from H.C. Doss, the plant manager, who denies that men work overtime at his branch without pay. Doss recalls talking to the letter writer before he left and that his only stated reason for leaving was the noise in the plant, which was more than he could endure.

Doss also ridicules his former employee as someone, "looking for a soft snap." He concludes his letter by saying, "It will no doubt be easy for you to understand that in employing a great many men we will occasionally have someone who, for some reason or other, will try to justify his own laziness or improper attitude by offering the alibi that he did not receive fair consideration."

Another worker started at the Highland Park plant in 1928 at five dollars a day and, about a year later, was transferred to the Rouge with a raise to seven dollars a day. In a letter to the *Detroit Free Press*, cited by David Lewis, Emil Moresi, a Swiss immigrant, writes that the wage was great but the work was hard. "I worked on the assembly line drilling out the front axle spindle," he says. "They were very strict. A person never left the assembly line unless there was an emergency (this was indicated with one or two fingers). When permission was granted, the worker took one step back with another worker immediately taking his place. The same rule applied when the shift ended. The assembly line never stopped."

Initially, enthusiasm for the new Ford was just as strong abroad as it was in the United States. More than 125,000,000 people saw the Model A during its introduction in foreign countries and thousands of orders were placed. In time, however, problems surfaced, not the least of which were the slow growth of production and the fact that Ford had to contend with strong competition from General Motors and Chevrolet as well as small, cheap but very good foreign cars such as the Austin and Morris in England, the Fiat in Italy and the Citroen in France.

Ford Canada began production on February 1, 1928, and, according to Mira Wilkins and Frank Ernest Hill (*American Business Abroad*), totaled 74,798 units for the year. A new assembly plant with a two hundred-twenty-five car capacity was completed in Yokohama,

1928 Model A Tudor.

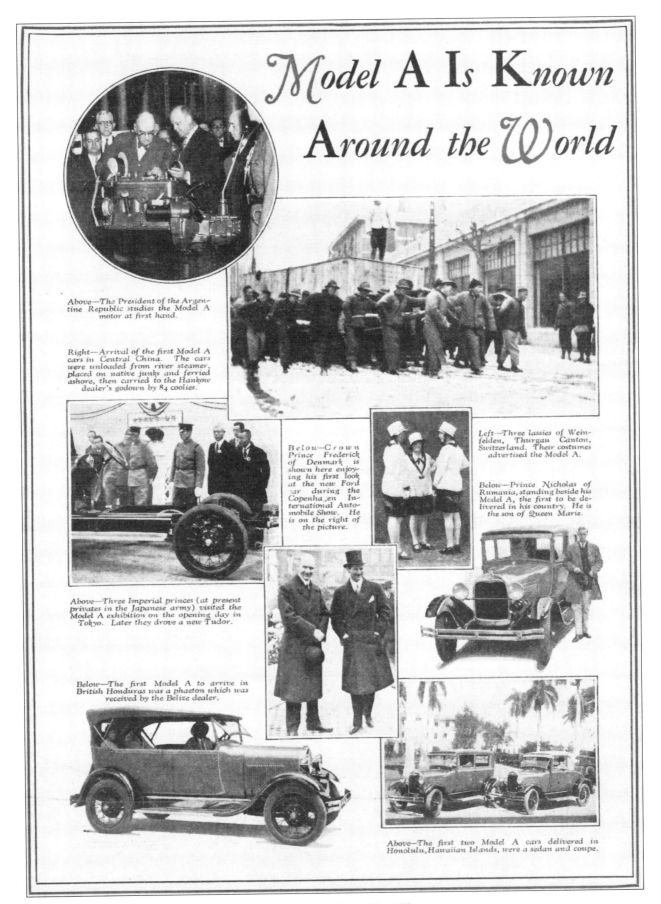

Model A Is Known Around the World

Above—The President of the Argentine Republic studies the Model A motor at first hand.

Right—Arrival of the first Model A cars in Central China. The cars were unloaded from river steamer, placed on native junks and ferried ashore, then carried to the Hankow dealer's godown by 84 coolies.

Below—Crown Prince Frederick of Denmark is shown here enjoying his first look at the new Ford car during the Copenhagen International Automobile Show. He is on the right of the picture.

Left—Three lassies of Weinfelden, Thurgau Canton, Switzerland. Their costumes advertised the Model A.

Below—Prince Nicholas of Rumania, standing beside his Model A, the first to be delivered in his country. He is the son of Queen Marie.

Above—Three Imperial princes (at present privates in the Japanese army) visited the Model A exhibition on the opening day in Tokyo. Later they drove a new Tudor.

Below—The first Model A to arrive in British Honduras was a phaeton which was received by the Belize dealer.

Above—The first two Model A cars delivered in Honolulu, Hawaiian Islands, were a sedan and coupe.

Ford News, June 1, 1928, "Model A Is Known Around the World."

Japan, and Ford added a fourth sales and service entry in the Asiatic field with a new service plant in Shanghai, China. In Latin America business improved as knockdown models became available and assembly plants went on-line. By the end of the year, nine assembly plants in Europe, Mexico, South America and Japan were in operation.

The most serious situation for the Ford Motor Co. abroad was in Europe where imports of the Model A did not begin until May 1928. It was not until October 1,

Service department employees at Keller Motors, Oneida, New York, in 1928-29.

1928, that all the European factories were producing the new car. Sales of both the Model A and AF were slow. The AF was equipped with a special engine with taxable horsepower of 14.9 designed to meet the demands of the British market for a small, inexpensive automobile of sixteen horsepower or less. Nevins and Hill caution that we need to remember here that British horsepower has more strength per unit than its American counterpart.

On the plus side, the 50,000th Ford car sold in Sweden left the Stockholm service plant of the Ford Motor Co. on December 3, 1928. Led by a 1908 Model T and Ford car No. 30,000, the Model A Tudor attracted wide attention as it was driven over the streets of Stockholm.

In addition to the late startup of production, the reasons for lagging overseas sales included high prices that had to be charged due to tariffs as well as rivals who were outselling Ford. In France, for example, the cheapest Model A sold for nine hundred dollars and in Germany the high tariff virtually killed production. "On the continent," write Wilkins and Hill, "because of low-priced, low-powered rivals, Ford was not in first, second or third place in France or Germany, the most important markets."

In England, the Model A was upstaged by small cars such as the Morris and Austin, which were lower in horsepower, cheaper and more economical to operate than the Model A and AF. For the year, Ford's English sales declined to 6,224 cars and trucks against a total production for the country of 211,877 vehicles.

Keenly aware of the problem, Henry Ford and his executives decided to systematize distribution through three great mass-production factories in Dearborn,

A salesman hands over the keys for a 1928 Tudor to a new owner. (Photo courtesy of AACA Library and Research Center)

Admiring a new 1928 Tudor. Visor is covered with artificial leather matching the top material. Belt molding and upper back are painted a dark color.

Pioneer motion picture producer Cecil DeMille poses with his 1928 Tudor. (Photo courtesy of John A. Conde)

Ontario and England in order to produce and distribute cars as economically as possible. Early in 1928, Henry Ford traveled to England and appointed Sir Percival Perry to head the Ford reorganization in Europe. The following December, Ford Motor Company Ltd. was formed to unify all western European interests.

Although 1928 production and sales were up dramatically, the company's report for the year still reflected a loss of $70,640,628 to add to the $30,447,190 deficit the previous year (Federal Trade Commission figures cited in *Giant Enterprise* by Alfred D. Chandler, Jr.). In March, when Ford was struggling with production problems, factory cost sheets showed that the company was losing an alarming $318.79 on each Tudor and $335.84 on every Phaeton produced. Henry Ford himself said that the company did not reach a satisfactory profit until production reached a half-million units. For the year, Ford's annual figures show an overall loss of $84.40 per car.

Over the last nine months of 1928, a steady increase in production and sales, price increases, improvement in plant efficiency and solving of difficulties with suppliers combined to bring the losses under control and point Ford into a profitable 1929. Lowered costs through changes in production, such as the shift to the more liberal use of malleable castings and stampings to replace steel forgings were also instrumental in this turnaround.

The story of Ford dealers during the early months of 1928 was one of patience and perseverance in the face of severe financial difficulties due to the continued lack of new cars to sell. *Automotive News* characterized their loyalty and faith as "amazing." Nevins and Hill point out that although some dealers went under, the mortality rate was only slightly higher than normal.

A December 1, 1928, Branch Check-Up Sheet lists a total of 8,384 dealers in the 35 Branches. Of these, 817 were in cities with populations of 50,000 or more and 7,567 in smaller towns. The Twin City Branch with 444 dealers was the largest and Salt Lake City the smallest with 87.

The financial statement of the Hughson Motor Co. of San Francisco, California, cited in *The Ford Agency* by Henry L. Dominguez, shows the sale of only three hundred-sixty new Model A units in 1928. That compares with a total of 9,500 Model T Fords sold in the years 1925-26-27. Income from the sale of parts was almost as high as that from new auto units.

Another dealer, quoted by Dominguez, wrote that he only lost one hundred-fifty-two dollars in the month of August. After receiving thirty-nine units for September he said, "I feel confident that we will be out of the red and if deliveries keep on increasing it won't be long before we are making a profit again."

Cazenovia, New York, dealer D.D. Norton did not receive his first Model A, a Tudor, until January 6, 1928, and had to wait another month for his second car, also a Tudor. In both cases he was instructed to send a representative with a cashier's check for four hundred-fifty dollars and a blank check for the difference to the Kearny, New Jersey, plant for a driveaway (when a dealer or his representative pick up a car at a Ford plant and drive it to the dealership). Another dealer, Miner's Garage of Oriskany Falls, New York, waited until February 16 to take possession of a Sport Coupe as the dealership's second Model A.

During the early weeks of 1928, dealers in the Green Island Branch, Troy, New York, and probably elsewhere, were instructed that after the Model A they received served its initial exhibition purpose, they should get the car out on the highways and demonstrate it continually, but not sell it. "We want every individual in your community and your logical sales area to receive a practical demonstration of the new Ford car," urged a January 6, 1928, letter from the Branch. In particular, dealer's were instructed to contact bank presidents, lawyers, physicians, businessmen and fleet owners.

On January 30, 1928, G.E. Walrath, the manager of the Green Island Branch, informed his dealers that every agency in the Branch now had its first Model A Ford car to use as a demonstrator and that the Branch was preparing to supply a second car to use for exhibition in the showroom. He warned the dealers not to sell either car

December 1, 1928, Branch Check Up Sheet. (Photo courtesy of Henry Ford Museum and Greenfield Village)

until told to do so because the Branch was arranging distribution to fleet owners and other large commercial users and did not want to slight them by making delivery at random to private individuals.

Desperately looking to make a dollar, some dealers nevertheless sold their demonstrators and, in some cases, made an extra hundred or two hundred dollars by selling through a third party. In reaction, probably to this kind of thing, the Buffalo (New York) Branch sent a special letter to its dealers stating that some of them "had misinterpreted our wishes in the way of handling their first Model A cars. We do not think the first car should be delivered as a retail sale, but should be used as a demonstrator and as an example of mechanical precision." This letter was dated February 20, 1928, showing that after almost three months, production was a long way from meeting demand and that at least some dealers were getting restive.

A February 24 letter informed dealers that enough cars were available that they could begin to make deliveries of units in their possession "to individuals having oldest retail orders on file with our dealers." The only exceptions to this were their demonstrators, which were the original cars furnished to them. Dealers were also reminded that large fleet owners were to continue to receive preferential deliveries.

For small town dealers such as Norton and Miners, the number of new Model As available to them continued to be limited well into the year. For example, in October, Norton was allotted seven units and Miners just five. Norton's allotment for November was eight.

Again and again Norton and the other dealers were cautioned to keep their cars in prime operating condition, paying particular attention to the finish, upholstery, steering wheel, throttle control, emergency brake lever and gear shift lever. The dealer himself, the Branch warned, should check the demonstrator each morning making sure that it was properly cleaned, oiled, greased and that the tires were inflated to the required thirty-five pounds of air pressure. "Don't forget," cautioned the Branch, "that you are merchandising a high quality automobile and that your demonstrator must reflect this quality."

In hope of receiving orders and excited by the Model A's obvious appeal and the intense interest in it, Ford dealers wasted no time in showing the cars to as many people as possible in their communities. Photos and articles in local papers showing prominent people driving or buying a Model A were prime opportunities for positive publicity because of the prestige these important citizens gave the car.

Throughout the year, Ford would reap an advertising bonanza from photos of prominent Americans with their

Starlet Dolores Del Rio with her early 1928 Model A Sport Coupe. Wind wings, radiator cap and spare tire cover were accessories.

Model A Fords. A sampling of these includes New York State Governor Franklin D. Roosevelt, humorist Will Rogers, golf champion Bobby Jones, movie producer Cecile B. DeMille, baseball star Lou Gehrig, actress Billie Dove, columnist Christopher Morley, movie star Wallace Beery and industrialist John D. Rockefeller.

In letters to *Model "A" News* (September-October 1997) and the author, eighty-seven-year-old Ed Kallel of Chesterfield, Illinois, reminisces about his impressions of a demonstration ride he took in a new 1928 Model A rumble seat coupe in Carrollton, Illinois, early in 1928. On that day, a dealer was taking advantage of an opportunity to show the car to a lot of people. He would take a few for a ride a mile or two up the road and back, let them off and then take another group.

Kallel recalls that the upholstery seemed "nice and soft" and had that odor only a new car has, especially with a cloth interior. "I remember," he writes, "how quiet it was and how smoothly it rode compared to other cars, especially the Model Ts and the 1927-'28 Chevys." Kallel says that he was impressed with his ride and marveled at the car's indicated speed of seventy miles per hour although, he confesses, "I have since wondered if they didn't doctor the speedometer."

It appears that some dealers let their zeal for the new Ford and its advertised speed get the best of them, drove them recklessly particularly on driveaways, and did not maintain them as well as they should have. A June 21, 1928, letter from the Green Island Branch admonishes dealers to treat their cars with care so that they could be placed in owners' hands in the best possible mechanical condition. "The Model A will do almost unheard of things when called upon to do so," the letter stated, "but let us insist that you hold your speed down, preferably below recommended speeds, thereby giving this wonderful car the consideration it is entitled to. Give it a chance."

Whenever the Model A which established a new record between Los Angeles, California, and Phoenix, Arizona, appears on the streets of Los Angeles, it proves a constant advertisement for the car's performance and stamina. The same car averaged 62.51 miles per hour in a 500-mile sustained speed test on one of California's dry lakes; and is probably the best-known Model A in the Southwest. The accompanying picture shows how it has been decorated by the Los Angeles dealers, in order to 'tell the world' of its power and prowess.

Phoenix Flyer, *Ford News*, July 2, 1928.

Displaying typical American ingenuity dealers vied for ways to dramatize the stamina and reliability of the new Ford by organizing long distance runs and other events. Many of these performances were written up in the pages of *Ford News*, the company's in-house organ.

On the evening of February 6, 1928, a Model A Tudor, piloted by two Ford dealers, arrived in Seattle after a seventy-six-hour-and-fifty-minute run from the Fordson plant in Michigan. The car traveled a distance of 3,064 miles over long stretches of snow covered prairie country and through snowy Rocky Mountain passes. The only stops made were for refueling, shoveling snow and mud, two full meals and two hours of sleep every twenty-four hours.

In January, a stock Model A Tudor (Engine No.1283) with standard equipment carried three Los Angeles dealers to Phoenix in eight hours and fourteen minutes. After being refueled, it then returned home in eight hours and fifty minutes. The dealers traveled about four hundred-fifty miles each way over rutted, rough roads crossing desert country long considered a severe testing ground of motor cars. The car established a new record and demonstrated that neither road difficulties nor desert sand could interfere with its performance.

Not long after this the same car again proved its stamina by racing around a six-mile circle on Muroc Dry Lake on the Mojave Desert, a distance of 500 miles, at an average speed of 62.51 mph. After the test, an examination showed the car to be in perfect running condition. Finally, the dealers decided to test the car's hill-climbing ability. It was sealed in high gear and driven 36.2 miles out of San Bernardino in one of the stiffest hill-climbing tests possible. For one stretch of 5.7 miles, the grade rose from 3,000 to 6,075 feet with absolutely no chance for relief during the climb. This series of events, the dealers boasted, "establish beyond any reasonable doubt that all-around performance is a built-in characteristic of the Model A car and are convincing proof of its quality, performance and durability."

A dealer in Mt. Morris, Illinois, drove his Model A Tudor with four passengers up a hill with a nearly forty percent grade. On the way down he stopped the car at will to demonstrate the brakes. The hill had never been climbed by an automobile before. Elsewhere, in Pennsylvania, a dealer demonstrating a Tudor to four prospective buyers was run off the road by a speeding car. The Model A turned over three times and tore up thirty-five feet of fence before it was finally stopped by a tree. Although the roof and fenders were badly dented the car remained intact and none of the glass was broken. The five occupants, although shaken, were not injured.

More than 17,000 people tested a new Ford while it was displayed in downtown Syracuse, New York. A total of 3,642 miles of hard driving, quick stopping, second-gear work and turning sharp curves was registered. After the test the upholstery did not show any wear and the car was still in excellent mechanical condition.

In New Berlin, New York, Palmatier Motor Sales ran a Model A continuously for 3,232 miles. Three passengers rode in the car the entire trip. The car delivered an average of 20-1/2 miles on a gallon of gas and did not require any oil to be added. At the end of the run the oil was still in good condition. On a similar run, a Windsor, Missouri, Ford dealer drove a new Model A coupe a total of 2,845 miles at a mean speed of 41.23 mph and an average of 20.2 mpg. Regardless of speed, the car did not overheat. Three tire changes were the only trouble experienced.

In the months dealers had few if any Model As to sell, they scrambled to keep their sales and service staffs busy demonstrating the new Ford, signing advance orders and attending Model A service schools. They were also advised to arrange showings of the "New Ford Car" film, a revised edition of which was available in February at a cost of $26.50 to the dealer.

Since these efforts put little if any money in the bank, dealers also continued to sell Model T parts and service, Fordson tractors and accessories such as snow removal equipment, and supplies such as ammonium sulfate, nickel and body polishes, paints and batteries. The sale of Lincoln automobiles and used cars also helped many dealers keep their heads above water.

The company encouraged all these efforts and, in particular, counseled its dealers to properly display, sell and service batteries and look to the huge number of Model T owners for sales of parts and service. The Green Island Branch, which manufactured about 1,500 batteries a day in January, promoted a sixty day sales contest in competition with other Branches. Prizes were offered to those selling the most batteries, and dealers were encouraged to take advantage of the $3.65 gross profit they received from each battery sale (less about seventy-five cents allowance on the old battery). At the end of the contest Green Island announced that its dealers had sold 4,338 batteries. In the fall, upstate dealers netted $25,000 in profits during a second contest.

During 1928, the D.D. Norton agency received more than a dozen letters from the Branch regarding the approximately 8,000,000 Model T Fords still in service and the importance of reaching out to those Model T owners in its territory. Servicing Model T cars and selling parts was a good way for dealers to bring in cash even after Model A Fords became more readily available. The regular dealer discount of forty percent allowed them to make good money on the sale of parts in addition, of course, to profit from servicing their cars. A dealer could also make a twenty-five percent profit on the sale of a Model "T" engine, less starter, for one hundred-twenty-five dollars.

Ford News, **July 2, 1928.**

Ford News, **July 16, 1928.**

Ford did not just encourage the dealers to concentrate on Model T service. The company backed its words with concrete help including four sample letters to be sent to owners; "stuffers" to go out with the letters; lists of Model T owners, which dealers could purchase at $7.50 per thousand names; and, ads that could be run in local newspapers. Dealers were also required to attend the showing of "Wake-Up," a three-reel film on the importance of Model T service.

Aware that increasing Model T parts and service sales was to their benefit, dealers responded positively to the focus by the company on continuing to provide for its Model T owners. One agency reported that it had added $1,017 in new Model T shop equipment over a period of eight months and that, in the first ten days of May, it had an increase of one hundred-fifteen percent in parts sales and ninety-two percent in labor sales. "This is largely," the dealer wrote, "because we have our men out selling parts and service to Model T owners, making personal calls as well as a follow-up with a series of letters."

During July and August 1928, Ford ran a series of ads in many newspapers throughout the country to reassure Model T owners that the advent of Model A did not mean they would be abandoned. In the Green Island Branch zone these ads were published in over one hundred newspapers. "We're making a new car," wrote the manager of the Green Island Branch, "but we're going to play fair with Model T owners. No Model T Ford will ever be an orphan. We're going to continue to make Model T parts for years to come."

Realizing that in the past much of the service work on Model T Fords was not done by Ford dealers, the company also made a concerted effort to stress with dealers the necessity of intelligent and efficient service so that the new Fords would be maintained exclusively by Ford dealers. Each Model A car and Model AA truck sold was entitled to free fourteen point inspections at 500, 1,000 and 1,500 miles. These were provided at no charge to the owner with the exception of the oil for an oil change.

The dealer who originally sold the car was responsible for these inspections and required to reimburse an owner for expenses incurred if the service was provided at another dealership. After the 1,500-mile checkup, dealers were encouraged to sell the service to owners at $5.00 net exclusive of oil. This included $2.00 for a car wash, $1.50 to lubricate and change the oil and $1.50 for the inspection.

Stressing that service would be the most important factor in merchandising the new Ford car and truck, Ford Branches sent out flyers and had their representatives pay personal visits to dealerships to stress the five important points of Ford Service: 1) Cleanliness. 2)

A 1928 half-ton panel truck operated by Purity Bakery.

Using Ford service equipment. (For a special rate of $72 dealers could purchase a complete set of twenty-three tools for the Model A.) 3) Adoption of a 60:40 bonus plan of pay for mechanics. 4) Using the suggested list of flat rates for labor. 5) Making money (this meaning that better service would be the greatest assurance for increased and continuous sales of Ford products).

The Branches also helped their dealers to provide outstanding service by sponsoring Service Schools at the factory. These schools offered instruction on the various adjustments on the Model A and Model AA together with how to remove, disassemble, and assemble the engine and other major components. Initially, each dealer had to send his shop foreman for a five-day school with the understanding that this individual would then train the other workers in the shop. Later, 2-1/2 day sessions were held for mechanics, sales people and the dealer himself.

At the beginning of Model A production, only five passenger body styles were available. These were a five-passenger Phaeton ($395 f.o.b. Detroit), Roadster ($385 or $420 with rumble seat), Coupe ($495 or $530 with rumble seat), Tudor ($495), and a Sport Coupe with landau irons and rumble seat standard ($550). Initially, all cars were offered in any of seven color combinations: dark or light Niagara Blue, dark or light Arabian Sand, dark or light Dawn Gray, and Gun Metal Blue. The prices listed did not include spare tire and tube ($12.15) and bumper ($15.00).

Throughout 1928, dealers would install bumpers on cars before they sold them, charge the customer the fifteen dollars extra and receive a twenty percent commission on each set. Ford did not encourage the sale of cars without bumpers, but did tell dealers that "if any of our dealers' customers insist on cars without this equipment, there is no objection to our dealers arranging accordingly, but it should be held to a minimum."

Commercial body types in early production included an open cab pickup ($395) and the 1-1/2 ton AA truck chassis, 131-1/2 inch wheelbase, with an open cab ($545) and a choice of three bodies: Platform ($595), Express ($600), and Stake ($610). A closed cab also became available in December 1927. For an extra fifty dollars these trucks could be equipped with a dual high transmission.

On August 30, dealers were informed that production of panel delivery bodies for both the Model A and Model AA chassis had been started. The Model A Panel Delivery would list at $575 f.o.b. Detroit and the AA at $850. Both prices included a fifth wheel, hand-operated windshield wiper and rearview mirror. Bodies only would also be available through service. Also announced in 1928 were nine- and fourteen-passenger buses and a taxicab.

Presented as a "New idea in truck transport," the 1928 Ford Model AA truck shared a common engine with Model A passenger cars. This was an inline, water-cooled, four-cylinder, L-head design powerplant capable of producing 40 horsepower at 2200 rpm. This engine had pump-assisted, splash-type lubrication and pump-circulated thermo-syphon cooling. It employed a three forward speed, selective sliding gear, lever-operated transmission. The optional dual transmission for heavy loads over rough roads, had six forward and two reverse speeds that increased the normal pull of the truck by forty-seven percent.

The AA truck was equipped with a cantilever rear spring designed to lighten unsprung weight, improve riding qualities and increase durability and semi-elliptic front springs with double-acting hydraulic-type shock absorbers. It featured steel spoke wheels, four wheel brakes and torque tube drive. The all-steel cab would easily accommodate a driver and two helpers. Both cab and body were finished in dark green Pyroxylin lacquer

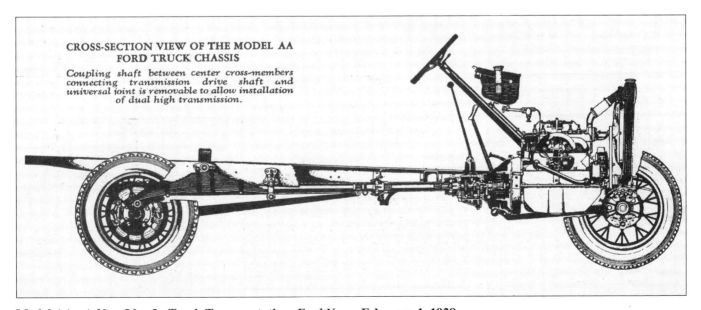

Model AA - A New Idea In Truck Transportation. *Ford News*, February 1, 1928.

Installing the DUAL DUTY UNIT
is a Simple Operation

Specifications of DUAL DUTY UNIT
for FORD TRUCKS

AXLE TUBE—3¼ inches in diameter, 10 gauge seamless steel tubing, capped with malleable iron caps for carrying bearing spindle. Caps are press fitted and riveted to tube.

BEARING SPINDLE—Nickel steel, heat treated and ground of ample size. Fitted to the tubular axle flange with a standard taper and securely locked with a castellated nut and cotter key.

BEARINGS—Bower Taper Roller, No. BT28156-28137 inner, and No. BT09074-09194 outer. Hub construction similar to standard front hub. These bearings are standard Ford bearings.

WHEELS—Standard Ford truck type steel spoke, mounted to hub the same as the front wheels.

FRAME—6⅜ inches in depth, with 3-inch flange extending approximately 48 inches back of the standard Ford frame.

SPRINGS—Standard Ford rear springs with additional graded leaves.

RADIUS RODS—The radius rods are of Silico-manganese steel. These rods are for the purpose of tying the axles together for maintaining alignment and at the same time allowing flexibility between the two axles.

TIRES—32 x 6-inch pneumatic truck type.

DUAL DUTY COMPANY
ALMA · MICHIGAN, U. S. A.

20M-11-28

Printed in U. S. A.

Installation instructions for a Dual Duty unit.

with black wheels. A thirteen-piece tool kit was included with each truck just as it was with the passenger cars.

Aware of the need to adapt the Model AA truck to larger loads, companies such as Dual Duty of Alma, Michigan, began to develop special equipment for Ford trucks. The Dual Duty Unit was a practical way of adapting the standard 131-1/2 inch truck chassis to larger loads. It consisted of an additional axle mounted in tandem with the driving axle. This was carried on four wheels instead of two and allowed for the installation of either an eleven- or twelve-foot body.

A 1928 Model AA platform/stake truck.

As previously stated, production in the early months was slow for passenger cars and, apparently, even slower for trucks. For example, in mid-February, the Norton agency was informed by the Branch that no definite date could be given for receiving a truck and that it would likely be early March before the dealership would be able to get one. As late as March 23, dealers received a letter indicating that the commercial line was still not available and that for "detailed descriptions of our proposed line of commercial body types," dealers should use the March 1, 1928, issue of *Ford News*.

In addition to the Detroit price, the actual cost of buying a Model A car or truck in 1928 reflected other charges including gas, oil, freight and tax. Each car contained nine gallons of gasoline at approximately fifteen cents per gallon and five quarts of oil at approximately fifty cents per gallon. The dealer discount was twenty percent for passenger cars and twenty-two percent for trucks. The truck discount was lowered to twenty percent in June and the excise tax eliminated effective May 29, 1928. The following prices for a Tudor Sedan are taken from the Green Island Branch driveout price list for February 16, 1928.

Tudor Sedan - list for Detroit - $495.00
net to dealers - $396.00
freight - $44.25
tax - $13.21
gas and oil - $1.98
total cost to dealer - $455.44
Green Island delivered price - $554.44

An early 1928 Fordor with celluloid visor. Note the cowl vent. (Photo courtesy of Henry Ford Museum and Greenfield Village)

A few other examples of Green Island delivered prices in February 1928 are $442.17 for the pickup, $610.76 for the Sport Coupe, $443.80 for the Phaeton and $652.73 for the 1-1/2 ton truck with a stake body.

As previously mentioned, Ford raised prices at times during 1928 to help offset losses incurred from production costs. In July, the price of Model AA trucks increased eighty-five dollars per unit. By late November, price increases were noted on a number of models. For example, the base price of the Model A Phaeton was four hundred-sixty dollars, an increase of sixty-five dollars from the previous December, the Roadster was priced at four hundred-fifty dollars, an increase of sixty-five dollars. At the same time the company now listed electric windshield wipers, windshield wings, windshield finger clips and outside and inside door handles as standard on the Phaeton and Roadster.

As production increased so did the number of body styles offered for the Model A. The two-window Leatherback Fordor advertised during the introduction in December 1927 was shown for the first time in early 1928 at the Ford Industrial Exposition held in New York City and Chicago. This show drew over one million people in New York and 400,000 in Chicago.

In addition to exhibits on all aspects of Ford's vast industries, including the cycle of Model A production, the exhibitions treated attendees to the first viewing of the new Fordor presented by Ford as the "deluxe car of the new passenger line." The Fordor, body by Briggs, was not available until late May 1928. Priced at five hundred-seventy dollars initially, it was up to six hundred-twenty-five dollars by July.

Other body styles added to the line during 1928 included the Business Coupe, Closed Cab Pickup, Taxi, Panel Deliveries, and, in December, the Town Car and 150-A Station Wagon. The Standard Coupe, which went out of production for a while in early 1928, was reintroduced in July with a change in the rear panel to leather from the belt up instead of metal as well as a fifty-five dollar increase in price to five hundred-fifty dollars. Although Ford initially referred to this slightly revised model as the Standard Coupe it eventually became known as the Special Coupe until phased from production in July 1929.

SALES   Subject:

General Letter to All Dealers   GREEN ISLAND "DRIVE OUT" PRICES   No. 3
MODEL "A" AND "AA"
CARS AND TRUCKS   P. 2

February 29, 1928.

MODEL	LIST FOB DETROIT	NET DEALER PRICE	ADV FRT ON BODY FREIGHT EQUIPT.	GAS TAX & OIL	TOTAL COST TO DEALER
Tractor	495	396	27.00		423.00
Tractor with Fenders	530	422.25	27.00		449.25
1½ Ton Truck					
Chassis	460	358.80	65.29	2.16	426.25
Chassis with Cab	545	425.10	"	"	492.55
Chassis with Cab and Express Body	600	468.00	"	"	535.45
Chassis with Cab and Stake Body	610	475.80	"	"	543.25
Chassis with Cab and Platform Body	595	464.10	"	"	531.55
1½ Ton Truck – Dual High Transmission					
Chassis	510	397.80	"	"	465.25
Chassis with Cab	595	464.10	"	"	531.52
Chassis with Cab and Express Body	650	507.00	"	"	574.42
Chassis with Cab and Stake Body	660	514.80	"	"	582.22
Chassis with Cab and Platform Body	645	503.10	"	"	570.55

NOTE: Spare Tire and Tube (32 x 6) when furnished with truck, will be $42.05 extra.

FORD MOTOR COMPANY

C. R. SHERWOOD

Chief Clerk

CRS C

SALES   Subject:

General Letter to All Dealers   GREEN ISLAND "DRIVE OUT" PRICES   No. 3
MODEL "A" AND "AA"
CARS AND TRUCKS   P. 1

February 29, 1928

This letter cancels and supersedes the following letters relative to prices to dealers under the Green Island Branch on New Ford Cars and Trucks obtained as driveaways from the Green Island Branch:

(On all cars and trucks obtained as driveaways from the Kearny Branch, freight rates, taxes, gas, oil, etc., shown on Kearny invoices will apply.)

LETTER – "DRIVE OUT PRICES", dated December 20, 1927.

GENERAL LETTER – SALES – "GREEN ISLAND DRIVEOUT PRICES" – No. 3, Pages 1 and 2, dated Jan 19 and Feb 16, 1928.

LETTER – "CONTRACT FREIGHT RATES", undated, from our Traffic Dept.

Effective immediately and until further notice, the following wholesale prices to dealers apply on all New Cars and Trucks driven out of the Green Island Branch:

MODEL	LIST FOB DETROIT	NET DEALER PRICE	ADV FRT ON BODY FREIGHT EQUIPT	GAS TAX & OIL	TOTAL COST TO DEALER
Phaeton	395	316	43.68	10.79 2.16	372.63
Roadster	385	308	"	10.79 "	361.95
Roadster with Rumble Seat	420	336	"	11.39 "	383.23
Coupe	495	396	"	13.19 "	455.03
Coupe with Rumble Seat	530	424	"	14.03 "	483.87
Sport Coupe (Rumble Seat Standard)	550	440	"	14.51 "	500.35
Tudor Sedan	495	396	"	13.19 "	455.03
Fordor Sedan	570	456	"	14.99 "	516.83
Chassis	325	260	"	9.11 "	314.95
Pickup	395	316	"	9.11 "	370.95

NOTE: The Excise Tax on the Pickup is the same as on the Model "A" Chassis, due to the fact that the seat, top and pickup box are non-taxable. The above prices do not include spare tire and tube and bumpers and rear guards.
Price of Bumpers is $15.00 less 20% = $12.00
Price of Spare Tire & Tube is   12.15
When cars are sold with bumpers and rear guards and spare tire and tube, the cost of same will be included in the cost of the car and Excise Tax of 72¢ added.
Each car contains 9 gals of gasoline @ .17 per gal and 5 qts of oil @ .50 per gal.

Green Island Drive Out prices for cars and trucks.

Another early 1928 Fordor. Note the Central Automobile Co. tire cover and the trunk.

Later production Fordor does not have the cowl vent and has a leathered covered visor. (Photo courtesy of John A. Conde)

In late January, Ford advised its dealers that they should not order accessories from outside sources until a decision was made about which ones the company would handle. The letter was accompanied by a list of fifty-five possible accessories and dealers were asked to indicate those for which they had a market. The following July, a list of eleven approved accessories was sent to dealers with a note that these would soon be available subject to the dealer's usual discount of forty percent.

Dealers were also warned that when they sold cars they were not to create the impression that the Model A was incomplete without accessories. "These approved accessories," the company stated, "are offered not as necessities, but to meet the demand of owners desiring additional equipment."

Included among the accessories was the famous quail radiator cap selling for $3.00 and designed to represent "quail in flight, symbolizing the quick acceleration of the Ford car." The others ranged from a tire gauge costing $1.50 to the more expensive windshield wings for open cars costing $8.50 per set. Also listed were a tire cover, tire lock, spare wheel lock for use with well fenders, top boot, electric windshield wiper, moto-meter, and spring covers. Fenders with wells for tires were also an accessory item.

By mid-September, the accessory list increased to more than twenty-five items. Added were such useful items as trunks, cowl and spotlights, an acme starter (push button on steering column) and even radio equipment. In October, a manifold heater was added costing $3.50 if self installed, or $4.50 including installation.

It appears that "approved" list or not, dealers continued to sell accessories not on the official list. B.J. Moore & Co. Inc. of Buffalo, New York, sent letters to Ford dealers advertising Limaco oil gauges costing $2.35 each, Pierce Model A governors for car and truck costing $15.00 each (customer cost: $3.50 and $22.50, respectively), and other items including choke extensions, heaters, air cleaners, trunks, steering wheels, shift handle knobs and a full line of ornaments, wind caps, etc. Moore advised dealers to "Sell the accessories at the time the car sale is made and get this extra profit, which is rightfully yours."

Hungry for increased profits to make up for the down time, some Ford dealers installed accessories without the approval of their customers and then forced them to pay more for their cars. Ford Motor Co. received a number of complaints about this practice and admonished dealers about it in a July letter. "We understand that a number of dealers are adopting a practice of this kind, taking advantage of the customer's keen desire for the automobile regardless of the extras installed or the extra cost. This is a bad practice on your part as it destroys customer goodwill."

In view of Henry Ford's long standing opposition to credit financing, the announcement to Ford dealers on May 3 that the company had organized the Universal

Credit Corp. (UCC) was a bit of a shocker. The purpose of the UCC was to organize the financing of sales to Ford dealers and their customers as well as to forestall efforts by others, such as the Manufacturers' Finance Corp. of New York, to persuade Ford dealers to join their finance plan. UCC officially opened its parent Detroit office on June 1 and by the end of the year had expanded to twelve Branches with more to follow.

Under the UCC plan a dealer only had to advance ten percent of the list price of a car or truck, the credit corporation financed the remainder. In *The Legend of Henry Ford*, Keith Sward argues that "under an arrangement known as 'floor planning,' the UCC promptly began to operate as the factory's most powerful weapon." The Fords, he maintains, now had the final answer for the dealer who tried to resist having to accept cars from the factory that he did not want because of an inability to pay. The factory advanced him the money. Sward also claims that in time UCC agents were given each dealer's blanket power of attorney and could accept or pay for consignments without waiting for the dealer's consent.

Retail customers could also avail themselves of the finance plan by placing a down payment of one-third of

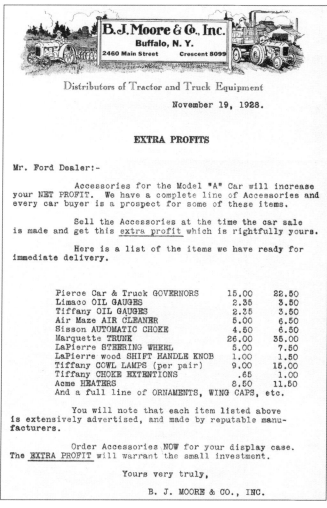

B.J. Moore & Co. letter regarding accessories.

the cash delivery price. They then had one year to complete payment at an interest rate of eleven or twelve percent. Included in the deal was a fire and theft insurance policy that covered eighty percent of the cash delivery price of the car for one year.

With the opening of UCC and the steady expansion of production, dealers began to see an improvement in their sales and financial situation. Those assigned to the Green Island Branch, Troy, New York, shared this improvement but their enthusiasm was tempered somewhat by the disruption of having their Sales and Service Branch close on August 20th. (However, manufacturing of Model A parts such as springs and radiators would continue at Green Island.)

On the face of it, this may not seem to be a huge problem since it was done by the company as part of its effort to curtail operating expenses and increase efficiency. At the same time one can sense the distress, even anguish, of G.E. Walrath, the Branch manager, in the personal letter he sent to each of his dealers.

"It was with the keenest regret that I was obliged to send you the letter today advising of the closing of the good old 'Green Island Branch.' I have come to feel as though we were just one large family of friends: Dealers and the Branch organization. Many of the boys here will no doubt be lucky enough to join the other Branches and continue to do business with a group of loyal, straight-shooting dealers, while others of them will remain at

Green Island, which will continue as a manufacturing plant." Walrath asked the dealers to meet with him personally at the Branch so he could express his appreciation and told them that at least one driveout during the rest of the month would be arranged for each of them.

In the rearrangement of dealers and Branches that followed the closing, D.D. Norton and over sixty New York State dealers were assigned to the Buffalo Branch. Others were added to the expanded territories of the New York City and Somerville (Massachusetts) Branches. As might be expected, the change in Branches also meant some changes in methods of operation.

One of these changes was that dealers such as Norton now had to keep the proportion of models ordered as near as possible to the percentage figures of the various models assembled at Buffalo. For example, for October 1928, Tudor Sedans were to constitute twenty-seven percent of his order, Fordor Sedans seventeen percent, Standard Coupes nineteen percent and Roadsters ten percent.

Fay Leone Faurote visited the Rouge in July 1928 to study the assembly and shipping of Model A Fords. Faurote was well-known as the author, along with Horace Lucien Arnold, of *Ford Methods and the Ford Shops*, the definitive study of Ford manufacturing in 1915. The results of Faurote's observations were articles published in August 1928 in the *American Machinist* magazine and in *Factory and Industrial Management.*

A late 1928 panel delivery. Note the optional mounted rearview mirror. This was the first Model A panel delivery car delivered in Michigan. It was purchased by the Herpolsheimer Co. of Grand Rapids, a leading department store in western Michigan. (Photo courtesy of John A. Conde)

Ford Motor Company

Manufacturers of Automobiles, Trucks and Tractors

GREEN ISLAND, N. Y.

January 5th, 1928

IN REPLYING REFER TO

TO ALL DEALERS:

ALL STATEMENTS OR AGREEMENTS CONTAINED IN THIS LETTER ARE CONTINGENT ON STRIKES, ACCIDENTS, FIRES, OR ANY OTHER CAUSES BEYOND OUR CONTROL AND ALL CONTRACTS ARE SUBJECT TO APPROVAL BY THE SIGNATURE OF A DULY AUTHORIZED EXECUTIVE OFFICER OF THIS COMPANY. CLERICAL ERRORS SUBJECT TO CORRECTION.

NUMBERING OF MODEL "A" CARS

On all Model A Cars the motor number will be stamped on the left side member of the frame at a point which will be covered by the cowl and gas tank assembly. Should it become necessary to change the number on a motor or frame the old number is not to be removed but a line stamped through and the new motor number stamped above or below the old one in the same manner as stamping a new car.

The number stamped on the motor or frame is to be preceded by stars, such as **A-090. A record is to be kept of this exchange of numbers and this Branch should be notified at once of any such change.

FORD MOTOR COMPANY

JOHN A. SEELENBRUCKER

Service Department

JAS Q

Letterhead of Green Island Branch.

Fordson Plant (Rouge) during the Model A era.

Rolling Mill at the Rouge.

The first article follows, step by step, the 76-1/4 operations required to assemble a Model A Tudor Sedan from the initial placing of the frame assembly on a stand to starting the engine, running the car off of the assembly conveyor and its final inspection.

In the second article, Faurote reviews how Model A cars and trucks were packed and shipped when they were not picked up by dealers as driveouts. At that time, in August 1928, cars were being shipped primarily in railway cars or boats either in complete assembly or as major and minor assemblies and parts. Shipments were being made both to domestic plants and overseas. According to Faurote, the company handled over 1,000 railway cars a day in its major and minor plants. Each of the box cars used was generally 36 to 40 feet long, 10 feet high and 8-1/2 feet wide with a capacity of 80,000 pounds.

An article in *Ford News* (August 15, 1928), states that more than eighty railway cars left the Pressed Steel building in the Fordson plant of the Ford Motor Co. every twenty-four hours. They contained fenders, hoods, running boards, shields, body parts and similar materi-

als. These shipments were consigned to Ford Branches and were that portion of the output that was not used for assembly within the Fordson plant.

Complete cars shipped in boxcars were commonly grouped as three closed cars and two open cars in one railway car. The accompanying diagram illustrates how the cars were arranged and the method used for unloading them. Model As were also grouped as four sedans or two sedans and two trucks. Since a Model A chassis took less room than a complete car, a railway car could hold seven regular Ford chassis or five regular chassis and one Ford AA truck chassis. Shipped separately, Model A engines were packed upright in a special shipping fixture, seventy engines in a forty-foot standard railway car. Smaller parts could be loaded over them to the weight capacity of the boxcar.

In some instances transporting Model A Fords by ship was cheaper than using the railroad. For example, one hundred-seventy-five Model A Fords were delivered to dealers in Rhode Island by freighter early in 1928. They were unloaded in Providence and then driven to the various dealers participating in the consignment. The cars

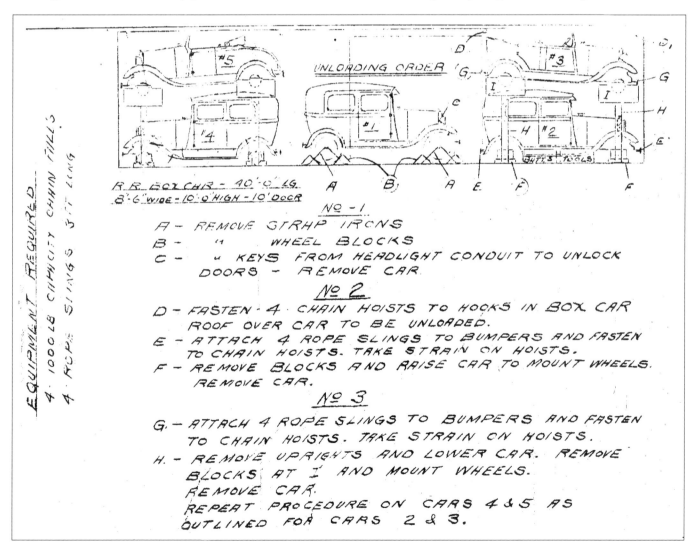

Ford Motor Co. diagram of how a boxcar was to be loaded with Model As in 1928.

were loaded at Kearny, New Jersey, and the expense of shipment was cut in half by using the water transport.

The significance of the growing number of women drivers and their interest in owning cars, was not lost on the Ford Motor Co. during the Model A days. In February 1928, *Ford News* alerted dealers to the importance of the woman driver or owner by featuring an article, "Women and the Model A," in its Dealer Supplement.

Interestingly, and probably in keeping with the thinking of the times, the article is stereotypical and does not mention any interest on the part of women in the mechanical aspects of the new Ford. As a matter of fact, it does not even mention beauty of line, price or interior comfort as factors influencing a woman's attraction to the Model A Ford, although clearly they were. As the following excerpt shows, the message to Ford dealers was that cleanliness was the key factor in a woman's decision about buying a Ford at a dealership.

"[Evidence of] Grease impresses a woman more than it does a man; she can detect dust where the average man

Women and the Model A

THE increase in closed car production to 70 per cent of the total in 1926; the trend toward greater beauty and style; improvements in riding quality and driving ease; the increase in two-car ownership; the constantly growing number of women drivers; and the 665 per cent increase in advertising investment in women's magazines from 1923 to 1926 by passenger car manufacturers—all are significant facts.

Woman's influence in American life —in work, food, dress, thinking, reading, entertainment and buying—has engulfed old notions and ideas and has swept new activities and methods into existence.

Like all other business men, the Ford dealer has had to adjust himself and his establishment, his sales methods and his service department, to care for this great factor in present-day merchandising. The woman owner or driver demands a clean place into which she can come for car repairs or to make further purchases. It is not enough to show her a freshly cleaned floor when new models are presented and have a dirty floor the rest of the year.

Grease impresses a woman more than it does a man; she can detect dust where the average man would never notice it. A pleasing arrangement of accessories or parts in the show cases and on the shelves will impress her very much more than it will her husband. A clean place to stand or sit down is essential if she is to favor your place of business.

Dirt has no charms for her; neither has an untidy exterior Water, soap, a paint brush and a broom, applied regularly in the proper places, will make everybody feel better and will result in a larger bank balance

You know the saying—*He profits most who serves best.'*

"Women and the Model A," *Ford News* **Dealers' Supplement, February 15, 1928.**

would never notice it. . . . A clean place to stand or sit down is essential if she is to favor your place of business. Dirt has no charms for her; neither has an untidy exterior. Water, soap, a paint brush and a broom, applied regularly in the proper places, will make everybody feel better and will result in a larger bank balance."

Taking an entirely different approach, Hazel Fahnestock wrote an article published in the October 1928 issue of *Ford Dealer & Service Field*, in which she tried to persuade women that it was easy to learn to drive a Model A Ford. Her humorous opening paragraph will be enjoyed by anyone who drives an "A."

"My husband tried to write an article on how to drive the new Ford. But it was as full of foolishness as most of the things men do. He said, 'Release the clutch,' when he meant 'Push down on the left-hand or Clutch Pedal.' Or 'Advance the spark,' when he meant to say in clear English 'Pull back the little rod under the left-hand side of the steering wheel.' I sometimes think mechanical men use these left-handed technical terms for the same reason that lawyers use Latin—to display a little learning to impress us women."

In addition to advertising the new Ford in newspapers in 1928, Ford began to target potential buyers through ads in more than forty magazines. These included several specifically aimed at women such as *Cosmopolitan*, *McCall's* and the *Women's Home Companion*. Ads in these magazines emphasized that the new Ford is the right car for women because it is "a splendid car for the busy mother," or because "smooth riding ease and restful comfort make the new Ford an especially good car for women to drive." Women see things that men do not, the ads claimed, and that is why, for example, they see that the Model A's upholstery has been made for long wear as well as appearance. A man would only say that it is "good-looking."

For 1927 and again for 1928, the Ford Motor Co. was awarded the Harvard Advertising Award for meritorious advertising. This award was bestowed each year by the Graduate School of Business Administration of Harvard University. The 1927 award was presented for the best advertisement of the year dealing with a specific product in the national field. The ad selected was one of those used to introduce the Model A. During 1928, the same body presented the company with an even more significant award for a "national campaign conspicuous in excellence of planning and execution." It was presented both for the Model A and in the general field of aviation.

The end of Model T and advent of the Model A were events of such importance that they were celebrated in song by well-known writers such as Walter O'Keefe who composed "Henry's Made A Lady Out Of Lizzie," arguably the most famous of the Model A songs.

Here's how the song begins:

"Have you seen her, ain't she great?
She's something you'll appreciate.
I'm sure you understand just what
  I mean.

Everybody, everywhere is falling
  for her now,
I'm talking 'bout the new Ford,
And boy, it's sure a wow!

Two other charming Ford songs written in 1928 were "I'll Be Ready to Marry When You Buy Me a Ford," written by Lawrence Lewis, and "Poor Lizzie," written by Abner Silver and Jack Meskill, which laments the end of the Model T with lines such as, "Poor Lizzie, what'll become of you, now that your sister is here?" Also noteworthy and probably written in 1928 is "Henry Ford's Model A," sung to the tune of "Casey Jones," by a man named Oscar Ford.

As more and more Model As came off production lines and were delivered to customers, letters of praise from all over the world began flowing into company offices. Following is a sampling as found in the pages of *Ford News*:

Model A Stands Test of Road

Myron T. Monsen took delivery of a Model A Tudor (Engine No. 129904) in New York City on May 28. Monsen broke the car in on an 1,100-mile jaunt through New England, and then drove it from Philadelphia to Chicago in 23 hours and 32 minutes. "I was particularly pleased," he wrote, "with the power and ability to maintain high speeds, as I have driven practically every car made in the last 21 years. Not one drop of water was added in the radiator after starting although I ran up the mountains and most of the way with the throttle wide open. . . I think you have a wonderful automobile entirely different from anything on the market so far."

Triplex Glass Does Its Job

One of the features of the Model A was its shatterproof windshield. This glass was made of three layers with an inner layer of transparent plastic binding two outside layers of fine, thin glass. The three layers were forced together under heat, pressure and chemical treatment so they were permanently a single, solid layer of the same thickness as ordinary glass. Under impact the glass would crack and score but not shatter. Under severe impact people were thrown through it, but avoided the injuries that come when glass shatters. Numerous examples of how well the glass worked were sent to Ford.

For example, one of the earliest accidents in a Model A was reported in a New York newspaper on January 14. A man driving his new coupe on the highway was cut off by another car, forced off the road and crashed into a pole. He was hurled

forward and his head struck the windshield, but he escaped serious injury. In Texas, two women driving on a lonely stretch of road were fired upon. The bullet struck the windshield directly in line with the face of the lady driving, and ricocheted off without penetrating the glass.

In another incident, a railroad crossing gate was lowered directly across the road in front of a traveling Model A and a fifteen-pound weight suspended from the gate dropped completely through the windshield barely missing the driver. The hole was clean-cut and there were no glass splinters.

Ford Company Wins Advertising Award

HARVARD ADVERTISING AWARDS

Founded by Edward W. Bok

ADMINISTERED BY THE
HARVARD GRADUATE SCHOOL OF BUSINESS ADMINISTRATION
GEORGE F. BAKER FOUNDATION, HARVARD UNIVERSITY

A Series of Annual Awards Offered to Encourage Merit and Stimulate Improvement in Advertising

Certificate for 1928 of the Award to

Ford Motor Company

For the National Advertising Campaigns of the Ford Motor Company,—deemed by the Jury of Award conspicuous for the excellence of their planning and execution in advertising both the Ford Motor Car and the general subject of Aviation

In Testimony Whereof, the Harvard Graduate School of Business Administration issues this Certificate of Award, signed by its Dean and approved by members of the Jury of Award who served during the year 1928

Dean

Approved by

MELVIN T. COPELAND NELSON S. GREENSFELDER GUY C. SMITH
ELMER ADLER JOSEPH B. MILLS PHILIP L. THOMSON
NEIL H. BORDEN WILLIAM F. ROGERS RICHARD J. WALSH
LEWIS C. GANDY THOMAS L. RYAN ROBERT R. WASON

Jury of Award

Certificate of merit presented by Harvard University.

One of the principal marks of recognition for meritorious advertising is the series of annual awards founded by Edward W. Bok and bestowed each year by the Graduate School of Business Administration of Harvard University. They are offered to 'encourage merit and stimulate improvement in Advertising.' Twelve men of wide experience and national repute sit on the jury which determines the winners annually.

One year ago the Ford Motor Company was given the prize for the best advertisement of the year dealing with a specific product in the national field. The ad selected was one of those used to introduce the Model A.

During 1928 an even more notable recognition was given the company by the same body, the Certificate of Award for a 'national campaign conspicuous in excellence of planning and execution' both for the Ford motor car and in the general field of aviation. It was presented to the company March 8.

Karl Dane usually travels in a Ford coupe when at home on his Malibu ranch property. George K. Arthur drives a new Ford coupe wherever he goes. Norma Shearer always uses a Lincoln, having a town car of special body design.

Ford Motor Co. wins advertising award. (Photo courtesy of Henry Ford Museum and Greenfield Village)

Why the Model A Is Superior

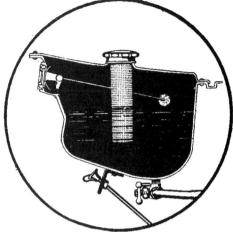

Cross-sectional view of welded fuel tank showing fire-proof filling sieve and gas gage.

Safe, simple, efficient, enduring—these are the outstanding qualities of the gasoline tank of the new Model A Ford car.

A fine-meshed circular sieve extends downward from the inlet opening of the tank, effectually eliminating all danger of fire from flames nearby, precisely as the famous Davy lamp has eliminated the hazard of gas explosions in coal mines. Many earnest experimental attempts to set fire to the gasoline within the tank through the sieve have failed without exception. Another safety feature of the tank is its strength. It has successfully withstood an internal air pressure of ninety pounds.

Built of terne plate, a rustproof form of steel, and fabricated by the seam resistance welding method, the tank is integral with the cowl of the car and provides a steady supply of fuel to the engine by gravity, the simplest and most dependable method. Simplicity and dependability, too, mark the gage, the indicator of which is connected directly with the float. Internal baffle plates prevent the gasoline from splashing.

The sieve which protects the fuel from external flame also filters it as it enters. Minute particles which do manage to escape through the sieve into the tank are removed by a gasoline filter between tank and carburetor.

"Why The Model A Is Superior," regarding the fuel tank, *Ford News*, January 15, 1928.

Saves Lives in Hawaii

Three Japanese youngsters were driving at high speed when the car left the road and rolled over into a five-foot ditch. The car tore up a length of fence and finally stopped upside down, with its engine still running. The fabric on the top of the sedan was torn, the body was scratched but barely dented and the windshield was full of cracks but unshattered. Both doors could be opened and closed and the windows raised and lowered as before. The only major items of damage was a bent front axle and a bent front fender. Despite reportedly driving almost seventy mph, the boys crawled out of the car without serious injury.

Splendid Service From His Car

While visiting Cincinnati, Ohio, a man received an urgent call to return home to Utah. After covering 2,660 miles he wrote, "I sincerely believe the car is as good today as when I took delivery. After driving six days through rain, snow and mud, the little car has proved to be a wonder. The mud in places was hub-deep due to continuous rain. At one place I passed eight cars and a bus all nicely settled in the mud for the night."

Model A Wins German Contest

A standard Model A Sport Coupe won the gold medal in a utility and reliability contest for automobiles held in Germany. It competed against a large number of cars, most of which were bigger and higher priced. The contest included a hill-climbing competition, starting test, cross country trial and tests for slow speed, brakes, acceleration with gear shifting and fuel consumption. The starting test was held at the beginning of each day's program. The cars were kept out-of-doors all night, had to be started within one minute after the driver touched foot to them, and had to leave the starting line under their own power.

Fire Tests Strength of Fuel Tank

Built of ternplate, a type of steel that resists rust indefinitely, and fabricated by the seam resistance welding method, the Model A fuel tank is integral with the cowl of the car or truck and provides a steady supply of fuel to the engine by gravity. A fine meshed cylindrical safety screen extends from the inlet opening of the fuel tank into the interior and eliminates all danger of fire from nearby flames. As mentioned elsewhere, Ford salesmen were fond of passing a lit match near the inlet opening of the tank with the safety

screen. A weak flame would appear and this would be easily and safely extinguished by placing a hand over the opening.

A dramatic example of the strength and safety of the fuel tank, occurred in Harvey, Illinois, when a fire broke out in a Model AA truck parked in a garage. The owner of the garage went to investigate a blowing horn and found the upholstery and the cab of the truck ablaze. By the time the fire was extinguished, the cab was completely gutted. There were four gallons of gasoline in the tank, and although the tank bulged from the terrific heat, the gasoline did not add any fuel to the fire.

Converted To The New Ford

A naturalist stationed on Mt. Washburn (altitude 10,346 feet) in Yellowstone Park, observed many different makes of cars as they struggled to the top of the mountain. In a letter to Ford headquarters he wrote, in part:

"Let me congratulate you. Of the thousands of cars to win the summit and make the pass, the new Ford Model A surpassed them all. I have checked up on this all the year. I make the statement without bias, malice, or reservation. Also, without influence from Ford agency or representative. Many makes of cars go over in second and many of the same makes do not go over. But I have never seen any style of the new Ford that could not go over without touching low, also without raising the mercury column one-half

Ford News
February 15, 1928

Windshield Glass Protects Owners

This standard Model A windshield has been struck twenty-five blows with a steel hammer. While the glass has cracked, not once has it been shattered. Right—Clipping from eastern newspaper, telling of actual accident in which Model A owner escaped serious injury largely through the use of Triplex.

All Ford Model A cars are equipped with Triplex shatterproof windshield glass. It is also available in the various Lincoln models as optional equipment. In case of accident there is no flying glass to injure or disfigure. The glass will do no more than crack.

During the World War, aviators were protected by goggles and windshields made of this material. Glass for submarines, and safety screens for high speed submarine chasers, were made of it.

Flying glass, usually from windshields, is responsible for 65 per cent of all injuries in the 700,000 annual automobile accidents. The shatterproof glass, which by actual test is 50 per cent stronger than plate glass of equal thickness, will not do more than crack. There are no flying splinters or jagged edges. It will also soften the direct rays of the sun and break headlight glare. It relieves condensation on the glass of closed cars during winter driving. Although flexible under impact, it cannot be cut with a diamond.

Seventeen distinct operations are re-

UNHURT IN NEW FORD SMASH-UP

NEW YORK, Jan. 14.—Distinguished by having the first accident in one of the new Fords, Edward Price, 25, of Everett, Mass is a hero today in his home town. Price was driving his new coupe along the highway through Norwalk, Conn., when a passing car abruptly cut in on him and forced him off the road on a hill. His car crashed into a pole and Price was hurled forward, his head striking the windshield.

Triplex, the flexible, non-shatterable glass, which is standard in the new Fords, stood up under the crash, according to Price, and an impact which might have caused him vital injuries brought him no harm. At the same time, the rubber composition steering wheel doubled up, according to witnesses, saving Price's chest from hurt. The car's body was badly smashed.

quired in its manufacture. Two pieces of thin specially selected ground and polished glass are coated with chemicals to make a cement coating; a layer of pyroxylin plastic is introduced between the two coated sheets, and by means of heat and pressure the two are united to form a single sheet of laminated glass.

The laminated sheet is finally sealed at all edges to prevent action of air and moisture on the plastic and the chemicals.

Shatterproof glass cannot be cut and fitted as ordinary glass, but must be manufactured to the size required. It is not truly unbreakable, but when broken, each small particle of glass adheres firmly to the pyroxylin inner layer with the result that flying pieces and jagged edges are eliminated. When severely damaged, the entire piece usually remains within the windshield frame.

Windshield glass protects owner, *Ford News,* **February 15, 1928.**

inch. I hope to buy a car before spring and my Mt. Washburn observations have converted me to the new Ford."

Speed In The New 1928

Walter E. Moore, Ford dealer in Manhattan, Kansas, used a novel advertisement to tweak the interest of prospects in the new Ford. His advertisement, reproduced in the March 1928 issue of *Ford Dealer & Service Field*, and cited in *The Restorer* (September-October 1967), mentions that one of his salesmen was fined ten dollars for speeding while trying out one of the new Ford cars. In the ad, Moore stressed the "easy riding qualities" of the Model A and concluded with a challenge: "Who's next to take a ride?"

So desperate were people to get a new Ford that they pulled out all the stops to try to get people with influence to help them find a car. In August 1928, for example, Alice Ford Bequette contacted R.H. Laird, an in-law of Henry Ford, who worked in Henry Ford's office gathering information for the Ford family tree. She wrote that her sons needed a four-door sedan right away, but were unable to find one within a radius of one hundred miles in less than ninety to one hundred-twenty days. Bequette asked Laird, whom she knew, to use his influence to help the young men.

Laird replied about a week later and told her to have her sons place an order with a Ford dealer and send the name of the dealer and information on the car wanted to him. "When I receive this information," he wrote, "I will refer it to our distribution manager and request him to have a car sent to this dealer tagged for delivery to your sons."

Subsequently, he received notice that an order for a four-door sedan with two fender wells, two extra wheels, medium-priced trunk and solid bumper on back had been placed with a California dealer. He then informed Bequette that she could expect delivery in about two weeks.

Model A equipped with steel pick-up body and open cab.

Pickup body is a popular type, *Ford News,* **February 15, 1928.**

On September 23, Mrs. Bequette wrote to Laird and told him that the car had been delivered on the 21st. Her sons wanted to be sure that the car was only driven twenty miles per hour for the first five hundred miles, so they and a salesman picked it up from the distributor and drove it to the dealer's shop. "They are sure proud of it," Bequette penned, "and the envy of all that have had their orders in so long." She asked Laird to remember her and her family to Henry and his family and "tell him how proud we are of the car."

The Model A Ford was a good car for its time, but it was not perfect. Nevins and Hill tell us that by mid-1931, halfway through the car's fourth and final model year, some 200 major and 19,000 minor changes had been made in its construction. Some of the more difficult problems with which Ford had to contend in 1928, involved the brakes, clutch and starter.

The Model A's four-wheel brake system was criticized by authorities in a number of states and foreign countries because it did not have an independent emergency brake system. Germany even refused to license the sale of the new Ford until this was changed. Ford eventually had to give in and, as early as January 1928, the company announced that it was planning to equip all new Ford cars and trucks with an emergency handbrake independent of the four-wheel service brakes.

This separate emergency brake system was phased into production beginning in February 1928 and, except for some commercial vehicles, completed by June. These commercial vehicles continued the early emergency brake arrangement into 1929. The change meant that the handbrake lever had to be relocated from the left of the driver to the center. In 1930, it was moved to the right of the gear shift.

Another brake matter that turned out to be a problem concerned stops that were discontinued when the change to solid brake rods was made. Since these stops prevented any possibility of the brake equalizer coming out of the brake operating shaft, dealers were informed in September that they should check on every car they delivered with the solid-type brake rods, and make certain that the stops were installed.

Six weeks later, the company followed up with a second letter stressing the importance of having this done, and lamenting the fact that stops had been installed on only a few cars. Not wanting to broadcast the problem, the company also told dealers to do the work without calling it to the attention of the owner. Obviously, the part and labor were being supplied without charge to the owner, but there is no indication in the letters whether or not the dealer had to pick up part or all of the cost.

In November, dealers were informed that a new single plate clutch was now standard on all Model A cars and AA trucks. This would replace the troublesome multiple disc, dry plate-type. The next month, the company told its dealers to offer truck owners having clutch problems a special material price of $18.50 to replace the multiple disc clutch with a single disc clutch. The dealer's labor charge should not exceed $10.00. This would amount to

Station Bus, mounted on the Model AA truck chassis.

Station Bus on Truck Chassis

THIS is a commodious body which will comfortably accommodate fourteen persons including the driver. It may be used as a delivery unit by folding up the side seats.

The body is steel, with three windows on each side, besides the door windows. The roof is covered with heavy rubber-coated material; exterior finish of the body is in pyroxylin in a variety of color options. The two folding front seats and the side seats are upholstered in brown artificial leather, and the interior finish harmonizes with the exterior. Rubber floor mats are provided. The rear door is wide; access to the bus is made easy by a step. The spare wheel is carried on a bracket over the running board on the right side. Dimensions are: Inside height 51 in.; width 50 in.; and length from back of front seat 92⅞ in.; length of side seats 92 in.; width of front doors 28³⁄₁₆ in.; width of rear door 32 in.; height 45 in.

Station Bus on Model A Chassis

THIS is an all-inclosed passenger and delivery car for use on estates and by clubs and schools. It will accommodate nine passengers besides the driver. There are two folding seats in front and side seats in the rear, all upholstered in brown artificial Spanish leather, deeply cushioned to insure full comfort for passengers. In addition to the door windows there are two windows on each side, as well as small panel windows in the rear door. The body is steel with wide belt running back from the dash. The roof is covered with heavy rubber-coated material.

Finish will be in a number of colors of pyroxylin, with interior to harmonize. The spare wheel is carried forward in a fender well on the left side. Dimensions show an inside height of 51 in., width of 50 in., and a length from back of front seat of 60 in. Width of front doors is 28³⁄₄ in., width of rear door 32 in., height 45 in. The height of bus from road is 77 in.

On the left is shown the driver's compartment of the Model AA Truck, Station Bus. This compartment is similar to that of the Station Bus mounted on the Model A chassis so far as seating arrangement is concerned. In center is the Station Bus mounted on Model A chassis. On the right, looking into passenger compartment of Model A Station Bus.

Station Bus, *Ford News* Dealers' Supplement, April 16, 1928.

Panel Body Types Fill Important Need

Model A light delivery with panel body.

Model AA truck with panel body.

THE panel type of body fills a special field of usefulness in delivery service. For department stores, bakeries, and all others who wish their goods transported in an inclosed truck or delivery car, it offers an ideal combination. Its two sides present opportunities for attractive advertising, either of the name or the slogan of the owner. Its method of construction affords protection and insures cleanliness and freedom from dust for the wares carried within.

Two styles of panel body types are offered by the Ford Motor Company as part of its standard equipment. One is designed for the Model AA truck; the other for the Model A light delivery.

The Model AA panel body is attractive in appearance. It is constructed of a combination of wood-finished interior and metal exterior. Two folding seats give the driver easy access to the interior of the body. Loading dimensions are, approximately: Width 50 inches; height 51 inches; length 93 inches. The spare wheel and tire are carried over the right running board, to the rear of the cab door.

The Model A light delivery panel body is likewise built with a wood interior and metal exterior. Its roof is covered with a heavy-coated rubber material. Double doors at the rear open the full width of the body and are provided with a handle lock.

The driver's compartment is fully inclosed. There are two folding seats upholstered in brown artificial leather. The loading space is approximately 50 inches wide, 47 inches high and 60 inches long.

Prices have been announced as follows: Model AA complete with panel body, $850; panel body only, $310; Model A complete with panel body, $575; panel body only, $250.

Two Cars for Every Family!

More and more families are coming to realize that one car is not enough to answer present-day needs. Dad needs a car for his own personal use if he is to keep all business appointments promptly. Mother needs a car for shopping, the theater, and social calls and then there are the children to take to school.

Some families in moderate circumstances find it economical to own three cars. Many of them have discovered that it pays to own two. Your family can own two cars just as well as not.

Because Model T Fords will play a conspicuous part in automotive transportation for many years to come, it will pay you to keep your Model T in first-class condition. Bring it to our service station for a complete overhaul NOW.

How? By purchasing two new Fords at a cost less than the price of one car of more expensive make. Or by keeping the Ford you now own and buying one new one. Why not use your faithful Model T for an extra or second car? Then you can have your new Model A as spic and span, always, as grandfather's Sunday surrey.

A message to owners from dealers' sales bulletin.

Panel Body types, *Ford News* Dealers' Supplement, August 15, 1928.

The Business Coupe

THE Model A Business Coupe instantly commends itself for use by business executives, salesmen and those in commercial life whose activities keep them on the road. It combines good appearance with service and is in every way a practical car.

It has a bit of the sport coupe effect. The roof covering which extends down over the rear quarters to the belt line of the car is of high-grade black artificial leather heavily coated with nitro-cellulose to withstand weather. This covering is mounted over padding and moisture-proof material and is supported by heavy wood bows.

The bow effect is carried out in the interior rear quarter with trimming in harmony with the cushions, giving the whole interior a most pleasing effect. Door pockets are convenient for papers or small books and there is a commodious parcel shelf behind the seat. The seat cushion is deep and comfortable.

The rear deck has a luggage space of 14 cubic feet and the deck opening 35 3-8 inches wide. The door, which is provided with a handle lock, lifts easily and is held in place by supports when raised. Hinges are fully protected from weather and rust, and the door closes into gutters which run down an opening with a spillway into the road, making the compartment fully waterproof. Rumble seat may be obtained at extra cost.

❧ ❦ BODY-DETAILS ❦ ❧

Number of passengers - 2	Number of doors - 2	Width of front seat 42½ in.	Color options - - 5
		Width of doors - 29¼ "	Exterior finish - *Pyroxylin*
Frame work material - *Steel with rear quarter of wood bows*		Height of body - 49½ "	Tire size - 30x4.50
		Height of car from	Wheels - *Steel spoke*
Top and rear quarter - *Black artificial leather, pyroxylin coated*		road - 71½ "	Windshield type *Tilts out*

EQUIPMENT: *Automatic windshield wiper, gasoline gage on instrument panel, spare wheel, sun visor, combination tail and stop light, door locks, ignition lock, 4 shock absorbers, speedometer, four-wheel brakes, rear-view mirror, dash light.*

Business Coupe, *Ford News* **Dealers' Supplement, April 1, 1928.**

a substantial savings for truck owners since the normal charge would be between $50.00 and $60.00.

The Abell-type starter drive initially used on the Model A proved unsatisfactory so, finally, about October 1st, Henry Ford bowed to the inevitable and the company obsoleted the Abell and went to one hundred percent production on the Bendix-type starter drive. Dealers could get the new unit from their Branches for an exchange price of $3.00. The price to the customer was to be $4.50, including installation. While dealers were not to campaign to get customers to change over, they were to point out that "because of its quieter, smoother operation, the Bendix starter drive constitutes a distinct improvement over the old type."

There was a scattering of criticism reflecting other problems including faulty speedometers, checks in the composition of some steering wheels, Houdaille (hoo-dye) shock absorber arms striking and indenting the front fender apron, oil pump difficulties when starting a cold engine at low temperatures and defective batteries.

The dealers also had to contend with complaints about a rumble in the Standard Coupe, leaking roof on the Business Coupe, problems with steering gears in cars previous to Engine No. A-15650, rusting landau irons used on the Sport Coupe and windows in closed cars having a tendency to lower slightly when the car was in motion. All of these as well as other problems were addressed and taken care of eventually.

A number of dealers reported that curtains or floor mats in Phaetons and Fordors were missing. The Buffalo Branch, however, found this hard to believe and suggested strongly that before they complain, dealers should check the car carefully, including the compartment in the rear of the front seat of the Phaeton for the curtains and behind the back of the rear seat in the Fordor for the carpet. If they did that the Branch believed they would most likely find the missing items.

Sensitive to the importance of providing a superior product and keeping Model A buyers happy, the Ford Motor Co., through its Branches, urged dealers to immediately report any complaints to their Branch Service Department. If the matter was sufficiently serious, they were to use the telephone rather than mail or wire. The Ford Motor Co. did not just seek to sell the Model A, it wanted happy and satisfied customers, which, of course, would generate more sales.

As 1928 ended, the company saw itself on the edge of a breakout 1929, and it would leave no stone unturned in the quest to return Ford to sales leadership. For a short time—two years—the Model A would make that happen.

A 1928 Tudor - owner Sam Aiello.

A 1928 Ford Speedster - owner Ed Sensbaugh.

A 1928 Sport Coupe - owner Lorch Wildenstein.

A 1928 pickup with box. For sale in the flea market at Dunkirk, New York.

A 1928 fruit peddlers truck - owned by the late Joe Doti.

A 1928 Leatherback Fordor.

A 1928 pickup - owner George Nowack.

Chapter Three

1929: The Golden Year

"He has caused more dirty dishes to be left in the sink after
supper than all of the Leading men in the Movies.

He has broke more people's wrists than all the Osteopaths in
the World combined.

And caused more Profanity than Congress and Senate combined.

First man to discover every Joke sold a Car, and every Joke
bought one.

Broke in more customers for other cars than necessity.

Only Millionaire that ever apologized for ANYTHING.

Gives more value for the least money. A marriage certificate
and a Ford car are the two cheapest things known.

Both lead to an ambition for something better.

IT COST HIM ONE HUNDRED AND FIFTY MILLION TO
GET AMERICA OUT OF ONE FORD AND INTO ANOTHER."

Will Rogers, *The American Magazine*, December 1929

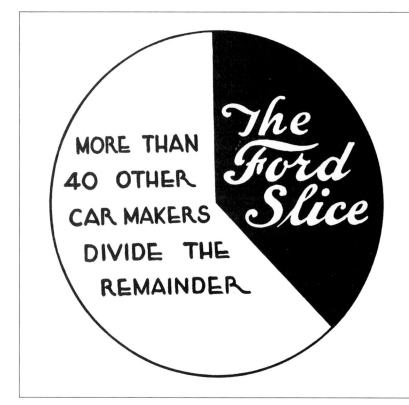

The Automotive Pie of 1929

IN the old days we were accustomed to graphs which showed Ford car production as constituting half of all car output. But when Model A came into being naturally Ford production fell below that of many other makes.

The old ratio is returning rapidly. Here, is a chart showing the "automotive pie" for 1929. Notice the generous slice which was served to Ford while the remainder was divided variously among other car builders.

Expressed otherwise, it means that during the year Ford output reached 37% of total production of all makes of cars, and it is certain that the percentage will greatly increase during 1930.

The total Ford production for 1929 was 1,951,092 cars and trucks—an increase of 138% over 1928.

Next in the race came Chevrolet with 1,301,166. The difference is easily computed as 649,926—the Ford lead.

"The Automotive Pie of 1929," *Ford Dealer & Service Field*, **February 1930.**

Written at the end of the Model A Ford's signature year, humorist Will Rogers' words are part of an article in which he lists all the reasons why Henry Ford is his "Grand Champion," as he calls him. In his own unique style, Rogers mirrors the high esteem that many people around the world had for the automobile industrialist who had followed one success, the Model T, with another, the Model A.

Despite the stock market crash in October 1929 and signs that the good times enjoyed by many Americans were quickly coming to an end, the Ford Motor Co. and its Model A ended the year on a roll. Allan Nevins and Frank Hill say that government figures show that Ford made a profit of $91,522,000 in 1929 (after taxes), "a figure all the more impressive," they add, "when the substantial profit reductions of other companies were considered." It was Ford's best profit year since 1924, and the company's high-water production and sales mark for the next quarter century. Profit per car is listed by *Automobile Trade Journal* (1932) as $41.90.

A 1930 issue of the Utica (New York) *Observer-Dispatch*, lists Ford production for 1929 as 1,851,092 machines, as do Nevins and Hill. Two sources from the Henry Ford Research Center ("Production By Body Type" and "World Production for 1903-1943"), and data published in *Ford Dealer & Service Field* (1930) and *Automobile Trade Journal* (1932) place the total Model A

and AA production figure at 1,951,092 units for 1929. Recent research by Steve Parageter (*The Restorer*, May/June 1991) sets the number at 1,961,092 units worldwide. These numbers, although not far apart, indicate the difficulty of determining exact Model A production figures.

Whatever the number, it is clear that, after two years in second place, Ford rebounded with a vengeance in 1929, capturing thirty-seven percent of total production of all makes of cars and once again became the sales and production leader of the industry. Ford production of almost two million cars and trucks, was an increase of one hundred-forty-two percent over 1928. Next in the race came Chevrolet with 1,301,166. Nevins and Hill list Ford's sales for the year, as distinguished from factory production, as 1,710,734 units.

A review of 1929 shows that production and sales moved upward steadily. In late January, Ford announced a daily output of 7,418 units had been reached and, on June 26, the production lines established a one day record of 9,100 units. Model A Engine No. 1,000,000 was assembled on February 4, 1929, slightly less than fifteen months after production was started. On July 24, less than six months later, a Cabriolet, the 2,000,000th Model A, rolled off the Rouge assembly line. In contrast, it took more than seven years to build the first one million Model Ts and eighteen months and a few days to complete the second million.

F O R D   F A R   A H E A D   I N   1 9 2 9   T R U C K   S A L E S

	Position 1929	Position 1928	Total Retail Sales for Twelve Months 1929	Total Retail Sales for Twelve Months 1928	Per Cent of Grand Total of Retail Sales 1929	Per Cent of Grand Total of Retail Sales 1928	Gain or Loss in 1929 Over 1928 Number of Units	Gain or Loss in 1929 Over 1928 Per Cent
Ford...............	1	2	223,085	65,270	42.38	19.13	+157,815	+241.77
Chevrolet..........	2	1	160,940	133,682	30.57	39.19	+ 27,268	+ 20.39
I. H. C.............	3	4	31,274	26,196	5.94	7.68	+ 5,078	+ 19.38
Dodge.............	4	3	28,646	36,542	5.44	10.71	— 7,896	— 21.60
G. M. C...........	5	5	14,221	17,569	2.70	5.15	— 3,348	— 19.62
Reo...............	6	6	13,218	16,325	2.51	4.78	— 3,107	— 19.03
Mack..............	7	7	6,865	6,898	1.34	2.02	— 33	— .48
White.............	8	8	6,084	6,273	1.16	1.84	— 189	— 3.01
Fargo.............	9	11	3,368	1,175	.64	.34	+ 2,193	+186.64
Autocar...........	10	10	2,987	2,191	.57	.64	+ 796	+ 36.33
Federal............	11	9	2,772	3,111	.53	.91	— 339	— 10.90
Pierce-Arrow........	12	12	483	803	.09	.23	— 320	— 39.85
Miscellaneous.......	..	....	32,447	25,088	6.16	7.35	+ 7,359	— 29.33
TOTAL.............	..	....	526,390	341,123	.....	.....	+185,267	+ 54.31
TOTAL without Ford	..	....	303,305	275,853	.....	.....	+ 27,452	+ 9.95

"Ford Far Ahead in 1929 Truck Sales," *Motor*, March 1930.

At the end of the third quarter, Ford announced that total car and truck production for the first nine months of 1929 was 1,633,498 units and that advance schedules for the full year indicated production in excess of 2,000,000. As previously mentioned, Ford did not quite reach the magic two million plateau in the model year, but the company did celebrate a total of 2,033,202 units built by Ford plants between December 2, 1928, and December 1, 1929. *Ford News* described this as a "truly phenomenal record for the second year's production of any car," and "a new high mark for the industry."

In foreign countries, as in the United States, the year 1929 was characterized by a spirit of expansion. On May 16, 1929, Edsel Ford broke ground at Dagenham, England, and the construction of a huge Ford manufacturing center was underway. Plans called for the plant to begin some manufacturing in 1930, but it did not open until March 19, 1931. Wilkins and Hill say that 107,113 Model A and Model AF cars and trucks were sold in England and on the continent by the end of 1929.

Ford sold 84,952 units during the year in Latin America and Asia and its Canadian subsidiary managed to sell 87,830, including units delivered to South Africa, India, Australia, Malaysia and New Zealand. Ford interests in Australia included a large manufacturing facility at Geelong, assembly plants in five states and three hundred-thirty-three Ford dealers. As in the United States, the company's books at the end of 1929 registered profits wherever the Model A was sold abroad. The reorganized British and continental companies showed a net earning in excess of $10,280,000 and the Canadian company a profit of $5,461,000.

Ford's Model A overseas story for 1929 also included an agreement with the Soviet Union to help organize Model A production there and to sell 72,000 knockdown (unassembled) Ford cars and trucks to the U.S.S.R. in the next four years. The agreement involved $30,000,000 worth of Ford products and the construction of a Ford factory by the Soviet Government, with technical advice and assistance from Ford.

In the summer of 1929, Rouge production boss Charles Sorensen traveled to the Soviet Union to review the plans for Model A and AA production. Sorensen gives the details of this trip and what happened subsequently in a fascinating chapter on "The Russian Adventure," in his 1956 autobiography. More on the Russian story is included in later chapters of this book.

As 1929 moved along, Ford Branches and the parent company received letters and cables from around the globe detailing achievements of the Model A in tests, competitions and just ordinary driving. Non-stop endurance runs were among the favorites. Early in 1929, a Model A Tudor with its hood sealed and carrying a driver and his relief, successfully completed a six-day, six-night non-stop run through difficult Alpine passes in Switzerland. In South America, Ford Phaetons finished a two hundred-hour non-stop run in Brazil and a one hundred-hour run in Venezuela without any problems.

To demonstrate the efficiency of the Ford engine, a Phaeton was tested over one hundred hours of non-stop running on the streets and highways of Brisbane, Australia. Throughout the test a normal passenger load of four persons was maintained and at times five or six made up the load. After the run, the car was taken to the showroom of the Brisbane dealer where the cylinder head was removed and the crankcase lowered.

Official observers representing the Motor Trader's Association made the following report: "Total mileage 2,563. Petrol consumption 29.12 miles per gallon, Exceptionally economical in view of full passenger loads. . .speeds maintained (averaging throughout the test 25 mph). Less than one cup of water added to radiator. The oil proved to be wholly satisfactory—the condition of the engine provides abundant proof of this."

On May 4, 1929, three Model A Fords took first, second and sixth place in the 1,440-mile Copenhagen-Paris-Copenhagen automobile and motorcycle test. The winning car, a Tudor, drove the route in thirty-two hours, five minutes, an average speed of 47.25 miles per hour. The car's driver said, "We just went, that was all. No matter how deep the ruts, or whether we had to go into the fields, crossing a crude railroad track with deep ditches, we just flew over everything, and we did not have one single mishap, aside from a couple of punctures, on the trip."

Another report of a difficult test came from French Equatorial Africa where a driver was forced to run his Model A Phaeton for five hundred miles on the left front rim because he had ruined two tires and had no spare left. While using the rim he drove at a speed of about

Danish Winners

Herewith are shown the Model A owners who won the first two places in the recent Copenhagen-Paris-Copenhagen race in which a large number of cars took part. Three out of the first six places went to the Model A.

In the top picture the driver seated on the right is the owner of the Tudor, Mr. Tholstrup. Before the race his car had gone 23,000 miles.

The winner of the second place appears in the lower photo on the right, minus his hat.

Above—Winners of the Copenhagen-Paris race in Model A Tudor.

Below—Winners of second place in Model A phaeton.

"Danish Winners," *Ford News*, July 1, 1929.

A 1929 family reunion at the Eckel homestead in Vienna, New York, is graced with a new 1929 Model A Roadster parked next to a damaged Overland.

Don Gendron poses with his new Model A Tudor in 1929 in Rhode Island.

A young lady sits on the fender of the family Model A Tudor in 1929.

A young woman poses in her 1929 Sport Coupe, August 30, 1929.

The Ford Phaeton

Features of the Ford car

Sturdy body construction ✧ ✧ *Mechanical reliability* ✧ ✧ *Unusual number of ball and roller bearings* ✧ ✧ *Alemite chassis lubrication* ✧ ✧ *Choice of colors* ✧ ✧ *Four Houdaille hydraulic double-acting shock absorbers* ✧ ✧ *Triplex shatter-proof glass windshield* ✧ ✧ *Fully enclosed, silent six-brake system* ✧ ✧ *Quick acceleration* ✧ ✧ *55 to 65 miles an hour* ✧ ✧ *Smoothness and security at all speeds* ✧ ✧ *Vibration-absorbing engine support* ✧ ✧ *Theft-proof ignition lock* ✧ ✧ *Economy and long life.*

Ad for a 1929 Phaeton from *The Country Gentleman*, September 1929.

A 1929 Oval Window Business Coupe - owner Ron Van Allen.

A 1929 Phaeton.

thirty-five miles per hour over an exceptionally hard road and covered the distance in two days. After arriving home he mounted a tire on the rim and drove twenty miles farther without difficulty. During the trip the car carried three drums of gasoline and a camping outfit.

As production and sales accelerated through 1929, the company finally announced that in March it was able, for the first time, to balance the manufacturing schedule at the Rouge to provide for full production of its entire line. The eighteen different passenger and commercial types then available were designed to cover almost every transportation need.

Among the passenger cars were two open types, the Roadster and Phaeton. A third, the Convertible Cabriolet, was listed by Ford with the closed car line that included the two-window Fordor Sedan, Tudor Sedan, Sport Coupe, Coupe, Business Coupe, Town Sedan, chauffeur-driven Town Car, Taxicab and Station Wagon. Each type was available in a variety of color combinations.

Commercial vehicles consisted of the Model AA truck with express, panel and platform bodies, the latter also available with stake, stock rack and grain sides; the light delivery pickup with either closed or open cab; the Panel Delivery and Deluxe Delivery. In 1929, light commercial vehicles were generally painted Rock Moss Green although several other colors were available. The heavy iron was painted either green or black. Wood parts were painted Commercial Gray Spar varnish.

For the first year and a half of Model A production, truck orders were lost because of the company's inability to increase production sufficiently to limit the wait time to an acceptable amount. By May 1929, truck production was up sufficiently so that Branches could promise ten day delivery on orders. The following July, production reached the point where all dealers could arrange to stock at least one low speed and one high speed truck as samples, sell these as soon as possible, and then get replacements. By the end of the year, Ford surged far ahead in truck sales moving 223,085 units or 42.38 percent of the total retail sales to 160,940, or 30.57 percent for Chevrolet.

In December, the Buffalo Branch sent out a list of dealers who had AA trucks in stock and suggested that dealers who did not have any should continue to try to sell them and obtain the needed unit from the nearest dealer who had it. The number of chassis available at dealers ranged from eight to zero. The majority had only one or two or none. Stake bodies predominated with express, panel and platform also available, but in much smaller quantities.

In addition to the attractiveness of the Model A and its performance and quality of workmanship, there were a number of standard features that, Ford boasted, "make it beyond doubt the greatest value ever offered in Ford history." These were the Houdaille hydraulic two-way shock absorbers, five steel spoke wheels, the extensive use of steel in the construction of the body itself, the greater use of steel forgings and of electric welding throughout the chassis and Triplex shatterproof windshield glass. Added to these were the six-brake system, the Twolite head-lamps, the stop-light signal, the gasoline gauge on the dash, the headlight control on the steering wheel, the electro-lock in the ignition switch as well as others.

Interest in the new type of Ford bodies announced late in 1928 peaked at the Ford Service Exposition in New York City early in January 1929. These types were the Convertible Cabriolet, Town Sedan, Taxicab and Town Car.

The Cabriolet was advanced as a car for all seasons adaptable as a closed car for inclement weather and an open car when the weather was fair. The top was able to be folded compactly when lowered and lie flat in back of the seat. Door windows, which fit snugly into the top, were in nickeled frames and could be raised to act as windshield wings when the top was lowered. Its list price was six hundred-seventy dollars f.o.b Detroit.

The Town Sedan, a three-window Fordor type, with body by either Murray (155-A) or Briggs (155-B), listed at six hundred-ninety-five dollars. It was equipped with nickeled cowl lamps and a finish strip at the juncture of

A 1929 Roadster Pickup - owner Al Mattei.

A 1929 Town Sedan - owner Charles Storm. An original car photographed at Hershey '98.

Ernest Portner and friends load scrap on a Model AA stake rack and another truck.

Carrying Coke in an early Model AA Truck.

The new Ford Town Sedan

OF ALL the many features of the new Ford, there is none that means so much to the woman motorist as the comforting assurance that everything is just right.

You have confidence in the mechanical performance of the car because it has, to a greater degree than ever, the reliability that has always been associated with the name Ford. Equally important is your confidence in the safety of the car.

Your first impression of the new Ford is one of sturdy strength. This is due not only to the substantial, well-built frame and the extensive use of steel in the body, but also to the carefully-planned balance of the car. The way it holds the road is particularly noticeable on curves and in traveling at more than average speed.

The six-brake system of the new Ford, is, of course, one of its outstanding features. It is unusually reliable and effective because the surfaces of all six brakes are fully enclosed. There is thus no possibility of water, dirt or oil entering the brake mechanism and interfering with brake action under ordinary driving conditions. Silent, easy operation is another feature you will appreciate.

A further factor in the safety of the new Ford is the Triplex glass windshield. This is so made that it will not shatter or fly under the hardest impact. Such protection becomes increasingly necessary as traffic increases and is an important point to remember in the purchase of an automobile.

Ease of steering and of shifting gears, quick acceleration, abundant speed and power for every emergency, and full vision front, side and rear also contribute to the safety of the new Ford and are among the reasons why it is such a good car for a woman to drive.

Ad from *The Farmer's Wife*, August 1929 showing 1929 Town Sedan.

the hood and cowl. The interior was luxurious with armrests on either side, a center armrest that could be folded when not in use, right and left assist cords, a flexible robe rail on the back of the front seat, pockets on the doors, pull-down silk curtains on the rear and rear quarter windows, and a dome light. Production of this type and the Cabriolet was not scheduled to begin until March.

In a letter to dealers, Ford said that the Cabriolet and Town Sedan were designed to reach a market "we are not thoroughly covering with present types." These were people who could afford paying hundreds of dollars more for luxury and beauty but, according to Ford, did not get the "motor car performance that only the Model A can give."

Ford News profiled the Model A Taxicab and Town Car in December 1928. Figures compiled by Leslie R. Henry (*Henry's Lady* by Ray Miller) show a production of 89 Town Cars and 264 Taxicabs in 1928, and 913 and 4,576, respectively, in 1929. Only a small number of each were produced after that. The Taxicab provided ample room for three passengers on the back seat and a fourth on a folding rear facing jump seat. It was ruggedly built to withstand the hard use to which cars in taxi service are subjected. The driver's seat was separated from the passenger compartment by a sheet metal partition with windows of triplex shatterproof glass. A February 22, 1929, letter to dealers states that special colors for taxicabs were available for an extra charge of ten dollars subject to the dealers' regular twenty percent discount. There was no charge if the order was for ten or more. The Model A Taxicab was listed at eight hundred dollars.

Offered for discriminating (read, wealthy) motorists, the all-weather Town Car had a Briggs custom-made body mounted on the Model A chassis. It had room for three in the back and one next to the chauffeur and was listed at $1,400. The Edward Lowe Motors Co. of San Francisco offered a Town Car with Triplex glass throughout for $1,550 delivered complete.

The interior of the Town Car was trimmed with high grade English Bedford cords or French broadcloths,

Telegram received by D.D. Norton regarding the sale of Town Cars.

Pair of 1929 Town Cars at the 1996 Rochester National Meet of the Model "A" Restorers Club.

Distinguished Appearance   *Exceptional Riding Comfort*

ANNOUNCING

THE NEW FORD TOWN CAR

Here is a fashionably designed, chauffeur-driven car created to meet the difficulties of city traffic conditions.

Its striking smartness has made it the instant choice of thousands of distinguished families throughout the United States.

It will be welcomed by those who already own larger cars of this type. The Ford Town Car is admirably suited as a personal car for down-town shopping, theatre—in fact it adequately will fulfill any service now performed by your larger cars, and with greater facility.

Price $1550 Del'vered Complete
Triplex glass used throughout.

A telephone call will bring this car to your residence for demonstration.

Walnut 2000

EDWARD LOWE MOTORS COMPANY

Van Ness Avenue at Jackson
SAN FRANCISCO

SACRAMENTO   OAKLAND

Ad from *Ford Dealer & Service Field* showing 1929 Town Car.

A 1929 Town Car. (Photo courtesy of John A. Conde)

A 1929 Station Wagon.

optional to the purchaser and was described by Ford as "offering all the lavish features found in the finest cars." The passenger compartment had several accessories including a pocketbook-type vanity set, a center bow light, a clock, a pair of hassocks and a cigar lighter and ashtray combination.

According to George DeAngelis, Edward Francis, and Leslie Henry (*The Ford Model "A" as Henry Built It*), Ford projected 2,500 Town Cars but sales were not strong. Even a price reduction of two hundred dollars on November 1, 1929, did not help. Eventually, only 1,198 units were delivered. At first, sales of this model were reserved to Lincoln dealers, but weak returns eventually prompted the company to encourage Ford dealers to sell them.

D.D. Norton, for example, received a telegram on February 13, 1929, explaining that the Town Car "has enjoyed an excellent reception by owners of big cars for use as a small second car." He was advised to immediately place a three-month order for this model. There is no record of how the dealership responded.

In May, dealers received word that a Standard Three-Window Fordor Sedan, list price six hundred-fifty dollars, was being added to the line and that it would be furnished in the same colors and upholstery as the two-window Fordor. More ordinary than the Town Sedan, the Standard Fordor had an adjustable front seat but did not have cowl lights, nickel cowl band and armrests in the rear compartment. Both of these new types proved popular and were continued in production into 1931. In 1929, 53,941 Standard Fordors and 84,970 Town Sedans were manufactured.

On January 4, 1929, dealers in the Buffalo (New York) Branch were informed that Station Wagon production would begin the following week and that the list price for this model would be six hundred-ninety-five dollars. This new unit would have comfortable seating accommodations for eight passengers. Seats in the rear compartment could easily be removed if it became necessary to convert the wagon into a hauling unit.

The following October, concerned that dealers were not promoting the general utility use of the Station Wagon, the Buffalo Branch sent them a letter reminding them to emphasize the fact that this type was an all-purpose car practical for use by landscape gardeners, telephone and telegraph companies, ranches and plantations, farmers, contractors and others.

The wood body parts for the Station Wagon were milled at Ford's Iron Mountain plant on Michigan's Upper Peninsula. They were shipped to the Murray Corp. where they were assembled and shipped to Ford plants for final assembly on the chassis. The 150-A Station Wagon, characterized by a square profile with a sun visor, was built through May 1930. Total production was 6,529 units with 4,954 of these built in 1929.

A 1929 Panel Delivery.

Panel Delivery bodies mounted on the A or AA chassis were not available in sufficient quantities during the early months of 1929 causing the company to lose considerable business. A May letter from the Buffalo Branch informed dealers that the company was now in position to increase production of these two types, and asked that they survey their areas and try to close as many Panel Delivery sales as possible. At that time the list price for the Model A Panel was six hundred-fifteen dollars, while the Model AA Panel was more expensive at eight hundred-fifty dollars.

Dealers were also notified that a limited number of panel bodies only were available "through Service." These could be purchased for approximately two hundred-fifty dollars for the Model A and three hundred-ten dollars for the AA and installed on any surplus chassis they might have on hand. Production figures for the 1929 Panel Delivery, body by Budd, as cited by Lorin Sorensen in *The Commercial Fords* were 22,012 for the Model A and 5,166 for the Model AA. Sorensen also says that "except for 1950, the 1929 Model A would hold all Ford Panel sales records through 1956."

Another panel type, the Deluxe Delivery, began production in 1928 and became available in 1929 due to a request from the Jewel Tea Co. for a light-duty delivery car with a back door. Essentially a windowless Tudor with a door cut out of the back body panel, the DeLuxe Delivery was priced at five hundred-ninety-five dollars. Access to the loading compartment was through the wide rear door, which also had a window to give the driver rear vision. All doors had locks giving full protection from theft. The spare wheel was carried in a fender well on the left side. According to Sorensen more than 7,000 of these cars were produced by the end of 1929 production.

In 1929, the Ford Motor Co. began to supply Model A and Model AA chassis to the U.S. Post Office. Regional Post Office garages would then mount postal vehicle bodies constructed of oak or white ash and painted "Post Office Olive Green" to these chassis. *The Model A Judging Standards* (published jointly by the Model "A" Restorers Club and the Model A Ford Club of America) list five companies that made mail truck bodies: York-Hoover Body Co., York, Pennsylvania; Mifflinburg Body Co., Mifflinburg, Pennsyl-

A 1929 photo showing a 1929 Panel Delivery. With the truck are the grandchildren of the owner, A.F. Hubler.

A 1929 Deluxe Delivery.

vania; August Schubert Wagon Works, Syracuse, New York; Metropolitan Body Co., Bridgeport, Connecticut; and General Motors Truck Co., Pontiac, Michigan.

Production of Model A Mail Trucks is listed by the *Model A Judging Standards* as 400 on the 1929 Model A chassis and 1,000 on the 1931 chassis. Total production of Model AA Mail Trucks was 400 on the 1929 chassis and 2,500 on the 1931 chassis. Model A and AA Mail Trucks were built from June 1929 to March 1932.

Many Ford commercial Model A and AA vehicles seen on the highways in 1929, as well as during all the Model A years, had colorful and unique bodies designed for special needs. These were ordered in volume by fleet purchasers including A & P, Armour & Co., Bell Tele-

phone, and Railway Express. Bodies were built by suppliers such as York-Hoover, Stoughton, Martin Parry, Lee Trailer & Body, the Geneva Body Corp., Wood Hydraulic Hoist and Body Co., and numerous others. Many were also built to order in small local shops located all around the country.

Some bodies for the Model A were built by individual owners. A 1929 Model A Roadster, for example, was assembled with an aluminum body crafted by W.L. Walton of Indianapolis, Indiana. Walton bought a 1929 chassis at the Rouge, installed a seat and drove it home. He then hand-built the body and had the engine reworked by the Miller race team for which he did bodywork at the time. His work, says John Young, one of the current own-

A 1929 Snowmobile.

A 1929 Model A mail truck.

Depot Hack, body by John Vandenberg & Sons, Hawthorne, New Jersey.

A March 4, 1929, photo of a Model A with special body and six wheels. (Photo courtesy of John A. Conde)

Panel truck, body by John Vandenberg & Sons, Hawthorne, New Jersey.

A wrecked Huckster.

A 1929 Model AA Delivery truck.

A 1929 Model AA Large Platform Stake truck with four wheel extension.

LAUNDRY OFFICE

DE LUXE CURVED SIDE PANEL
For Ford Model A Chassis
Model No. 1909—Loading space, Length 70″, Width 44″, Height 51″.

A double insulated body with curved sides and pressed in steel moulding—V. V. type windshield and air deflector, automatic windshield wiper and rubber floor mat, double spring cushions with folding spring backs beautifully trimmed and finished—Ternstedt remote control hardware.

Page 6   STOUGHTON COMMERCIAL BODIES

Stoughton Bodies catalog.

T.A. Kimball with his special body Model AA "grinding" truck.

ers, "is exquisite and masterful. The detail and craftsmanship is unmatched in today's time given the limited tools of that era that Mr. Walton had to work with."

John Young first saw the car in the 1940s. Many years later he ran across it again and, over a period of years, tried to buy it numerous times. Finally, in 1986, he was successful. He and his brother, Ralph, restored the car from the ground up doing all the work themselves except the paint and upholstery. They consider the car to be a "museum piece."

From February 1929 through October the list price of the various Model A types remained fairly constant. There was a twenty dollar reduction in the price of a closed cab pickup on April 10, but no significant change after that until all prices were lowered in November.

As anyone who has ever bought a car knows, the list price for the various Model A types was rarely the actual price paid. That was as true in 1929 as it is today. To find out the delivered price of a Model A in 1929, information was pulled from an actual sales invoice (courtesy of *The Cowtown "A"*) for a two-window Fordor sedan, Engine No. A1692550, sold by the Harris Motor Co. of Fort Worth, Texas, on June 26, 1929.

The Fordor was listed at $625 but the buyer actually paid $893.93. This price included fifteen dollars for a spare tire and tube, fifteen dollars for bumpers and fifty-seven dollars for accessories (tire lock and cover, spring covers, pedal pads, quail, trunk rack and trunk). There were also charges for freight and delivery, gas and oil, insurance, license and a light test. The customer traded in a used car for $190.53 and took a note for $703.40 payable in twelve installments over the next year. The carrying charge for the note was $64.40 or slightly over nine percent.

In addition to keeping a supply of parts adequate to handle the normal workload, dealers were expected to display and sell a percentage of approved accessories based on their allotment of cars. In March, for example, with every ten cars delivered they were to sell five moto-meters, five spring covers, eight tire covers and wheel locks, eight pedal pads, three radiator ornaments, etc. In August, they were warned that "under no circumstances should tire covers furnished by outside manufacturers be installed on Model A cars, new or used, either on a charge or gratis basis."

Based on quotas established by Ford, one hundred percent accessory sales would equal $7.55 per car at the dealer's net price. At the end of six months not one Branch had reached one hundred percent quota. The highest was seventy-seven percent (three Branches) and the lowest twenty-one percent (three Branches). At the same time the company revised the quotas or percentages of cars for which accessories should be sold. The tire cover, for example, had a one hundred percent quota. The lowest was fender lamps assigned a quota of two percent. Other examples were the Quail radiator cap at twenty-five percent, pedal pads at sixty percent and spring covers at thirty percent.

Dealers received a discount of forty percent on accessory sales and were urged to pass along at least five percent, if not ten, to encourage salesmen to sell accessories to their prospects. Selling accessories in groups was highly encouraged. In April, the tire cover, tire lock, tire gauge, moto-meter and cap, spring covers and pedal pads were offered at a group price of $16.25. A price, by

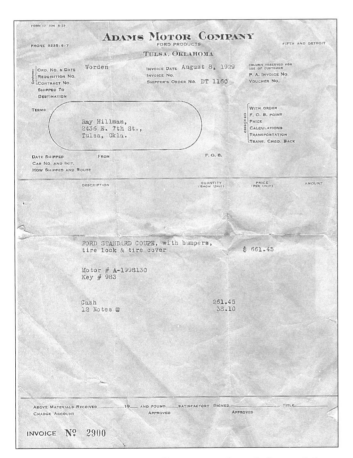

Invoice for a Standard Coupe purchased from Adams Motor Co. of Tulsa, Oklahoma.

A 1929 aluminum-bodied Roadster originally built in 1929 by W.L. Walton. Current owners are John and Ralph Young.

the way, which was not a savings for the buyer over the individual prices of these items.

Each month the dealer was required to submit an inventory of the accessories he had on hand and a list of his requirements for the next month. The company played hardball on this issue, warning dealers that if they did not submit the inventory and requirement list they would have to take what the Branch shipped them. They were told that they must establish monthly quotas for their salespeople and do everything possible to show a marked increase over previous months sales. At one point, Norton was admonished for a shortage of seventeen tire cover sales on the one hundred-eight units sold to date and told to take immediate steps to remedy the situation. It is clear that Ford pressured dealers regarding accessory sales.

At the end of 1929, the list of approved accessories sent to dealers was not a whole lot different from that of 1928. Some of the items introduced during 1929 were an air filter, distributor heat baffle, fender lights, eight day clock, folding trunk rack, trunk, cigar lighter, seat covers and sport light. On July 2, dealers were informed that "The idea of an automobile dealer trying to merchandise a side line like a radio is out of the question." The company suggested that dealers already had more than enough to do and that "the day of handling radio as a side line has passed."

The use of radios in Model A cars, however, especially for police departments, was lauded by Ford in an article in *Ford News* about one hundred-twenty-five Model A Ford cars ordered by the Chicago Police Department. These were to be radio equipped but, based on the letter sent to dealers, probably not by the dealer who took the fleet order.

Only one major body style change was made during Model A production. This distinguishes the 1928-29 models from the 1930-31 versions. As noted in the previous chapter, however, there were hundreds of major and minor changes in the Model A and AA during their four model years. Some of these resulted from Ford

engineers and production line people discovering better, frequently less expensive, ways to do things. Others were due to feedback from dealers reacting to complaints from their customers.

Among the complaints that surfaced in 1929 were reports that Station Wagons had problems with water leaks, that small accidents were being caused by the sharp lower corner of open body doors, and that gear shifts in Model A cars were coming out of second and into neutral unassisted. There were also reports that customers were alarmed by certain noises they heard in the engine and that there were overheating problems in some units.

These complaints and other problems and changes were addressed by the company in service letters from the Branches to dealers (not to be confused with Service Bulletins), and in other letters sent almost daily from each Branch to the dealers in its territory.

To solve the Station Wagon water leaks, instructions were given to use rubber weather strip or windlace on the door sills and door jams. To prevent cuts from sharp lower edges of open car doors, the remedy was to round off the lower corner on the lock side of all doors.

The gear shift problem was the result of an engineering compromise so that drivers would have an easy shift. The company claimed that the problem was never encountered on level surfaces and only infrequently

---

Form 3027
500M—7-10-29

NEW CAR DIRECTIONS

SPEED Avoid high speeds while the car is new. To obtain best results, IT SHOULD NOT BE DRIVEN FASTER THAN 30 TO 35 MILES PER HOUR FOR THE FIRST 500 MILES.

OIL Keep the oil at "F" on the measuring rod, especially during the first few hundred miles. Never let it get below the mark "L." Remove measuring rod and wipe with a dry cloth before testing the level. OIL SHOULD BE CHANGED AFTER THE FIRST 500 MILES AND EVERY 500 MILES THEREAFTER. Summer oil should conform to S.A.E. specification 40, and Winter oil to S.A.E. specification 20.

BRAKES this car is equipped with 4-wheel mechanical brakes which are quick and positive in action. Keep the car under control at all times to avoid the necessity for sudden application of brakes which might result in discomfort to passengers or collision from rear.

FAN BELT Do not tighten fan belt. The V-type fan belt does not require tight adjustment for proper operation. Too tight an adjustment will result in excessive wear on fan belt and generator bearings, particularly at higher speeds.

TIRES For easy riding qualities, proper braking and long life keep the tires, both front and rear, inflated to 35 pounds. (4.75—21 tires should be inflated to 40 pounds.)

INSPECTION To insure best results have an Authorized FORD DEALER inspect this car and make necessary minor adjustments after the first five hundred miles of running.

TRIPLEX SAFETY GLASS Triplex Safety Glass is used in this car for your protection. Do not replace Triplex Safety Glass with plate glass. If replacement is necessary use TRIPLEX SAFETY GLASS.

DRIVE SAFELY

In 1929, the Ridgewood (New Jersey) Garage catered to all makes of cars including this Model A Sport Coupe.

Break-in instructions given to the owner of a new Model A Ford in 1929. (Photo courtesy of *The Restorer*)

while climbing hills and that correct shifting techniques would normally solve the difficulty. Dealers were instructed to use diplomacy in handling the situation and, in the event they determined there was something wrong with a car, to make the necessary repairs without charge to the customer.

Dealers were also told to disregard ninety percent of the noises they heard while an engine was idling, "as not indicating anything wrong." They were advised to point out to their customers that "the new Model A is built to run up to sixty miles an hour and that sufficient clearance between the parts has been provided to handle the expansion from the heat developed at sixty miles per hour, and since several miles running will scarcely make the motor warm, that it is only natural to expect minor valve, piston, wrist pin end play or bearing noises to be audible when idling or when cold."

Most engine noise complaints were made while the new car was in the ninety-day free service period and dealers were told to assure their customers that if the diagnosis was wrong and there really was a problem, it would be fixed free of charge, even after the ninety days.

Regarding overheating problems, which seemed more likely to relate to truck engines, Branches were informed in May that some radiators were coming through with poor connections of fins to tubes. This meant that the fins were of no value in conducting heat from the tubes.

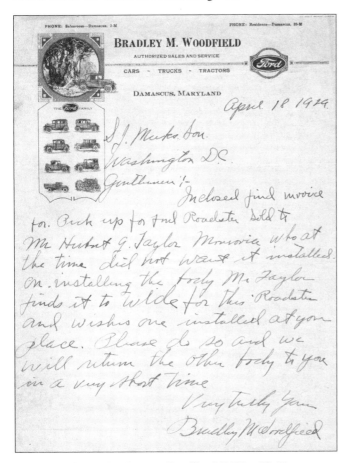

Example of a dealer letter - Bradley M. Woodfield.

Dealers were told to first check for conditions that ordinarily cause a problem such as timing, fan belt, water pump end play, cylinder head gasket, carbon, spark plug gap, clearance between valves and push rods, radiator fins, etc. As a last resort the radiator would be replaced gratis provided it was within the ninety day service period.

After the ninety days, the standard radiator could be replaced with a special Flintlock four-row tube radiator, a Long three-row flat tube-type radiator or a McCord five-row tube radiator in exchange at nine dollars net to the dealer and ten dollars net to the customer. The list price of these radiators was twenty-one dollars.

While it is fair to say that 1929 was a much better year for the approximately 8,275 Ford dealers than 1927 and 1928, some of them continued to struggle even as others did well. An article on Model A discount changes in the March 1931 issue of *Automobile Trade Journal* claims that the 1929 operating statements of one hundred Ford dealers show that, "even on a 20 percent margin, their combined new and used car operations were conducted at a loss."

Keith Sward says that one dealer, overloaded with more cars than he could sell, was forced to close out 1929 by selling one hundred-fifty cars at a loss. Nevins and Hill, however, maintain that the "limited stocks of Model A in 1928 and the keen demand for it throughout most of 1929 had made it unnecessary to overload dealers, and then hammer them to sell." They also point out that in 1929, for the first time in its history, Ford began market analysis to gear production schedules to long-range sales possibilities.

Although there were unhappy dealer stories in 1929, there were also good ones. C.J. Crimmins, who worked in accounting for Ford during the Model A years, says in his "Reminiscences" that the top dealership in New Haven made over $100,000 in 1929. Getz Motors, Inc. of Fort Wayne, Indiana, sold more than 2,100 Ford cars and trucks during 1929 and, in San Antonio, Texas, the ten-man sales staff of Morgan-Woodward Ford dealers sold 1,935 Ford cars and trucks during the year. The firm's 1929 sales were greater than those of any Ford dealer in the entire Southwest.

In another case, a salesman working for the Stevenson Motor Co. at Fort Bragg, California, earned $1,068 during the month of June. He was paid on a basis of five percent for new car sales and ten percent for accessories and other sales. In New York City, "walk-in" patronage at the Ford Motor Co. showroom on Broadway totaled 48,822 visitors from January 22, 1929, to December 1. Sales averaged one for every twenty-two persons or about 2,219 units.

Our featured dealer, D.D. Norton of Cazenovia, New York, delivered one hundred-eight passenger cars from January 1929 through October and purchased one hundred-thirty-nine from the Branch by the end of November. During each month he received a "Dealer's Monthly Allotments" form telling him how many units he would receive next month and whether they would be drive-

D. D. NORTON, Inc.

SALES and SERVICE

Cazenovia, New York

Oct 18 1929

Ford Motor Co.
Buffalo
New York

Gentlemen:

Regarding a 10 % agreement with Mr. Earl Stockton
of DeRuyter, N. Y., and, in answer to your letter regarding same of Oct. 16, please be advised that we believe
that in as much as DeRuyter is part of our old original
territory and several years ago Mr. Stockton had a 5%
selling agreement we do not see why he is not entitled
to a 10% agreement now.

We do not believe he will interfere with the dealer
at Cuyler N. Y. for most of his sales are made in the
other direction towards Cortland where he came from and
is better known. We also believe that your records will
show he has delivered very few cars in DeRuyter.

Mr. Stockton will take in a lot of trade ins on
Whippet cars which he has sold a lot of especially
around Georgetown which is remote from any dealer and
we believe it would be to the advantage of the Company
to let him have a 10% agreement.

We understand Morrisville has a 10% agreement under
Leland Motor Car Co. which comes nearly as close to us
as Cuyler is to DeRuyter.

Mr. Stockton has a couple of deals pending now,
one for delivery in DeRuyter and one in Sheds but we
are not allowing him to deliver same until we are advised
by you that it is O.K.. We ask for your cooperation and
feel that with the proper investigation you will deem
it advisable for us to sign up Mr. Earl Stockton on a
10% selling agreement.

Yours very truly

D. D. Norton, Inc.

By

Example of a dealer letter - D.D. Norton.

aways or shipped by convoy. He also received a letter telling him what percent of his 1929 monthly estimate he could expect to receive and what percent of each type the Branch would produce that month. He was then supposed to tailor his model order as closely as possible to the percentage allocated to each body type.

For example, Norton was informed that in April he would receive ten units and given the dates on which he could arrange to drive them away. The ten units were eighty-five percent of the estimate assigned for that month. He also received a body percentage list indicating that twenty-nine percent of the types being produced that month were Tudors. He was expected to conform his body order as closely as possible to the percentage sent to him and, therefore, knew that the Branch expected his order to reflect three Tudors.

Based on letters received by Norton it appears that Buffalo Branch production was running sixty to ninety days behind orders during the first quarter of 1929. By May this was down to thirty to sixty days.

It was not until August that the Branch was finally able to announce that dealer allotments that month would rectify all unfilled orders. During the early months Norton received at most eighty-five percent of his allotment. In September, Buffalo reported that for the first time in two years sales were running slightly behind production. "Last month we built 5,000 cars, and sold 4,200."

In October, Norton was forced to accept two units more than his estimate. His original order for that month included two Standard Coupes, one Sport Coupe, two Tudors, one three-window Fordor, one Town Sedan, one closed cab pickup and one closed cab stake truck. To these he had to add a Tudor and a chassis with a closed cab only.

Also that month Norton received several letters from the company that indicated that production and sales were going so well that Ford fully expected that production of Model A cars and Model AA trucks for the full year would exceed 2,000,000 units provided that he and all other Ford dealers sold one hundred percent of their October estimate. If they accomplished that then it would only be necessary for the thirty-five Branches to build and sell fifty percent of their monthly estimate or 100,000 cars in November and 100,000 in December to reach the 2,000,000 total.

As it turned out the magic sales plateau was never attained. The stock market crash at the end of October and other factors weighed against it. Norton's November allotment was reduced to seven units since production at Buffalo was limited to about forty percent of normal. The Branch closed its production lines for the last two weeks of the month. On December 19, he was told that "Your job is to deliver 50 percent of your estimate during the month." Gone was any mention of the 2,000,000 mark, although, perhaps trying to put a good face on a worsening situation, the company reminded Norton that "With the knowledge that our production program on the Model A calls for thirty million, your salesmen should be in position to counteract false rumors and keep new car sales moving."

Early in 1929, Ford dealers received a list of eighty-seven "important duties which should be observed by every Ford dealer in the conduct of a Ford dealership." These duties were generally categorized under sales, service, business and building or location. Sales, of course, were a priority. The dealer was expected to employ one full-time salesman for every seventy-five units of his yearly estimate.

Larger dealers were required to have four salesman for each three hundred units. Each salesman was to be provided with a "clean, attractive, up-to-date" portfolio of literature, testimonial letters and sales material to use when soliciting a sale. All new salesmen were to receive training at a three-day sales school run periodically at the Branch and each salesman was to make twelve calls a day.

The training of salesmen was not left to chance. Each Branch was required to run schools for sales training. By August 1, 1929, a total of 14,155 salesmen had been trained in these schools nationwide. This, however, left the parent company unsatisfied because some 8,093 salesmen had not as yet received the schooling. Branch managers were admonished to take note of this and see to the required instruction for all salesmen.

The company was also concerned that demonstrators be well-maintained and that each retail salesman drive a Model A car in first class operating condition and appearance. Occasionally, dealers said that some men could not as yet afford to buy a Model A, but this excuse got little sympathy from the sales department. Salesmen were to drive Model A Fords, end of discussion. "We should not have a single salesman calling upon prospects in other than a Model A car."

The sales operation of each dealership depended heavily on maintaining an up-to-date card system with the names of active prospects to at least equal twice the yearly estimate. The dealer was also required to hold daily sales meetings, show films at the dealership and elsewhere, provide free literature to prospects and insist that all his people use the four-step sales plan.

The four-step sales plan, constantly hyped by the company to its dealers, consisted of the following:

1) Present the prospect with a copy of the Ford booklet, *The Story of a New Car.*

2) Take the customer for a ride in a Model A that, the company insisted, was to look like new and run like new. Also, the car was to be a Tudor or a Fordor not a two-passenger or an open job. This was deemed so important that the Branches checked on each dealer's demonstrator. For example, in January 1929, Norton was required to submit to the Branch a list of his demonstrators with engine number, model, date put in service and mileage to date. He notified Buffalo that he had just sold a Tudor demonstrator with two hundred-twenty-five miles and still had in service a Fordor with three hundred-fifty miles, which was also his personal car.

3) Give the prospect a tour of the dealer's establishment, if possible during the demonstration.

4) Hand literature to the customer and record his/her name for a direct mail follow-up. Folders for the follow-up and other mailings were provided to dealers by the Branches. Thirteen booklets were made available to dealers in January and several more were added during the year. Ever aware of cutting costs, a Branch letter emphasized, "that literature should be kept out of sight (except *The Story of a Great Car*). Care should be taken to give out only the folders describing the model in which the customer is interested."

A rather unique sales tool provided to dealers was a Fordex miniature chassis that salesmen could use to describe features such as transverse springs, torque tube drive, radius rods, etc. Each demonstrating model was 12 inches long and 6-1/2 inches wide from right to left wheel. Wheels were equipped with miniature balloon tires and the entire chassis was finished in a bright aluminum. Springs were of steel to give easy flexible action. The price of these models, as quoted by the Sales Equipment Co., was $4.95 for one, and $4.50 if two or more were purchased.

While sales were concentrated on the Model A, some dealers also sold Lincolns and all of them sold used cars and were required to service the estimated seven million Model T Fords still on the road. Model T owners were considered prime targets for upgrading to a Model A and dealers were continually urged by the company to demonstrate the Model A to these owners.

Following policy as requested, Brown & McCooey of Randolph, New York, reported to the Branch on July 15, 1929, that there were four hundred-seventy-five Model T owners in its trade area and that one hundred-thirty-nine demonstrations had been made to these Model T owners to date. The rest would be completed by August 1st.

Although most of the burden of selling the Model A fell to individual dealers, the company did what it could to help market its cars and trucks through advertising and showing of cars. Up to November 1, 1929, Ford salons had been staged in eighty-six cities across the United States, with a total attendance of 575,038. At these salons the complete line of Model A passenger and

The new 4-STEP method is the basis for uniform sales action in 1929

The four steps in this plan are listed below and are pictured and explained in detail on the following pages:

1 Presenting the New Ford Sales Portfolio

2 The Road Demonstration

3 Inspection of Parts and Service Departments

4 Presentation of Current Ford Literature

THE proper application of these four steps permits the salesman to adequately meet all sales points which usually arise during the process of selling a Ford Car. They are arranged in logical sequence, the first step being designed to get the prospect's interest and arouse his enthusiasm for the Model A to the point where he readily agrees to take a ride in the New Ford—Step No. 2, the Demonstration, thus being accomplished.

If the salesman follows, as prescribed in this plan, a previously selected route for the road demonstration, it will conclude at the establishment of the dealer where the next, or third, step begins. The salesman should know each feature of the shop and equipment thoroughly and explain it intelligently. Most prospects are eager to learn something about the maintenance of a car and its mechanical construction. If this step is properly covered "Selling Service" later becomes easier, also the sale of the second and third Ford. Following inspection of the shop and parts department, the time payment plan is discussed and of course the salesman asks for an order—in fact, the order should be requested several times during the sales process, depending upon the prospect's interest.

Should the prospect decline to sign an order at the conclusion of Step No. 3, the salesman naturally makes another appointment, preferably for that evening at the prospect's home. Current company literature is then handed the prospect—Step No. 4—and the latter's attention directed to certain features which seem to be of outstanding importance to the particular prospect.

Should the order be obtained prior to or during the process of the 4-Step Plan, the salesman should nevertheless make every effort to complete the first three steps—*unless immediate delivery can be effected.* The reason for this is obvious. Should the prospect have to wait a week or two, or perhaps longer, for delivery he may be influenced to cancel and purchase another make. We know that if the first three steps are properly covered, the prospect's interest in and desire for the Model A will be so strong it will preclude any possibility of cancellation. In other words, there will be less likelihood of the prospect changing his mind when he has had the benefit of the well-rounded selling which the 4-Step Plan provides.

There may be instances where the order of the 4-Step Method procedure will be reversed or varied. Circumstances might arise where Step No. 4, or perhaps Step No. 3, would be taken first. The important thing is to include all four steps in whatever sequence.

Read the following pages carefully, and be sure they are thoroughly understood by your sales force, and followed to the letter. Your branch will be glad to give you any further particulars desired.

New 4-Step Sales Method For Ford Dealers.

commercial cars and Model AA trucks was presented so that the public could see the large number of body types available and have an opportunity to ride in a Ford car.

There were some innovative displays at these salons. In Buffalo, New York, for example, a sedan was tipped to a great angle to show "balance," and a Tudor was hung by its fenders. In another display a closed car with one wheel set twenty inches high was used to demonstrate "rigidity," the ease with which doors open and close, etc.

As part of its regular sales campaign each dealership was encouraged to pay particular attention to soliciting and servicing multiple sales to fleet owners, a major sales interest for Ford throughout the Model A years. These were divided into three classifications: Limited - five or more cars; State - fifty or more in one state; National - fifty or more in ten or more states.

On all group purchases by authorized fleet owners, delivery of which was taken at one time, a five percent discount was given. Large fleet owners (those buying 1,000 cars per year) were given a ten percent discount. Fleet owners purchasing cars in smaller than units of ten received the discount on the eleventh delivery and after. A twenty-five percent discount on forty percent items and ten percent discount on twenty-five percent items was provided fleet owners for the purchase of parts.

It is interesting to note here that the discount provided fleet owners came from the dealer's margin—it was not

an extra discount from the company. For example, a 1,000-car fleet owner would get a ten percent discount and the dealer got the other ten percent. In the case of two dealers, one selling and one delivering, they split the discount, each getting five percent. The dealer took a smaller discount but, of course, got the advantage of multiple sales.

The company never paid anything extra, deducting only the usual twenty percent as it did on all cars through most of 1929. Each year dealers received periodic lists and updates of those qualified as fleet owners. In 1929, the number of qualified fleet owners listed by the Buffalo Branch easily exceeded 1,000.

The second, but equally important, category of dealer duties was "Service." Dealers were expected to employ a sufficient number of capable mechanics and provide them with the necessary shop clothing, tools, parts and training so that customer needs would be adequately handled. Cleanliness of the shop was a high priority as was training, regular meetings and study of the Service Bulletins by shop foremen and mechanics. In addition, it was mandatory for each dealer to provide the services of at least one qualified mechanic at night, until 9 p.m. This was to be done, the company said, "in order to uphold the high standard of Ford Service."

Each shop was required to maintain up-to-date service records of car owners. New owners were to be followed for the 500, 1,000 and 1,500 mile free inspections and after that contacted every sixty days unless they came into the shop themselves. Fleet owners were to be contacted every thirty days. To encourage owners to continue their lubrication service at Ford dealers after the initial three checkups, the company arranged a Ford Recorded Alemite Service plan or F.R.A.S with the Alemite Manufacturing Corp.

Under this plan, owners could purchase special cards that entitled them to twelve lubrications for the price of ten. Shortly after it began, the plan was upgraded to thirteen lubes for the price of ten or six for five. Shipment of all F.R.A.S. material was made by Alemite to individual dealers after they submitted a list of their customers. Dealers were not required to use this service, but, if they did, they had to use Alemite chassis and gear lubricants. The benefit to the dealer was that he got an advertising and merchandising program at a price of twenty-four cents per car that actually cost forty-four cents. Dealers who did not subscribe to the service were required to use another plan that was equally as good or better.

A "Special Check-Up Service" form that incorporated all of the essential maintenance operations suggested by the Ford Motor Co. was made available to dealers through the Sales Equipment Co. of Detroit. This form covered forty-three operations that the company suggested dealers sell to owners on the basis of 1,000-mile service. Many dealers also used the form for checking new cars before they were delivered to the customer.

Persuading dealers to equip their shops with the machines and tools necessary to properly service and

The 1929 Fleet Owner's Agreement with the Ford Motor Co.

maintain Ford vehicles, was a Service Department priority. Most of this equipment was provided by K.R. Wilson although similar equipment from other sources could be used. Dealers were given a list of sixteen items they should have in their shops. Some of those listed were a combination machine complete with Model A attachments, the seventy or seventy-two dollar group of tools, master ammeter, all position engine stand, high-pressure auto washer, valve refacing machine, etc.

Ford's list of duties for dealers also covered the building that housed the dealership and stressed the importance of an adequate size building with good location, clean throughout, and with sales and service oval electric signs conspicuously displayed. To show what dealers were sometimes asked to do, D.D. Norton received a letter from Edsel Ford asking him to cooperate in marking the roof of his building, or another building, with the village name for the purpose of assisting aerial navigation. Directions on how to do this were included with the letter.

Norton, who was at that time the supervisor of the Town of Cazenovia, New York, wrote back to say that he was able to have this done on the roof of the town machinery building the previous summer. He also men-

IN THE Ford Motor Company we emphasize service equally with sales. It has always been our belief that a sale does not complete the transaction between us and the buyer, but establishes a new obligation on us to see that his car gives him service. We are as much interested in his economical operation of the car as he is in our economical manufacture of it. This is only good business on our part. If our car gives service, sales will take care of themselves. For that reason we have installed a system of controlled service to take care of all Ford car needs in an economical and improved manner. We wish all users of Ford cars to know what they are entitled to in this respect, so that they may readily avail themselves of this service.

Signed, HENRY FORD

Henry Ford on Service, *Ford News*, January 15, 1929.

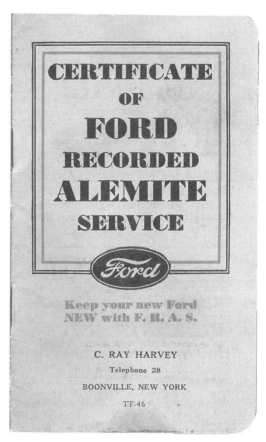

Certificate of F.R.A.S.

Mechanic at Keller Motors, Ford dealership in Oneida, New York, turning brake drum.

Ford dealership Service Department mechanics working on a Model A Roadster.

Special Check Up Service $3.00
(Material Extra)

Ford

Model A.................... Date ....
Model AA .... Lisc. No. ....

Customer's Name.................... Address .... Speedometer Reading.................... Motor No. ....

No. Description Operation	G	F	P
1—LUBRICATE All Pressure Connections			
Spray Springs			
2—DISTRIBUTOR—Hone Points			
" Set Gap .018 to .022			
" Oil Shaft			
" Vaseline Cam			
3—SPARK PLUGS—Clean			
Set Gap .027			
4—CHECK TIMING—Reset if necessary			
5—FAN—Adjust or replace belt			
6—SEDIMENT BULB—Drain			
" Clean Strainer			
7—CARBURETOR—Clean Strainer			
" Check Idle—Adjust			
8—GENERATOR—Check charging rate			
9—RADIATOR HOSE—Tighten			
" " Condition top			
" " " side			
" " " lower			
10—WATER PUMP—Condition packing			
Tighten if necessary			
11—STARTER—Tighten 3 studs			
12—MOTOR—Road test			
" Knocks—Rods			
" " Pistons			
" " Bearings			
Compression No. 1			
" No. 2			
" No. 3			
" No. 4			
Tighten Cyl. Head Nuts			
CARBON			
VALVES			
13—CRANK CASE OIL—Quantity			
" " " Quality			
Drain and Change IF INSTRUCTED			
14—FRONT SYSTEM—Check front wheels			

No. Description Operation	G	F	P
Align and adjust—1/32" to 3/32"			
15—FRONT BUMPER—Tighten			
16—SHOCK ABSORBERS—Make seasonal adjust.			
(Also see No. 41) Tighten arm clamp bolts			
17—BATTERY—Add water			
G—Fully charged 1250 to 1300 Gravity Cell No. 1			
F—Fair 1225 to 1250 " " " 2			
P—Low 1200 and under " " " 3			
Tighten cable connections			
Clean off any corrosion			
Tighten carrier			
Tighten battery in carrier			
18—TRANSMISSION—Check lubricant level			
Add lubricant if necessary			
19—CLUTCH—Adjust—lubricate bearing.			
20—UNIVERSAL JOINT—Tighten bolts			
21—BRAKE EQUALIZER—Spray with oil			
22—REAR RADIUS RODS—Tighten			
23—MUFFLER—Tighten to frame			
24—REAR SPRING—Condition bushings			
" " " perch bushings			
" " " hangers, tighten			
25—REAR BUMPER—Tighten			
26—WIND SHIELD WIPER—Adj. or replace bush.			
27—HORN—Adjust, clean and oil			
28—HEAD LAMPS—Align and focus, check others			
29—TIRE PRESSURE—Inflate if necessary			
" " R F 35 lbs.			
" " L F recommended			
" " R R pressure			
" " L R Red spot at			
" Spare valve			
30—BRAKES—Inspect, adjust if necessary			
31—GENERAL APPEARANCE—Paint Top			
Roof... Glass... Upholstery... Window lifts...			
Fenders... Hood... Floor Mats...			
Floor boards... Spare bulbs... Accelerator...			

No. Description Operation	G	F	P
License... Card...			
32—TIGHTEN BODY BOLTS			
BODY—Inspect doors for rattles—adjust			
Inspect Rubber Door Bumpers			
AT 5,000 MILES (extra charge $2.50)			
In addition to 500-mile check-up			
33—FRONT SYSTEM—Remove hubs			
Clean hubs and bearings			
Examine bearings			
" brake drums			
" spindle bearings			
" brake shoes			
34—GREASE AND REPLACE—Adjust, align			
35—STEERING GEAR—Tighten arm clamp bolt			
Tighten ball sockets, all connections			
Adjust sector shaft			
36—TRANSMISSION—Drain and flush			
Inspect gears			
1 pint new lubricant			
Grease thrust bearing and adj.			
37—HORN—Sand commutator, clean			
Oil and adjust			
38—GENERATOR—Clean commutator			
Adjust charging rate			
39—REAR AXLE—Test for wear			
Drain and flush			
Renew lubricant, 3 pints			
Tighten all housing studs			
40—BRAKES—General inspection			
Adjust if necessary			
41—SHOCK ABSORBERS—Check glycerine			
Quality and quantity			
42—SPEEDOMETER—Lubricate flexible shaft			
43—GAS TANK—Clean Filter Screen			
Note—Always use special lub. in steering gear case.			

DEALER'S NAME.................... ADDRESS .... MECHANIC .... SERVICE SUPT. ....

Check-Up Service Form used by Ford dealers.

tioned that the Town of Cazenovia had received recognition for this marking from the Daniel Guggenheim Fund for the Promotion of Aeronautics. Cazenovia was one of 2,000 communities that placed markers by mid-1929.

In regard to finances, the company expected each dealer to be properly financed, have the support of his banker, pay his bills promptly and submit monthly financial statements to the Branch office. In a January 1929 letter, dealers were assured that rumors Ford was trying to force them to use the Universal Credit Corp. (UCC) at the risk of losing a franchise or having car deliveries restricted, were unfounded.

At the same time, the company made it crystal clear that Ford dealers were supposed to do everything possible to build up the UCC Authorized Ford Finance Plan. Kansas City Branch Manager H.C. Doss said that "I

pretty definitely told the dealers that we wanted them to patronize the Universal Credit Company."

Shortly before June 1, 1929, the one-year anniversary of UCC, each dealer received a lengthy news release extolling the virtues of the plan and was instructed to have it run in the local newspaper. The release said that UCC had purchased installment contracts in excess of $75,000,000 and expected to do an additional $25,000,000 a month from then on. At this time, UCC was operating in twenty offices in the United States and one in Mexico City.

During 1929, as in all the Model A years, it was common for satisfied owners to send photos and letters about their cars and trucks to their dealer, or their Branch office or Detroit. Although some of these came from the rich and famous, mostly they were testimonials from ordinary people enjoying their Fords in the relative obscurity of their daily lives. They had nothing to gain by writing but, obviously, felt strongly enough about their Model As to want to share their experience with the people from whom they bought the cars and the company that built them. Following is a 1929 sampler of these letters.

Ford

MORGAN MOTOR CAR CO.
FORD FACTORY DEALERS
NEWARK
ALL NIGHT SERVICE

Important To FORD Owners!

Special Repair Reductions

Your used Ford (the old model) should have the best of attention, as it will last for years if given same. There are few used Fords for sale in this territory, a sterling tribute to the old car. Don't take your car to an inexperienced repair shop as it may be damaged. Bring it to Ford-trained shop employees.

Come to us any hour of the day or night and take advantage of these extraordinary offers on your Ford car at a greatly reduced price:

No. 1—Install new transmission bands—Labor and Materials $2.95

No. 2—Replace rear brake shoes, tighten both rear wheel axle nuts, grease rear end and universal joint and drive shaft bushing, 1920 to 1925 cars—Labor and Material 3.25

No. 3—Reline rear brake shoes, tighten both rear wheel axle nuts, grease rear end and universal joint and drive shaft bushing—Labor and Material 4.25

No. 4—Rebush front steering spindle bodies and arms. Also tighten front system—Labor and Material 5.50

No. 5—Grind valves and clean carbon. Install new gaskets, new timer, roller and case and 4 pair coil points—Labor and Material 5.45

No. 6—Install all new piston rings, tighten all 4 connecting rods, tighten center main bearing, grind valves and clean carbon, tune motor and change motor oil. Material includes new motor gaskets, timer case and roller, 4 complete coil points, piston rings and 1 gal. oil—Labor and Material.... 16.25

No. 7—Have your car painted, wide choice of color combinations—
Runabout 22.50
Touring 25.00
Coupe 27.50
Sedan 30.00

Genuine Ford Parts Installed Exclusively

Morgan Motor Car Co.
"THE HOUSE OF SERVICE"

Morgan's Message.

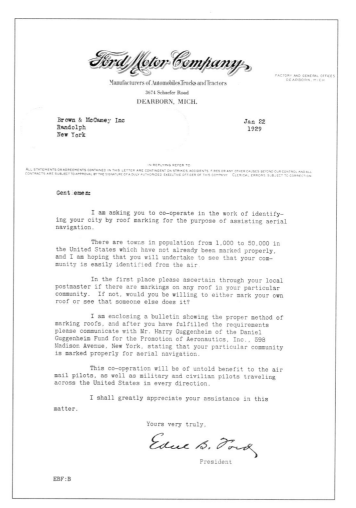

Letter from Edsel Ford regarding marking a town for airplane navigation.

NEW FORD FINANCE COMPANY MAKES IT EASIER TO BUY A FORD

Universal Credit Company Developing Great National Organization To Handle Model A Time Payments

One of the developments of the past year which created national interest in both automotive and financial circles was the organization of Universal Credit Company for the purpose of financing exclusively the time sales of Ford products thruout the country. Ultimately service of a similar nature will be provided in all countries where Ford products are sold.

Universal Credit Company is a specialized financial institution created to provide uniform and authorized time payment plans at low cost for the purchase of Ford products on an instalment basis. The Company in the first year of business just closed has made sound and gratifying progress. The reception accorded the authorized Ford Finance Plans by the public and Ford dealers in the 21 large cities where branch offices have been established is indeed impressive.

Today UCC has purchased instalment contracts in excess of $75,000,000 which establishes a new record in instalment financing for an institution which has only been in operation for one year. It is anticipated that the volume of business handled will exceed $25,000,000 monthly from now on. In the short space of a year, the UCC organization has grown from an organization of ten people to one employing almost a thousand.

Already there has come a realization that the Universal Credit Company was created primarily for the sound financing of the Ford dealer and the purchaser, and not with the primary object of profit. Its establishment is thus squarely in conformity with the reiterated Ford policy of creating and developing every possible economy from mine to consumer, for the benefit of the public.

The purpose is to reduce the cost of credit, to the individual who buys on time, commensurate with sound business policies. This reduction in the cost of credit is made possible by the many economies that arise from the operation of an authorized plan, on the basis of nation-wide volume, and dealing exclusively with the Ford dealer organization. Simplicity of forms, special bookkeeping and statistical machinery and general uniformity of procedure all under centralized control and management, are constantly contributing to cut these costs.

This cost of credit is just as vital as the cost of any of the material that goes into the building of the automobile. It is in every sense a commodity which becomes a part of the completed article before it is ultimately sold to the public.

Thus the Universal Credit Company's low finance charges are equivalent to a price reduction on the Model A car and other Ford products.

Then there is that important matter of good will. A buyer delights in dealing with an organization that gives him prompt, courteous service, that deals fairly with him, that maintains scrupulously the standard of its product and that is constantly instilling in that buyer a sense of reliability and confidence and appreciation of the seller and his product.

UCC is serving a still greater purpose in the economic and social phases of our national life. In addition to adding to the advancement of organized industry, UCC is at the same time contributing substantially to the happiness and contentment of society. By extending credit to every deserving person in the nation at the lowest possible cost, UCC is helping to bring greater health and happiness to a large group of American people, heads of families as well as their children. In the process of transition from the crowded city to the healthy country districts, UCC is aiding the American family to establish itself with economic advantage in more desirable locations and is thus helping to raise the standard of American living conditions.

Thomas A. Edison, an outstanding genius of our time has recently said on the subject of instalment selling:

"What we call instalment buying is one of the methods by which we are preparing to take immediate advantage of the opportunities for a higher standard of living thru machine production. That is a method of saving in goods instead of saving in money. In the old days a man spent most of his life getting ready to die. He saved against a rainy day—against old age. Now, altho it is a nice thing to have a fund to fall back on, a family thinks more of living than of dying.

"People who work for wages seldom come into the possession of considerable funds. Unless they save, they can hardly ever buy an article costing over $50 or $100. Their incomes, however, justify the possession of more expensive articles that contribute to their comfort or their enjoyment, such as automobiles, phonographs, radios and books, as well as many household conveniences. There is no reason why the manufacturers of these articles should not aid in the purchase by shifting the point of saving from before purchasing until after purchasing.

"If the cost of living goes down—and invention and engineering are bound to drive it down—and wages go higher—and they are bound to go higher with more efficient production—then still more attention can be paid to living rather than dying. This whole instalment system which is gradually developing along business lines will be a necessary part of the job of having consumption both increase and diversify in order to take care of production.

"Saving by people of moderate means, in order to provide funds for investment, is not so necessary as it used to be. The big companies are able to provide their own investment funds to a considerable degree out of their own earnings. We are getting a new slant on savings by the individual of comparatively small earnings. One evidence of that is the giving of more attention to living than to dying. That means that people in general have greater confidence in the future than they used to have."

Sound spending by the recipients of American high wages logically follows. If industry is to continue to create products they must be consumed. To make this consumption possible by the wage earner who helps create the product, the manufacturer presents low cost finance plans and makes available credit where credit is due. A sound instalment plan is now one of the necessary elements of our modern business system and is so recognized.

The institution of instalment selling has contributed a monumental share in the development of industry. The cost of credit to the consumer is of paramount importance to prosperity and to the individual. In the operation of the Universal Credit Company, they are always aiming at lower costs and broader markets with high standards for the specialized banking field in which it has embarked. Thru these lower costs for financing service, the use of motor cars is made available to that great section of society who most benefit by every economy. With these ideals of service paramount in mind, Universal Credit Company is making a contribution to the economic and social phases of American life.

UCC is operating at this time 21 complete offices, located in the following cities: Atlanta, Boston, Buffalo, Charlotte, Chicago, Cincinnati, Cleveland, Dallas, Detroit, Houston, Jacksonville, Kansas City, Memphis, Minneapolis, New York, Norfolk, Philadelphia, Pittsburgh, St. Louis, Washington and Mexico City.

UCC Press Release of May 23, 1929.

Ford News profiled five enthusiastic Model A owners in their eighties in an early 1930 issue. One of them, M. Nowls, owned a 1929 Tudor, which was his first car. "The reason I bought a Ford," he told the dealer, "is that, physically, I was down and out, unable to work. I would take my morning walk but that was not sufficient exercise. I was 88 years old and had never tried to run a car. I bought the car for exercise and pleasure. I got both and now I am young again."

In a letter to *Ford Life*, a reader recalls driving from Chicago to Detroit in his Model A and stopping at the Ford service station near the Rouge to fill up with Benzol before he returned home. On the way over he got about eighteen miles per gallon, but on the return trip, after filling his tank with Benzol, got as high as twenty-three. Benzol was a by-product fuel, described in *Ford Life* as "a blend of one part Light Oil recovered from the coal to coke operations at the Rouge, and three parts ordinary gasoline." It was only available in the immediate Detroit area.

Five hundred hours and one minute comprised the non-stop endurance run performed by a stock Model A roadster on the Cincinnati and Hamilton speedway track. The car traveled a distance of 14,540 miles in temperatures sometimes below zero and through heavy rain and snow. Gasoline was supplied by the use of containers filled by guards on the grounds, and handed the drivers while the car was passing by. Oil was changed while the car was in operation by using a small board platform attached to the front bumper and supports. The two drivers never left the car, eating their meals while the car was in motion, and sleeping on the roomy rear deck of the car.

A Model A owner living in Duluth, Minnesota, credited his Tudor's sturdy body construction with saving his life. While rounding a horseshoe curve along the cliffs near West Duluth, he turned in his seat to look for something in the back and drove directly over the bank. The car fell about eighty-five feet, somersaulting several times, but landed right side up and crossways of a small stream. The principal damage to the car was two bent fenders. Not a window was broken and the driver was uninjured.

While waiting for the insurance company's adjustment for his wrecked large car, a Knoxville, Tennessee, man bought a Model A Ford to tide him over. When he purchased the Ford, he had his mind made up to dislike it but, as he drove it, found his prejudice gradually vanished. "It pulls like a bay steer, operates as smoothly as an Elgin watch and is as comfortable to ride

in as a Pullman car," he said. "I'm going to admit that I was wrong at first. I am delighted with the car."

A Model A Tudor won both the grand sweepstakes award and first prize in its own class in a gasoline economy contest among women drivers held in Southern California. Thirty-seven cars of various makes participated covering a distance of one hundred-seventy miles including mountain driving. The contest was open only to private owners driving strictly stock cars. The winning Tudor, carrying the driver and four passengers, used 7-1/2 gallons of gasoline and no oil or water.

Rogers Motor Sales of Jackson Center, Ohio, named thirty-seven satisfied owners of new Model A Fords whose cars together traveled 129,730 miles at a total repair cost of $13.92. That amount included $6.90 for lamp bulbs and only $7.02 for actual repairs.

An unusual accident brought this account from a Forrest City, Arkansas, man who had parked his car beside a stretch of road while he helped a driver repair a truck. Suddenly he saw the oncoming headlights of a car. As he watched, he was startled to see the car strike a gravel dump, soar bottom side up with all four wheels spinning

and land with a thud on the ground fifty feet by actual measurement from where it left the earth. Landing on its top, it bounced over again and settled right side up in the swampy grass beside the road. There was no sound of splintered glass nor flare of ignited escaping gasoline. The man and his companion ran to the car expecting to extricate bodies of the dead. Instead, when they opened the door, a tousle-headed Boy Scout greeted them with a big grin. Investigation proved the lad was not even scratched. No glass was broken, every light was still burning, the body was undamaged save for a few scratches on its shiny surface—it was a new Model A. The engine still purred quietly. The young driver had fallen asleep. In his letter to Dearborn describing the incident, the man stated that he wished the car had a hand so he could have shaken it. Instead, he went down and bought a new Ford the next day.

Three stories of Model A Fords submerged underwater for varying lengths of time were sent to *Ford News* during 1929. In one case, a mail carrier's Tudor was covered with flood water for better than a day. In another case, a Model AA truck was completely submerged for

Owes Life to Car

Harold Spindler, Model A owner living in Duluth, Minnesota, credits the sturdy body construction of his car with saving his life. While rounding a horseshoe curve along the cliffs near West Duluth, he turned in his seat to observe something in the rear and drove directly off the bank. The car toppled over a straight drop of approximately eighty-five feet and rolled to the bottom.

During the descent, the car broke off several birch trees as well as a number of smaller saplings. It finally landed in the position shown in the accompanying picture, right side up and crosswise of a small stream. Not a window was broken and the driver was uninjured although the car had turned over seven times. The principal damage to the car, according to A. H. Lord of the Lord-Fisher Company, Ford dealers, was two bent fenders which were easily straightened out.

"Owes Life To Car," *Ford News*, **April 1, 1929.**

Two women and their 1929 Model A Coupe.

Mom and daughter pose with the family's Model A Coupe.

Sport Coupe with proud owner.

Young couple and their Sport Coupe.

Well-used Model A Coupe and its owner.

thirty-six hours. In both cases, when the cars were pulled from their watery graves, their owners stepped on the starter and the engines started as though they had not been submerged.

Still another report said that five Model A Fords were lost in the harbor of Buenos Aires, Argentina, when the riverboat carrying them was rammed and sunk. They were underwater for fourteen days, then retrieved and left on a dock for another three weeks before they were reconditioned and sold and, reportedly, gave excellent satisfaction to their purchasers.

In all three examples the emphasis is placed on the fact that the cars ran after being submerged. There is no mention of other problems such as the effect of the water on the upholstery. Waterlogged upholstery cannot have been an easy matter to bring back. But then, the cars ran, and, at least in the view of the Ford Motor Co., that was all that really mattered.

An often overlooked part of the Model A story revolves around the Rouge plant, the men and women who worked there, and the task of transferring men and machines from the Highland Park plant to the Rouge—a major effort in 1929.

Located on the River Rouge just west of Detroit, the Rouge plant occupied 1,096 acres. With 7,000,000 square feet of floor space it was said to be one of the largest, if not the largest, industrial enterprises in the world. In 1929, Ford Motor Co. employed approximately 200,000 workers in the United States, about half of them at the Rouge.

So huge and well-publicized was the Rouge that it became America's most visited factory and, according to David Lewis, entertained 121,811 tourists in 1929—a record that would remain unbroken until 1936. Previously known as the Fordson plant, the Rouge received its new designation of "Rouge Plant, Dearborn, Michigan" in early 1929.

The *New York Times*, in its October 20, 1929, issue, listed the total number of visitors to Ford Motor Co. plants in Detroit, Michigan, at an estimated 500,000 for the year. During the summer there were between 1,300 and 1,600 a day. The largest in a single day was 8,000. Two buses and thirty-five guides were busy from 8:30 in the morning conducting tours.

The production cycle at the Rouge began with the docking of an ore boat from Marquette and ended when a dealer paid cash for a new Model A and drove it away. Here there was a conversion of raw materials into cash in approximately fifty hours, twenty-four of which were consumed in shipping and handling. Edwin P. Norwood, in *Ford Men and Methods*, his 1931 study of the Rouge, says that the assembly time for a Model A engine, from cylinder block to completely assembled power unit, was exactly two hours. This involved the placing of seven

"Trim Line," *Ford Industries*, 1929.

"Building Model A Bodies," *Ford Industries*, 1929.

SHORTENING THE

1

One of the most noteworthy accomplishments in keeping the prices of Ford products low is the gradual shortening of the production cycle. The elapsed time between the receipt of raw material and its appearance as finished merchandise in the hands of the dealer bears strongly on the retail prices. The longer an article

2

MONDAY 8:00 A. M.

1 After a trip of approximately 45 hours from Marquette the ore boat docks at the Rouge plant. Hulett unloaders start removing the cargo which is transferred to the High Line and from there to the skip car which charges the blast furnaces. By continuous process this takes 10 minutes.

TUESDAY 12:10 A. M.

2 In sixteen hours the ore has been reduced to foundry iron, which is carried in a molten state to the foundry. In less than an hour it has been mixed with the proper proportion of scrap and poured into moulds.

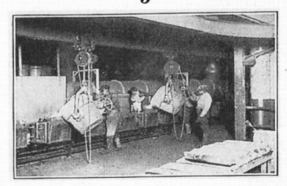

3

TUESDAY 1:10 A. M.

3 As the conveyor brings the molds past the pouring station the hot metal is cast into cylinder blocks. These go to the shake out station and are taken away to be cooled and cleaned. The cooling and cleaning process requires an average time of five hours.

TUESDAY 6:10 A. M.

4 The casting now goes to its first machining operation. It takes two hours and forty minutes to machine the casting. This machining is performed in the foundry building in line with the Ford practice of continuous operation. It arrives at the motor room at

4

"Production Cycle," *Ford Industries*, **1929.**

PRODUCTION CYCLE

is in the process of manufacture and the more it is moved about, the greater is its ultimate cost.

During the period of business depression in 1920, the Ford production cycle was cut from 21 to 14 days. Today the Ford production cycle has been further reduced as here illustrated.

5

6

7

8

TUESDAY 9:25 A. M.

5 It requires two hours to assemble and block test the Model A engine. Except for "running in" to loosen it up, everything is done on the move until it reaches the testing block.

TUESDAY 11:25 A. M.

6 The finished and inspected motor comes out on a conveyor and is loaded into a freight car and shipped to an assembly plant. It takes about 10 minutes to convey and load in the car.

WEDNESDAY 6:35 A. M.

7 By this time the motor should have reached an assembly point 300 miles distant. It takes approximately 35 minutes to unload the car and carry the motor to the assembly line.

WEDNESDAY 7:35 A. M.

8 It takes one hour to assemble the complete car, so by 7:35 A. M. the car is ready for the dealer.

WEDNESDAY NOON

Long before noon the dealer will have taken delivery of the car and paid cash for it. Here is a conversion of raw materials into cash in approximately 50 hours. Of this 50 hours, 24 are consumed in shipping and handling. Even this record-breaking cycle is often shortened.

"Production Cycle," *Ford Industries*, 1929.

hundred-fifty parts requiring seventy operations and many inspections.

A prominent feature of the plant was its extensive conveyor system that, according to Norwood, was a sixty mile long maze at the time he studied the plant. The installation of various conveyor systems throughout the different departments resulted in speeding up production, but sometimes had a negative effect on unskilled jobs. In a 1929 letter to Charles Sorensen, the Rouge production boss, one engineer said that the installation of new conveyor systems resulted in the elimination of almost six hundred jobs.

The workers at the Rouge who built the Model A represented almost every state and nation. They were old and young, black and white, American and foreign born. A few were women and some were handicapped. As reported by Ford R. Bryan in *The Ford Legend* (Henry Ford Heritage Association), as early as 1911, Henry Ford paid particular attention to the assimilation of the handicapped into the workforce.

In February 1929, H.M. Cordell, Ford's secretary, named specific jobs in Motor Assembly, the Gasket Department and the Valve Bushing Department where blind men were employed. Fifteen years later, Helen Keller commended Ford and the company for these efforts. "Truly the service of the Ford Motor Company to the blind is unique in the annals of handicapped humanity," she said.

In his doctoral dissertation on Black Americans at Ford, David Lewis says that in 1929, 7.7 percent of Detroit's population was black and eight percent of Ford's Detroit area employment was black. In 1926, according to Lewis, approximately forty-seven percent of the black population was supported by Ford paychecks but, by 1931, this had fallen to twenty percent. Both Lewis and Nevins and Hill see the story of Black Americans at Ford as a generous one.

Nevins and Hill argue that Ford practiced real equality, giving blacks the same wages and chances as whites and enabled them to share in all the manufacturing operations. Lewis agrees, and also points out that Ford promoted Black Americans to "foremanships and other positions in which they supervised both blacks and whites." Writing in the *Michigan History Magazine* he

states "To this day, (Ford) remains one of the greatest benefactors of African-Americans."

Lewis' view is supported by the *Journal of Negro History* published by the National Association for the Advancement of Colored People, which, at the time of Henry Ford's death, declared that Ford "endeavored to help humanity by offering men work at living wages and making it comfortable for them in his employment. In this respect he was a great benefactor of the Negro race, probably the greatest that ever lived."

In fairness, however, it should be noted, as Joyce Shaw Peterson points out in her 1987 study *American Automobile Workers, 1900-1933*, that the bulk of black workers, between sixty percent and seventy percent at the Rouge, were still employed in the foundry. "At Ford," she writes, "there was only a greater possibility that a black worker might acquire skill and training and be promoted to skilled and supervisory positions."

Former Ford worker Robert Cruden sees little positive in the situation for black workers at Ford, saying that there were few blacks on the assembly lines, in the tool rooms or in other skilled work. He claims that most blacks swept the floors or labored where the work was hard and body-killing—in the rolling mill, the foundry and the steel mills. Cruden's highly critical comments on Ford are contained in a small pamphlet, *The End of The Ford Myth*, published by International Pamphlets, a Communist publishing house, in 1932.

By 1928-29, the hiring rate at Ford was $.62.5 an hour, which, according to Nevins and Hill, was at the top of the automotive industry. On December 3, 1929, Edsel Ford announced that the minimum wage would be increased from six dollars a day to seven dollars and that all wage earners whose wage rate exceeded the minimum would receive an increase of five cents an hour. The dollar a day increase benefited 24,320 employees while another 113,643 were given the additional five cents an hour. The new hiring-in rate was increased to seventy-five cents per hour.

Employees on salary also received a five percent increase. The new hiring-in rate for salary roll employees over twenty years of age was one hundred-thirty-five dollars per month and the minimum rate after two months service was one hundred-sixty dollars per month. Minors (twenty years and two months or younger) received increases ranging from four to ten dollars a month depending on age.

Automobile Topics, in its December 1929 issue, quoted Edsel Ford who said that "Employees to the number of 113,643 have received increases which bring their daily wage between $7.20 and $10 a day." Full-time employment at Ford in October was 144,990, which meant an average raise of about one hundred-twenty-eight dollars a year per employee, if working full-time. Overall, the increase meant an addition of approximately $20,000,000 of buying power a year.

Ford's wage increases at the end of 1929 were in sharp contrast with hiring policy at the beginning of the

"Final Assembly Conveyors," *Ford Industries*, **1929.**

No.24

THE END of the FORD MYTH

by

Robert L. Cruden

5c

INTERNATIONAL PAMPHLETS

799 Broadway   New York

The End of the Ford Myth. **According to this pamphlet's author, Robert Cruden, the Ford myth was the legend of high wages, safe working conditions and contented workers at Ford Motor Co.**

year. As 1928 was drawing to a close, the company announced that an additional 30,000 workers would be hired at the Rouge over a three month period. Keith Sward says that on January 2, 1929, when hiring was supposed to start, 32,000 applicants came to the Rouge. Most of them were turned away. Four months later only 8,000 had been hired. Eventually, however, more were hired as production escalated.

One of the Ford workers at that time was Walter Reuther, later to become the president of the United Automobile Workers from 1946 to 1970. At the age of nineteen, Reuther was hired in April 1927 to work at Highland Park as a tool and die maker at $1.05 an hour. About six months later he was transferred to the toolroom of the B-Building at the Rouge, arriving just in time for the Model A. In 1929, he was classified as an "A-1 Diemaker Leader," at $1.40 an hour. Reuther's experience at the Rouge is chronicled in Nelson Lichtenstein's biography, *The Most Dangerous Man In Detroit* (1995).

Working conditions at the Rouge were far from 1990s standards. Physically, Nevins and Hill say, both Highland Park and the Rouge "stood decidedly in advance of most American factories. Good light, ample ventilation, cleanliness and efficient safety precautions were maintained."

The Ford safety record, although not perfect, was the best in the business. First aid stations and a hospital were located on the premises. "Ford was particularly concerned with safety," writes Joyce Shaw Peterson, "and both the Highland Park plant and the River Rouge plant ranked first among all auto companies in its safety record and sometimes first among all companies."

In late 1928, Ford announced that it would run its factories on a six-day week while maintaining a five-day week for employees. However, if one believes Robert Cruden, "The five-day week has itself been abandoned as occasion demanded—in 1929, I worked many weeks on the six-day basis."

Work rules at Ford were essentially the same as in the factories of other automobile companies. Workers were not allowed to sit while working and could not smoke. They were supposed to be completely silent, although this rule was not fully enforced. The lunch period lasted only fifteen minutes and included the time to wash hands and get food from one of the two hundred-twenty lunch wagons, if so desired.

Norwood, who spent many days at the Rouge and ate fifty meals from the wagons, was impressed with the freshness and quality of the food and the price. A boxed lunch containing a spread, such as jelly, a New York ham sandwich, a piece of fruit and either a slice of cake or a cupcake sold for fifteen cents. A pint bottle of milk cost seven cents and a pint of coffee or tea, five cents.

Shifts rotated every two weeks without regard to seniority or any reason other than illness There were three shifts starting at staggered times so that too many would not enter or leave at one time. Shift changes were made on a signal as described by Phillip Bonosky in his biography of Bill McKie, a Ford worker, communist and union organizer (*Brother Bill McKie*).

"Bill had to be inside the gates before the 3:30 bell. The men came with reluctant hurry. They raced down through the departments until they reached their own, as Bill did to the tin shop. They only carried their lunches. They were already dressed in work clothes, since there was no place or time to change. As 3:30 neared, they lined up behind the men on the belt. Bill was at his bench, his apron tied, toolbox out, tools ready.

"The signal!

"For a split instant a shudder spread through the plant. The workers on the belt fell back as though they had been shot, and the new workers stepped into their places. Not a motion lost!"

The happiness and satisfaction of the workers who built the Model A depended on many factors. There were those who were unhappy such as Cruden who maintained that talk of Ford's paternal interest in his workers is "the sheerest hypocrisy." He claims that after

the seven dollars a day wage was introduced workers were told by their bosses to "Go like hell. If you're gonna get that raise you gotta increase production."

In an article in the *New Republic*, Cruden says that to qualify for his seventeen percent increase in pay he had to raise his personal production quota by forty-seven percent. The speed-up, he maintains, resulted in a high accident rate. He also disputes claims that there were no wage cuts at Ford, saying that it was common for workers to be shifted to other departments at a lower salary, or fired and then rehired at a lower wage.

As the conveyors speeded up the work they also contributed to the elimination of unskilled jobs. In a 1929 letter to Rouge boss Charles Sorensen, one engineer said that they were able to eliminate four hundred jobs in the B building and almost two hundred more in other departments as more conveyor systems were completed. (Cited in *Autowork* by Robert Asher and Ronald Edsforth.)

Unhappiness on the part of some workers was evident, but there does not seem to have been organized attempts to strike or walkout during the Model A years. One walkout that did occur was at an outside supplier, the Briggs body plant in 1929. According to Peterson, when Briggs cut piecework rates, the workers simply refused to go back to work after lunch and just sat around waiting to see what would happen. The company brass appeared, made threats and were greeted by tough talk from their employees. The result was that the old rates were restored and the men went back to work.

In Cruden's opinion Ford was not a popular employer. Nevins and Hill, however, say that many Ford workers preferred working at the Rouge to any other plant and that many "cherished a sense of personal or institutional loyalty" to the company. "The fact remains," they state, "that to the end of the 1920s many workers felt themselves fortunate to have a job in the Ford plants." In general, Norwood and others quoted by Nevins and Hill seem to agree with this position.

Another negative perspective is presented in a telegram sent to Fred Rockelman, Ford sales manager, on October 29, 1929, by a twelve-year Ford employee working in the chassis department at the Memphis plant. The man claimed that men were working ten-hour days and being paid for five hours; that they were working in carbon monoxide fumes, but the management would not allow windows to be opened; that they were virtually on a piecework basis since pay time was marked according to the number of cars produced. He also said that six men at the plant were laid off two days each for lying down resting on their own time. "The remedy," he wrote, "is beyond our control, but the cure is obvious."

Outside the factory, the living conditions for many Ford workers were modestly acceptable, but never with a wide margin of security. During 1929, Ford asked the Bureau of Labor Statistics to conduct a study of Ford workers in Detroit regarding their standard of living. Some of the conclusions of this study, cited by Peterson, follow, but must be understood in the context of the criteria established by Ford, which eliminated many workers with lower standards of living.

From a pool of 1,740 married workers earning approximately seven dollars per day, one hundred families were chosen for the study. Most of the families (sixty-eight percent) rented their homes and lived in four or five rooms plus a bathroom with indoor plumbing. Their diets were sufficient in quantity and balanced in nutrition. Most used public transportation to get to work, although slightly less than half owned an automobile.

The average income of these families was $1,711.87, while their average expenditures were $1,719.83. Food, housing, clothing, fuel and light absorbed eighty percent of the family budget. The study revealed among other things that forty-four percent of the families were living above their income; fifty-nine percent made installment purchases; eighty-six percent spent some money on motion pictures; and every family spent money on newspapers.

Tempering what seemed to be a basic but far from luxurious life for most of these workers, was the fact that many of them came home from work so fatigued that about all they could do was sleep. Additionally, after 1929, this modest standard of living was greatly eroded for most by the realities of the Great Depression.

The other part of the Rouge story in 1929, was the immense task of moving men and machines from the Highland plant to the Rouge. More than 7,000 machines had to be moved and others, already in place had to be transferred. Prior to June 1, 1929, more than 4,250 were in place and operating. And all this was done without interrupting the flow of production of Model A cars and Model AA trucks.

In *Moving Forward*, Henry Ford wrote that "This moving was one of the biggest moving jobs the industrial world has ever seen, yet it was accomplished so easily that even in the city where it was being done few persons noticed it." Just one example of what was done, is the move of the die-casting department in which small production parts were cast directly from dies. During two weekends, seven hundred men, three hundred machines and an entire tool room department were moved and making die-cast parts in the new location by the end of the second weekend.

On October 24, 1929, and again on October 29, stock market prices plummeted. With their fall came the end of the prosperity of the "Roaring Twenties." The crash was the opening event of what is known as "The Great Depression." During the rest of 1929 and into 1930, the Ford Motor Co. initiated a series of measures designed to help weather the storm. These included price reductions, a cut in the dealer discount, increasing the number of Ford agencies, plant expansion, raising wages and improvements in the design of the Model A.

Price reductions affecting all Model A cars and AA trucks went into effect on November 1. With them came a rollback in the dealer discount from 20 percent to 17-1/2 percent. Cuts ranged from a low of fifteen dollars for the Roadster to twenty-five dollars for the Tudor, Fordor and

While Ford workers struggled to make ends meet, Edsel Ford enjoyed his new 130-foot yacht "Sialia" photographed on November 12, 1929. (Photo courtesy of International News Photos)

Town Sedan to a high of two hundred dollars for the Town Car. A sampling shows the Phaeton now selling for four hundred-forty dollars, the Sport Coupe for five hundred-thirty dollars, the Town Sedan for six hundred-seventy dollars and the Station Wagon for six hundred-fifty dollars. Truck prices were also cut back. For example, the Model AA Panel Delivery was reduced from eight hundred-fifty dollars to eight hundred dollars and the Model AA truck chassis from five hundred-forty dollars to five hundred-twenty dollars.

In announcing the reductions, Ford President Edsel Ford said, "The company believes that, basically, the industry and business of the country are sound. Every indication is that general business conditions will remain prosperous. We are reducing prices now because we feel that such a step is the best contribution that could be made to assure a continuation of good business throughout the country." Under different circumstances this effort might have worked. Unfortunately, much more was needed, not only from Ford but from industry as a whole.

Shortly after the price reductions were announced, each dealer received a letter in duplicate requiring him to sign one copy and return it to his Branch office so that there would be a record of his agreement with the discount reduction. That letter was followed by a three-page justification of what Ford was doing and a statement that the price changes would not have been possible without the discount revision. What this meant, as dealers well knew, was that they, not the company would finance the bulk of the price reductions.

On the Tudor, for example, by lowering the price to $500 from $525 and changing the discount from 20 percent to 17-1/2 percent, the dealer's gross profit was reduced from $105 to $87.50. In effect, he was picking up $17.50 of the reduction and the company $7.50. As might be expected, the change in the discount caused widespread dealer resentment forcing the company to adjust its discount three more times in the next fifteen months.

The discount reduction was not the only problem facing dealers in late 1929 and through the following

months. They also had to contend with Ford's attempt, orchestrated by Rouge boss Charles Sorensen, to increase the number of dealers from 8,300 to 10,000. This not only increased competition for established dealers, but in some cases meant that they had to contend with a new agency planted as little as three blocks away from their location.

Two other steps taken by the company were plant expansion and a raise in wages. Early in 1930, Ford announced a $25,000,000 plant expansion program. At the end of November 1929, at the conclusion of a White House conference of business leaders to discuss possible solutions to the economic situation, Ford made his sensational announcement of the seven-dollar-a-day wage minimum mentioned previously. It marked the third time in its history that the Ford Motor Co. raised its minimum wage. In 1914, it increased it from $2.34 to $5; in 1919, from $5 to $6.

In announcing the increase in pay, Henry Ford said, "There is nothing about business for the country to fear, and if everyone will attend to his own work the future is secure." He further stated that, "In this country the purchasing power of the people has been practically used up, and still they have not been able to buy all that they must have. I, therefore, suggest the need of increasing the purchasing power of our principal customers—the American people."

Another measure taken by Ford to offset the increasingly serious economic decline was already in the planning stage and involved the first important change in the lines of the Model A Ford since its introduction in December 1927. While keeping the mechanical features that distinguished the car since 1927, the Model A entered 1930 with a new and distinctively beautiful line of body types. The following excerpt from the 1930 edition of the *Ford Sales Manual*, intended solely for the use of Ford dealers and Ford salesmen, indicates some of the changes.

"The entire front of the car is raised. Moulding treatment is new and fenders are of more generous dimensions, streamlined to flow with the lines of the car. There is a new treatment in the sweep of the bodies, giving an impression of fleetness. From the new-type flat radiator cap to the tip of the low, graceful curve of the rear fenders, every line is new, clear cut and extremely smart.

"Introduction of rustless steel for such exterior exposed metal parts as the radiator, headlamps, taillamp, hubcaps, the cowl finish strip, etc., is an outstanding feature. Polished to a high lustre, it retains its brilliancy indefinitely.

"As one looks at the new Ford car the first thing that catches the eye is the new radiator. Still retaining the Ford individuality, it is high and narrow, and in excellent style. This with the higher and longer hood and the shorter cowl give the front of the car a distinctly new and pleasing appearance, to which an added touch of brightness comes from the finish strip at the juncture of the hood and cowl.

"Head lamps of a new style, set higher on a new design arched tie rod, also contribute to better appearance.

"There is a new atmosphere of stability in the smaller steel spoke wheels and larger tires. They bring the bodies closer to the ground, producing a lower center of gravity and consequent great safety on the road, especially in rounding turns at high speed. Riding quality also is improved."

In December, dealers were informed that the new body styles would be shown in their showrooms on December 31st. They were also given specific instructions on how to display the new Ford and told that they were to keep an accurate record of daily attendance at their showing and of the orders taken either for immediate or spring delivery. This information was to be wired to the Branch on January 1st. They were warned not to show the cars in advance.

D.D. Norton was notified on December 26 that he would receive a Tudor with the new body type for display purposes only. He was given the number of the freight car in which his car, and a Tudor and a Town Sedan intended for neighboring dealers would arrive. The cars were to be unloaded and driven-away to each dealership after dark only, and then kept under cover and out of sight until the national announcement and the showing.

On December 31, 1929, a total of 3,951,612 persons attended the introduction of the new body types. About ten million people visited dealerships on the first five days, according to actual count. An enthusiastic reception was reported from all parts of the country. A wire from Louisville was typical: "Reports from all sections indicate public well pleased and in receptive mood for new body types."

Kansas City noted that an average of 1,500 visitors, including a fair number of women, viewed the new models in each of the city's twelve Ford showrooms. This was remarkable considering that the opening was on Tuesday, a regular work day. The Galigher Motor Sales Co. of Huntington, West Virginia, reported that "The new Ford body changes made a tremendous hit with the crowds that viewed the new Ford bodies. . . . Many of them made the remark that the new Ford was now the ultimate car."

People who viewed the cars appeared most interested in the new look of the Ford, the mechanics seemed taken for granted. In one instance, one hundred-sixty-five men and women passed around the bright Tudor sedan on display before a single person lifted the hood to view the engine. Drawing the most interest were the higher radiator, the steering wheel, the wheels and the two-tone color schemes.

The public also commented on the fact that though the car was changed some in appearance, it was not changed enough to make the older models look out of date. "That's a thing I have always liked about Fords," a woman said. "You can buy a car and feel sure it is not going to look obsolete right away. As long as you keep the paint looking good the model stays in style. I was afraid the new styles would be a lot different from the original Model A, but I see they are not." (*Ford Dealer and Service Field.*)

The following is an exact duplicate of an original letter sent to all Ford Dealers by the Ford Motor Company in 1929

General Letter No. 31   November 1st, 1929

	List	Disct.	Net to Dealer	Bumpers	Freight	Gas & Oil	Net Cost	Del.
Phaeton	440.00	17½%	363.00	12.38	28.25	2.60	406.23	525.00
Roadster	435.00	17½%	358.88	12.38	28/25	2.60	402.11	520.00
Sport Roadster	470.00	17½%	387.75	12.38	28.25	2.60	430.98	550.00
Standard Coupe	500.00	17½%	412.50	12.38	36.25	2.60	463.73	590.00
Sport Coupe	530.00	17½%	437.25	12.38	36.25	2.60	488.48	620.00
Business Coupe	490.00	17½%	404.25	12.38	36.25	2.60	455.48	580.00
Tudor Sedan	500.00	17½%	412.50	12.38	36.25	2.60	463.73	590.00
Fordor Sedan 2-window	600.00	17½%	495.00	12.38	36.25	2.60	546.23	690.00
Fordor Sedan 3-window (Std.)	625.00	17½%	515.63	12.38	36.25	2.60	566.86	715.00
Town Sedan	670.00	17½%	552.75	12.38	36.25	2.60	603.98	760.00
Cabriolet	645.00	17½%	532.13	12.38	36.25	2.60	583.36	735.00
Town Car	1200.00	17½%	990.00	–	36.25	2.60	1028.85	1275.00
Taxicab	725.00	17½%	598.13	12.38	36.25	2.60	649.36	815.00
DeLuxe Panel Delivery	550.00	17½%	453.75	12.38	36.25	2.60	504.98	640.00
Station Wagon	650.00	17½%	536.25	5.78	36.25	2.60	580.88	735.00
"A" Chassis	350.00	17½%	288.75	5.78	28.25	2.60	325.38	425.00
"A" Chassis, Closed Cab	440.00	17½%	363.00	5.78	30.80	2.60	402.18	515.00
Pick-up, Open Cab	430.00	17½%	354.75	5.78	30.80	2.60	393.93	505.00
Pick-Up, Closed Cab	460.00	17½%	379.50	5.78	30.80	2.60	418.68	535.00
"A" Panel Delivery	590.00	17½%	486.75	5.78	36.25	2.60	531.38	675.00
"AA" Panel Delivery	800.00	17½%	660.00	5.78	38.80	2.60	707.18	895.00
"AA" Truck Chassis	520.00	17½%	429.00	5.78	30.80	2.60	468.18	745.00
Closed Cab	90.00	17½%	74.25		1.65			
Open Cab	65.00	17½%	53.63		1.35			
Stake Body	65.00	17½%	53.63		3.05			
Pick-up Body	30.00	17½%	24.75		.70			
Express Body	55.00	17½%	45.38		1.40			
Platform Body	50.00	17½%	41.25		2.40			
"A" Panel Body	250.00	17½%	206.25					
"AA" Panel Body	310.00	17½%	255.75					
Rumble Seat	35.00	17½%	28.88					
Stock Rack	40.00	25%	30.00					
Grain Sides	35.00	25%	26.25					

Tray with sliding screen for DeLuxe Panel may be obtained through Service at $10.00 list less discount of 25%.

Price list, November 1, 1929, including dealer delivered price.

Despite ominous economic signs, the crowds filling Ford showrooms across the nation must have been heartening to the typical Ford dealer and certainly to company executives. They could hope that conditions might improve. But, alas, although 1930 would be a relatively good year for Ford, it would also bring increasing hard times for the company and its dealers as well as the industry and nation as a whole.

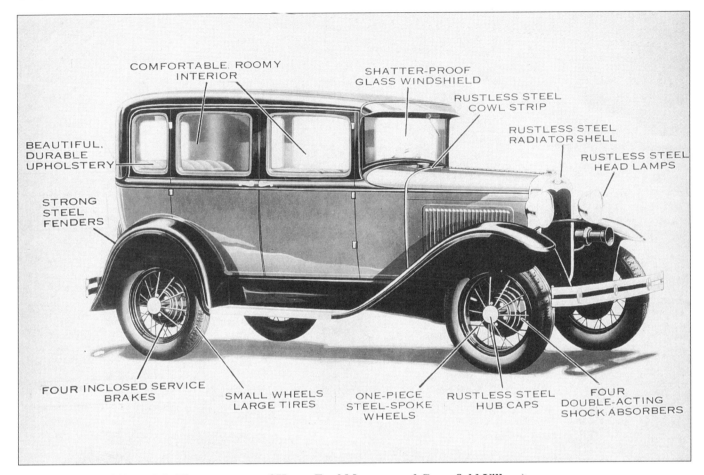

The New Ford, 1930 model. (Photo courtesy of Henry Ford Museum and Greenfield Village)

Chapter Four

1930: Year of Expansion

"SHE'S a BEAUTY! That is one's prompt and logical impression at first sight of the 1930 Model A Ford—with the redesigned bodies.

The best part of it is that the improved Model A Ford really is as good as it looks! Road-tested by nearly three million actual owners, the Ford car has definitely earned the approval of the American public, which asked for no improvements or chassis changes, but only that the quality and mechanical features through which the Ford gained its remarkable record of performance always should be kept."

Murray Fahnestock, technical editor
Ford Dealer and Service Field magazine

Appointments of the New Ford

TRIPLEX SHATTER-PROOF GLASS

FIVE STEEL WHEELS

RUSTLESS STEEL

NEW STEERING WHEEL

SMALLER WHEELS—LARGER TIRES

"Appointments of the New Ford," from booklet "Beauty of Line."

Writing in the January 1930 issue of the magazine, Fahnestock lists the new improvements of the Model A, which he predicts will build big sales in 1930. Among these are the liberal use of rustless steel, smaller wheels and bigger tires—which give the car a lower center of gravity and consequent greater safety when rounding corners—a new radiator, headlamps, higher, narrower and longer hood and redesigned front and rear fenders. He also cites a better way of setting the gasoline tank into the body and says that the size of this fuel tank "has been increased from the 10-1/2 gallons of earlier Model A Fords to a little over 11 gallons for these new 1930 Ford cars."

"Mechanically," Fahnestock wrote, "the 1930 Model A Ford is practically identical with the improved Model A powerplant as used on the more recent Model A Ford cars. Briefly, about the only change is that the top hose connection is now 8 inches long, instead of 6-1/4 inches long, as formerly." Although various changes in the engine components were made in 1930 as in the previ-ous model years, the basic 40 brake horsepower at 2200 revolutions per minute remained constant.

Ford Facts, published by Ford in 1931, enthusiasti-cally claims that, "Although 40 horsepower is developed at 2200 revolutions per minute, the engine will turn up to about 2700 revolutions per minute with almost no loss of power, corresponding to about 65 miles in high, 35 in second and 20 in low." Elsewhere, *Ford Facts* hedges its bet somewhat by claiming that the Model A should be able to be driven as high as fifty-five to sixty-five miles per hour. Arguably, sustained speeds of sixty to sixty-five miles per hour were as unlikely in the 1930s as they are in the 1990s.

In its February 1930 issue, *Ford Dealer & Service Field* reported that Ford dealers around the country "expected the biggest business in Ford history," as a result of the enthusiastic public reception of the improved Model A. The improvements are, said the magazine, "a practical painting of the lily; making the best car even better." A Salem, Oregon, dealer's com-ments were typical: "The new bodies were received very favorably by 2,000 patrons on December 31. We booked 26 orders in 10 days. We expect to sell 40 percent of all cars sold in our county this coming year." Dealers were helped greatly in their efforts through the year by the company, which spent almost $8,700,000 advertising the revised Model A.

See the New Ford Bodies at Our Showrooms

From the new deep radiator to the curving tip of the rear fender, there is an unbroken sweep of line---a flowing grace of contour heretofore thought possible only in an expensive automo-bile. Now, more than ever, the new Ford is a "value far above the price."

Condit Motor Sales Co.
INCORPORATED

12 Moran Street

Newton, N. J.

MORE VALUE
FOR YOUR MONEY

See the new Ford body lines and colors at our showrooms. ⁊ We also have a few 1929 new cars for sale at a substan-tial discount.

Morang-Robinson Co., Inc.
Tel. 57   *Bar Harbor*

Ads from Ford dealers for the new showing, *Ford Dealer & Service Field*, June 1930.

Rustless Steel Protects the Ford Against the Attack of Depreciation

Cartoon "Rustless Steel Protects the Ford Against the Attack of Depreciation," *Ford Dealer & Service Field,* **September 1930.**

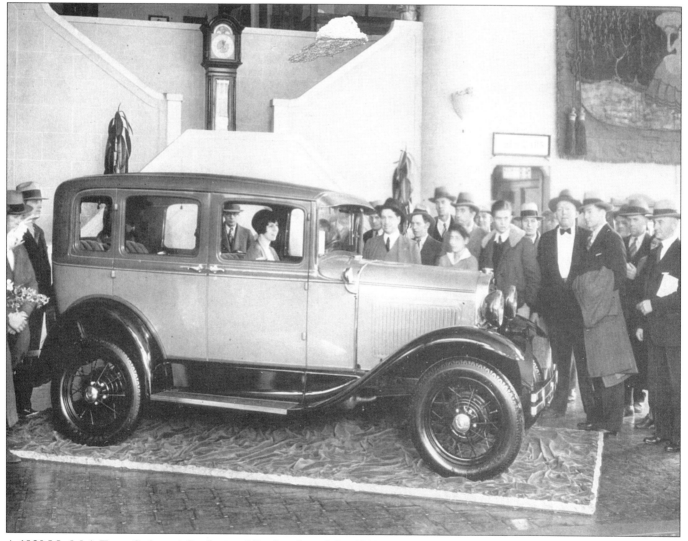

A 1930 Model A Town Sedan at the first public showing of the 1930 models.

At the time of the 1930 Ford's introduction nine revised body types were available: Tudor, Standard Coupe, Sport Coupe, Phaeton, Roadster, Cabriolet, Town Sedan and the two- and three-window Fordor Sedans. In addition to these, five new types were announced by the company during 1930. They were the DeLuxe Coupe (five hundred-fifty dollars), DeLuxe Sedan (six hundred-fifty dollars), DeLuxe Phaeton (six hundred-twenty-five dollars), DeLuxe Roadster (five hundred-twenty dollars) and the Victoria (six hundred-twenty-five dollars)—all prices f.o.b. Detroit. The Model A Station Wagon adopted the 1930 style in June and, at about the same time, the price was reduced by ten dollars to six hundred-forty dollars. By the end of August 1932, domestic, Canadian and foreign production of this type would total 11,881 units.

As explained to Ford dealers, the DeLuxe Coupe and Sedan were "provided to meet the constantly growing demand, particularly from women buyers, for smart, richly trimmed body interiors." Ford also hoped that these two types, as well as the DeLuxe Phaeton and Roadster, would impress owners of medium- and high-priced cars enough to claim some sales among them.

The body lines of the DeLuxe Coupe were similar to the Standard Coupe. The DeLuxe Sedan was similar to the two-window Fordor and was intended to replace that model after the stocks of two-window Fordor bodies on hand and in transit were used up in production. The interior trim was like that of the Town Sedan. For both models, cowl lights and a dome lamp assembly were standard and the purchaser had the choice of either Mohair or Bedford cord upholstering.

Standard equipment on the Model A DeLuxe Phaeton included rearview mirror with chrome-plated bracket; chrome-plated windshield frame; chrome-plated vacuum windshield wiper; cowl lamps; trunk rack with chrome-plated platform; and spare, steel spoke wheel mounted in a well fender on the left side. This model went into production at the Buffalo plant in June 1930, but only at the rate of one per day for the first month. The DeLuxe Roadster was furnished with the same equipment as the Phaeton. It also had as standard, a full-length bumper, front and rear, rumble seat and a top boot.

Standard colors for the DeLuxe Phaeton and DeLuxe Roadster were Raven black and George Washington blue with genuine leather upholstery. For both models any passenger car color combination was optional if, as Instruction And Assembly Change Letter #74 (June 13, 1930) explained to Branch offices, there is sales resistance to the standard blue or black. In November, Ford

An early 1930 Town Sedan with Murray body shows the classic 1930-31 style of the Model A. Photo dated October 16, 1929. (Photo courtesy of Ford Motor Co. Archives)

Late-1930 Model A Station Wagon - owner Zane Zander.

In 1931, the author and his Mom pose with the family 1930 Model A Tudor. Note the tire chains on the rear wheel and the accessory moto-meter.

A boy poses in the family 1930 Sport Coupe.

A 1930 DeLuxe Roadster.

A 1930 DeLuxe Phaeton.

announced an additional standard color combination for these two DeLuxe models; body and hood in stone brown, moldings in stone deep gray and the wheels and striping in Tacoma cream.

With the introduction of the four DeLuxe models, dealers were encouraged to loan them to prominent persons as a "courtesy" car program to enhance sales. A successful example of this is explained in the following letter from the Bonneville Auto Co. of Idaho Falls, Idaho, to the Salt Lake City Branch.

"Gentlemen:

For the past six months we have kept a DeLuxe Coupe busy in the hands of prominent people and large car owners and through this activity have acquainted many people with the quality, ease of riding and control, of the new Ford. This has resulted in sales to three bankers, two physicians, and several other people who have previously driven nothing but expensive cars. In every case the sale of a DeLuxe Model to this class of trade has resulted in a straight deal with no trade.

The DeLuxe Coupe that we kept in this service has been driven approximately six thousand miles, and we have made eighteen sales to which positive credit can be given to this activity. We sold the coupe just yesterday and found it necessary to reduce the price only $75.00, so it is evident that this process is not an expensive one."

An additional DeLuxe type, the Victoria Coupe, with a "bustle back" (luggage space reached from behind the rear seat cushion), was added to the Model A line in late October 1930. The Sales Department described the Victoria Coupe as "a four-passenger model extremely attractive in appearance, and the only one of our closed cars to have a slanting windshield; an effect that adds much to its appearance. The top and rear quarter down to the belt line are covered in a heavy tan colored pyroxylin coated material. . . . The spare tire is set at an angle, which adds a final touch of smartness. . . ." Later, a steel back Victoria became available. *Ford News* described the Victoria as having "an atmosphere of jauntiness."

Domestic assembly of the Victoria during 1930 totaled 6,306 units. Another 141 were assembled at Walkerville in Canada. Production for 1931 reached 35,830 units with 1,096 assembled in Canada and an additional 828 outside North America. In 1932, Victoria production was down to two hundred-fifty units with only one of these assembled in the United States. During the first week of December 1930, Ford ran newspaper advertising featuring the Victoria in all cities of 25,000 population and over in the United States.

In addition to the above there were several other Model A-types assembled in 1930. These included a Taxicab, Town Car, Panel Delivery, DeLuxe Panel Delivery and Pickup (open and closed cab). A Sport Roadster (probably with rumble seat) is listed on early sales letters, but removed by August. A few Business Coupes were assembled overseas. A small number of DeLuxe Tudors, Special Delivery and Drop Floor Panel Delivery-types were also assembled in 1930, as was one Town Car Delivery.

There were also a number of custom-built Model A Fords assembled in 1930. One of these by Gordon Buehrig is described later in this chapter. Another, the so-called "Gourmet Model A," is profiled in the March-April 1990 issue of *SAH Journal* (publication of the Society of Automotive Historians). This 1930 Sport Phaeton was designed by Edsel Ford and built by the Lebaron Detroit Co. of Detroit. It utilized the entire—though

A 1930 DeLuxe Coupe. (Photo courtesy of Henry Ford Museum and Greenfield Village)

A 1930 Pickup in use today by the Galuski Plumbing and Heating of East Syracuse, New York.

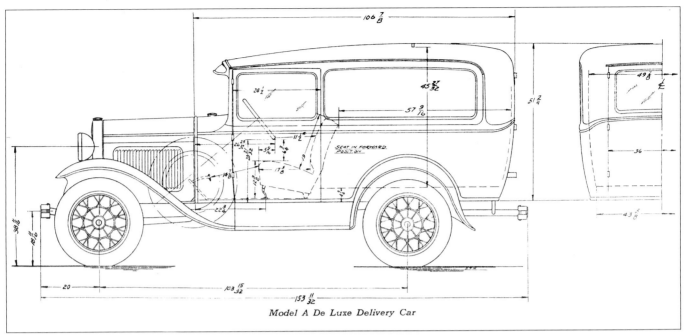

Model A De Luxe Delivery Car

Diagram of a Model A DeLuxe Delivery car. From the Ford Sales Manual for 1930.

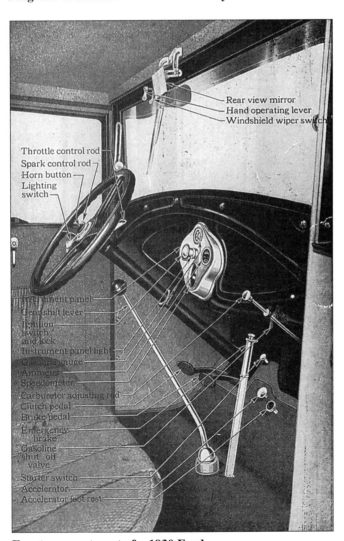

Rear view mirror
Hand operating lever
Windshield wiper switch

Throttle control rod
Spark control rod
Horn button
Lighting switch

Instrument panel
Gear shift lever
Ignition switch and lock
Instrument panel light
Gasoline gauge
Ammeter
Speedometer
Carburetor adjusting rod
Clutch pedal
Brake pedal
Emergency brake
Gasoline shut off valve
Starter switch
Accelerator
Accelerator foot rest

Front compartment of a 1930 Ford.

SPECIFICATIONS AND LICENSE DATA

Engine	Type of engine . . . . 4 cylinder Cylinder bore . . . . $3\frac{7}{8}$ inch Stroke . . . . $4\frac{1}{4}$ inch Horse Power . . . (S. A. E. rating) 24.03
Transmission	Selective sliding gear type. Car, three speeds forward and reverse. Truck, four speeds forward and reverse.
Clutch	Single plate dry disc.
Brakes	Four wheel internal expanding service brakes operated by the foot brake pedal. Also an emergency or parking brake on both rear wheels operated by the emergency brake lever. The emergency brakes are entirely separate and distinct from the four wheel service brakes. Total braking surface: Car, $225\frac{1}{2}$ sq. inches; Truck, $474\frac{7}{8}$ sq. inches.
Steering Gear	$\frac{3}{4}$ Irreversible, worm and sector type, ratio 13 to 1.
Oiling System	Engine lubricated by gear pump, splash and gravity feed. Oil pan capacity 5 quarts.
Cooling System	Pump and thermo-syphon. Capacity, 3 gallons.
Gasoline Tank	Capacity, 10 gallons.
Rear Axle	Three-quarter floating type. Torque tube drive. Spiral bevel drive pinion and gear.
Tires	Car, 19 x 4.75 Balloon. Truck, 6.00 x 20 and 32 x 6.
Wheel Base	Car, $103\frac{1}{2}$ inches. Truck, $131\frac{1}{2}$ inches.
Turning Radius	Car, 17', circle 34'. Truck, 23', circle 46'
Tread	56 inches.
Road Clearance	9 inches.

ENGINE NUMBER

The engine number is stamped on the left side of the cylinder block just above the cylinder inlet connection. The engine number is also the serial number of the car.

Specifications and License Data for a 1930 Ford.

Form 331

FACTORY AND GENERAL OFFICES
DEARBORN, MICH.

Ford Motor Company

Manufacturers of Automobiles, Trucks and Tractors
BUFFALO, N. Y.

BUFFALO BRANCH DEALERS   IN REPLYING REFER TO   Aug 28 1930

Supplement to Sales Letter No. 6 of 8-28-30

ALL STATEMENTS OR AGREEMENTS CONTAINED IN THIS LETTER ARE CONTINGENT ON STRIKES, ACCIDENTS, FIRES, OR ANY OTHER CAUSE BEYOND OUR CONTROL, AND ALL CONTRACTS ARE SUBJECT TO APPROVAL BY THE SIGNATURE OF A DULY AUTHORIZED EXECUTIVE OFFICER OF THIS COMPANY. CLERICAL ERRORS SUBJECT TO CORRECTION.

1   Superseding "Supplement to Sales Letter No. 6 of 6-2-30" sent you under date of June 2nd, 1930, the following current prices are furnished for the information of the dealers in the different discount classifications. These prices include standard equipment as itemized below:

MODEL "A" AUTOMOBILE AND CHASSIS

Starter	Mirror	Complete Tool Set
Speedometer	Ammeter	Four Balloon Tires
Gasoline Gauge	Dash Light	Four Shock Absorbers
Rear and Stop Light	Ignition Lock	Five Steel-spoke wheels

| | | F.O.B. DETROIT | - | DEALERS' | | |
	List	17½% 1-50	18% 51-100	19% 101-150	20% 151-500	21% 501-Over
Phaeton	440.00	363.00	360.80	356.40	352.00	347.60
DeLuxe Phaeton	625.00	515.63	512.50	506.25	500.00	493.75
Roadster	435.00	358.88	356.70	352.35	348.00	343.65
DeLuxe Roadster	520.00	429.00	426.40	421.20	416.00	410.80
Standard Coupe	495.00	408.38	405.90	400.95	396.00	391.05
Sport Coupe	525.00	433.13	430.50	425.25	420.00	414.75
DeLuxe Coupe	545.00	449.63	446.90	441.45	436.00	430.55
Tudor	495.00	408.38	405.90	400.95	396.00	391.05
Fordor, 3-Window	600.00	495.00	492.00	486.00	480.00	474.00
DeLuxe Sedan	640.00	528.00	524.80	519.40	512.00	505.60
Town Sedan	660.00	544.50	541.20	534.60	528.00	521.40
Cabriolet	625.00	515.63	512.50	506.25	500.00	493.75
Town Car (including bumpers)	1200.00	990.00	984.00	972.00	960.00	948.00
Taxicab	725.00	598.13	594.50	587.25	580.00	572.75
DeLuxe Delivery (less tray)	545.00	449.63	446.90	441.45	436.00	430.55
Station Wagon	640.00	528.00	524.80	518.40	512.00	505.60
"A" Chassis	345.00	284.63	282.90	279.45	276.00	272.55
"A" Chassis, Closed Cab	435.00	358.88	356.70	352.35	348.00	343.65
Pick-up, Open Cab	425.00	350.63	348.50	344.25	340.00	335.75
Pick-up, Closed Cab	455.00	375.38	373.10	368.55	364.00	359.45
"A" Panel Delivery	570.00	470.25	467.40	461.70	456.00	450.30
Rumble Seat for Roadster, Standard and DeLuxe Coupes, (installed)	25.00	20.63	20.50	20.25	20.00	19.75
"A" Panel Special Polish	20.00	16.50	16.40	16.20	16.00	15.80
Front Bumper and Rear Fender Guards	15.00	12.38	12.30	12.15	12.00	11.85
Front Bumper	7.00	5.78	5.74	5.67	5.60	5.53
Well Fender	9.00	7.43	7.38	7.29	7.20	7.11

August 28, 1930, Ford Motor Co. price list.

modified—Model A chassis, including frame, drivetrain, wheels, muffler, dash panel, steering column, radiator, and a blend of the 1929 and '30 radiator shells.

Rumble seats, much prized today on certain models, were standard equipment on the Cabriolet, Sport Coupe and DeLuxe Roadster, according to Ford's Sales Letter #6 (August 8, 1930). They were optional on the Standard Coupe, DeLuxe Coupe and Standard Roadster at an extra charge of twenty-five dollars installed. The Model A chassis listed at three hundred-forty-five dollars. It included cowl tank assembly, instrument panel, instruments, front fenders (well in left front fender), spare wheel, carrier bracket, running boards and running board shields, but not the rear fenders.

Among the more interesting and visible changes made in the interior of the Model A during 1930, was the mid-year adoption of a new design instrument panel with the lamp mounted on the underside of the front belt rail, instead of in the center as previous. The cowl tank was also redesigned to accommodate the instrument panel. The effect of this change was to give a softer, indirect light more convenient to the driver.

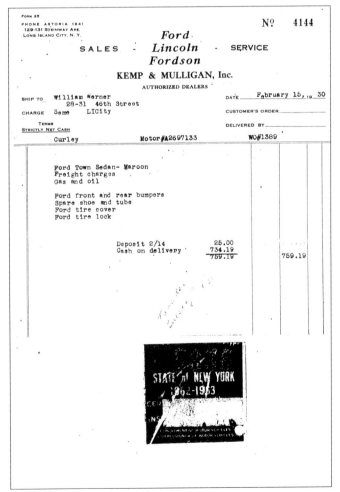

Bill of sale for a 1930 Town Sedan. This car, a low mileage original, is currently owned by Don Maines, LaFayette, New York.

Another example of a change was the letter to dealers on March 27, informing them that the Tudor would be supplied in "leather trim" and the Standard Coupe in "leatheret trim" at the customer's option. Dealers were urged to make this option known to commercial users and to use this feature to build the farmer's trade, particularly on the Tudor, since the use to which the average farmer put the Tudor Sedan was hard on any type of cloth upholstery.

In July 1930, the company updated its "Guarantee Service and Replacement Policy for the Model A & AA" from that of April 4, 1928. As in the past the general guarantee period was for ninety days. Shocks, vacuum windshield wipers, windshield glass and clutch pressure plate assemblies, for example, all carried a ninety-day warranty. In other cases the guarantee period was adjusted.

Electric wipers received by dealers on cars or through service stock after June 1, 1930, were guaranteed for one hundred-twenty days. Top decks on Tudors, Fordors and Coupes were guaranteed for one year if, the instructions stated, "there is no indication that the condition is due to the use of an unsatisfactory top dressing." This guarantee only applied to leaks through the material and not through the seams. As part of an ongoing campaign to sell Ford batteries, the guarantee period was extended to six months and was retroactive to March 1, 1930. Speedometers were guaranteed by the manufacturer for 4,000 miles. After that, repairs were to be authorized on a sliding mileage scale.

During 1930, Ford was forced to adjust prices in response to the worsening economic situation. A general price decrease took effect on June 2nd, lowering prices from five to twenty-five dollars depending on the model. The Panel Delivery, now sold for five hundred-seventy dollars, down from five hundred-ninety dollars while the Standard three-window Fordor was reduced by twenty-five dollars to six hundred dollars. These prices were f.o.b. Detroit and, as listed on Sales Letter #6 of August 8, 1930, included the following as standard equipment: starter, speedometer, gasoline gauge, rear and stop light, mirror, ammeter, dash light, ignition lock, complete tool set, four balloon tires, four shock absorbers and five steel spoke wheels.

The final amount paid by the buyer depended on the additional costs such as freight, gas and oil, bumpers, accessories and possibly the cost of a license and insurance. Provided are two examples of the actual cost of a Model A in 1930. On Long Island, Kemp & Mulligan, Inc. delivered a maroon Town Sedan on February 18, 1930. The new car price f.o.b. Detroit was $670. The buyer paid $759.19, which included freight charges, gas and oil, front and rear bumpers, spare tire and tube, a Ford tire cover and a Ford tire lock. Today, this car, still in mostly original condition and with only 30,000 miles on the odometer, is owned by Don Maines of LaFayette, New York.

Across the country, in San Diego, California, Stubbs Motor Corp. sold a Cabriolet on July 17, 1930, for a total price of $793.18. At that time the car's list price was $625. A copy of the Bill of Sale, reproduced in *The*

A B.T.C. PRODUCT

Tuxaway

PAT. PEND.
COPY. 1930

The Disappearing Always-Ready Rumble Seat Top for Fords . . .

Out of sight when not in use.

Up or down in half a minute from the seat.

Allows easy entrance and exit.

Harmonizes with the rest of the car.

Does not interfere with leg room or storage space.

Neat, snug-fitting side curtains are available for complete comfort and protection.

Cash In On This Ready Market!

Out of sight when not in use. It does not interfere with leg room or storage space.

Can be put up or down in half a minute from the rumble seat — a handy protection from sun or sudden showers.

Tuxaway can be pushed forward for easy entrance or exit. A convenient top from every viewpoint.

EVERY owner of a Ford rumble-seat car has long recognized the need for a rumble-seat top. And every owner will buy just as soon as he finds a top which is attractive and convenient.

That top is the Tuxaway. The Tuxaway conforms to the lines of the car and is smart looking as well as protective. It is the first permanent rumble-seat top designed by factory engineers — no straps, loose rolls of fabric, or pieces to match.

The Tuxaway is easily installed—only four holes need be drilled, and these are readily located with a template. Every Tuxaway you install will be an excellent advertisement for you.

The Tuxaway retails at $35 with the side curtains. Liberal dealer discount allowed. Send the coupon today and get ready for additional profits.

Manufactured by
THE BREWER-TITCHENER CORPORATION
Cortland, New York

Tuxaway
PAT. PEND.
COPY. 1930

THE BREWER-TITCHENER CORP.
Cortland, New York.

GENTLEMEN:

☐ I should like to try a Tuxaway and am enclosing my check for the special price of $35.

☐ I should like further information on the Tuxaway.

Name ....

Street ....

City .... State ....

Example of a non-Ford accessory, The Tuxaway, *Ford Dealer & Service Field*, August 1930.

A 1960 photo of a Tuxaway installed on a Model A Cabriolet.

Restorer, shows that the price included gas and oil ($3.50), Mexican insurance coverage ($8.18), and a license ($3.00). No accessories are listed. The buyer was given a trade-in allowance of $213.64 for a car of unknown make.

A study of prices in twenty-six cities across the country in mid-1930 appeared in *The Ford Dealers News* and reflected a wide disparity in the cost of Model A Fords. As one example, the Phaeton (list four hundred-forty dollars) sold for as little as four hundred-eighty dollars in Detroit and as much as five hundred-sixty-eight dollars in Savannah, Georgia. A Tudor (list four hundred-ninety-five dollars) could be bought for five hundred-thirty-five dollars in Detroit, but, at six hundred-thirty-one dollars, was almost one hundred dollars more in Savannah. These prices were delivered prices including

How Do *You* Sell Accessories?

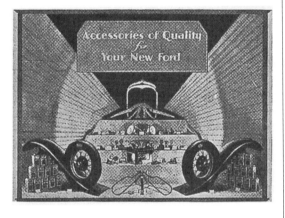

ACCESSORIES give the car owner a chance to get *individuality* into his car, and to include some non-standard equipment for which he may have taken a fancy. While accessories are a very profitable line for the dealer, many dealers have a tendency to let accessory sales "just take care of themselves." And then wonder why such car owners buy their equipment elsewhere. There is keen competition for the sale of accessories, just as for the sale of anything else, but the Ford dealer is in a wonderfully advantageous position to sell accessories, through the fact that he sells the car.

To make a success of selling equipment, a definite plan is required, and one Ford dealer has found the following plan very successful:

For instance, quote the price of the car as follows:

Ford Tudor Sedan, f. o. b. Detroit....	$495.00
Freight	35.00
Bumpers	15.00
Gas and Oil	3.00
Total	$548.00

This figure is used in all advertising, by salesmen, and in all answers to inquiries by telephone or otherwise. It represents the lowest price any other dealer can quote in the same area, having the same contract freight rate.

In selling the car to the customer, however, after the ord has been signed, the following minimum list of necessary accessories is added:

Spare tire	$13.00
Spare tire lock	3.00
Spare tire cover	2.00
Spring covers	3.50
Pedal pads (two)	.35
Total	$21.85

To this is added the $548.00 delivered price of the car, making a total of $569.85.

However, before commencing the sale of accessories, the salesman should ascertain whether the prospect is going to use the car for: 1. Business; 2. Sport; 3. Touring.

The salesman should have a list of the esesntial accessories needed for "business." Another list should be made for use on "sport" cars, including various fitments to doll up the car, regardless of whether or not they are essential to the operation of the car. The sport accessories can be divided into two groups, those for the roadster and phaeton, and those for the enclosed models.

If the car is to be used for touring, then there will be certain fitments such as trunks and trunk racks, reserve gasoline and oil cans, etc., which will be especially desirable for this use.

To increase the sale of accessories, it is obviously necessary to display them. This includes placing them in a window that is clean and well lighted at night.

Display boards can often be used to advantage on both the shop and salesroom floor for the display of accessories.

Every buyer of a new car should be consulted with regard to his choice of suitable accessories.

All Ford salesmen's cars should be equipped with approved accessories.

The Ford Motor Company has consistently emphasized "The Model A Ford, Serviced Completely by Ford Dealers." Which obviously includes such fitments and accessories as are needed for the use—or pleasure—of the owner in driving the car.

"How Do You Sell Accessories," *Ford Dealer & Service Field*, August 1930.

Prices shown are Delivered Prices, including Spare Tire, Tube, Bumper	Toledo, Ohio	Atlanta, Ga.	Cleveland, O.	Boston, Mass.	New York City	Wilmington, Del.	St. Louis, Mo.	Milwaukee, Wisc.	Minneapolis, Minn.	Grand Rapids, Michigan	Indianapolis, Ind.	Denver, Colo.	Dallas, Texas
Phaeton	$491	$540	$505	$526	$517	$514	$515	$508	$526	$505	$507	$564	$559
Phaeton Deluxe	661	725	690	...	...	...	700	693	...	...	...	749	...
Roadster	486	535	500	...	512	509	510	503	521	500	502	559	554
Roadster—Rumble Seat	511	560	525	546	537	534	535	528	546	525	525	...	579
Standard Coupe	550	603	568	589	580	577	573	571	589	563	570	627	622
De Luxe Coupe	600	653	618	639	630	627	623	621	639	613	620	677	672
Sport Coupe	580	633	598	619	610	607	603	601	619	593	600	657	652
Cabriolet	680	733	698	719	710	707	703	701	719	693	700	757	752
Tudor	550	603	568	589	580	577	573	571	589	563	570	627	622
3 Window Sedan	655	703	673	694	685	682	678	676	694	668	675	732	727
De Luxe Sedan	695	748	713	734	725	722	718	716	735	708	715	772	767
Town Sedan	715	768	733	764	745	742	738	736	754	728	735	793	787
"A" Chassis	388	...	404	...	416	514	414	405	...	402	...	472	441
"A" Panel	617	...	635	...	647	644	639	638	656	630	...	...	689
Pick Up Open Cab	470	...	469	...	496	494	493	488	508	484	...	552	544
Pick Up Closed Cab	500	...	494	...	526	524	524	518	538	514	...	582	574
De Luxe Delivery	600	...	618	...	630	627	622	621	...	...	...	677	672
Station Wagon	687	...	705	...	717	714	...	708	...	700	...	764	759
"AA" Chassis, Standard	540	...	...	...	...	564	562	...	574	...	...	...	606

Prices Shown are Delivered Prices, including Spare Tire, Tube, Bumpers	Mobile, Ala.	Erie, Pa.	Richmond, Va.	Savannah, Ga.	Topeka, Kansas	Portland, Me.	Jersey City, N. J.	Kansas City, Mo.	Louisville, Ky.	Detroit, Mich.	Bismarck, N. D.	Springfield, Mass.	Scranton, Pa.
Phaeton	$556	$515	$521	$568	$522	$530	$517	$532	$510	$480	$564	$528	$527
Phaeton Deluxe	...	700	760	...	707	...	...	702	...	665	749	713	712
Roadster	551	510	516	563	517	525	512	527	505	475	559	523	522
Roadster—Rumble Seat	576	535	541	588	552	550	537	552	530	500	584	548	547
Standard Coupe	617	575	581	631	585	590	580	595	573	535	627	588	584
De Luxe Coupe	667	625	631	681	635	640	630	645	...	585	677	638	634
Sport Coupe	647	605	611	661	615	620	610	625	603	565	657	618	659
Cabriolet	747	705	711	761	715	720	710	725	703	665	749	718	714
Tudor	617	575	581	631	585	590	580	595	573	535	627	588	584
3 Window Sedan	722	680	686	736	...	685	685	...	678	640	732	693	689
De Luxe Sedan	762	720	726	776	730	735	725	740	718	680	772	733	729
Town Sedan	782	740	746	796	750	755	745	700	738	700	792	753	749
"A" Chassis	459	410	415	535	430	432	417	434	410	377	...	429	424
"A" Panel	685	640	634	688	650	...	647	662	640	602	...	655	651
Pick Up Open Cab	...	490	487	542	506	512	497	514	490	457	...	509	506
Pick Up Closed Cab	...	520	517	572	536	532	527	544	520	487	...	539	536
De Luxe Delivery	...	625	...	671	635	632	630	645	623	585	...	637	634
Station Wagon	755	...	704	758	723	732	717	732	...	655	...	725	721
"AA" Chassis, Standard	606	607	...	607	589	580	...	582	...	525	...	624	574

Delivered prices from twenty-six cities for various models of Ford cars and trucks, *The Ford Dealer News,* **August 15, 1930.**

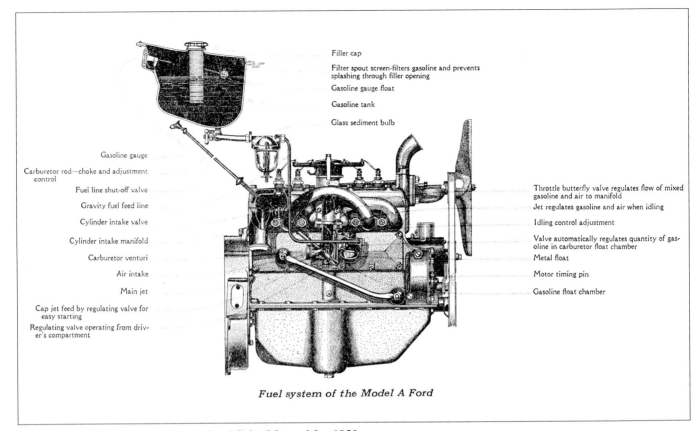

Filler cap

Filter spout screen-filters gasoline and prevents splashing through filler opening

Gasoline gauge float

Gasoline tank

Glass sediment bulb

Gasoline gauge

Carburetor rod—choke and adjustment control

Fuel line shut-off valve

Gravity fuel feed line

Cylinder intake valve

Cylinder intake manifold

Carburetor venturi

Air intake

Main jet

Cap jet feed by regulating valve for easy starting

Regulating valve operating from driver's compartment

Throttle butterfly valve regulates flow of mixed gasoline and air to manifold

Jet regulates gasoline and air when idling

Idling control adjustment

Valve automatically regulates quantity of gasoline in carburetor float chamber

Metal float

Motor timing pin

Gasoline float chamber

Fuel system of the Model A Ford

Fuel system of the Model A Ford, Ford Sales Manual for 1930.

spare tire, tube and bumpers. There is no mention of freight or gas and oil although it is likely that these were also included.

Ford accessories as listed in the 1930 Sales Manual were: tire cover, tire lock, spare wheel lock for use with well fenders, radiator cap with quail ornament, radiator cap with moto-meter, tire gauge, spring covers, fenders with wells for tires, clock, pedal pads, cowl and fender lamps, sport light, cigar lighter, seat covers, trunk rack and trunk. This list was augmented at times with others such as a spare wheel guard, radiator locking cap with quail, and a metal tire cover.

Of course, the Ford approved accessories were only a small part of the Model A accessory story in 1930 as in other years. *Ford Dealer & Service Field* carried ads for more than one hundred-seventy different non-Ford accessories in its twelve 1930 issues. These included familiar items such as heaters, trunks, air filters, oil filters, directional lights, luggage racks and many others. Less familiar, perhaps, to the reader are the ten-inch Fulton accelerator pedal, a deluxe walnut finished instrument board, the Victory combination oil gauge and choker extension, a Tietzmann reflector to light the gas gauge, and nineteen-inch wood wheels.

There was also the "Pedal Bloomer," a heavy piece of rubber that fit around the steering post and pedals to lock out those wintry blasts of cold air. Or, for those prone to drive in foggy conditions, how about the "Foggone," an English device that, it was claimed, removed fog from twelve to fifteen feet ahead of the car? And, if you were a dealer, why not install Venti-Shades, the perfect combination of ventilator and sun shade, on the side windows of every car on your showroom floor?

Dealers selling Model A and AA Fords made money from the discount they received on the car, as well as the accessories they were able to sell at a forty percent discount. During 1930, however, the company's policy on the sale of non-Ford accessories was a bit nebulous. A weekly service letter (April 25, 1930) from the Chicago Branch, for example, clearly states Ford's continuing opposition to the sale of accessories that directly compete with the approved Ford materials of similar design. It does not, however, explain the policy on non-Ford accessories that did not compete with those approved by the company.

In September, a service letter from the Indianapolis Branch was more precise. Commenting on a reduction in price on most accessories, the letter states, "Since this reduction has gone into effect we do not believe that there should be any Model A cars equipped with any but standard Ford accessories. We believe that our dealers should take advantage of this situation and reap the harvest which is theirs by selling the Model A accessories when the new cars are delivered." Unresolved here is the question whether this reflected only a Branch policy or a Ford Motor Co. policy.

A different point of view is expressed in an editorial in *Ford Dealer & Service Field* (October 1930), which claims that the magazine investigated the accessory situ-

ation and found that Ford dealers may sell non-Ford accessories. "The Ford Motor Company," states the magazine, "recognizes the right of the car owner to equip his car with such accessories as may add utility, service and enjoyment of this purchase. The Ford dealer is the logical one to supply his customers with such needs. If a car owner desires certain extra equipment, it is obviously poor business to send him to some other dealer, possibly one unfriendly to Ford products. . . . Ford dealers who use judgment and adopt a sensible policy in accessory merchandising will find that their methods will win approval." In weighing the merits of this statement it is important to note that *Ford Dealer & Service Field* was a monthly magazine devoted to the interests of Ford dealers, but was not connected with the Ford Motor Co.

Another interesting twist to the Ford accessory story has to do with the use of the word "accessory" itself. The Wattis-Kimball Motor Co. of Ogden, Utah, claimed that the word is obsolete. People who bought new Fords from that company did not buy "accessories" and think they were paying for something that was not essential but "handy" and "nice to have." They bought "additional equipment."

In the opinion of W.S. Hall of Wattis-Kimball, "Equipment sells easier than accessories." People thought of "accessories" as something not necessary and to be bought later, but buying "equipment" carried an entirely different meaning to the purchaser. "The result is," Hall said, "we have definitely increased the average sale of equipment with each new car by substituting the word equipment for accessory when making a sale."

The Ford Sales Manual for 1930, states that the Model A Ford is "economical on gasoline and will average better than 20 miles to the gallon, depending, of course, on the driver." In cases of poor gas mileage the company maintained that the fault was not in the car or the carburetor, but due to a combination of other factors such as distributor or spark plug gaps that were not properly set, the car was timed late, brakes were dragging, the carburetor was not properly adjusted or the tires were not properly inflated.

Disturbed by reports of poor gas mileage, the company reiterated its claim that the Model A Ford's standard carburetors would give eighteen to twenty miles to the gallon at a speed of forty-five miles per hour and twenty-two to twenty-five miles at twenty-five miles per hour. In August 1930, each dealer received a letter about this matter and was asked to invest eight dollars in a testing outfit, so that he could test cars and show owners that the Model A would give the mileage as claimed or better. In making the tests he was to check consumption in both directions on the same road, checking at each twenty-five miles per hour and forty-five miles per hour.

The Payne Motor Co. of Washington, North Carolina, ran its test over a ten day period from November 17 to 27, 1930. Each owner who took the test paid one dollar for a seven point checkup prior to the test. He was promised return of the dollar if the car failed to get twenty-two miles per gallon. Ten dollars in gold was to be given to the Ford owner getting the most mileage per gallon during the contest. A Zenith Ford carburetor tester accurate to the fraction of a tenth of a mile was installed on each car, and a company representative accompanied the driver during the ten to fifteen minute test.

A total of one hundred-twelve Model A owners participated in the contest. The average miles per gallon

A 1930 Tudor at a local service station in Milwaukee, Wisconsin. Note the gas pumps, Kelly tires and Coke for sale.

registered by the cars was twenty-four plus. The highest, and consequently the winner of the ten dollars, was thirty miles per gallon achieved by a Tudor that had been driven 13,489 miles prior to the test. The winning car and driver were featured in an advertisement and local news story following the conclusion of the contest. Another outstanding performance was that of a contestant who registered twenty-four miles per gallon in a car with 48,947 miles on the odometer.

During 1930, as in the other Model A years, testimonials regarding operating costs and miles per gallon appeared from time to time in the pages of *Ford News*. One of these came from the Director of Safety in Louisville, Kentucky, who reported a total operating cost averaging 1.073 cents per mile for five Model A roadsters used by the Police Department in his city. The average mileage of each car was 174,276 miles and gas consumption was over twenty-one miles per gallon per car.

Another owner who did ninety percent of his driving in the city of Denver reported that the one year average for his Model A was 20.63 miles per gallon. "You will note," he wrote, "that my cost per mile for operating is well under three cents. The car has given me the most automobile satisfaction I have ever enjoyed and I have owned cars costing much more than the Ford."

The author's experience with Model A Fords for the past forty years, makes him doubtful that our seventy-plus year cars can consistently attain gas mileage averaging in the twenties as is reported from 1930. John Hargrave, writing in *The Restorer* as technical director of The Model A Ford Club of America in 1991, says that "There is a 'lot of rubber' in the gasoline mileage claims of many Model A owners!" In his opinion, at normal highway speeds, "the average Model A owner is doing well if he can average more than 17 or 18 mpg. . . ."

Hargrave reports on a test of a new Model A Tudor with a full passenger load of seven hundred-fifty pounds, run by Ford in 1930. The results were: "32 mpg at 15 mph, 29 mpg at 25 mph, 28 mpg at 30 mph, 22 mpg at 40 mph." In Hargrave's view, "for speeds in excess of 40 mph, Model A gasoline mileage of less than 20 mpg is to be expected."

In response to a suggestion published in *Ford News*, owners and dealers from all over the world wrote to Dearborn during 1930 to share their experiences and feelings about the Model A Ford. These are published here without comment, leaving it to the reader to draw his (or her) own conclusions about them.

From Chicago, Illinois, a new convert:

C.C. Millett wrote to say that he had never driven a Model A until a Ford salesman persuaded him to sit behind the wheel of a Coupe. "There are not enough superlatives in the English language to do this car justice," he declared after his experience. He placed an order with the dealer for a Convertible Cabriolet.

Proud owners Rolland Wyke and family pose with their new 1930 Tudor on December 7, 1930.

From Vandalia, Illinois:

"I want to tell you about Model A No. 1,071,388. It was bought in April 1929 and has been driven 33,000 miles. The spark plugs have never been out and the rings and valves have not been touched. The only expense I have had was one dollar for a broken generator support and seventy cents for a fan belt. This car will go from five miles an hour to seventy most any time. I had it tested for gas mileage. It went seven miles on one quart of gasoline. This may not be of interest to you, but I am well pleased." The letter is signed by Glen O. Walter.

From Iron Mountain, Michigan, Alfred Berrutti comments on a previous letter:

"I saw an article by Mrs. C.K. Palmer of Los Angeles, stating that her car has cost her forty cents for repairs with 14,000 miles of running. Well, I have that beaten. My car has cost me eighty-five cents and for half of that cost I was to blame. My car now registers 23,500 miles and is still performing very nicely. It is the same make of car—Standard Coupe 1929 model."

An "easy riding" story from England:

A Model A Ford owner set out to drive from Bristol to Malverne, England, a distance of sixty-one miles, and by mistake left a packet of cigarettes and box of matches on the running board. When he got out of the car after almost completing the journey, he was astonished to discover both cigarettes and matches still lying on the running board. "We had driven over rough roads," the driver commented, "and there was nothing to prevent the packets falling off—what wonderful springs this car must have!"

Tested by fire:

An unusual illustration of the quality of the Model A body was sent in from Mesquite, Texas, where the interior of a Standard Coupe caught on fire. The problem was not discovered until the next morning when the owner found that the upholstery had been consumed, but that the fire had then extinguished itself due to lack of oxygen. Apparently a cigarette had been left in the car the night before. After new door panels and seat cushions were obtained and the windows washed, no trace of the fire could be seen.

Letter to a Connecticut dealer:

Mrs. _____ had her car stolen a week ago and I believe you can sell her a Model A, as she has ridden in my car and likes it very much. The writer wants no commission, as he is merely trying to pay back to the Ford company a debt of gratitude for the splendid car you are making and the unexcelled service you are giving." The dealer reported two sales from this tip.

Endurance run by driver chained to the car:

A 100-hour endurance run was the main feature of a "Trade at Home Week" staged by the Sanford (North Carolina) Merchants' Association. Driver Roy Roberts was handcuffed to the steering column of a Model A DeLuxe Sedan selected from the stock of the Triangle Motor Co. He drove the car a total of 1,055 miles during the 100 hours stopping only, with engine running, to have gas added and to eat. I leave to your imagination as to how the other necessities of life were handled.

After sixty hours, Roberts issued a statement to the newspapers saying, "Tell the world that I am certainly well pleased with this Ford, and it is a pleasure to be able to have this smooth running car on this long drive. For power, speed and economical transportation, it can't be beat." Following the run, a mileage of 21.9 miles per gallon was registered and less than one quart of oil was needed to bring the level up to the "full" mark.

An Italian run proves reliability:

A team of twelve Model As took first prize for reliability in performance in a popular winter race held in February each year in Italy. To win the trophy the cars had to travel a distance of one hundred-nineteen kilometers at a speed as nearly uniform as possible, the minimum being fifty kilometers an hour. The course chosen included straight road, narrow winding highway with dangerous curves and mountain climbing with hairpin turns and steep gradients. A total of two hundred-twenty cars were entered in the test.

$50.00
REWARD

Will be paid for the recovery of our NEW FORD DEMONSTRATOR, the first NEW MODEL A Tudor Sedan ever entered Marshall, Saline County, Missouri. Color Anti-Lu-Site Blue, looks like new, runs like new, and has registered on the speedometer more than 48,000 actual miles and still good for that many more miles.

ANOTHER $25.00 REWARD will be given to the thief who stole this Car for his good judgement in selecting this car as his choice of more than 1,000 cars parked in Marshall that night, and also for the daring chance he took by stealing the car from in front of our Sales and Service office, the most conspicuous place in Marshall.

Motor Number of this NEW FORD TUDOR is 2823 and since it was manufactured more than 2½ million Model A Fords have been built and delivered. An automobile in the value of $1,000.00 but sells to the customer for $500.00 F O. B. Factory.

Reward for Ford Thief

A CLEVER newspaper advertisement, part of which is reproduced herewith, was used recently by the W. P. Thomas Motor Company, of Marshall, Mo. The advertisement occupied about a quarter-page of a local newspaper and besides the portion shown here presented many Ford quality features.

Clever newspaper advertisement for a Ford thief, *Ford Dealer & Service Field,* **January 1930.**

STOLEN

One Model A Ford Tudor Sedan, Engine No. A3249097.
Kansas License—No. 27-C-450.
Royal Master Cord Tires all around and on spare.
Color of car, Thorne Brown.
Wire Wheels.
Two suit cases in car.
Stolen at Kingman, Kansas, June 28, 1930.
Owner offers reward of $25 for car if not stripped, burned or wrecked, and $25 for conviction of thief.
OFFICERS: Search garages, repair shops, etc., in your city, and be on the lookout for strangers who want to sell a car; notify all reliable garages in your city.
Send or Wire all Information to M. F. FISHER, Sheriff, Kingman, Kansas.

Ad for a stolen Ford from Kingman, Kansas.

King likes Model A

In an interview in *Cosmopolitan* magazine, June 1930, King Alfonso XIII, Monarch of Spain said that he liked his Model A Ford. ". . .best of all I like to drive my little two-seater Ford. It's so easy to jump in and go off hunting or rambling anywhere in the country."

"It was a Ford" from Australia:

As reported in *Ford Dealer & Service Field*, a Model A Ford, traveling at an excessive speed failed to negotiate a difficult turn. The car ran off the road, missed a deep culvert by nine inches and crashed into a four-foot bank. The stump it dislodged was thrown ten feet away.

The impact diverted the car's course across the road again, causing it to leap over a six-foot embankment and land on its wheels. The total distance between the take-off and the landing place was thirty-six feet. It fell with such force that it turned a double somersault sideways, again landing on its wheels. The car was then driven up the hill again and to a nearby town. Here it was examined in a local garage and found to be mechanically perfect. Chassis, springs and engine were intact, only the body was damaged. Fortunately, no one was injured.

Where the FORD Gets Its SNAPPY PICKUP!

The Ford Gets Away Like a Trained Sprinter

H·M·F

REASONS FOR RAPID ACCELERATION OF FORD		
	FORD	**CHEVROLET**
Car weight _____	2,375 pounds	2,500 pounds
Piston displacement per 100 lb._____	8.35 cu. in.	7.76 cu. in.
Piston weight _____	Aluminum	Cast iron
Less piston motion _____	7,500 feet per mile	10,920 feet per mile
Lighter wheels _____	One-piece wheels	Wire wheels
Rear axle design _____	¾-floating axle	Semi-floating axle
Transmission and drive bearings___	4 roller bearings	4 plain bearings
Engine design _____	High-torque engine	Higher-speed engine
AND MANY OTHERS.		

"Where the Ford Gets Its Snappy Pickup," *Ford Dealer & Service Field*, December 1930.

Proof

that the

FORD Car

Has

Less

Depreciation

CHEVROLET
and
FORD OWNERS

Trade in Your 1928-29-30 Cars
and Get a *Brand New* HUDSON
or ESSEX at Present Low Prices

NO FURTHER DOWN PAYMENT!

Why drive the old car through the winter? Why put more money into it—when we will accept it as Down Payment on a *brand new* Hudson or Essex, if it is in salable condition? Get a NEW and *better* car during our big TWO WEEKS' SALE! Hudson-Essex is famous for brilliant, dependable performance!

Best allowances of the year! If you are in the market for any car priced from $500 to $1500—COME IN—no matter what m' you now are driving. You actually put n' in your pocket! GET OUR PROPOS' Learn how extremely liberal o'' on the unpaid balance!

FORDS

	1930	1929	1928
Coupe	$510	$385	$300
Tudor	510	375	300
4-Door Sedan	520	400	310

— for cars in salable condition.
NO FURTHER DOWN PAYMENT!

CHEVROLETS

	1930	1929	1928
Coupe	$515	$400	$285
Coach	510	385	265
4-Door Sedan	525	410	285

— for cars in salable condition.
NO FURTHER DOWN PAYMENT!

Get Our Special Proposition on YO''''
Equally Liberal Allowances on A'

ESSEX "6" CHALLENGER MODELS,
HUDSON GREAT EIGHT, '8''

PIERPOINT MC

5001 BAUM BOULEVARD   Distributors of Hudson-E   Phon-

Reproduction of Newspaper Ad Used by Dealer

THERE ARE MANY good and sufficient reasons why the Ford should depreciate less than cars of other makes, including excellent design, high quality of material and workmanship, large number of ball and roller bearings, etc., etc. But these are sometimes a little difficult to put on an actual dollars-and-cents basis.

However, the distributors for one of the largest automobile makers have expressed the difference so neatly (in newspaper advertising appearing in some of the larger cities) that the comparison is of keen interest to Ford dealers and makes a fine sales argument for Ford salesmen.

Let's compare 1930 prices. A *used* Ford coupe is valued at $5 less than a Chevrolet—but wait! A new Chevrolet sold for $70 more, which means that it suffered $65 more depreciation in less than a year! If bought in May, the depreciation on the Chevrolet was $2 a week *more* than on the Ford.

Notice that the used valuation of the Ford Tudor is exactly the same as that of the Chevrolet coach, though the first cost of the Chevrolet is $70 more. May we not ascribe part of this $70 difference to the excellent quality of the Ford all-steel body?

The allowance for used 1930 Fordor sedan is $5 less, but then the first cost of the Fordor sedan was $75 less, which means the Fordor sedan suffered $70 less depreciation than the Chevrolet.

Briefly, the depreciation on a 1930 Ford is $68 less than on a car of the second most popular make.

The 1929 Ford did not have rustless-steel trimmings, the smaller wheels, etc. But even so, the depreciation on a 1929 Ford is $68 less than the depreciation on the second most popular make.

Most of the 1928 Ford coupes sold were business coupes and so we have listed the Ford coupe at $495, the same price as the Tudor. Durability begins to show up within the third year, and the 1928 Ford shows $108 less depreciation than another make.

	CHEVROLET		FORD		Less Depreciation
	New	Used	New	Used	of Ford
1930					
Coupe	$565	$515	$495	$510	$65
Tudor or Coach	565	510	495	510	70
Four-door Sedan	675	525	600	520	70

1930 Ford has $68 *less* depreciation

	New	Used	New	Used	of Ford
1929					
Coupe	$595	$400	$500	$385	$80
Tudor or Coach	595	385	500	375	85
Four-door Sedan	675	410	625	400	40

1929 Ford has $68 *less* depreciation

	New	Used	New	Used	of Ford
1928					
Coupe	$595	$285	$495	$300	$115
Tudor or Coach	595	265	495	300	135
Four-door Sedan	675	285	625	310	75

1928 Ford has $108 *less* depreciation

Proof that the Ford car has less depreciation, *Ford Dealer & Service Field*, **December 1930.**

Contest between Ford truck and Chevrolet truck:

A crowd of four hundred to five hundred persons showed up to witness a contest between a Ford and a Chevrolet, arranged to settle a dispute between the two owners as to which could pull the heaviest load up a hill. J.V. Flynn put 6,875 pounds of fertilizer in his new Ford Model AA with four men, making a total weight of 7,520 pounds. He pulled the hill without any problem at all. The fertilizer was then loaded in a Chevrolet truck owned by Mr. Arnsparger. His truck did not even get to the steepest part of the hill before it quit, making the Ford an easy winner.

Service during storm:

The following letter from the Yellow Cab Co. of Richmond, Virginia, testifies to that company's satisfaction with its Model A Ford Tudor Sedans:

"I feel that in justice to you and the Ford Motor Company I should give you the experience which we had this morning during one of the hardest rainstorms that I can ever remember in the city of Richmond.

"During the rain of several hours duration, cabs of every make operated by us were drowned out on the streets, which caused considerable delay in our service. At one time we had as many as eighteen cabs standing still with motors drowned out. But during all of this time, the ten Ford sedans recently purchased from you were all operating without any trouble whatsoever. While I have been very well pleased with the operation of our Ford cars, I am indeed more so since the experience of this morning." The letter was signed by the Richmond Yellow Cab Co. manager.

Stories of satisfied Model A owners are not limited to period publications such as *Ford News* and *Ford Dealer & Service Field*. Following are two more, the first with thanks to *Parade* magazine and the second to *Reminisce* magazine.

Seeing America backward

In 1930, two enterprising St. Louis youths successfully drove in reverse from New York City to Los Angeles and back again. With the car's gears locked in reverse and the headlights attached to the rear of the roadster the pair drove nearly nonstop, at speeds of eight to eleven miles per hour. Their only problem occurred when leaving New York and a taxicab ran into the Model A, bashing its fender and damaging the running board. Needless to say, the young men were quite proud of their car and their accomplishment.

An Open Road Adventure for Two Girls

In the summer of 1930, two young women, ages eighteen and twenty-four, roamed west from Pennsylvania to California and back in a new, trouble-free, 1930 Model A Tudor Sedan. The girls slept in the car, carried their provisions in food boxes bolted to the running board and loaded down the car with a gas stove, folding table, burlap bag filled with canned goods and draw curtains for the windows. They had bad luck only on one day. First, a car drove out from a side street and smashed into the front door, shattering the glass and destroying a food box. Undaunted they found someone who repaired the door and built a new food box for thirty dollars. On the same day, the bag filled with canned goods, which was tied to the rear bumper wore through and they left a trail of broken cans strewn along the road.

Proof of Ford ability

A new world's nonstop automobile endurance record was established by a Model A Panel truck on November 24, 1930. On that day, Ralph and Rolland Davis, brothers, completed a 2,775 hour and 46 minute continuous driving run in Des Moines, Iowa. The car was equipped with a special dolly for changing wheels while moving, in case of punctures, and had an extra emergency brake, so that the rear wheel could be stopped to permit changing of the wheel.

The Ford traveled a total of 47,138 miles between August 1 and November 24. In addition to eleven tire changes due to punctures, the only repairs made during the entire run were a replacement of spark plugs when the car passed 30,000 miles, and the replacement of generator brushes and a nut on the petcock drain of the crankcase.

Buehrig's Model A

In 1930, at the age of twenty-six, well-known automotive designer Gordon Buehrig was the chief body designer for the Duesenberg Co. in Indianapolis, Indiana. Unable to afford a Duesenberg he decided to custom build a distinctive Model A Ford. "The Model A Ford," Buehrig writes, "was probably the highest quality small car ever built, and I could see in it the possibility of altering its proportions and making a blind quarter convertible Victoria, which would be distinctive and beautiful."

Buehrig bought a 1930 Model A Cabriolet on September 27, 1930, and brought it to the Duesenberg plant where it was reworked and completed on December 21. "There is nothing I have ever owned that gave me as much pleasure, as much satisfaction or greater pride than this beautiful little car," Buehrig wrote. "Its quality in every respect was equal to a Duesenberg and that was pretty good!"

In 1972, Buehrig wrote an article for *Model "A" News* in which he described the conversion. He wrote that he drove the car about 90,000 miles until he sold it in 1934. After that he lost track of it and, in 1972, believed that it had been destroyed.

Copy of the original drawing of the Buehrig Model A. (Photo courtesy of *Model "A" News*, November-December 1972)

Testimonials to the Model A Ford not withstanding, the 1930 version was not trouble free. On the other hand, the problems that surfaced were mostly of the nagging kind, which did not keep people from buying Fords. Following is a sampling of these problems and the solutions for some of them suggested by Ford.

A common criticism had to do with carburetors and usually occurred in cars driven less than five hundred miles. A service letter sent to the Branches and forwarded to dealers, contained the following comment on the problem. "Recently complaints have been received of difficulty experienced in adjusting carburetors on new cars for idling speeds, excessive gas consumption and motors stalling when stopping cars at street intersections. In most cases, this happens on cars driven five hundred miles or less.

"As motors now being built have highly polished crankshaft main bearings, this is sufficient mileage to limber them up. In fact, so little wear takes place with these polished bearings, it sometimes requires considerably more driving before the motor is well broken in." The solution was to be patient, the company said, and once the engine reached the point where the bearings produced the least amount of friction, then make sure to adjust the carburetor carefully, time the engine accurately and set the spark plug gaps and distributor points properly.

In May, the company's Instruction and Assembly Change Letter #71, noted that two or three Branches had reported trouble with Thorn brown pyroxylin not adhering to the surface of the body. The reason was that the surface coat had not been properly baked, due either to the wrong temperature of the oven or the length of time in the oven was not to specification. The company also

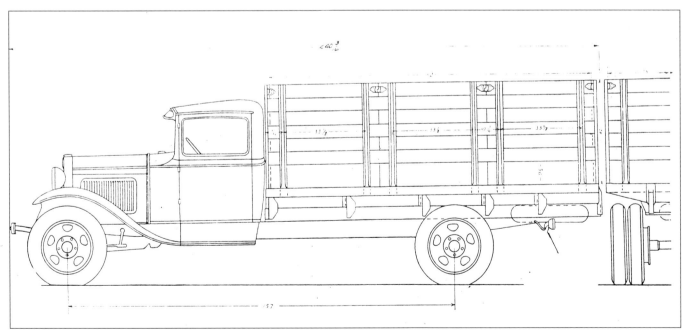

Stake body on 157 inch wheelbase chassis. (Photo courtesy of Ford Archives)

The Ford is a good-looking truck

Ford 1½-ton truck with panel body

THE Ford truck, with new bodies of greater beauty, is designed to be a fitting representative of your business in any community. The new radiator and hood are higher and narrower, in more pleasing proportion to the overall height of the body and cab. Front fenders meet the running-boards in a more sweeping and graceful line.

The radiator, hood, cowl and cab are unified in appearance, joining in a line which seemingly lengthens the truck, increasing the impression of fleetness. A smart-looking visor of military shape adds further to this impression.

Greater comfort for the driver is provided by roomier cabs, with wider seats. The windshields, of Triplex shatter-proof glass, operate by swinging out from the bottom. Both open and enclosed cabs are offered with the stake and platform bodies.

Valuable as these body improvements are, they are second in importance to the excellent performance, long life, and rugged strength which the Ford truck offers at low cost. Features of the chassis which contribute to these are the 4-speed transmission; the new three-quarter floating rear axle; the option of two different gear-ratios; the larger brakes; and the dual rear wheels available at small additional cost.

Panel, stake and platform bodies are standard. They are sturdy and rugged, designed to give ample loading-space. With the important new chassis features, they adapt the Ford truck for a wide variety of purposes.

More handsome appearance

Greater comfort for the driver

All-round sturdiness

Ample loading-space

Ford

Ad for 1-1/2 ton Model AA truck with panel body, *Saturday Evening Post*, July 19, 1930.

found that the proper clean up had not been given to bodies before the prime coat was sprayed on.

There were other complaints, such as defective rear roof rail assemblies in Murray bodies, a rattle caused by the speedometer and ignition cable, noisy truck rear axles, the front stake rack bolt rubbing against the cab on the AA-157, and complaints about blemishes on the upholstery, which sometimes appeared on panels that were tacked on with small brads.

This last complaint is interesting for the way in which the company handled the problem. Ford told dealers to explain to their customers that what appeared to be moth eaten, was really "a slight mark" left by the tool used to pull the cloth over the head of a brad that held the cloth to the panel, or by the brad piercing the cloth. Nothing was said about repairs. Apparently the matter was considered too minor to do more than explain what happened to the customer.

At the beginning of 1930, four standard Ford AA truck bodies, equipped with either the open cab or all-steel enclosed cab were available. The bodies were the Express, Panel and the Platform which could be converted into a Stake body. These trucks were equipped with several new features that had been incorporated into the Model AA 1-1/2-ton truck to improve its performance. Among them were: a new front axle, heavier front springs and radius rods, greater braking power due to enlarged front brake drums, new rear axle and a new four-speed transmission.

Murray Fahnestock was impressed by the total braking surface of 474-7/8 square inches. "Cut that out, and paste it in your hat," he wrote in *Ford Dealer & Service Field*, "for this is a very unusual amount of braking surface for a 1-1/2 ton truck, or indeed any truck selling at twice-the-price of the Ford Model AA."

Typically, other changes and additions were made as the year moved on. In March, the company announced that a high-speed rear axle with a ratio of 5.14 to 1 would shortly be in production. This would permit higher road speeds than currently available with the standard 6.6 to 1 gear ratio. In May, dealers were informed that a 157 inch wheelbase truck chassis had

HEAVY HYDRAULIC DUMP BODY

Length of body, 84"; width, 60"; depth, 14½"

Dumping Angle 45°

Heavy Hydraulic Hoist

The body is made of one-piece of 10-gage blue annealed steel. It has no center or bottom seams. There is nothing to prevent free flow of material. Provision is made for 6" side-boards. Channel-iron is used throughout to assure long, heavy-duty service.

The end-gate is double-acting and is operated by a control-lever near the cab. The lever is positive-operating, permitting the end-gate to be tightly and securely locked.

The heavy hydraulic hoist has an ample margin over its operating capacity of 1½ tons. It will lift body and load with motor idling.

The hoist locks instantaneously in any position, regardless of load, when the clutch is released, or if the motor accidentally stalls. This prevents the body from falling back to deliver a jolt to the chassis.

Because of the fact that more power is required for lift at certain points than at others, equalizing links are used. These links act as a governor and so maintain uniform oil pressure at the pump, prolonging the life of the mechanism.

From Ford original booklet "Five Dump Bodies" for 1-1/2 ton truck chassis.

been added to the line of commercial units. The price was set at five hundred-forty-five dollars f.o.b. Detroit. Henceforth, the 131-1/2 inch chassis would be known as the AA-131 and the 157 inch chassis as the AA-157. The capacity of 1-1/2 tons applied to both the 131-1/2 inch and 157 inch chassis.

The company believed that the AA-157 would have a ready market and make it unnecessary to convert the present 131-1/2 inch wheelbase chassis by adding extensions to take care of furniture dealers, department stores, moving vans, warehouse bodies, school buses, motor coaches, etc.

In June, the company announced changes in the truck front end, and in the cab. The lines of the truck front would now resemble the improved Model A's, which were introduced the previous December. "The radiator is higher, the fenders are wide and flowing, and a black cowl strip has been added," stated the letter to dealers. "The new enclosed cab is all-steel, low in appearance, and has ample headroom."

A sampling of other changes included the availability of a polished finish on panel bodies at an additional cost of twenty dollars for the A Panel and twenty-five dollars for the AA Panel. Customers now had a choice of colors along with the polished finish. Previously, panel bodies were available only in "satin finish." In August, a Stake body for the AA-157 and improvements in the size of the DeLuxe Delivery car were announced.

Another important development in the truck line during 1930 was the beginning of a policy to create a line of bodies comprehensive enough to fulfill almost any business need. The first announced were five types of dump bodies, each of 1-1/2 yards capacity, added to the Model AA-131 truck line. These included a gravity dump body, hand dump body, mechanical dump body, regular hydraulic dump body and a heavy-duty hydraulic dump body. Prices ranged from one hundred-fifteen to two hundred-twenty-five dollars.

In November, a 1-1/2 yard light- and heavy-duty hydraulic dump body and hoist manufactured by the

Model No. 93-F for Ford AA-157" Truck

The New Open Express Body for general utility purposes--a regular "He Man" body, designed for heavy work--day in and day out. It's good looking too, and lacquered to match cab. -- The body is 10½ ft. long, 72 in. wide, and 15 in. high on the panels. Same body can be furnished with top if desired.

From "Genuine Geneva Bodies" folder.

Wood Body Co. became available. In December, dealers were informed that four coal bodies and a garbage body were being added to the line of commercial bodies for the AA-131 chassis. The most expensive of these, the High Lift Coal Body, listed at five hundred-seventy-five dollars f.o.b. Detroit.

Outside body builders also continued to provide units for the Ford truck chassis. The Martin-Parry Corp., for example, released a price list in July 1930 listing thirty-six bodies available for the truck chassis. The most expensive of these was the 530-B Panel body, which had a retail price of $356.51 including fenders, mounting or crating and freight from the factory. Martin-Parry also sold equipment such as parcel racks, screen sides, drop end gates, sliding door partition, and extra seats.

With demand heavy on its truck production facilities, Ford called back into service as Model AA assembly plants, three former Branch buildings located in Philadelphia, Pennsylvania; Long Island, New York; and Cambridge, Massachusetts. Each plant would serve dealers in the area in which they were located. Each of these plants was also the location of a permanent truck exhibit that, along with a National Truck Week, a National Salesmen's Contest and Ford Road Shows,

were part of the company's strategy in merchandising its commercial lines.

Permanent truck exhibits were of assistance to dealers in fitting the product to the needs of the prospect. The exhibit at the Philadelphia plant, for instance, had fifty-three different units on display, including equipment for twenty-four different lines of business. In an area of nearly 30,000 square feet, the Branch displayed the complete Ford commercial lines, both Model A and AA. All of the body types of special equipment were mounted on the Ford chassis. Among those displayed were fire apparatus; dump bodies of all types; hand, gravity and power lift; semi-trailer attachments; special house-to-house delivery bodies; street sweeper attachments; school bus and motor coach bodies; as well as equipment for every municipal use and many types fitted to special agricultural needs.

On August 4, 1930, a permanent exhibit of Ford commercial cars and trucks, special equipment and bodies designed for use in conjunction with Ford trucks opened in a building at Highland Park, formerly used as a power house. Included was a display of the merchandise of twenty-four body and equipment manufacturers who specialized in equipment for use with the Ford 1-1/2 ton

A Chart of Comparative Truck Specifications for Dealers

As additional sales help to accompany the detailed facts in this article we offer this chart of comparative specifications of trucks which may be considered in competitive range with the Model AA Ford. The chart should provide a ready answer to many questions met by the dealer or the salesman.

Capacity	Chassis Price	Chassis Weight	Wheelbase	Fuel	Number Cylinders	Bore and Stroke	Taxable Horsepower (Piston Displacement)	Brake Horsepower and Revolutions	Make and Model	Compression Ratio	Piston Make	Type of Rear Axle	Gear Ratio	Reduction in Low	Bearings Countershaft	Tires, Front and Rear	Engine Revolutions per Mile
1½	$ 520.00	2282	131½	Grav.	4	3⅞x4¼	24. 200.5	40 2,200	Ford AA	4.22	Aluminum	¾ float	6.6	42.24	Roller	32x6	4171
1½	$ 520.00	2375	131	Pump	6	3⁵⁄₁₆x3¾	26.3 194.	50 2,600	Chevrolet Utility	5.02	Iron	Semi.	5.43	33.2	Plain	30x5	3649
1½	$1345.00	3695	150	Vac.	6	3⅜x3⅞	27.3 207.9	58 3,000	Dodge	5.18	Aluminum	Semi.	5.67	36.8	Roller	32x6	3583
1½	$ 895.00	3075	127¾	Pump	6	3⁵⁄₁₆x3⅞	26.3 200.	58 3,000	G. M. C. T-19	4.9	Semi-steel	Semi.	6.20	34.4		32x6 34x7	3608
1½	$1450.00	3520	140	Vac.	4	3¾x5	22.5 220.9	43 2,500	International 6-Speed			Semi.	5.29	22.6 3-speed		30x5 32x6	3343
1	$ 795.00	2785	133	Vac.	6	3 x4⅛	21.6	55 3,000	Fargo 1-ton Freighter	5.	Aluminum	Semi.	5.66	37.19	Plain	32x6	3477
1½	$1295.00	3525	137	Vac.	6	3⅜x5	27.3 268.3	67 2,800	Reo Speedwagon FA	5.3	Aluminum	Semi.	5.2	22.96	Roller	32x6	3286
1½	$ 645.00	2540	131	Vac.	6	3⅛x3⅞	23.4 178.3	40 3,200	Whippet C-101	5.12	Iron	Semi.	6.38	33.5		30x5	4287
1¼	$2725.00	3755	146	Vac.	4	4 x5¾	25.6	45 1,600	White "57"			Aluminum	Semi.	4.67	19.3		32x6	2951

Comparative truck specifications for dealers, *Ford Dealer & Service Field,* **May 1930.**

truck. More than one hundred body types were displayed. *The Ford Dealer News* characterized it as the largest showroom in the world.

Sixty Ford dealers in the Detroit vicinity participated in the show, with each required to furnish a man for the show on certain days. Organized in two shifts daily, this meant that ten Ford dealers' salesmen were on the floor during a shift. Each manufacturer of special equipment exhibiting its merchandise in this display was required to furnish a representative at all times, who would be available to provide Ford truck salesmen with the necessary knowledge to enable them to sell Ford trucks properly equipped to suit the customers' needs.

The first Ford National Truck Week to be held by Ford dealers since the introduction of the Model AA, was held from June 9 to June 16, 1930. During the week, Branches and dealers across the country went all-out to emphasize the unusual values in Ford commercial car and truck types. A set of five special posters advertised the week in every community. Parades were organized. Special displays of the transmission, front and rear axle assemblies of the AA chassis, and demonstrations of the new Ford truck features were arranged in showrooms as well as on the street.

Parades were a popular activity during the week. In Memphis, Tennessee, for example, seventy-eight Model AA trucks and seventeen Model A commercial units paraded for three miles through the main business section of the town. Thirty-six trucks representing different business houses of the city, were led by a band along the main street of Harrisburg, Virginia. In Louisville, Kentucky, a lengthy parade of over forty Ford units were led by two police vehicles, a motorcycle with sidecar and a 1930 Model A Roadster. Many of these parades featured a Model AA chassis with a large sign advertising the new features of the Ford truck as "a value far above the price."

Commenting on the week, *Ford Dealer & Service Field* stated that dealers won the attention of thousands by their displays, demonstrations and parades, and, more than that, "they registered many sales." This truck week, the magazine said, "went far to focus the attention of the public on the fact that business is good in the Ford field."

On November 21, 1930, Ford salesmen in approximately 10,000 dealerships across the country received a catalog explaining a National Sales contest that would begin that day and terminate on January 31, 1931. The purpose of the contest, of course, was to stimulate flagging sales in both the Model A and AA lines.

The catalog listed prizes that could be selected according to the number of points won. Furniture and other articles for the home, apparel, musical instruments, sterling silverware, a fur coat and many other prizes

A 1930 Ford canopy-top Express. (Photo courtesy of John A. Conde)

were offered. In addition to the prizes, the winning car and truck salesman in each Branch and the national winners would receive trophies from the Ford Motor Co.

Contest rules were simple: For each new car sold two hundred-eighty points would be credited to the account of the person making the sale; for each new truck, three hundred-thirty-five points; and for each used car, two hundred-twenty-five points. Points could be applied to prizes at the contest's end and, therefore, everyone enrolled was likely to win at least something. The cost of the contest, was borne jointly by the company and the dealers with Ford contributing fifty cents for each new car or truck sold.

Dealers had the option of expanding those eligible to participate to other people in their organizations. For example, if a mechanic was enrolled, and turned over a new car prospect, he would receive two hundred-eighty points if the sale was made within five days. The salesman selling the car would also receive two hundred-eighty points. Ford, however, still contributed only fifty cents per car while the dealer's expenses were double, as points for two prizes were awarded covering only one sale.

Ford kept the pressure on during the contest, turning it into a horse race for the top prizes. Telegrams, letters and lists of leading salesmen were sent periodically to the Branches and through them to dealers. It was a race in which both the consistent leaders faded at the end. The winner in the car division was Earl Murphy, employed by George Holzbaugh Co., Detroit, who delivered one hundred-eighty-six cars or an average of three sales per working day.

The National Truck Salesman's contest was won by P.T. Manning of McComb Motors, Des Moines, with eighty-four deliveries. In addition to their trophies, the successful national winners were given trips to the Ford headquarters at Dearborn. Trophies to the winners in each Branch were given out in the Branch city at a special presentation held during a meeting of salesmen.

A fourth marketing strategy used by Ford to sell trucks as well as cars, was the traveling road show (sometimes called Tent Show). The first of these was held in April 1930 in Albany, Georgia, from which it began a tour of the Atlanta Branch territory. Due to the widespread interest in and success of this show wherever it went, a second was added in June. Eventually there were six of them showing in various areas of the country.

Essentially, the traveling shows were groups of five or six Ford trucks that would travel to a small community, set up a tent, and, with the help of local dealers, arrange a display of the entire line of Ford passenger cars, as

Five Model As headed to an auto show on a Nuway car carrier, May 7, 1930. Four of the cars are apparently 1929 models. The covered car is a 1930 Ford, but with 1929 wheels and bumper. (Photo courtesy of Henry Ford Museum and Greenfield Village)

well as a representative sampling of truck body types and light commercial units. Visitors were invited to look over the exhibit of Ford products featuring a cutaway Tudor Sedan and Ford parts, as well as the cars and trucks, and view an innovative (for its time) sound motion picture. By the end of December 1930, more than one-and-one-half million persons visited the shows in different parts of the country. A total of three hundred-

A 1930 Police Patrol.

forty-eight shows were given by the six "circuses" in the field during 1930.

By late August, the list price for the Model AA chassis f.o.b. Detroit was five hundred-ten dollars for the AA-131 and five hundred-thirty-five dollars for the AA-157. Dual wheels cost an extra twenty-five dollars. The chassis included cowl tank assembly, instrument panel, instruments, front fenders, running boards and running board shields (long or short optional), but not rear fenders.

These prices included standard equipment as follows: starter, ammeter, speedometer, gasoline gauge, six-brake system, five disc wheels, dash light, rear and stop light, mirror (truck with cab or panel body), ignition lock, complete tool set, two 20 x 6.00 balloon tires in front, two 32 x 6.00 tires in the rear and a hand windshield wiper in a truck with a cab or panel body.

Bodies for trucks were additional. The AA-131 mechanical dump body, for instance, listed at one hundred-ninety dollars. Other prices were fifty-five dollars for the Express body and sixty-five dollars for a Stake body. The Panel Delivery with single wheels, however, was listed at seven hundred-eighty dollars complete.

On November 26, 1930, Branches were notified that fifteen commercial bodies would shortly go into production. Prices, some definite and some tentative, and pro-

A 1930 Model A Coupe.

Sales (State)	1929			1930 (6 Mos.)		
	Ford	Chevrolet	Essex	Ford	Chevrolet	Essex
Alabama	25,190	14,639	1,241	7,600	5,080	206
Arizona	5,560	4,046	553	2,200	1,495	75
Arkansas	16,775	8,528	616	5,500	3,352	126
California	83,290	39,128	11,208	45,150	20,707	2,306
Colorado	14,480	6,937	1,905	7,049	4,615	406
Connecticut	12,541	8,430	3,577	8,031	4,682	1,096
Delaware	3,200	1,736	424	1,994	1,052	107
District of Columbia	8,029	3,831	1,278	4,985	2,385	328
Florida	15,950	9,334	1,362	9,186	5,114	432
Georgia	19,370	10,442	703	8,445	4,872	148
Idaho	6,152	3,690	485	2,725	1,957	116
Illinois	70,153	39,802	11,861	42,962	23,767	2,724
Indiana	40,172	25,062	7,619	20,554	11,468	1,688
Iowa	41,045	27,710	4,168	19,715	15,496	899
Kansas	28,072	16,620	2,996	10,776	7,448	596
Kentucky	19,840	13,201	2,851	10,420	6,693	665
Louisiana	19,280	11,020	886	7,063	4,492	198
Maine	6,660	4,105	2,122	3,725	2,275	728
Maryland	15,250	11,001	2,556	8,898	6,643	677
Massachusetts	37,230	20,234	10,696	27,625	11,387	3,492
Michigan	91,830	47,620	20,169	49,630	19,192	3,066
Minnesota	35,788	17,190	3,395	20,112	11,732	856
Mississippi	18,698	11,064	392	7,038	4,776	83
Missouri	39,640	26,530	5,004	24,462	17,735	1,508
Montana	6,599	4,716	928	2,725	1,972	183

Sales (State)	1929			1930 (6 Mos.)		
	Ford	Chevrolet	Essex	Ford	Chevrolet	Essex
Nebraska	26,020	15,540	1,324	10,993	7,992	346
Nevada	1,293	788	208	550	314	76
New Hampshire	3,773	2,576	851	2,521	1,548	255
New Mexico	4,162	3,312	208	1,717	1,152	43
New York	76,030	53,750	18,502	56,195	29,165	5,291
North Carolina	29,163	14,802	2,312	9,165	4,783	397
North Dakota	9,895	5,282	604	3,789	2,706	135
Ohio	83,196	50,940	17,556	42,739	22,332	3,155
Oklahoma	37,930	23,117	1,740	14,123	10,681	276
Oregon	12,872	6,980	1,322	5,845	3,281	317
Pennsylvania	76,782	45,015	16,895	46,654	24,634	3,825
Rhode Island	4,792	3,539	1,275	3,219	1,984	304
South Carolina	15,276	8,761	720	5,290	3,439	172
South Dakota	10,998	7,053	866	4,749	3,445	214
Tennessee	23,020	14,455	1,812	10,776	6,803	414
Texas	84,294	56,111	3,815	32,363	22,538	665
Utah	6,132	3,571	882	2,965	1,662	217
Vermont	2,820	1,970	935	1,938	1,108	278
Virginia	24,546	15,004	2,386	12,535	8,066	616
Washington	18,804	9,046	2,483	9,599	4,503	628
West Virginia	12,714	9,117	2,056	6,833	4,733	535
Wisconsin	31,944	20,084	6,064	18,407	12,356	1,332
Wyoming	2,834	1,752	413	1,198	778	84

(All Figures closely approximate)

Sales by states, *The Ford Dealer News*, August 15, 1930.

duction dates to help in promising delivery were included. A few examples are: Ambulance body with side door priced at $1,800 with the AA-131 chassis (production date - February 14, 1931); Funeral Coach at $1,750 (production date - February 14, 1931); Drop Floor Panel on the Model A chassis at $590 (production date - November 25, 1930).

The 1930 Model A Ford was born into a world troubled by a steadily weakening economy as the Great Depression tightened its grip on the nation and the world. Because of the popularity of Model A, Ford was able to stave off its moment of reckoning during much of the year only to have the other shoe drop with a vengeance in 1931.

Publicly, the Ford Motor Co. was upbeat in its end-of-the-year survey of company accomplishments, which included the following:

* On June 16, Ford celebrated the completion of the twenty-seventh year in its history and, seeking to boost the confidence of its employees and dealers, centered its publicity of this event on the accomplishments of the first six months of the year rather than recapping the past.

* More than $60,000,000 was expended or reserved for expansion and development.

* Two large, modern assembly plants were completed at Edgewater, New Jersey, and Long Beach, California.

* New foreign plants were opened at Istanbul, Turkey; Perth, Australia; and Port Elizabeth, South Africa.

* Construction on the largest automobile plant in the world—outside the United States—at Dagenham near London, England, moved forward rapidly. This plant would have a capacity production of about 200,000 units a year and employ 15,000 men.

* Eight new plants were announced during the year. These would be located at Richmond, California; Seattle, Washington; Buffalo, New York; Mexico City, Mexico; Cologne, Germany; Antwerp, Belgium; Rotterdam, Holland; and Stockholm, Sweden.

* By the end of 1930, more than 4,000,000 Model A cars and AA trucks had left the Ford assembly lines. The three-millionth engine was assembled during March and the fourth was passed in October.

* A new high mark in daily production for the Model A was set during April when 9,565 cars and trucks were built in one day. April also achieved the highest monthly total with 206,340 cars and trucks assembled.

* Major improvements at the Rouge plant included increasing the power supply by remodeling the main power house and building a water-intake tunnel two miles long between the plant and the Detroit River. When operated at capacity, this tunnel was capable of pumping one billion gallons of water per day into the power house.

* In February 1930, experiments to salvage old or useless motor vehicles began at the Rouge. By November, more than 30,000 had been salvaged and the dismantling line was averaging six hundred cars and trucks a day. The derelicts were bought from Ford dealers at a fixed price of twenty dollars per car. There were no restrictions on make, age or condition except that all cars had to have tires and a battery. On the salvage line everything was reclaimed. Spark plugs, batteries, headlight lenses, horns, lamp bulbs, wheels, tires and hubcaps were removed. Artificial leather was made into aprons, upholstery into hand pads, floor boards became crate tops, glass was used for window panes, and metal was utilized in the making of steel.

Edwin Norwood describes the scrapping process in detail in his book, *Ford Men and Methods*. Here is his eloquent description of a car's final moments as it reaches the crusher at the end of the conveyor line. "There is no escape for this victim. Slowly and with deadly intent, the weighted ceiling—twenty-two tons of it—moves downward. There is a crack like a pistol shot; then another. A crunching of wood, a whining of resisting steel greets the ear; a last sigh as little breaths of air are sent outward under the tremendous pressure. Then the ceiling, once more operated by the turn of a lever, recedes, leaving the distorted mass still writhing in its wake."

With $58,000,000 in new orders after the first few days showing of the revised 1930 models, Ford seemed headed for a record year. New Ford registrations peaked at 402,364 for the second quarter and Ford sales for the first six months of the year totaled approximately 700,000 cars as compared with approximately 400,000 for the nearest competitor. Compared with the first six months of 1929, Ford sales figures indicated an increase in business of slightly more than 1,000 cars, but then, as the economy weakened, fell off considerably during the second half of the year.

By year's end, Ford assembly records show a total worldwide production of 1,485,602 units, down 465,490 from 1929. At the same time, production was about 300,000 units higher than the entire General Motors line and the Ford Motor Co.'s market share increased from thirty-five to forty-two percent.

Despite the fact that the high hopes of January were not realized, 1930 still was not a bad year for Ford. Worldwide, car and truck output was down more than two million from 1929, but Ford still led the industry in car and truck production for the second year in-a-row. Ford's per car profit for the year was $29.70. The total profit was $39,996,121 (*Federal Trade Commission Report*, 1939). Ford managed to stay out of the red ink for the second straight Model A year.

FORD'S INDICATED EARNINGS AND PRODUCTION 1923-1930

These earnings figures are compiled from the profit and loss surplus statement submitted by the Ford Motor Co. each year to the Massachusetts Commissioners of Corporations. They do not include dividends, if any, withdrawn by owners.

Year	Invested Capital	Net Income	Per Cent Return on Investment	Production—Cars & Trucks	Profit Per Vehicle
1923	......	$82,263,483	....	2,090,959	$39
1924	......	100,435,416	....	1,993,419	50
1925	......	79,890,396	....	1,990,995	40
1926	$733,910,000	75,270,895	10.3	1,810,029	42
1927	685,860,000	—42,786,727	...†	454,601	..
1928	605,010,800	—72,221,498	....	854,818	..
1929	688,020,000	81,797,861	11.9	1,951,092	42
1930	736,650,000	44,460,823	6.0	1,530,000	29

Average return on investment 1926-1930, inclusive—2.5 per cent.

Ford's indicated earnings and production 1923-1930, *Automobile Trade Journal*, **July 1931.**

Although Henry Ford's initial response to the Depression was to bolster consumer confidence by lowering prices, raising wages and increasing production, the fact is that the economic problems were too far reaching and severe for these remedies to have the effect he sought. As 1930 moved on it became increasingly evident that, as David Lewis has pointed out, Ford was baffled by what was happening and unable to provide any ready answers.

In August 1930, Ford said, "We are better off today than we have been for three or four years past. It was a mighty good thing for the nation that the condition which was misnamed 'prosperity' could not last." In October 1930, he announced that "the Depression is a good thing," and, the following March, proclaimed that "these are really good times, but only a few know it." These comments shocked those who saw around them what was really happening.

Attempting to buoy dealer confidence, Edsel Ford sent a letter to them on October 22. "You recall," he wrote, "when the Model A was introduced three years ago we stated we would make more Model A cars than we had made of the Model T. We still intend to do that. In fact, we look forward to the day when the 30,000,000th Model A will come off the line. When the Model A was offered to the world it was years in advance of its time. Since, we have constantly added to value by improving design, materials and workmanship, and in the last twelve months we have made two price reductions. We shall continue to improve quality in every way possible, but no major changes in the cars or trucks are contemplated."

In the letter Edsel appealed to Ford dealers to "make a vigorous drive" for increased business. "The road to general business recovery," he said, "lies in increased sales, and we look to the Ford dealer to do his share by putting his shoulder to the wheel and working as he has never worked before."

The foreign story was much like that in the United States, with the full effect of the Depression not kicking in for Ford overseas until 1931. In June 1930, the Hawley-Smoot tariff created a high wall against imports and led to foreign retaliation against American automobiles and other products and the situation increasingly worsened.

Although the Depression hit earlier in Latin America, Ford still managed to claim an average sixty-two percent of the market there. In Canada, production for 1930 was down twenty percent and in Australia by more than fifty percent. On the other hand, English production inched up by about 2,100 units and Ford-Japan did comparatively well in 1930 with 6,551 new registrations compared with General Motors' 4,445.

The Russian experiment got under way slowly. According to Robert Scoon, "The first Ford assembled in Russia, a 1929 AA, rolled off the AMO Moscow line on February 1, 1930, followed by a 1930 Phaeton." Scoon tells us that the Russian Model A engine would have a seventeen year lifespan with the last ones manufactured in 1947. Scoon's in-depth study of "Those Communist Model As" can be found in the March-April 1970 and March-April 1971 issues of *The Restorer* magazine.

In September 1930, Henry Ford traveled to Europe to inspect the progress at Dagenham, England, and, on October 2, laid the cornerstone for the new factory at Cologne, Germany. He also went to Rotterdam to lay the cornerstone of the new Dutch plant but refused to participate when he found out that the plant was located a half mile from water. "No water, no plant," he said. Ford-Holland was forced to abandon the project.

Henry Ford laid the cornerstone for Cologne, Germany, Ford plant on October 2, 1930.

The Ford Cologne plant.

New Ford Model As come off the Berlin-Westhafen assembly line in 1930.

While in Germany, Ford was interviewed by the *New York Times*, which ran quotes from the interview in its October 3, 1930, edition. Ford said that the trouble behind the present Depression was laziness. "They wanted something for nothing," he asserted. "They wanted to gamble on the Stock Exchange. They didn't want to work. The crash was a good thing; it has made them start working and thinking again. That will lead to new levels, new attainments in quality and a new era of prosperity. You watch. It is coming."

As mentioned in the previous chapter, the workers who manufactured and assembled the Model A Ford at the Rouge and the thirty-four other U.S. Branches, were a mix of native born and foreign born whites with a small percentage of blacks. In 1930, the Detroit auto workers were 40.8 percent native born white, 43.3 percent foreign born white and 13.9 percent black. About three out of four black auto workers in Detroit worked at Ford. (*American Automobile Workers 1900-1933*, by Joyce Shaw Peterson).

By far, the majority of workers were men although women were employed by Ford on certain jobs. These were likely to be young, single women who were supporting someone else. Henry Ford explained his philosophy regarding women workers in *Moving Forward*, published in 1930.

"Our experience with women workers is not large— although it is considerable. We have no objection to the employment of women, but only a small portion of our work is suited to them, and we also have the very definite policy of not employing any women who do not have others dependent on them. On the whole I share the feeling that women's least valuable contribution to life is made through industry."

As listed by Nevins and Hill, the annual average U.S. employment at Ford in 1930 was 152,362, with approximately sixty percent of these workers employed at the Rouge and Highland Park. These figures were down almost 22,000 from 1929, and would fall even more in 1931 to about 108,000.

An age distribution study at the Rouge dated February 20, 1930, reveals that the workers who made the Model A ranged in age from eighteen to eighty-three, with about ninety-one percent age fifty or younger. There were more men over sixty than under twenty. They worked in three shifts, with the second shift, 3:30 to 11:30 p.m., the largest.

While Ford made much of the seven dollar day introduced in December 1929, the fact is that not all payroll employees were paid at that rate. The wage schedule for hourly workers started with a hiring-in rate of six dollars per day or seventy-five cents an hour. Minors (eighteen and nineteen year olds) received forty to fifty-five cents an hour, depending on age. The maximum was one dollar an hour for skilled labor and ninety cents an hour for unskilled. After two months, employees hired-in at seventy-five cents an hour were raised to eighty-seven-and-one-half cents or seven dollars a day.

Salaried employees were paid according to position, with a minimum hiring-in rate for employees over twenty years of age of one hundred-thirty-five dollars per month. This was increased to one hundred-sixty dollars after two months of employment. The highest listed on the February 1, 1930, salary schedule was assistant manager at a maximum of eight hundred-fifty dollars per month. The superintendent of an assembly branch could make as much as six hundred dollars while the maximum salary for a traveler, who would represent the Branch to its dealers, was four hundred dollars.

The lowest paid salary, other than that of a minor, was for a female clerk whose maximum was two hundred dollars a month, or fifty dollars less than a male clerk. This was for jobs such as an assistant cashier, payroll clerk, stenographer, etc. These and other "clerk" positions were filled with female help, "when competent male help is not obtainable."

Minors (office boys, mail clerks, messengers, etc.) started at sixty-five or seventy-five dollars if they were younger than eighteen years of age, reaching the hiring-in rate at age twenty. As a general rule, recommendations for salary increases were considered either January 1 or July 1.

While the seven dollar day was definitely a plus, Nevins and Hill caution that there were two factors that exerted a downward pressure on real wages; the Depression reduced the size of the workforce and the company increasingly diverted work to outside suppliers who paid less than the Ford wage scale.

As the Depression deepened, Ford, like all manufacturers, had to cut back and lay off workers, or in many cases put them on a three-day week. "In that period of soup lines and lengthening relief rolls," say Nevins and Hill, "men employed even three-fifths of the time felt lucky." During this period Ford's use of outside suppliers increased considerably. Henry Ford tells us that in 1930

A 1930 Model A Coupe - owner Ray Cousins.

the company had 5,800 suppliers available and constantly used 3,500 of them. It appears that these companies paid less than Ford.

An example of this, as related by Nevins and Hill, was the Murray Body Co., which in the spring of 1930, employed five hundred women on a Ford contract and paid them on a piecework basis as little as three dollars a day. Another example, related by Ford critic Robert Cruden, was the Briggs Co., manufacturer of over forty percent of Ford bodies, which put through a fifteen to fifty percent general wage cut early in 1930 and piecemeal cuts from five to thirty percent later in the year. At the same time, Cruden says, Briggs earnings for the first half of 1930 increased by almost forty-six percent over the similar period in 1929.

As described in the previous chapter, working conditions at Ford for those who managed to keep their jobs during the Depression were not easy and certainly a long way from what they are today. Henry Ford's philosophy toward the working man can be understood, at least in part, by reflecting on two statements in his book *My Life And Work* (1922), written in collaboration with Samuel Crowther: "We make no attempt to coddle the people who work with us;" and, "A great business is really too big to be human."

Workers at Ford during the Depression were subject to increasing pressure to speed up their work and, in fear of losing their jobs, had to be careful to obey work rules. As mentioned previously, these included: no talking on the job, being on time, not smoking, not staying too long in the men's room, and not leaving their work stations early. Edmund Wilson quotes a worker's feelings in "Detroit Motors," published in the *New Republic*, March 25, 1931: "Ye get the wages, but ye sell your soul at Ford's—ye're worked like a slave all day, and when ye get out ye're too tired to do anything—ye go to sleep on the car coming home. But as it is, once a Ford worker, always a Ford worker." (See *The Best Of Ford* by Mary Moline for the complete article.)

As Ford and other automakers cut back, the situation in Detroit and elsewhere steadily worsened. Joyce Shaw Peterson says that by April 1930, the Detroit Department of Public Welfare was swamped with 728,000 persons for which to care. "In the winter of 1930," Peterson writes, "the city's municipal lodging homes sheltered 5,000 each night and fed up to 10,000 each day."

Henry Ford steadfastly ignored the existence of a major Depression. He did manage some efforts including offering his workers garden plots to supplement their incomes with homegrown vegetables, and working out an agreement with the city of Dearborn to shift unemployed Ford workers to Ford relief. This allowed workers to get sixty cents worth of food a day at the Ford commissary with the understanding that if the worker was later re-employed by Ford, his relief debts would be deducted from his paycheck.

Another, limited, effort was made by Ford's Sociological Department, which, according to Peterson, visited 1,040 families between March and November 1930 and

As Ford workers struggled during the Depression, Edsel Ford looked forward to the delivery of his new yacht, the 125-foot Onika, in Palm Beach on December 31, 1930.

arranged jobs for 367. During this time the department paid out $9,921 for groceries, fuel, clothing and hospital care. At the same time, investigators arranged for $14,615 in assigned wages to be paid to the company in return for hospital care.

Ernst Toller, a German correspondent, visited the Ford factories and wrote an article about them, which was published in the May 1, 1930, issue of *Living Age*. The article is also in *The Best of Ford*. Toller's commentary presents a foreigner's highly critical perspective on the dichotomy he found in the lives of Ford workers.

On the one hand, Toller found that Ford workers were better paid, lived in nicer homes, ate better and had more of the comforts of life than workers in his homeland. On the other hand, they had virtually no protection if they became sick or lost their job. At work they were subject to the restrictions detailed elsewhere in this book and had to spend their day essentially repeating the same gesture again and again.

"In the Ford factory," Toller writes, "no one can leave his place or go to another part of the building. The result is that a man may spend his whole life executing the same hammer stroke on the same part of an automobile without ever seeing with his own eyes the complete automobiles on which he has labored."

The Ford dealer story for 1930, was a mix of controversy and struggle to maintain sales and profits. As reported in a 1931 survey of more than four hundred-fifty car distributors and dealers by the Curtis Publishing Co., thirty-four percent reported profit in 1930, while fifty-three percent reported losses and thirteen percent said they broke even. Nevins and Hill state that "our available evidence suggests that between one-quarter and one-third of the nation's automobile dealers went out of business this year (1930)." In view of Ford's leading sales situation, Ford dealers arguably did somewhat better than the average, but that still was not an outstanding record.

A major cause of discontent for the Ford dealer was the reduced discount that had gone into effect in November 1929, and the relentless effort by Charles Sorensen to increase the number of dealerships, often to the harm of existing franchises. The lowering of the discount to 17-1/2 percent meant that in 1930, the average dealer saw his gross profit cut 12-1/2 percent.

"Few people realize the bitterness," commented the *Automotive Daily News* in its April 30, 1930, issue. Nevins and Hill say that, "As indignation spread among the Ford dealers, their outcry reverberated across the country. . . . One Detroit newspaperman termed the clash of interest 'the biggest factory-dealer battle in the automobile industry since its start thirty years ago.'"

Ford Dealer & Service Field, however, took a different view stating that "There is always a reason—and a good one—for Ford policies. And the company is not beyond changing policies according to the needs of the situation." The magazine quoted a dealer with a moderate-size franchise who said he refused to get on the "wailing wall." In his view, "volume sales of the Ford would result in my having a decidedly higher gross profit than the other fellows will have. You know that many times $17.50 is more money than a few times $22.50 or $25.00."

Two executives, Fred Rockleman, in charge of sales since the Model A's introduction and Henry Doss, Branch manager at Kansas City, openly opposed what was happening. In his "Reminiscences," Doss explains that he could not go along with the program and resigned in April 1930. "I wired Mr. Edsel Ford," he said. "Can't sell this program. . . . I won't sell this program because I don't believe in it. It's disastrous. I resign." Finally, in March 1930, Ford and Sorensen, concerned by the loss of dealers due to the new program and the continued outcry, retreated from their position and, making Rockelman the scapegoat, dismissed him from his position. He joined Chrysler shortly after.

On April 25, 1930, Ford dealers received a telegram from their Branch managers informing them that a sliding scale of discounts would take effect the next day, as follows:

1 to 50	17-1/2 percent
51 to 100	18 percent
101 to 150	19 percent
151 to 500	20 percent
501 and over	21 percent

How Ford Dealers Profit By New Discounts

UNITS	NEW DISCOUNT	GROSS PROFIT	OLD DISCOUNT	GROSS PROFIT	GAIN
FIRST....50	17½%	$ 4,331	17½%	$ 4,331	$ 000
SECOND .50	18%	4,455	17½%	4,331	124
THIRD...50	19%	4,702	17½%	4,331	371
NEXT...350	20%	34,650	17½%	30,317	4,333
TOTAL..500		$48,138		$43,310	$4,825

Note—This compilation is based on an average list price of $495.

"How Dealers Profit by New Discounts," *Motor*, **June 1930.**

Although few Ford dealers would qualify for the higher rate, there were many who sold more than one hundred-fifty and, therefore, would receive at least some relief from the new discounts. According to Nevins and Hill, the average gain was expected to be about eight hundred dollars a year. The authors also point out that this program helped city dealers in particular, and did not satisfy those in small towns and farm areas.

In January 1931, the discount was changed again so that the eighteen percent discount became effective with the twenty-sixth car and the twenty-one percent with the four hundred-first unit. Finally, on February 6, 1931, the dealer discount was raised to a flat twenty-two percent, meaning that on an average sale of one hundred-forty-two units, and assuming an average list price of five hundred-twenty-five dollars, a Ford dealer could expect to earn a gross profit of $16,401, or a 24-1/2 percent increase over the flat 17-1/2 percent basis. The letters received by dealers contained no reason for the change although it seems certain that growing discontent and negative publicity were causes. The *Automobile Trade Journal* suggested that, "The fact that Chevrolet led Ford by 1,958 in December passenger car sales for the first time since August 1928, also may have been a factor."

Commenting on the change, *Automobile Trade Journal* stated, "There is no doubt that February 6 was a day of rejoicing among Ford dealers. Their chances of earning a satisfactory net on car sales, with proper regulation of production, are very much better than at any time since November 1929, when discounts were cut from 20 to 17-1/2 percent."

Overall, 1930 was a year of significant change for many Ford dealers. Nevins and Hill place the number of dealers at 8,275 at the beginning of 1930. During the year 829 voluntarily dropped their sales contracts and 395 had contracts canceled by the company. At the same time 2,400 new dealerships were authorized during the year, so that the company began 1931 with 9,451 dealers, a net increase of 1,176.

To get a sense of what was happening in Ford dealerships around the country during 1930, following is a review of dealer activities culled mostly from the pages

Buffalo, New York, meeting of Buffalo Branch Ford dealers held on March 11, 1930. (Photo courtesy of Nortz & Virkler, Lowville, New York)

of 1930 issues of *Ford Dealer & Service Field*, *The Ford Dealer News*, *Ford News* or letters sent by the company to its Branches and by the Branches to the dealers.

Undercover Testing

During February 1930, employees of various Branches, traveling incognito, drove Model As in need of repairs to dealers to find out how well they were merchandising their service departments. The results were discouraging at best. For example, the Buffalo Branch reported that a Model A with a slight piston slap visited eighty-nine dealers. Only three noted that one fender was damaged and needed replacing, that the rearview mirror was missing, headlamp bulb burned out, taillamp bulb missing, dash light bulb missing and that the car needed greasing and washing. Not a very good record, but there was one positive result the Branch letter stressed: "All the men were very courteous and this is commendable."

Champion Ford Sellers of Texas

Houston, Texas, dealer Ray Pearson reported in *Ford Dealer & Service Field*, that his crew of sixteen salesmen sold five hundred-fifteen new cars and three hundred-forty-seven used ones in the first one hundred-four days of 1930. During 1929, his sales force moved 2,480 cars; 1,628 new and 852 used. Including parts and labor, the dealership's total volume for 1929 was $1,570,000.

Ladies Sales Club

The Logan Auto Co. of Philadelphia employed thirty young women and eighteen men on its sales staff. The young women did not sell on the showroom floor, but instead drove cars to prospects or located new prospects, left a company card and tried to bring the prospects into the agency to look over the desired model and have the deal closed. Here are the qualifications for the job as outlined in *Ford Dealer & Service Field*: "Naturally, it is deemed desirable to select women of attractive personality, but successful sales experience and ability are placed above beauty in cases where the entire combination might not exist."

One of the more successful salespersons on the staff of the Gray Motor Co. in Hollywood, California, was a woman, Grace Poundstone. She sold cars mostly to men, but concentrated on wives when dealing with "back-sliding" prospects or following up a lead by telephone. "It is (women) who give the final O.K. to the sale," she said, "usually on the basis of color selection, so I do a bit of preliminary work along that line over the phone."

Chromium-plating Sold Fords

Ford dealers in Detroit outsold the nearest competitor six to one in June 1930, registering nearly sixty-eight percent of all the new passenger cars delivered as against eleven percent for Chevrolet. The dealers also won new friends for used Ford cars by the simple process of chromium-plating the bright exposed parts, including the radiator and fuel tank caps and the radiator shell and headlights on the earlier models that did not have rustless steel. They also added new hubcaps. Through the service department of the Dearborn Branch, dealers were able to obtain a rate of less than five dollars for the chrome work in quantity lots. Reports from Detroit indicated that the brightly shining and newly plated finish helped move a lot of used cars.

SERVICE

I̶N THE *Ford Motor Company we emphasize service equally with sales* ⅄ *It has always been our belief that a sale does not complete the transaction between us and the buyer, but establishes a new obligation on us to see that his car gives him service* ⅄ *We are as much interested in your economical operation of the car as you are in our economical manufacture of it* ⅄ *This is only good business on our part* ⅄ *If our car gives service, sales will take care of themselves* ⅄ *For that reason we have installed a system of controlled service to take care of all Ford car needs in an economical and improved manner* ⅄ *We wish all users of Ford cars to know what they are entitled to in this respect, so that they may readily avail themselves of this service.*

Ad recommended for the use of Ford dealers.

Novel Way of Closing Sales

The Caro Motor Co. of Burkburnett, Texas, took prospective buyers of Model A Fords to Dallas in a Ford tri-motor airplane and showed them through the Ford assembly plant in that city. They were then placed behind the wheel of a Model A car the dealer wished driven to Burkburnett. During the one hundred-sixty-seven mile trip they usually sold themselves on the performance and roadability of the car. Many sales resulted, according to the dealer.

Ford Credit

The Universal Credit Corp. (UCC) observed its second anniversary in June 1930, and by the end of the year registered its one-millionth retail transaction, a Phaeton bought by a Miami (Florida) woman. During 1930, the UCC accepted 522,423 notes with volume exceeding $325,000,000. The average new car note was for $418.43, and the average down payment was 39.5 percent.

By September 1930, nearly 7,000 dealers had UCC services available and they, and their customers, were served by thirty-two complete UCC branches with over 1,800 employees. Dealers were given credit to a certain amount and paid a finance charge. Their credit was checked at the local branch of the UCC before cars were shipped or delivered. Retail buyers who financed through UCC, paid one-third down in cash and/or trade-in allowance, and the balance in not more than twelve equal monthly installments.

> UCC has twenty-five complete branches in operation, serving over 5,300 Ford dealers in the thirty-five states in which it is now doing business. The UCC plans are rapidly becoming familiar to motor car prospects, who recognize that they provide lower cost and standard insurance with courtesy and dependable service.
>
> UCC branches will supply dealers with time-sale aids in the form of UCC advertising mats, leaflets for mail campaigns, and circulars for salesmen, showing terms on all types for information of the prospect.

UCC has twenty-five complete branches, *Ford News*, February 15, 1930.

Form #1847

Among the paperwork that dealers were required to submit to their Branches was form #1847, "Dealer's Monthly Requirements." This informed the Branch of the dealer's new car requirements for the following month. The number requested was figured on the basis of the cars on hand, the total number expected to be sold during the current and following month and cars needed for stock or sample. After deducting estimated cancellations, the balance represented the dealer's requirements for the month. This number then had to be sub-divided to show the models requested and the total passenger, total truck and total commercial units needed.

When cars were available, the allotment was kept in line with the requirement figure. When production would not allow for that, the dealer's allotment was made on the basis of orders, size of territory, monthly estimate, etc.

Fleets

On February 20, the Buffalo Branch reminded dealers that a fleet owner's agreement, form #927, should be executed with any customer who had accepted delivery of twenty or more Ford cars. The five percent customer discount would apply on the twenty-first and subsequent deliveries during the remainder of the calendar year. Agreements with State Governments would be handled by the Home Office of the company. These governments would be entitled to a seven percent discount, as would companies on total purchases of five hundred and over Model A cars and AA trucks. For large volume customers such as American Telephone & Telegraph the discount was ten percent. AT&T had 8,207 Model A units in 1930.

Fleet sales, such as this 1930 Roadster used by the Philadelphia police, were common.

Newsletters

Leaving no stone unturned to attract business, some Ford dealers published and distributed newsletters highlighting their dealerships, cars and services. Examples are *Norton's Ford News*, published by D.D. Norton, Cazenovia, New York; *Good Auto News*, distributed by Harry Sandager, Inc. of Cranston, Rhode Island; *Campbell's Ford Exhaust* from C.H. Campbell Ford dealers of DeLand, Florida; the *Enon Ford and Fordson News* from the Ford dealership of George R. Andrews of Enon Valley, Pennsylvania; and *Morgan's Message*, a monthly, thirty-two page magazine from the Morgan Motor Car Co. in Newark, New Jersey.

Instead of publishing their own home-grown variety, dealers could also use a bulletin service such as that provided by the Krieg Letter Co. of Minneapolis. Krieg published bulletins for Ford dealers that were tailored to fit the dealers' needs and their pocketbooks. An example of a bulletin produced by a service is *Highways and Byways*, which was used by both the W.J. Irish

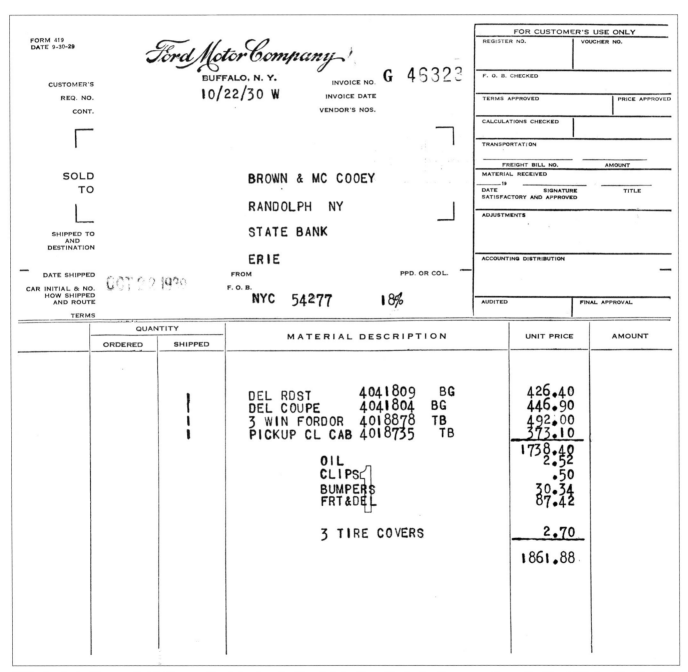

Bill of sale to Brown & McGooey, Ford dealers in Randolph, New York, for four cars from the Ford Motor Co. Buffalo Branch, dated October 22, 1930. Prices charged the dealer reflect the 17-1/2 percent discount.

Motor Co. of St. Paul, Minnesota, and the Keller Motor Co. of Oneida, New York.

Unique Advertising

An enameled finished cardboard 8-1/2 inches long by 2-1/2 inches wide was used by the Association Motor Co., Trinidad, Colorado, to advertise the Model A. The reverse side of this cardboard folder gave "Ten Reasons Why to Buy a Ford: 1 - Low first cost. 2 - Low upkeep. 3 - More miles to the gallon. 4 - It gets you there and brings you back. 5 - Has greater trade-in value. 6 - Can be serviced anywhere. 7 - Is comfortable and safe to ride in. 8 - Is a good looking car. 9 - You can own a home and own a Ford. 10 - It is common sense. Come in!"

2,700 Demonstrations

When the Beatrice Motor Co., Ford dealers in Beatrice, Nebraska, decided to demonstrate the Model A to more prospects, they announced their intention to present a new Tudor Sedan to one of the prospects who participated in the demonstration by driving a Model A for thirty minutes accompanied by a salesman. The route laid out covered extremely rough pavement, loose gravel, a hill climb and traffic stops.

"After completing the demonstration," *Ford News* stated, "the prospect returned to the dealer and filled out a card which was dropped in a locked container. In about ten weeks a total of 2,700 actual demonstrations were made. On some days, as many as six demonstrators were busy. On July 4, the container was unlocked and one of the prospects was presented with the Tudor." No word on how many cars were sold because of this sales initiative.

What Mechanics Earned

Mechanics at the Petersburg Motor Co., dealers at Petersburg, Virginia, were paid a straight salary of thirty dollars per week after working for the company one month. In order to hold their jobs they had to produce seventy-five dollars in labor sales per week. They also received a bonus of twenty-five percent of all labor in excess of the seventy-five dollars, provided they put in a full week's work. If a man failed to make his minimum quota for four consecutive weeks, he was either let go or shown how to go over the top. "All the mechanics seem to like this plan," the dealer said, "inasmuch as he knows each week that he is going to get money to pay his regular expenses. He also knows that he can make his salary anything he chooses by hard work and application."

What a Dealer Actually Paid His Employees

At the end of 1930, ten employees were listed on the weekly time book of the Nortz & Virkler Agency in Lowville, New York. One of these, a female secretary, was paid twenty dollars a week for five days of work. The highest paid man earned $2,126.50 in 1930. Using the week ending December 26, 1930, as a typical week, Nortz & Virkler paid $256.97 to nine employees. The total wages paid out for the entire year was $14,274.62 to ten employees. Many of the workers put in a six-day week.

As 1930 ended, it was clear to most people, and probably even to Henry Ford, that the good times were gone and the Ford Motor Co. and its dealers were in for some hard times. The Model A Ford, however, would continue to do yeoman service in transportation and haulage, even as it was slowly phased out of production. As we will see in a subsequent chapter, its legacy will be enduring and the stuff of legend. Following is one of those legends about a 1930 Model A, contained in a letter to the company, and printed in the March 1945 issue of *Ford Times*.

"A farmer drove his Model "A" 1930 Coupe into town and parked it beside a curb. About the same time the fire whistle blew. The fire engine came along in high speed and, the streets being a little slippery, the engine veered toward the Ford. In spite of the driver's efforts, the truck struck the Ford and turned it over a few times. The fire truck turned over, too. The farmer and a few men turned the Ford up on its wheels, and he got in, 'stepped on it,' and the car started right off. He drove to the next block, parked and walked back to the wrecked fire engine. The fire chief was standing looking at his wreck. The farmer said to him, "Next time buy a Ford.""

Chapter Five

1931: A Moment of Truth

"I felt that Henry Ford was the most surprised person in the world over this tremendous introduction of the Model A; the great public acclaim, the hundreds of thousands of orders that banked up convinced him, and I'm saying this through things he said himself, that he had another 15 year model. He had another Model T in terms of public acceptance. That was brought out in December 1927. We ran through 1928 and '29 quite satisfactorily. Then, as I remember, we made some changes, more or less minor. Sales began to fall off and I think Mr. Ford was really astonished, and tremendously disappointed when he realized that something had to be done."

Fred L. Black, former editor of *Ford News*, "Reminiscences"
Henry Ford Research Center

Period street scene in Milwaukee, Wisconsin, with a 1931 Tudor (left).

Arguably, the greatest second act in automotive history, the Model A Ford fell far short of both the more than fifteen million Model T Fords that preceded it, and the thirty million Model As confidently predicted by Edsel Ford. Nineteen thirty-one, the last of the four model years for Model A, was marked by a fifty percent decline in sales, and word that the Model A would be replaced by a new four and an eight. Contrary to popular perception, however, it would not be the last year in which Model A Fords were assembled.

On the whole, the Ford Motor Co., its workers and dealers, had a rough year in 1931, as the Depression caught up with the Model A. Since it was a buyer's market, it is likely that those people with money available to buy a new Ford were able to negotiate good deals. Unfortunately, there were not enough of them. The reality of the Depression, meant that the average car owner could not afford to buy a new car and was forced to make do with what he had. For millions of Ford owners, that meant driving, using and enjoying their 1928, 1929 and 1930 Model A and AA Fords, or their Model Ts.

In fairness, before we get into the dismal production/sales situation for 1931, it should be pointed out that the Ford picture for this year was not entirely negative.

Here's to—

the prosperity, growth and progress of Ford field factors during the year which is before us. And by "factors" we do not mean organizations or machines: we mean individuals — men.

¶ We are in a particular position to realize that, colossal though it has become, the Ford industry is no huge robot, but a group of human beings — and very good ones at that.

¶ We have visited with the central figure and founder of this group; with his highest executives and on down through to dealers in small cross-roads points and to their mechanics back in the shops.

¶ We have found them all showing a most human interest in their endeavor to design, build, sell or service a product of which each individual is proud because of its unsurpassed quality. And to their efforts the public humanly responds.

¶ These factors have secured Ford success and will assure its permanence and growth. The industry never can grow beyond the individuals who make it. The human factor always will be there.

¶ That is a thought for everyone in the field to hold. It is something for the "home-office" to consider in dealing with branches; for the branches to ponder in their relations with dealers; and, in turn, for the dealer to remember in working with his men and the public. Surely each group is essential to the other and the whole will thrive if moved by human and common-sense impulses.

¶ Big things have been done; greater things can be done through a spirit that avoids bureaucratic and mechanical operation and develops the man-to-man idea of continuing Ford world growth in

1931

Cover text of *Ford Dealer & Service Field*, January 1931.

There was some progress in the Ford world as can be seen from the following:

* In January, Ford happily announced that its employees would receive approximately $2,000,000 on their deposits during 1930 in the company's investment fund; a return of ten percent.

* Although the balance of the automobile industry in Canada suffered a forty percent drop in business during 1930, sales of the Model A were sustained at a level within ten percent of the record for 1929.

* Two new modern assembly plants in the United States opened at Richmond, California, and Buffalo, New York. A third, at Seattle, Washington, was practically finished. The company also announced plans to buy land at Painesville, Ohio, to build a plant with a capacity of four hundred cars a day.

* An assembly plant in India and a service plant in Sweden were placed in operation, and construction continued on new plants in Mexico, Belgium and Holland.

* On October 1, production began at the huge new Dagenham plant near London, England. The 1931 output was token rather than volume and, except for five-passenger cars, included only commercial vehicles. When completed in 1932, this plant, with an annual capacity of 200,000 units, was projected to be the largest automobile manufacturing plant in the world next to the Rouge plant.

* On May 4, the first Model A Ford—a combination of assembly and home-made product—ran off the assembly line at the Cologne plant in Germany. Plant capacity was estimated at one hundred-eighty vehicles and seventy-five sets of engines in eight hours.

* The Ford presence in Europe was designed to involve the people of the various countries in the ownership (through stocks), management and work of the Ford plants. Wilkins and Hill point out that "All the new Ford factories in continental Europe and Britain had been built by local labor, and by May 1931 not one of the European assembly plants used more than fifty percent American material (in value) in making a standard Tudor." For example, in Spain, the total cost of a Tudor was $947.79. Of this, thirty-seven percent was American material, one percent was European material and sixty-two percent was local duty, labor and overhead.

* In his survey of Russian Model A history, Robert Scoon tells us that a modern manufacturing plant, Nihni Novgorod, was completed in November 1931 in Russia. Popularly, it was called the "Russian Fordville" by Americans and "Gorky" by the Russians. The first vehi-

NEW FORD PLANT AT DAGENHAM · ENGLAND

A production capacity of 200,000 units a year is planned for the great new Ford plant at Dagenham, near London, which will be completed this year.

Top—
Close-up view of exterior

Center—
Foundry extension, showing steel work

Above—
Blast furnace

The Ford plant at Dagenham, England, *Ford Industries*.

cle, a Gaz AA truck, as the Russians called it, came off the assembly line in February 1932.

* At the Rouge, the huge 12,000-foot water tunnel from the Detroit River, begun in 1929, was officially opened in May 1931. It was said to be the largest tunnel serving the needs of a single industry and had a capacity of 650,000,000 gallons daily. The tunnel was one of four major additions that helped to increase the Rouge power generating capacity to 231,000 kilowatts, a net increase of 86,000. This power was used in the manufacturing of Ford cars and trucks, or in operating machinery incidental to their production (*Ford News*).

* In the United States, Ford's annual average employment for 1931 was 108,572 (Nevins and Hill). *Automotive Industries* quoted a Detroit newspaper report of September 9, which stated that employment at Ford stood at 65,000 in that area. Joyce Shaw Peterson says that only 37,000 were working in August. Without questioning the accuracy of these figures it should be noted that not all these workers worked full-time. The positive spin on this is, of course, that thousands of Ford workers were receiving at least some income as the Depression accelerated.

* On June 1, 1932, the Universal Credit Corp. (UCC), which handled authorized Ford credit plans, began its fifth year of operation. By June of 1932, there were thirty-three complete UCC Branches serving Ford dealers. During the first four years, UCC handled a volume of $801,961,000 comprised of more than 1,500,000 retail transactions and 650,000 floor plan accounts. In the early 1930s, in the midst of hard times, UCC was able to provide credit without increasing the actual cost of financing to its dealers and retail customers.

To give an idea of how the plan worked in 1931, a Tudor Sedan purchased through the Detroit Branch of the UCC, had a cash delivery price of $535.50. The UCC

You can purchase the Ford Car of your choice on the lower cost UCC Plans of Universal Credit Company which offer you the advantages of the

Authorized Ford Finance Plans

BRADY MOTOR CORP.
1033 Chicago Avenue
EVANSTON, ILL.

University 4883
Rogers Park 1516

Sales Representative

Salesman's card designed by Universal Credit Corp. (UCC) for Brady Motor Corp.

The Authorized Ford Finance Plans of

Paying for transportation as it is used has met with public approval because it makes it unnecessary to disturb the purchaser's existing investments and encourages more efficient handling of income in order to meet the payment terms of the contract. Accordingly, it has become the practice of automobile dealers to quote two prices—

1—The **Cash Delivered Price**, and
2—The **Time Delivered Price**

The Time Delivered Price usually includes the cost of insurance protection against fire and theft during the period of the contract for the protection of the interests of the various parties to the transaction.

The difference between the Cash Delivered Price and the Time Delivered Price represents the cost of handling the time payments, which include credit investigations of dealers and purchasers and the maintenance of organizations for collection of the balances due and keeping proper records of the accounts and incidental insurance. These costs vary by territories and also according to the company which furnishes the credit.

Conforming with established Ford policy the Universal Credit Company naturally puts forth every effort to help purchasers of Ford Cars to secure the Ford Car of their choice at the **lowest possible cost**. A large volume of credit

business handled through economical operating methods develops economies in financing costs for the benefit of the public.

In four years Universal Credit Company has handled $801,961,000 of business. Its credit standing is of the highest. Because of this high standing UCC is enabled to effect important economies in one of the largest items of cost in the operation of any finance company, namely the cost of the funds which it secures for its operations.

Similarly, because of—

(1) The high type of merchant selling Ford Products

(2) The well known quality of Ford Cars, and

(3) The exceptionally satisfactory credit experience with time purchasers

it is not necessary to increase the actual cost of financing to provide for abnormal credit losses. Ford Dealers do not on UCC Plan transactions add extra amounts to the UCC financing costs as an extra credit protection for themselves.

There are hundreds of finance plans available with different financing costs for the purchaser to pay and different policies with respect to methods of handling collections and protection of the customer's interests.

Likewise, occasionally, there are transactions completed which include excessive charges under the representation that these charges are required by the finance company.

However, any Ford Dealer will tell you, that in order to be absolutely sure you are not paying a higher Time Delivered Price than is justified by the conditions in your territory, it is advisable for you to request the Dealer to give you the benefit of the *"Authorized Ford Finance Plans"* of Universal Credit Company.

You can tell very easily whether or not you are receiving the benefit of a Universal Credit Company Plan by the following facts—

(1) The finance cost will be low.

(2) The contract forms will state that the payments are to be made at the office of Universal Credit Company.

(3) On the back of the contract forms is shown the seal of Universal Credit Company, similar to the one on the front cover of this leaflet.

(4) You will receive an official UCC coupon book for mailing payments and bearing the name and emblem of Universal Credit Company.

When you are considering the purchase of any car **investigate** and know definitely what you are paying for financing.

You will receive low cost financing service on the purchase of your Ford Car by insisting upon the benefit of the *Authorized Ford Finance Plans* of Universal Credit Company.

Universal Credit Company are Economical

Original Universal Credit Corp. leaflet that explains the plan.

Drying machine for aluminum borings salvaged from scrap

Finishing ingot cores in production foundry. The dried halves are assembled here in pairs

SALVAGING METAL SCRAP

THE tremendous production of steel at the Rouge plant is accompanied by the salvaging of more than 600 tons per day of steel scrap. Electric furnaces are particularly adapted to the reclaiming of valuable alloys in alloy scrap steel.

One of the advantages of the electric furnace lies in the absolute control of heat. Molten steel may be kept in the furnace at a given temperature for long periods.

At the Rouge two ten-ton units produce ingots and castings from which are cast locomotive frames and wheels, grinders for the glass house, cyanide pots, machine frames, furnace doors, turbine castings and hundreds of other special steel castings used in the Ford plants.

This work is largely done in a building known as the electric furnace building, one of the best equipped of its kind in America.

Although this is but a department of the Rouge plant and handles no production work, it pours from 70 to 80 tons of steel every day. The larger castings are made in huge pits to lessen chances for accident.

Most of the castings required by the Ford industries for repair and maintenance are made in the jobbing foundry. It is equipped to handle castings of any weight that might be required and one authority has said of it that "it is doubtful if any other general jobbing foundry in the country equals the wide range covered."

Ford engineers have developed original methods to accomplish many phases of the work. Among those is the method of forming the ingot mold and core as pictured above. Ordinarily, these are formed in an upright position.

Salvaging metal scrap, *Ford Industries*.

plan required a down payment of one hundred seventy-nine dollars and twelve monthly payments of thirty-three dollars. Finance cost for the year was $39.50 or about eleven percent.

   * Demonstrating its commitment to providing the best possible training for dealers and their servicemen, and the best service to Model A owners, Ford opened a factory research station in its Highland Park building. The purpose of the station was to provide a clinic at which service problems could be studied. The station also had cars on display and salesman available to give information about them to anyone interested. Deliveries, of course, were made through the dealer designated by the purchaser.

   * Salvaging old materials and converting them into useful articles netted the company profits running between $4,000,000 and $5,000,000 a year. This provided jobs and helped to decrease production costs, which, in turn, meant lower prices to the public. Very little was thrown away: used lumber became boxes and crates for shipping; cardboard pieces were used in packing; waste paper was converted into cardboard; glass salvaged from old motor cars was used for glazing in factory windows; five gallon paint cans became mop

buckets; burlap was sewn into bags; scraps of cloth were made into aprons and hand-pads, and thousands of tools that became worn in the shop were sent to salvage and reclaimed.

   * Two milestones in the manufacture of Ford automobiles were passed during the year. On March 24, 1931, a Town Sedan, the One Millionth Ford of Canada-built vehicle, was assembled at the East Windsor plant of the Ford Motor Company, Limited. Wallace R. Campbell, president, punched the serial number "CA-1,000,000" into the engine block and then drove the car off the final assembly line. This car made a nine month tour of Eastern Canada, covering slightly more than 20,000 miles.

The Twenty Millionth Ford car, a black 1931 Town Sedan, rolled down the line at the Rouge plant on Tuesday morning, April 14. From there, Henry Ford drove it to his home where it was displayed alongside the quadricycle, Ford's first car. Later the car was photographed with "999," the famous Ford racer and the Fifteen Millionth Model T, and then placed on exhibition in the company showrooms at the Highland Park plant.

One week later, the Twenty Millionth Ford, accompanied by a convoy of twenty new Fords, began a country-

Newspaper ad of May 6, 1931, for the Twenty Millionth Ford.

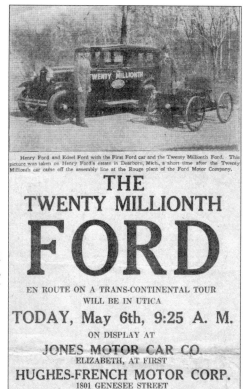

Henry Ford and Edsel Ford with the First Ford car and the Twenty Millionth Ford. This picture was taken on Henry Ford's estate in Dearborn, Mich., a short time after the Twenty Millionth car came off the assembly line at the Rouge plant of the Ford Motor Company.

THE TWENTY MILLIONTH FORD

EN ROUTE ON A TRANS-CONTINENTAL TOUR
WILL BE IN UTICA

TODAY, May 6th, 9:25 A. M.

ON DISPLAY AT

JONES MOTOR CAR CO.
ELIZABETH, AT FIRST

HUGHES-FRENCH MOTOR CORP.
1801 GENESEE STREET

wide publicity tour during which it visited Ford dealers in each of the company's Branch territories. Along the way it was greeted by governors, mayors, prominent persons, massed bands, parades and hundreds of thousands of excited viewers.

License plates bearing the figures "20,000,000" were presented to the car in practically every state traveled. It was driven by Eleanor Roosevelt and received the checkered flag at the Indianapolis Motor Speedway. The tour was completed and the car returned to Dearborn shortly before the Christmas holidays. Writing in *Ford Life*, David Lewis states that this milestone Ford "has not survived."

Although Ford put a smiling face on its accomplishments, as the above examples show, the fact is that, by and large, 1931 was not a good year for the company where it counts most—in production and sales. According to the "Ford Motor Company World Production Report 1903-1943," Ford car and truck production in 1931 totaled just 762,058 units worldwide, a drop of almost forty-nine percent from 1930. Production peaked at 119,626 in April and then fell steadily to a low of 12,656 in December. Except for a scattered few units, this would be the last month for the domestic production of Model A passenger cars.

The sales picture was worse because arch rival Chevrolet came out of the gate ahead and eventually topped

The Twenty Millionth Ford on Liberty Mall in Kansas City. (Photo courtesy of Henry Ford Museum and Greenfield Village)

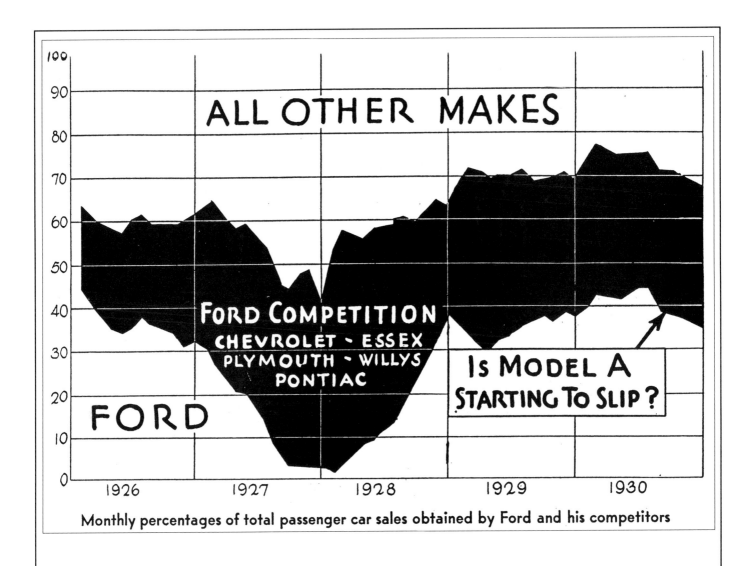

How the Model A Stacks Up With 1931 Competition						
	Ford	Chevrolet	Essex	Plymouth	Pontiac	Willys Six
Prices—2-Door Sedan	$490	$545	$595	$565	$675	....
4-Door Sedan	$590	$635	$695	$625	$745	$625
Wheelbase	103½	109	113	167*	112	110
Number of Cylinders	4	6	6	4	6	6
Piston Displacement	200.5	194	175.3	196.09	200	193
Maximum Horsepower	40–2200	50–2600	60–3300	48–2800	60–3000	65–3400
Tire Size	4.57/19	4.75/19	5.50/19	4.75/19	5.00/19	5.00/19

* Overall length.

Charts from *Automobile Trade Journal*, February 1931, demonstrating the Model A slipping in sales.

Ford. For the three months from December 1930 through February 1931, Chevrolet had the lead in domestic passenger car sales for the first time since August 1928. At year's end, Ford was again number two with domestic sales of 528,581 passenger cars compared to Chevrolet's 583,429. Ford's market share of about forty percent in 1930 fell below twenty-eight percent in 1931, while Chevrolet's share rose about seven percent.

Adding insult to injury, the upstart Plymouth cut into Model A sales with a forty-seven percent increase to 94,289 units. On the plus side, Ford did manage to retain its number one position in truck sales, selling 138,633 units to Chevrolet's 99,254. Even here, however, Ford was down by approximately thirty percent from 1930 while Chevy was only down seventeen percent. (Sales figures are based on data compiled in 1932 issues of *Automobile Trade Journal* and *Motor* magazine.)

Alert to various methods of increasing sales, Ford executives fostered competition among the Branches by keeping statistics and displaying these on charts used at Branch Managers' meetings. Branches were rated in seven areas including retail and wholesale deliveries. In 1931, the Edgewater (New Jersey) Branch was first in retail deliveries but, during the period from October 1 to December 31, was twenty-eighth in wholesale deliveries. The Salt Lake City Branch was last (thirty-fifth) in retail deliveries, but placed a little better at twenty-ninth in wholesale deliveries. Seattle led the pack in Branch standing based on wholesale results.

The significant slide in sales for 1931 meant that Ford ended up in the red for the second time in the four-production-year history of the Model A. A newspaper dispatch concerning the final balance sheet of the Ford Motor Co. for 1932, indicates that Ford lost $53,568,000 in 1931. The Federal Trade Commission lists the loss as $37,181,192. Kennedy says that the company lost about seventy-five dollars every time it sold a Model A Ford in 1931. Clearly, no matter which figures one accepts, the Model A was in trouble and, as a matter of fact, by the fall of 1931, its end had already been decided.

The question is, why? Why did a car that offered so much promise in 1928, 1929 and 1930 lose consumer appeal so quickly? Certainly, the economic slump played a role, but that reason is tempered by the fact that the Depression adversely affected all the car manufacturers. No, there is more to the end of Model A than hard times and the erosion of consumer buying power.

Model A got in trouble because, despite its advantages in quality, speed and low price, it did not keep up technologically. It was left behind because it did not adequately answer the growing competition of Chevrolet and Plymouth. Both of these cars offered smooth and comfortable motoring with advanced features at prices

Ford-Chevrolet Six Comparison

Specifications Released in January, 1931

FORD	CHEVROLET	More than Ford
Roadster......$430	Roadster..$475	$ 45
Phaeton........ 435	Tour...... 510	75
Coupe......... 490	Coupe.... 535	45
Tudor......... 490	Coach.... 545	55
D.L. Sedan.... 630	D.L. Sed.. 650	20
Spt. Coupe.... 500	Spt. Coupe 575	75
Fordor Sed..... 590	Sedan..... 635	45
Town Sedan.... 630	Spl. Sed... 650	20
D.L. Coupe.... 525	5W. Coupe 545	20
Cabriolet....... 595	. . . .	
D.L. Phaeton... 580		
D.L. Roadster.. 475	Spt. Rdstr. 495	20
Victoria....... 580	5 P. Coupe 595	15

REAR AXLE

¾ Floating relieves axle of all carrying strain	Semi-floating. Load strain is carried on axle

DRIVE

Torque tube and radius rods carry driving thrust and keep axle at right angles to frame	No radius rods. Road imperfections cause axle to be thrown out of alignment with frame

SPRINGS

Transverse spring suspension eliminates body wearing and twisting	Ordinary type spring suspension. Irregularities of driving surfaces transmitted directly to chassis and body

SHOCK ABSORBERS

Houdaille Hydraulic —two way action	Delco Lovejoy—one way action

FINISH BRIGHT METAL PARTS

Rustless steel	Plating

WINDSHIELD

Shatterproof glass	Ordinary plate glass

Ford-Chevrolet Six Comparison, *Ford Fax,* February 1931.

A 1931 Roadster clearly shows the painted inserts on the radiator shell, one of the identifying characteristics of 1931 Model As - owner Chuck Nelson.

Harold Newton's early 1931 DeLuxe Fordor is an original car with only 29,800 miles on the odometer.

Selling in the 1930s. A salesman points out the features of a 1931 slant window Model A Town Sedan. (Photo courtesy of Henry Ford Museum and Greenfield Village)

within range of the Model A Ford. Chevrolet and Plymouth represented the thinking of the 1930s while the Model A was, as Paul Woudenberg states in *Ford In The Thirties*, the "final flowering of the Twenties."

Except for the slanting windshield design on some types, the 1931 Model A Fords were not significantly different from their 1930 cousins. They are commonly recognized by painted panel inserts at the top and bottom of the radiator shell and the pressed stainless emblem. Commercial shells were magnetic steel and painted black except for some DeLuxe 1931 models. Other 1931 characteristics, such as the stainless, oval dash panel with ribbed center and round speedometer, one-piece splash apron and separate running boards can also be found on some 1930 models. The author's late-1930 Standard Fordor, for example, which is original except for new paint and mechanical overhaul, has the one-piece splash apron and separate running boards.

Another identifying characteristic sometimes cited for the 1931 models, is the indented firewall with the gasoline shutoff valve located on the engine side of the firewall. This feature, however, did not reach one hundred percent production until May 1931 and, therefore, not all 1931 cars have it. An example, is a two-window DeLuxe Fordor (170-B) owned by Harold Newton, which is an original car and has the traditional flat firewall.

The paradox of the 1931 Model A is that at the same time sales were plummeting, Ford was trying desperately to cut its losses by introducing new styling on some models, increasing its marketing of the DeLuxe types and expanding its commercial and truck lines. The new styling trend was introduced in November 1930 with the Victoria. It featured the slanting, visorless windshield

A 1931 DeLuxe Coupe - owner Don DeWolfe.

Convertible Sedan (A-400).

THE NEW FORD CABRIOLET

Smart style and utility are combined in this beautiful new Ford Cabriolet with the slanting windshield and sloping, swagger top. It is really two cars in one—so easily can you change it from a roadster to a coupe. The enduring body finish is offered in a variety of rich, attractive colors. Radiator shell, headlamps and other exposed bright metal parts are made of Rustless Steel. Seat and seat back is a fine quality Bedford Cord or crushed grain leather. Seat is adjustable. There is also a comfortable rumble seat upholstered in artificial leather. Attractive top material is fast-color, non-shrinking, with a sliding seam fastener for the wide rear window.

THE NEW FORD CONVERTIBLE SEDAN

An entirely new Ford body of impressive grace and style is the five-passenger Convertible Sedan. Great care has been taken to make the top sturdy and substantial, yet easy to raise or lower and quiet in either position. Only four clamps are needed to hold it securely in place . . . two at the windshield frame and one on each of the rear quarter side frames. Snaps fasten the non-shrinkable, fast-color top material to the sides. Upholstery of seat cushions and seat backs is genuine leather, with a narrow piping trim. Driver's seat is adjustable. Side fender well for spare tire is standard equipment. There is a choice of de luxe body colors. The slanting windshield is made of Triplex safety glass.

Ford Motor Co. original folder showcasing two dashing new Fords, a Cabriolet and Convertible.

A 1931 Convertible Sedan - owner Harold Rickles.

A 1931 Victoria - owner Cliff Howard.

A 1931 DeLuxe Tudor - owner DeVerne Breed.

and a lower roof line. Bodies for the slanting windshield types were made by Murray and Briggs.

In March, the company informed Branch managers that the DeLuxe Sedan was being built with the slanting windshield design the same as the Victoria and Town Sedan. They were also told that production of the Standard Sedan with the slanting windshield would begin in early April and that the Cabriolet was scheduled for about May 1st. At the same time, Ford emphatically stated that there were no plans to incorporate the slanting windshield design on either the Tudor or Coupe types.

Encouraged by the fact that the demand for the DeLuxe models was stronger than for the Standard types, Ford urged dealers to arrange displays of the DeLuxe bodies and to direct attention to what the company called the "smartness of type" that characterized these cars. By the end of the year it was clear that sales of the DeLuxe models held up much better than the Standard models. The DeLuxe Coupe, for example, sold at eighty percent of its 1930 level while the Standard Coupe could only manage thirty-six percent. DeLuxe Roadster sales increased five times while the Standard Roadster sales dropped by more than ninety-three percent from 1930 levels.

In June, Ford began to offer colored steel spoke wheels to match body stripe at no extra charge on all DeLuxe closed passenger types, including the Convertible Sedan, but not including the Victoria, Town Sedan or Cabriolet. On those models, as well as the Standard passenger types, the extra charge of five dollars to the public was continued.

The Convertible Sedan, a brand-new type of continental origin possessing at the same time the comfort of a closed car and the advantages of an open one, was announced in May 1931. It was designed to open a new field for dealers, enabling them to attract prospects who might otherwise be in the market for cars in the higher priced field.

Standard equipment for the A-400, as it is popularly called, included the following: cowl lamps, left well fender, top boot, chrome exterior windshield frame, chrome windshield wiper, upholstery of seat cushions and seat backs made of a deep tan color genuine leather with a narrow piping trim, armrests for rear seat passengers, two ashtrays, and adjustable driver's seat. Full length bumpers, front and rear, were supplied at the regular price of fifteen dollars list. Standard colors were the same as for all other DeLuxe closed types.

The Buffalo Branch manager was so excited by the Convertible Sedan that he wrote to his dealers the day the first job arrived, praising the car and telling them that when they show the car the first thing their prospects would say would be what he said, "I want one of these." He told his dealers to place orders for one of these cars immediately and when they received it to "put it on your showroom floor, run some advertising, then start an intensive demonstrating campaign. The people who will buy this car have money and there is no reason why every dealer can't build up some extra deliveries through this model."

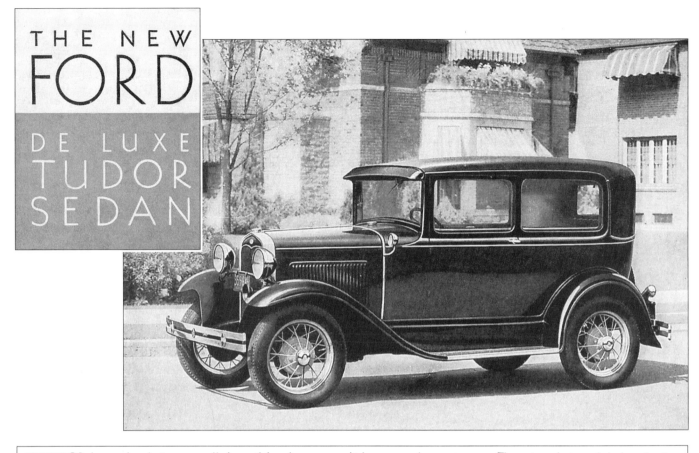

THE NEW FORD

DE LUXE TUDOR SEDAN

FOR those who desire unusually beautiful and attractive interior and exterior fittings combined with the utility and comfort of a coach, the New Ford De Luxe Tudor Sedan offers a happy choice. Upholstery is optional in rich Mohair, Bedford Cord, or Broadcloth. The entire floor is heavily carpeted. Cowl lights and a dome light are regular equipment. There is a choice of de luxe body colors with wheels to harmonize. The windshield is of safety glass, fenders and wheels are bonderized to prevent the spread of rust, radiator shell, headlamps and many other bright metal parts are of Rustless Steel. Here indeed is a car which appeals to those who want de luxe but economical transportation.

De Luxe Tudor Upholstery is of fine quality—durable as well as luxurious. There are arm rests on both sides of the spacious, deeply cushioned rear seat. Five adult passengers may ride in this car with comfort

The driver's seat is fitted with the new quick adjustment mechanism and is easily regulated, even when occupied, to accommodate the long or short reach. Mothers who, because of small children, prefer the two-door type appreciate this convenient feature

Original leaflet for a DeLuxe Tudor.

The fall season with its dropping leaves lends a nice background for this early-1928 Model A Roadster.

A fine example of a 1928 Model A Roadster Pickup. (Photo courtesy of Long Island Auto Museum)

Ford Motor Company created brochures for its 1928 models including the Model A Phaeton. An artist rendering of the automobile in use graced the cover of each brochure while inside, the particular car was shown inside and out in color. In this case, the Phaeton was recreated in profile and with its rear compartment in close-up.

Frank Hartmaier is the original and only owner of this 1929 Model A Standard Roadster.

Another beautiful 1929 Model A Roadster, this one photographed at a 1968 Ford meet, is owned by Bruce Wheeler.

George Dossena of New Jersey displayed his immaculate 1929 Model A two-window Fordor at a recent Hershey (Pennsylvania) Fall Meet.

The cowl location of the Model A's gas tank makes for convenient fill-ups, as demonstrated by George DeLaRoche (left) and Norm McGowan on DeLaRoche's 1929 Tudor.

American Telephone & Telegraph was a fleet purchaser of Model A commercial vehicles for servicing its phone equipment. One of the AT&T fleet, displayed at the 1978 Hershey (Pennsylvania) Fall Meet, was this 1929 Model A truck equipped with an extension ladder.

Ford Motor Company also created brochures for its 1929 models including the Model A Sport Coupe. An artist rendering of the automobile in use graced the cover while inside, the particular car was shown in color. In this case, the Sport Coupe was recreated in profile and with its rumble seat in close-up.

Complete with a weigh scale hanging in back, Robert Fischer of Olean, New York, displayed his 1929 Model A Huckster at a recent Hershey (Pennsylvania) Fall Meet.

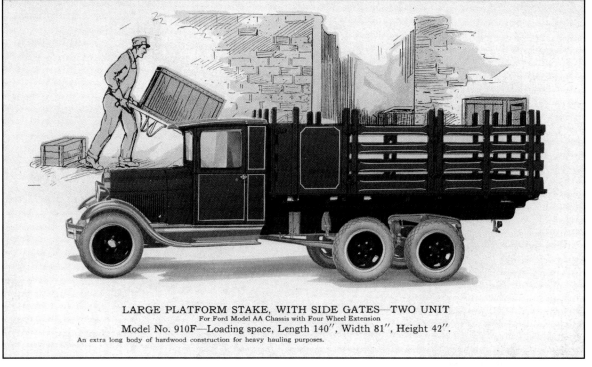

LARGE PLATFORM STAKE, WITH SIDE GATES—TWO UNIT
For Ford Model AA Chassis with Four Wheel Extension
Model No. 910F—Loading space, Length 140″, Width 81″, Height 42″.
An extra long body of hardwood construction for heavy hauling purposes.

The Stoughton Co., established in 1865, manufactured commercial bodies and cabs for both the Model A and Model AA. This Large Platform Stake with four wheel extension was one of the many applications produced for the 1929 Model AA, pictured in the Stoughton catalog that year.

A beautifully restored 1930 Model A Panel Delivery.

Marc Liddic has owned this
1930 Model A Tudor since 1962.

Douglas Maidment has
owned this 1930 Model A
Fordor since the 1940s.

Owner James A. Wild displayed his 1930
Model A Standard Fordor in the original class
at a recent Hershey (Pennsylvania) Fall Meet.

Cozad, Nebraska, is the home of alfalfa and this 1930 Model A Sport Coupe owned by Norman Beans. Displayed at the Hershey (Pennsylvania) Fall Meet, as nice looking a car as this is it is hard to believe Beans drives this car on a regular basis, but he does.

This combination metal and wood Model A is a 1930 Fruit Wagon.

A 1930 Model A Roadster competing in the gymkhana at the 1996 MARC National Meet in Rochester, New York.

Dennis Shenk of Indiana is the proud owner of this 1930 Model A five-window DeLuxe Coupe.

1930 Model A Pickup owned by Greg Sgroi of Canastota, New York. The emblems on the Pickup's doors promote the Mohican Model A Ford Club.

Displayed at the Hershey
(Pennsylvania) Fall Meet is
New Yorker Michael Vitale'
1931 Model A Pickup. Note
1931 New York commercial
license plate attached to the
light bar.

This 1931 Model A recreati
of a police patrol vehicle of
1930s is owned by Guy Pea
and Steve Eisenman. Note t
windshield frame-mounted
spotlight and light bar-mou
warning light/siren.

ob Baker is the proud owner of this 1931 Model A Town Sedan.

is 1931 Model AA gas truck represents the Haxtun Co-Op Oil Co.

Miscellaneous

An example of a Model A club involved in a public service project— the "Adopt-A-Highway Program" so popular across the United States. The Model A in the photo is the author's 1930 Fordor.

A heavy-duty Model AA truck with Tuthi overload springs mounted front and rear. Definitely a candidate for a little TLC. (Photo courtesy of Doug Maidment)

The 1998 Great American Race made an overnight stop in Syracuse, New York, on its way to the finish line in Haverhill, Massachusetts. Car #38 was a 192 Model A Speedster with Fred Secker as driver and Chuck Boblasky as navigator.

Participating in the 1996 Great American Race was the shop-built Model A Speedster of the Astro Auto Tech team from Astronaut High School in Titusville, Florida. Given the name "The Astro Flyer," five adults and five students completed the Model A project car that finished fifteenth in the Rookie Class of the cross-country race. Navigator Dave Mark and student Chris Burke are shown with the trailered Model A after it was pulled from a palmetto grove. The school's shop course students gave the derelict Ford a thorough restoration (shown in the shop) modifying it into a Speedster model. The Astro Flyer earned the Doc Fuson "Spirit of the Event" award at the 1996 Great American Race.

In the 1930s, Model A toy cars, such as this Fordor (left) and Sport Coupe made by Arcade, were a popular item. The gasoline station is by Gibbs.

A cast iron Model A Fordor made by the Champion Hardware Co.

A small collection of Arcade toys includes:
a Model A Fordor, Model A dump truck, Model T Fordor and a 1936 double-decker b

Touring is a big part of Model A club activities as evidenced by this lineup of Model As on a recent tour: (top, l-to-r) 1930 Coupe owned by Ray Cousins, 1930 Pickup owned by Norm McGowan, 1930 Fordor owned by the author and 1929 Tudor owned by George DeLaRoche.

Miscellaneous

Both Model A and AA vehicles were used in several types of conversions, including tractors and this unique camper unit.

Harold McAdam poses with his unusual two-door Model A Phaeton.

Form 331

Ford Motor Company

BUFFALO, N. Y.

FACTORY AND GENERAL OFFICES
DEARBORN, MICH.

BUFFALO BRANCH DEALERS

IN REPLYING REFER TO

Jan 19 1931

Sales Letter No. 6 (Revised)

     Below are current car and truck prices based on discount of $17\frac{1}{2}\%$, this list superseding the one sent you under date of August 28th, 1930.

     To the prices below are to be added the varying contract freight on the different models, applicable at your point. Where one gallon of alcohol has been supplied, add 80¢ to the net cost.

	List	Less $17\frac{1}{2}\%$	Bumpers	Gas & Oil	Net Cost to Dealer
Phaeton	435.00	358.88	12.38	2.80	374.06
DeLuxe Phaeton	580.00	478.50	12.38	2.80	493.68
Roadster	430.00	354.75	12.38	2.80	369.93
Roadster - Rumble Seat	455.00	375.38	12.38	2.80	390.56
DeLuxe Roadster	475.00	391.88	12.38	2.80	407.06
Standard Coupe	490.00	404.25	12.38	2.80	419.43
Standard Coupe - Rumble Seat	515.00	424.88	12.38	2.80	440.06
Sport Coupe	500.00	412.50	12.38	2.80	427.68
DeLuxe Coupe	525.00	433.13	12.38	2.80	448.31
DeLuxe Coupe - Rumble Seat	550.00	453.76	12.38	2.80	468.94
Victoria Coupe	580.00	478.50	12.38	2.80	493.68
Tudor Sedan	490.00	404.25	12.38	2.80	419.43
Fordor Sedan	590.00	486.75	12.38	2.80	501.93
DeLuxe Sedan	630.00	519.75	12.38	2.80	534.93
Town Sedan	630.00	519.75	12.38	2.80	534.93
Cabriolet	595.00	490.88	12.38	2.80	506.06
Station Wagon	*625.00	515.63	5.78	2.80	524.21
"A" Chassis	*340.00	280.50	5.78	2.80	289.08
"A" Chassis, Closed Cab	*435.00	358.88	5.78	2.80	367.46
Pick-up, Open Cab	*425.00	350.63	5.78	2.80	359.21
Pick-up, Closed Cab	*455.00	375.38	5.78	2.80	383.96
DeLuxe Panel Delivery, "A"	*540.00	445.50	12.38	2.80	460.68
"A" Panel Delivery	*535.00	441.38	5.78	2.80	449.96
"A" Drop Floor Panel Delivery	*560.00	462.00	5.78	2.80	470.58
"A" Natural Wood Panel Delivery	*615.00	507.38	5.78	2.80	515.96
"A" Town Car Delivery	1150.00	948.75	12.38	2.80	963.93
AA-131 Panel Delivery, Single Wheels	730.00	462.00	5.78	2.80	470.58
AA-131 DeLuxe Delivery, Single Wheels	950.00	783.75	12.38	2.80	798.93
AA-131 Chassis, Single Wheels	495.00	408.38	5.78	2.80	416.96
AA-131 Chassis, Dual Wheels	520.00	429.01	5.78	2.80	437.59
AA-157 Chassis, Single Wheels	525.00	433.13	5.78	2.80	441.71
AA-157 Chassis, Dual Wheels	550.00	453.76	5.78	2.80	462.34

*including left well fender

Buffalo Branch price list dated January 19, 1931.

The Convertible Sedan listed at $640 effective May 22, 1931. In November, Dearborn Branch dealers paid $499.20 plus $11.70 for the front and rear bumpers. They delivered the Convertible Sedan to fleet owners for $564.20 and retail purchasers for about $715. Only 5,072 were assembled worldwide in 1931 and 21 units in 1932.

Also in May, the company announced that the Victoria models of the DeLuxe line of vehicles were now coming off the assembly line with metal rear-quarters and roof side panels, instead of the fabric quarters and panels used previously. The price of the Victoria remained at five hundred-eighty dollars list.

The Tudor, the mainstay of the Model A passenger car line, experienced a decline in 1931 to forty percent of its 1930 level. This was offset, but only a little, by the new DeLuxe Tudor added to the line in June and which sold 23,490 units during the remainder of 1931 and 28 in 1932. The DeLuxe Tudor listed for five hundred-twenty-five dollars f.o.b. Detroit, or thirty-five dollars more than the Standard Tudor. A November 10, 1931, Rouge price list shows the dealer paying $409.50 for the DeLuxe Tudor with his then twenty-two percent discount. Fleet owners paid $474.50 and the retail purchaser $600.

The following was standard equipment for the DeLuxe Tudor: cowl lamps, dome light, mohair upholstering, toggle grips, side armrests in rear seat, driver's seat and front passenger seat of the same type as those in the Convertible Sedan, mahogany grain garnish strips, floor carpet instead of rubber mat and five steel spoke wheels in color to match the stripe. An extra fifteen dollars was charged for the front bumper and rear fender guards. The standard colors were the same as for the Model A Town Sedan: Black, Chicle Drab, Kewanee Green, Maroon, Brewster Green Medium.

Model A car prices remained stable through much of 1931. In January, for example, at the Buffalo Branch, the Phaeton was listed at $435 with a 17-1/2 percent discount to the dealer for a dealer cost of $358.88. The cost of bumpers ($12.38) and gas and oil ($2.80) made the net cost to the dealer $374.06. To this the dealer had to add the contract freight on the different models applicable at his location.

The list price at the Rouge (Dearborn) in November for the same model, was still $435 but the dealer now paid $339.30 because his discount had been raised to twenty-two percent. To this was added the cost of bumpers ($11.70), but there is no indication of a charge for gas and oil. Freight likely was minimal since it is possible that many of the dealer purchases were drive-aways. The fleet owner price at the Rouge on the Phaeton was $394.30 and the price to retail purchasers was $500.

The November prices also include a note about equipment: "Five colored steel wheels and safety glass throughout will be standard equipment on all DeLuxe types and also the Sport Coupe, Cabriolet, Victoria and Four-Passenger Convertible. Rumble seat will be standard equipment in the DeLuxe Roadster, Sport Coupe and Cabriolet and can be supplied in the Standard Road-ster, Standard Coupe and DeLuxe Coupe as optional equipment at $25.00 list extra."

The following are examples of final costs to Ford buyers in 1931. On May 28, 1931, Walter Moon bought a 1-1/2 ton Model AA truck from Nortz & Virkler Inc., Ford dealers in Lowville, New York. He paid six hundred-sixty-six dollars for the chassis; seven dollars for bumpers; four dollars for gas and oil; two hundred-sixty-two dollars for a dump body; and ten dollars balance due on a license. The total cost was nine hundred-forty-nine dollars. Moon paid for the Model AA by trading in his Chevrolet truck for four hundred-eight dollars, and taking a loan from the Universal Credit Corp. for the balance of five hundred-forty-one dollars. During the

THE FORD MOTOR COMPANY announces a REDUCTION in PRICES

The following prices are effective Monday, January 19, 1931

	New Price	Old Price	Reduction	Delivered
De Luxe Roadster	$475	$520	$45	523
De Luxe Phaeton	580	625	45	670
Phaeton	435	440	5	525
Roadster	430	435	5	520
Sport Coupe	500	525	25	590
Coupe	490	495	5	586
De Luxe Coupe	525	545	20	621
Tudor Sedan	490	495	5	586
Fordor Sedan	590	600	10	686
Town Sedan	630	660	30	726
Cabriolet	595	625	30	691
Victoria	580	625	45	670
De Luxe Sedan	630	640	10	726
Station Wagon	625	640	15	712
Model A Chassis	340	345	5	422
Model AA Truck Chassis, 131½-inch wheelbase	495	510	15	58

Newspaper ad for a reduction in prices. Of interest is the handwritten delivered prices written in by a salesman.

same time period, Nortz & Virkler sold other Model A Fords including a Tudor for five hundred-ninety dollars; a three-window Fordor for six hundred-seventy-six dollars; a closed Pickup for five hundred-thirty-three dollars and a Panel truck for six hundred-thirteen dollars.

On December 24, 1931, a school teacher in Smithburg, Maryland, purchased a 1931 Model A DeLuxe Fordor (160-C) from the Newman Auto Co. She paid seven hundred-twelve dollars less a three hundred-seventy-five dollar allowance for the trade-in, a 1929 Model A Cabriolet. The teacher was the only owner of the car until Smithburg resident, Joseph Miller, purchased it from the original dealership in 1978. The DeLuxe 160-C is easily identifiable by its blind rear quarter section and slant windshield.

After the order for a new car was obtained, Ford encouraged dealers to sell accessories to the new owner. In June 1931, the company issued a list of all the genuine accessories available for installation on both the A and AA since the introduction in 1927. This list contained eighty items. As in previous years, the accessories continued to carry a regular dealer discount of forty percent and were hyped as good money makers. For example, the Nortz & Virkler agency made $2.40 on the sale of a $6.00 moto-meter and cap and fifty cents on a tire lock that sold for $1.25. The dealer discount on a heater selling for $5.00 was $2.00 as it was for a trunk rack. A spare tire and tube selling for $13.00 in 1931, netted $5.20.

The *Pacific Coast Red Book* and the *Motor-Fax Price Bulletin* provide an interesting look at what people were paying for used Model As in 1931. The September 1 to November 1, 1931, issue of the *Red Book*, computed the appraised price of a Model A in "average as is condition" based on 15,728 used car sales. The 1931 Fordor was quoted at a factory price of five hundred-ninety dollars and an appraised value of four hundred-fifty dollars. The 1931 Victoria was listed at five hundred-eighty dollars and appraised at four hundred-fifty dollars.

A 1931 Pickup. Nortz & Virkler sold a model like this for five hundred-thirty-three dollars.

Eagle Baking Panel Delivery. Nortz & Virkler, Ford dealers in Lowville, New York, sold a model like this in 1931 for six hundred-thirteen dollars. (Photo courtesy of John A. Conde)

Motor-Fax for August 1931, did things a little differently, giving the factory list, the delivered price new and the current retail market value. Here, the Fordor, which also listed at five hundred-ninety dollars, had a delivered price of seven hundred-twenty dollars and a retail market value of six hundred-thirty-five dollars. The Victoria was listed at five hundred-eighty dollars, delivered new for seven hundred-ten dollars and its retail market value was five hundred-eighty-five dollars.

Used Model As from the earlier years were, of course, selling for considerably less. The late-1930 Standard Coupe (factory list four hundred-ninety-five dollars), was appraised at three hundred-fifteen dollars and had a retail market value of four hundred dollars. A 1928 Coupe was appraised at one hundred-fifty dollars and carried a retail value of one hundred-ninety-five dollars.

Arguably, the rarest and most distinctive Model A Fords for 1931 are the Gläser Model A Cabriolet and the Allegheny Steel Co. Tudor. Both of these cars are reportedly still in existence.

In 1930, the Model A Ford-Gläser Cabriolet was shipped as chassis number 3957780 from Detroit to Ford of Cologne, Germany. It was sold to Karosseriefirma Gläser of Dresden and, in 1931, a coachbuilder's body of oak and ash frame with steel over it was installed on the chassis. It was one of fifty built by Gläser on the Model A chassis. The car was shipped to the United States in 1965 and profiled in both *Antique Automobile* and *Model "A" News*.

A 1931 Model A Tudor, with body entirely of Allegheny metal, was one of three stainless steel Model As made by the Allegheny Metal Co., according to Fred Carlton, editor of *The Restorer*. Ford kept one and later cut it in half to make a display of it; Allegheny Metal Co. melted down the second one during World War II; the third is still around and, in 1995, was available for around $500,000.

In addition to introducing new styling and marketing the DeLuxe types, Ford's third major sales initiative to fight the Depression was an aggressive campaign to market its expanded commercial and truck lines. Although the production of commercial vehicles and trucks was down by one-third from 1930 to 1931, it was still almost twenty-eight percent of Ford's total production and good enough to best Chevrolet.

On January 28, 1931, Ford's Sales Department sent to Branch managers a list of thirty new commercial and truck body types. Ten of these were scheduled to start production by the end of February, the rest were listed as "production started." The addition of the new body types was made in line with the Ford Motor Co.'s policy of offering a complete line of commercial vehicles to meet all sorts of transportation requirements.

As the year advanced, Ford continued to announce new body styles so that, by November, fifty-eight were listed on the price list of Ford commercial types. Bodies for these units were made by equipment manufacturers such as Briggs, Murray and Budd. Ford was responsible for the production of the completed units.

Included in the new offerings mounted on the Model AA-131 truck chassis were five coal and coke bodies, three garbage bodies, ice body, Standard and DeLuxe police patrols, ambulance, funeral coach, two service cars for garages, stock rack body, express truck with and without canopy top, DeLuxe Delivery and heavy-duty express. On the Model AA-157 wheelbase a stock rack body, panel body, and express body with or without canopy top were available.

Three of the new Fords were mounted on the Model A passenger car chassis. They were the Town Car Delivery, Drop Floor Panel and Special "Natural Wood" Delivery.

Following is a sampling of the commercial and truck models introduced during 1931:

The Type 255-A Special Delivery, also known as the Natural Wood Delivery, had a birch and maple body built by Baker-Raulang Co. of Cleveland, Ohio. It was similar to the Station Wagon, but had two doors and roll-up windows. This unit was adapted for many delivery and other uses. It listed at six hundred-fifteen dollars and had a production of nine hundred-four units (including nineteen assembled in 1930 and forty in 1932).

Natural Wood Panel Delivery Details

DIMENSIONS

Height of inside............... 43 in.
Length of storage space...... 58 in.
Width of doors............... 50 in.
Overall length...............158¾ in.

EQUIPMENT

Here is offered a note of unusual distinction to those requiring a delivery body of smart appearance and appointments. It is built of hard maple and birch, finished in natural wood grain. Its sides and rear are painted. The seats are deeply cushioned and upholstered in cross cobra artificial leather. Bright metal parts are of rustless steel. Glass windows in the front doors can be opened or closed. There are two rear doors. All door handles have locks.

PRICE (F. O. B. DETROIT)....... **$615.00**

Panel "Natural Wood" Delivery, *Ford Fax.*

Ford Garbage Truck.

HIGH LIFT COAL BODY

BODY DIMENSIONS: Capacity of body is 72 cu. ft. It is made of 12-gage high resistance steel, welded at all joints. Sides are flared out at the top. A coal-door, chute, and deflector are built in the tail-gate. A telescope chute 18½ feet long slides under the body when not in use, and is held there by a screw arrangement which tightens it against the floor. Hoists are hydraulic, using two cylinders and a pressure-equalizing pipe. Body may be raised to three positions: straight end dump; rear end 88½″; front 120″; and rear end 99″; front 120″. Swinging partition for split deliveries is optional equipment. The center of gravity of the load is over rear wheels when in high lift position. Spare wheel is carried in left front fender well.

COAL BODY WITH HIGH END-GATES

BODY DIMENSIONS: Capacity 75 cu. ft., for coal, or 120 cu. ft., for coke. The body is made in four pieces: the front end-gate, rear end-gate, and two sections forming sides and bottom which are welded together through the center of the body. The end-gates extend above the sides, and channels are provided in the sides for sideboards. With this equipment, the body provides for deliveries of either coal or coke. Tail-gate chains permit dropping the tail-gate flush with the bottom, forming a platform from which to shovel. There is a coal-chute in the tail-gate, and a trip lever is provided, so that the entire load may be dumped at once. There is a swinging partition for split loads. The hoist is the heavy hydraulic type. Spare wheel is carried in left front fender well.

COMBINATION DUMP, COAL AND COKE BODY

COMBINATION DUMP BODY FOR COAL AND COKE

This unusually serviceable double-purpose unit is made by adding a Top Box of 14 gage steel to the Heavy Hydraulic Hoist Dump Body. The double acting tail-gate is equipped with chains and pin. It differs from the ordinary tail-gate in that it has an 18″ x 8″ coal door and a bagging chute. A swinging partition is mounted midway in the body for split deliveries and batch loads. The control lever is mounted outside. When this lever is turned, the partition is raised slightly. As the locking pins are then free from the holes in the floor, the load trips the partition and passes to the rear. The five sheets of steel which make up the ends, sides, and dividing partition of the top box are strongly joined through corner angles and reinforcing brackets. The lower edges of the top box are flanged to fit the top edges of the dump body at sides and ends. It is here that the two sections are securely bolted. The combined capacity totals 120 cubic feet. Spare wheel is carried in left front fender well.

Length of dump body 84″; width 66″; depth 12⅝″; dumping angle 45°. Length of top of box 84″; width at top 78″, width at bottom 66″, height 23¾″. Wheelbase, 131½″.

COAL BODY WITH HIGH END-GATES

HEAVY HYDRAULIC COAL BODY

BODY DIMENSIONS: Capacity of body is 75 cu. ft. The body is made of 10-gage high resistance steel, electrically welded throughout. It is made in four pieces. The sides have an 8½″ flare. The tail-gate is provided with chains, so that it can be lowered to shoveling position and may be lowered flush with the bottom, forming a platform from which to shovel. The chains are covered with leather to prevent rattling. The hoisting mechanism is the heavy hydraulic type, driven from a power take-off on the transmission. A body of this type is also available with a swinging partition for split deliveries, and with a door and chute in the tail-gate. Spare wheel is carried in left front fender well.

HEAVY HYDRAULIC COAL BODY

Ford Coal Trucks.

Among the more unusual uses of the Natural Wood Delivery were as a radio test car by the U.S. Department of Commerce and as an amplifier car in the Ford truck caravans that were visiting the cities and towns included in the territory of each of the Branches. Ford shipped amplifier equipment to each Branch with instructions to mount it in a Natural Wood Delivery.

To get the most out of the amplifier equipment the Branches were told to have the Natural Wood Delivery lead the caravan between dealer towns. Arriving at the town where the caravan was to stop, the amplifier car was to leave the caravan, proceed down the main street and then around the town to arouse the attention of the inhabitants. After that, the car returned to the caravan and led it into town to the dealer's place of business. All this time, of course, music was being broadcast and announcements made.

Ford encouraged its Branches to use broadcasting units with Ford shows and Ford car and truck caravans because this was an effective way of attracting attention and creating interest in Ford products. Aware, however, that the careless use of these units could be damaging to the company's image, Ford issued strict directives on how they were to be used. These included prohibitions against their use in residential areas after dusk, limiting the broadcasts to short periods so that they did not become a nuisance and remaining silent when passing a hospital or a home where there was an indication someone was dead. The bottom line the company warned, was that "Every precaution should be taken to see that nothing is done which will in any way offend public good taste."

A relatively unknown adaptation of the Natural Wood Delivery was the Travelers' Wagon, which is so unique that it is not even listed on the Ford Commercial Types price list for November 1931 and was not part of the regular line. This was a unit developed primarily for the use of travelers in South American countries. The standard natural wood panel was used with the side panels removed and replaced with a fine mesh insect screen. Long roll-type curtains could be raised or lowered to any desired position, and snap-on curtains were provided for the front doors. A rolled curtain was also installed above the windshield.

This early version of the motorhome was equipped with a folding front seat that formed the foot end of the sleeping berth. The case in back of the driver's seat was arranged to hold two one-quart thermos bottles. A metal wash basin was held in an anti-rattler bracket. The water tank under the roof had a ten-gallon capacity and was filled through a cap on the roof. All the doors could be locked from the inside. Branches were queried as to possible demand for this unit in their territories, but, based on the low production figure of only ten units, it appears that interest was minimal.

The Type 280-A Ford Ambulance with side door listed at $1,800 in January, but was selling for $300 less by the end of November. A total of eighty of these units were assembled in 1931. It was a popular item with the Kansas City (Missouri) Health Department, as the following letter to Ford from the superintendent of the ambulance division indicates:

"Replying to your inquiry as to the service the Ford Ambulances are giving us. Last week we purchased two more, making us (sic) five Ford Ambulances in our fleet of seven. And we expect to get two more in the next sixty days making our fleet 100 percent Ford. Our reasons for doing this are, the initial cost, the maintenance and upkeep along with the appearance and service. In our experience, making from 75 to 100 calls every 24 hours, we find the Ford Ambulance serves our purpose very satisfactory in every way."

In June, Branches were informed that the company was in a position to supply a Combination Ambulance and Funeral Coach similar to the regular Funeral Coach, but including the following additional equipment: window curtain, cot, mattress, tan mohair trim, heater, four rollers on floor, folding seat in rear compartment, front partition and linoleum floor covering.

Model AA Ambulance Details

131½' W. B.

DIMENSIONS

Length of loading space........102 in.
Height of loading space........ 55 in.
Width of loading space......... 54 in.
Width of rear doors............ 46 in.
Height of rear doors........... 49 in.

CONSTRUCTION

The body is of steel, and is covered in the inside with a composition panels finished in black lacquer. The ceiling has an imitation leather headlining. The floor is hard-wood and has metal skid-strips. Either full length double doors will be supplied at the rear, or a 20-inch tail-gate, with double doors above. Body is equipped with a dome light.

PRICE (F. O. B. DETROIT)..... $1800.00

Ambulance, *Ford Fax.*

"We are not planning to place this unit in our line," the company stated, "and we do not wish to carry any in stock, but if you have any customers who prefer this type instead of either our Ambulance or Funeral Coach we can supply as a custom body at a price of $1,950 list." Delivery would be made in about three weeks after the order was received. Just three of these were produced. Could it be that combining these two functions in the same unit just did not set right with prospective customers?

Listed at $1,150 f.o.b. Detroit, the Type 295-A Town Car Delivery was the most expensive and prestigious Model A Ford in the light delivery car line. Ford referred to it as "unquestionably the highest class body that has ever been available in the small car delivery field." Features of the car included slanting windshield, ornamental lights on either side of the body, cowl lamps, fender well for spare wheel and tire, extension mirror and open driver's compartment with canopy top for inclement weather. The body was fitted with veneer interior panels in natural wood finish over a strong wooden frame.

Some Branches attempted to stir up interest in this model by having the monogram or artwork of a pre-selected business lettered on a Town Car Delivery using water color paint. An employee dressed in a chauffeur's uniform would then drive the demonstrator to the business to show it off. Reportedly, there were some positive results from this effort, but, despite a one hundred-sixty dollar list price reduction in late-November, not nearly enough. Only one hundred-ninety-seven of these units were assembled, all but six in 1931.

At least one Town Car Delivery user was highly satisfied. On May 26, 1931, William Gordon of Gordon's Meats and Poultry in Atlantic City, New Jersey, wrote to the Chester (Pennsylvania) Branch as follows: "In reply to your query of recent date regarding our new Town Car Delivery, wish to say that it more than speaks for itself in the satisfaction it has given us so far. As you know, we are purveyors of quality meats, poultry and groceries, catering to a distinctive clientele, and a car of this type, creates exactly the impression that we are trying to con-

A 1931 DeLuxe Delivery - owner Don Maines.

vey to others, that is, 'Quality lends Distinction'. . . . You may use this letter as an authority to express our entire satisfaction in any manner you see fit."

Model A and AA delivery units were the workhorses of the Ford truck offerings for 1930-31. One of these, the drop floor DeLuxe Delivery was particularly unique because the floor actually dropped behind the axle to hubcab level and the panel below the door hinged downward for "walk in" ease of loading. In *Ford Life*, Lorin Sorensen writes that, "No rear bumper was available on these units and that is the prime reason for their early departure from the streets as they damaged easily."

An unusual and, as we shall see, controversial addition to the Ford truck line was the Type 315-A Standrive Delivery, which became available for limited distribution at the end of August 1931. The list price was $1,050 f.o.b. Detroit for the complete unit and $650 for the chassis alone. The body was manufactured by Baker-Raulang Co., and was constructed of a hard maple framework, covered by sheet metal on the sides and canvas on the top. It had a sliding door on each side and no doors in the rear unless these were special ordered in advance for an additional twelve dollars.

The Standrive Delivery had a capacity of forty-two standard size milk cases, and was designed primarily for house-to-house milk delivery although other service companies used them. A General Sales letter to the Dearborn Branch lists the vehicle's standard equipment as right-hand well fender, windshield wiper, rearview mirror and satin finish paint job. Standard colors were the regular commercial colors and white.

Mindful of the delivery man, the company recommended that in the majority of cases when this unit was to be used for milk delivery, a low-speed axle would serve to best advantage, "particularly in northern Branch territories as usually it is the milk delivery man who must make the first tracks through snow." Ford assembly records show a production of four hundred-fifty-eight Standrive bodies through December 1932. Less than half of these (two hundred-eight) were produced in 1931.

Model AA Funeral Coach.

Smart Town Car Delivery

Like the prestige that is given by an exclusive location or recognition for a valued name, there is distinction for these firms in the use of the Ford Town Car Delivery for running errands, making deliveries and carrying merchandise to an appreciative clientele. Many of the appointments and features of this type may be observed in the accompanying photographs, all of users of it.

How Town Car Delivery is serving Rep's, in Springfield, Missouri.

Town Car Delivery in the service of Lucile Lockwood, of Greenwich, Connecticut.

Doctors Byles and Bunker, veterinarians of Los Angeles, have a smart-appearing ambulance.

Used by Bacon, Stickney & Company, for factory deliveries, Albany, New York.

The Dollar Cleaning Company, of Pittsburgh, Pa., uses Town Car Delivery.

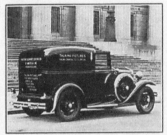

Town Car Delivery used by Photo-tone Equipment Corporation of America, in Indianapolis.

Mme. Julie of Brooklyn, N. Y., advertises its cleaning and dyeing business with Town Car Delivery.

W. J. Kennedy Dairy Company, of Detroit, Mich., uses many Ford units.

The King Del Florists are located in an exclusive section of St. Louis, Mo.

Thomas O'Brien & Sons, of Medford, Mass., is a men's store catering to exclusive trade in Metropolitan Boston.

Town Car Delivery, "Convenience in House-to-House Delivery" supplement to *Ford News*, February 1932.

A drop-floor panel body now brings Ford economy to new commercial fields

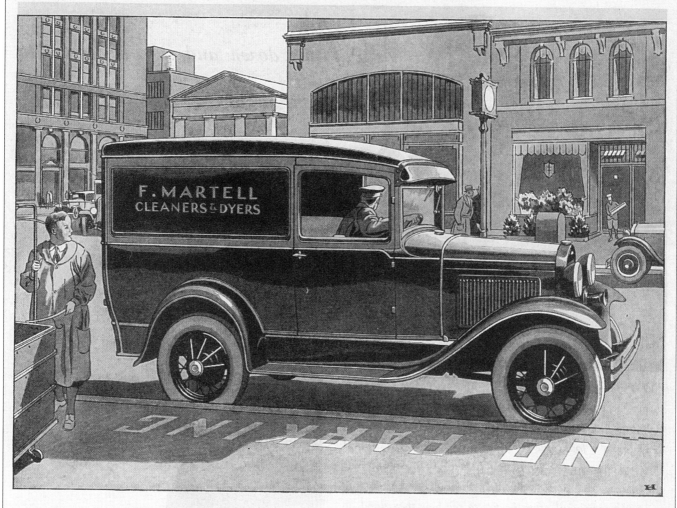

DAILY, throughout the country, Ford commercial units are doing new jobs. A steadily increasing range of body-types, a choice of two different chassis, and a variety of especially designed equipment, all help to adapt the Ford for service in many businesses.

It is possible to select a Ford truck, or a Ford delivery-car, which is exactly suited to almost any work required. Thus, the reliability, excellent performance, and definite economy of Ford units become directly available to a larger number of industries.

For example, a new body is offered on the light-delivery chassis. It is of the drop-floor panel type, a body of special convenience to cleaners and dyers, florists, radio dealers and others whose deliveries require unusual height from floor to roof. It is also used by specialty-salesmen, as it permits easy loading and removal of bulky samples.

In addition to a wide selection of commercial bodies on the Model A chassis, there is a range of types on the 1½-ton truck chassis, with either 131½- or 157-inch wheelbase. With the truck, there is a choice of open or closed cabs, of single or dual rear wheels, and of high or low rear-axle gear-ratios.

Your Ford dealer can show you a commercial unit, and equipment, suited to the requirements of your particular business.

FEATURES
of Ford Commercial Units

Four-cylinder, 40-horse-power engine. Torque-tube drive. Internal-expanding mechanical brakes, all fully enclosed. Sturdy frames, cross-members, axles, and springs. Forty different kinds of specific steels for special purposes. Extensive use of fine steel forgings. More than 20 ball and roller bearings. Precision built. Three different wheelbases. Two different chassis. Triplex shatter-proof windshields for safety. Low first cost. Low cost of operation and maintenance. Reliability and long life.

Complete Commercial Exhibits at New York, Philadelphia, Boston, Detroit, Dallas, and Los Angeles

Ad for a drop floor Panel, *Saturday Evening Post*, **January 24, 1931. This illustration is by the famous automotive artist, Peter Helck.**

A 1931 Standrive Delivery. (Photo courtesy of Henry Ford Museum and Greenfield Village)

A 1931 DeLuxe Pickup -
owner Jim Romanella.

The controversy about the Standrive stems from the remarks of California Ford dealer, John H. Eagal, Sr., who made the following comments about the Standrive in his "Reminiscences." "We did have difficulty with the model they called the Standrive. This unit was built, I think, piecemeal by some experimental employees who had never built anything before, and it was a terrible piece of merchandise. We had to rebuild it entirely and then sell it at a loss. We received three of those models which were the worst merchandise we ever received from the Ford Motor Company."

A unique and relatively rare Pickup was designed by Ford in collaboration with General Electric and introduced on May 1, 1931. General Electric wanted a unit combining exceptionally good appearance with genuine utility, for the use of branches and dealers of the General Electric Refrigerator Division. The result was the Type 66-A DeLuxe Pickup, which listed at six hundred dollars, was painted white and featured DeLuxe passenger car appointments. Standard to the model were fender well, five steel spoke wheels, rustless steel radiator shell, headlights, cowl molding and cowl lamps.

The DeLuxe Pickup featured a body made to match the Standard closed cab and to give the appearance of being an integral unit with it. To this end, the side panels at the front of the body overlapped those of the cab to provide unbroken continuity of line and contour. The box was supplied with a wooden floor with four bonderized steel skid strips to prevent wear and permit easy loading and was topped with chrome-plated brass side rails. Briggs produced two hundred-ninety-seven of these Pickups in 1931, and an additional fifty-five were built through June 1932.

To promote the sale of this unique Pickup, Ford Branches were asked to contact General Electric distributors in their territory and work closely with them in arranging demonstrations of the new unit to all G.E. dealers. In one Branch, the G.E. distributor purchased a DeLuxe Pickup and mounted a bronze replica of the "Millionth General Electric Refrigerator" on it. This unit traveled with the commercial caravan of the Ford Branch and was driven by one of the distributor's best salesmen.

When the caravan arrived in a town, the refrigerator was displayed on the local General Electric dealer's display floor while the truck was exhibited with the other Ford commercial units in a lighted area in the center of the business district. The next day, the G.E. salesman from the distributor helped the local dealer with sales by calling on prospects and displaying the refrigerator and the truck. During these calls dealers would inquire about the truck and a Ford salesman would swing into action. Reportedly, this program was carried out with excellent results.

Production of most body types, passenger and commercial, did not normally begin simultaneously throughout the thirty-five domestic assembly plants. The new Combination Grain and Stock Bodies for the 131 and 157 Model AA chassis, for example, were available at Dearborn in July, but in Buffalo not until August. They were shipped

Two 1931 Model AA trucks with stock racks. Right is a ten-wheeler with a tag-axle extension - owner Jim Eckel.

THE DELUXE PICKUP

on

The Ford Light Commercial Chassis

A DISTINCTIVE UNIT TO SERVE MANY BUSINESSES

THE DELUXE PICKUP CAR

Dimensions of loading space are: Length, 58¼ inches; Width at floor, 41½ inches; Depth, 22½ inches; Width of rear opening, 41½ inches.

Ford brochure for the DeLuxe Pickup.

from the body company completely painted and striped, and listed at one hundred-fifty dollars for the AA-131 and one hundred-seventy dollars for the AA-157.

General letter #35 from the Buffalo Branch describes this unit as follows: "These bodies are extra wide, 84 inches, are of hardwood construction throughout with exceptionally heavy flooring and the flare and side boards are rigidly supported by malleable iron brackets. Extension grain sides are provided making the body 26 inches deep. There is a hinged door in the tail gate. The sliding tail gate may be completely removed or fixed at any desired height. Stock rack fits into the same pockets as extension grain sides. Stock rack tail gate is painted white for visibility at night."

THE FORD ICE BODY

BODY DIMENSIONS: The Ice Body is designed for hard work and long service, day after day. The sides are 23½″ high and are constructed of steel panels over wood. The under-body is steel. The double-floor type of construction is used. The loading floor is of oak, and is equipped with 4″ oak skid-bars at the sides and in front, to prevent ice from pounding against the sides. The bottom floor is of yellow pine, and is water-sealed at all joints. In the front of this floor, there is a hole at either side for drainage. An 8″ tail-gate is provided as standard, while a full-height tail-gate is optional. Special equipment available at additional cost for this unit includes sign panels for sides of body, an ice scale bar and rear step. Standard equipment includes a canvas cover over the entire body. The cab may be either open or closed, and is equipped with a Triplex shatterproof windshield.

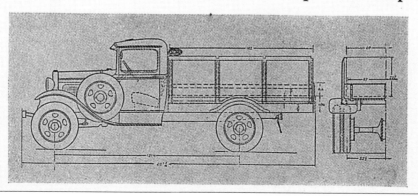

Ford Ice Truck.

Looking for more Profits?

Sell Commercial Jobs In *Fleets*, Instead Of One By One . . . . . . !

Schools and Bus lines need new Buses . . . but they must be low in price, economical to operate and easy to maintain.

. . . that's where the Model AA Ford chassis equipped with a 14 passenger body by Eckland comes in . . . it meets these rigid requirements like nothing else under the sun designed to deliver the same comfortable, low-cost transportation!

Ford Dealers are awakening to the fact that fleet business is easy to get if gone after in the proper way . . . and the proper way is to sell chassis equipped with comfortable, good-looking, long-enduring bodies by Eckland.

Free photographs, complete specifications and prices will be supplied on request.

READ THESE SPECIFICATIONS

1. Same sturdy construction as in large inter-state bus bodies, inside and out.
2. Door control operated from driver's seat.
3. One-piece windshield equipped with automatic wiper.
4. All side windows raise and lower.
5. Longitudinal or cross seats upholstered in Spanish leather over heavy duty springs.
6. Single unit Tropic-Aire hot water heater.
7. Bumper, tire rack, grab handles, dome lights, marker lights, rear danger lights and illuminated destination sign included.

SEND TODAY FOR COMPLETE SPECIFICATIONS, PHOTOGRAPHS AND PRICES

ECKLAND BROS. COMPANY
BUILDERS OF BETTER BUS BODIES SINCE THE INDUSTRY FIRST BEGAN
LYNDALE AT 28TH ST. SO. **MINNEAPOLIS, MINN.**

Advertising bus body for AA truck chassis, *Ford Dealer and Service Field*, July 1931.

A June 27, 1931, publicity release from Dearborn to Ford Branches and individual dealers reveals a Ford coup in obtaining a 1,500 unit order for the U.S. Postal Service. "The United States Post Office Department today," the release states, "placed an order with the Washington Branch of the Ford Motor Company for 1,500 motor truck chassis, of which 500 will be 3/4 ton carrying capacity and 1,000 of 1-1/2 tons carrying capacity.

"The purchase of the motor equipment was the largest made by a government department since the war. . . . The purchase marked another step in the Department's program of building up its fleet of several thousand trucks and also to replace some of the surplus trucks turned over to the Post Office Department by the Army at the close of the war.

"Deliveries are to start immediately and continue as rapidly as the bodies contracted for are ready for installation. The completed trucks will then be distributed to some 60 cities throughout the United States. The order was placed with the Ford company after an exhaustive test conducted by the Department with the cooperation of The Bureau of Standards. . . ."

Production on the Ford ice truck with tarpaulin began in February 1931, and reached a total of five hundred-thirteen units by the end of April 1932. Only one of these was assembled outside the United States and that at Buenos Aires. Built on the AA-131 chassis, the ice truck listed at Detroit for seven hundred-thirty-five dollars. Although designed and built primarily for hauling ice, its use was not restricted to ice alone. Really an open express body, this unit could easily be adapted to carrying wood, coal, grain, livestock, meat and other products.

According to a report from one of the Ford Branches, a representative driving an ice truck left the Branch to go to a city fifty miles away to demonstrate the unit to ice dealers. Along the way he noticed an ice retailer using a Model TT truck. He stopped, talked to the man and, finding that he had a prospect, contacted the local dealer and arranged for an appraisal. Within twenty-four hours the dealer sold an ice truck. This was cited by Ford's General Sales Department, as a good example of what could be done by alert and determined company representatives. The man in question saw an opportunity in the user of an ice truck whose equipment did not appear to be of the best, and made a sale possible.

A definite list price of $1,800 was established for the DeLuxe Passenger Bus on December 4, 1931. Standard equipment included: laminated glass throughout, three outside guard rails for side and rear windows, windshield wiper, rearview mirror, pillar mirrors, floor mat, polished finish, large generator, two batteries connected in parallel and a long muffler. This price included supplying 20 x 6.50 tires for dual rear wheels, but there was an extra twenty-five dollar charge for dual rear wheel equipment.

Ford marketed its trucks and commercial cars heavily and insisted that body companies live up to their agreed production schedules. Advertising folders for each model were prepared well in advance and shipped to Branches for distribution to dealers. The company also revised and updated its *New Ford Truck Book*. As an incentive to commercial concerns, Ford offered to paint passenger cars purchased by them for business use, in any combination of forty-six present or previous passenger or commercial car standard colors as shown on a list, at no additional charge.

In addition to adding new body types to its Model A and AA lines in 1931, the Ford Motor Co. also made many changes and improvements. For example, DeAngelis, Francis and Henry tell us that the first all-steel body (for a closed cab commercial vehicle) in automo-

A 1931 Fire Truck - owner Phil Giltner.

bile history was introduced in August 1931. Anticipating that some operators might think metal decks too hot, tests were run over a considerable period during hot weather. These showed that the temperature inside the metal cab was only four degrees above the one equipped with artificial leather when standing. No difference was shown when the units were moving.

A sampling of other changes includes a larger all-steel box for the Pickup, a canopy top to fit the box, improved front seat construction for the various coupe bodies as well as the Tudor and Town Sedans, heavy-duty truck tires (32 x 7.00 10-ply) for those who desired large capacity single wheel equipment on trucks and adapter plates to allow older AA trucks to use dual wheels.

Frames for the AA-131 wheelbase truck shipped after April 6 were approximately ten inches longer than the frame then in use, but the frames for use with dump bodies were supplied eleven-and-one-half inches shorter than the new standard frame length. Adjustable rear windows for Coupes, which lowered about two-thirds the width of the window, were placed in production in July. They were standard on the DeLuxe and the Standard Coupe with rumble seat. They could also be installed on the Standard Coupe without rumble seat, at an extra charge of five dollars list.

Ford trucks maintained their popularity, in part, because they were versatile and durable. "I've seen other trucks wear out in one season," said Clarence Mastellar of Sioux City, Iowa, adding that the Ford "stands the gaff." In 1928, Mastellar went into business hauling coal with his truck. He was so pleased with its performance that after 23,000 miles with two seasons of coal hauling and one summer of highway paving, he traded the truck in August 1930 for the new four-speed model. "I've seen many a truck of a different make worn out by only one season of paving work," he declared, "but the Ford stood it and the coal hauling for two winters besides." The cost of fuel was also in line. The truck traveled approximately five hundred miles a week using one quart of oil and less than fifty gallons of gasoline.

Speaking of gas mileage and operating costs, it appears that a major initiative by the company in 1931, as in previous years, was to prove the economy of the Model A and AA and disprove any competitive misstatements regarding excessive gas consumption. Service Letter #55, for example, sent to dealers by the Dearborn

Comparison Chart—Model A A Ford and One-Ton Trucks

Capacity	Chassis Price	Chassis Weight	Wheel-base	Gear Ratio	Rear Axle	Make and Model	Tires		Piston Displacement	Tax Horse-Power	Brake Horse-Power	Engine Speed
							Front	Rear				
1½	$510	2,723	131½	5.14	¾	Ford AA	6.00x20	32x6.00	200.5	24.0	40	2,200
1	$995	3,200	132	5.59	½	Brockway 60	30x5	30x5	214.7	27.3	61	3,000
1	$695	3,300	135	Opt.	½	Diamond T 216	6.50x20	6.50x20	224.7	27.3	56	2,400
1	$810	2,470	133	5.6	½	Dodge 4-Cyl.	30x5	30x5	175.4	21.	45	2,800
1	$675	2,670	130	5.83	½	G.M.C. T-15	7.00x20	7.00x20	200.3	26.3	58	3,000
1	$2500		138	4.86	½	Mack BL	6.00x20	D6.00x20	248.9	25.4	58	2,600
1	$1095	3,200	129	5.2	½	Reo DF Tonner	6.00x20	32x6	268.3	27.3	85	3,200
1¼	$1245	3,105	146	5.1	½	Studebaker 40	30x5	32x6	221.0	27.3	70	3,200
1	$1545	3,402	133	4.73	½	White 15-B	30x5	30x5	226.4	22.5	31	1,600

Comparison Chart - Model AA Ford and One-Ton Trucks, *Ford Dealer and Service Field,* **July 1931.**

South Hill Movers' 1931 Model AA truck.

Branch on March 6, 1931, stated, "Every opportunity to prove Model A and AA gas economy should be welcomed by the dealer, as proved economical fuel consumption has an important bearing on car and truck sales." And, dealers were reminded frequently to keep their mileage tester in use in demonstrations as well as to handle service complaints.

During 1931, a variety of gas tests, economy races and cost statements were used to get the point of Model A's superior fuel economy and low operating costs to the public. In one instance, a Utica, Michigan, dealer tested the gas mileage of forty-eight Model A Fords. The highest was 34 miles per gallon, the lowest 23 and the average was 26.1. The newest car had just 1,579 miles on the odometer while the highest mileage shown was 42,318. Still another example appeared in the *Kenya Weekly News* advertising the results of a Ford fuel economy race held at Nakuru, Kenya Colony in Africa. The best performance there was turned in by a Model A Roadster driven by a woman, which averaged over fifty-five miles per gallon.

On February 2, 1930, the U.S. Department of Commerce purchased a new Model A Tudor Sedan in

ROBAL INN
SAN PEDRO, CAL.

Thursday

Dear George:

I thought you might be interested in the dope on our trip because I think it sounds pretty good for the new Ford. In the first place I drove every foot of the way myself. We left Rockford Saturday morning and were in San Pedro, California, Wednesday at five o'clock p. m.

I kept track of the mileage, gasoline, etc., and the following figures are true:

First Day—Joplin, Missouri	607 Miles
Second Day—Mineral Mills, Texas	509 Miles
Third Day—El Paso, Texas	576 Miles
Fourth Day—Phoenix, Arizona	460 Miles
Fifth Day—San Pedro, California	492 Miles
Total Mileage	2654 Miles
Driving Time	67 Hours
Hourly Average	39.54 Miles
Total Gasoline Consumed	154 Gallons
Miles per Gallon	17.4 Miles

I might also say that we crossed the mountains in high gear and it was not necessary to run in second at all. The trip of course was hard, due to the time we made, but it would have been in any car.

Believe me a trip like this sells you more and more on the Ford.

Best regards to Dick and all the boys. "BUD" HUGHES.

"Another Ford Economy Record," *Ford Dealer and Service Field,* **May 1931.**

Atlanta, Georgia. It was driven 37,436 miles and then sold at El Paso, Texas, on April 23, 1931. The total operating cost for this car (gas, oil, repairs, tires, storage and miscellaneous) was $719.50. The original cost was $591.72 and the car was resold for $200, resulting in a gross expense of $1,111.22. The operating cost per mile was .0192 cent; the depreciation cost per mile was .0105 cent for a total gross expense per mile of .0297 cent. Although Ford would have loved to use these figures for advertising purposes, it was not allowed to do so but was instead given permission to pass the figures along to Ford dealers.

Beauty of line, durability, low price and low operating costs not withstanding, the 1931 Model A Ford was not problem free. In early February, dealers were notified that hubcaps used during 1930 and the early part of 1931 were of light material that was easily dented and, therefore, presented a poor appearance. These were to be replaced free of charge until April 10 with an improved version that was reinforced on the inside.

Another annoying problem was rain entering around the windshield on Town Sedans and Victorias and, later, the slanting windshield sedans. A liberal use of "Dum-dum" sealer was recommended to solve this complaint. Beginning in February, dealers were instructed to replace gratis on cars built since January 1, 1930, any windshield glass that was defective due to open spots or bubbles.

Among a variety of other problems were cracked or broken steel pillars used with Canopy Express models, complaints from fleet owners of excessive oil consumption, and problems with the cowl tank because steering column supports were breaking when the car was regularly used over rough roads.

One problem, not of the company's making, which was brought to the attention of dealers in 1930 continued to be a problem in 1931. This was the theft of Model A cars by thieves who were able to secure duplicate keys or key numbers from dealers. Dealers were advised to remind their employees of the company policy on this matter:

"Do not sell keys to strangers without proper identification or proof of ownership of the car. If the party making application of the key is not known by you, he should not object to showing the certificate of registration or some such identification.

A 1931 slant window Town Sedan - owner Dick White.

"Ford cars are equipped with locks for the owner's protection. Don't defeat this protection by careless selling of keys.

"Duplicate keys or key cutting machines should be accessible only to the dealer or a responsible employee, who fully realizes the importance of caution being exercised in the sale of these keys."

As 1931 moved along, it became obvious to even the most optimistic that depressed conditions were going to be around for a while. Industry-wide, production was down to its lowest level since 1921, and the industry as a whole (including Ford) was working at about one-third capacity. Total passenger car and truck registrations, which had gone up steadily every year since 1895, peaked in 1930, and then fell back for three straight years until they slowly began to climb again in 1934.

Naturally, the impact of this fell most heavily on the workers. At Ford, many were laid off or worked only three days a week. Higher paid workers often found themselves shifted to lower paying jobs in other departments. As cited by Sward, the *New York Times* reported this in its October 30, 1931, edition. "For some time past," stated the *Times*, the "Ford Motor Company has been laying off men in one department and rehiring them in another at lower pay." Work farmed out to outside suppliers was performed at sweatshop wages, as low as 12-1/2 cents an hour at Briggs, according to Robert Lacey (*Ford The Men and the Machine*).

During the winter of 1931, Detroit's relief rolls were adding three hundred families a day, at least half of which had never before sought welfare help of any kind. In 1931, an estimated fifteen percent of the families on Detroit's relief rolls were former Ford workers.

As mentioned in the previous chapter, Ford did manage some efforts to help alleviate the situation for its workers, but what was done was never enough. One of the more publicized Ford efforts occurred in 1931 when Ford offered to help some five hundred families who lived in Inkster, Dearborn's adjacent black community. Almost overnight streets were paved, homes were repaired, sewers installed and electricity provided. Ford also established a commissary, provided decent clothing and paid back bills.

Finally, and much criticized, was Ford's job offer to adult males who lived in Inkster. They would be hired at four dollars a day, but three dollars would be deducted to pay for the improvements in the community. According to David Lewis, "Ford pumped $884,035.37 into the community between 1931 and 1935." Payroll deductions and voluntary payments reimbursed the company all except $96,000 of this amount.

Another idea was initiated at the Norfolk Branch and then adopted by other Branches. Under the plan, workers were given the opportunity to assist dealers in selling cars during the days they were not regularly employed. From September 2, 1931, through the middle of October, forty-four new cars and thirty-three used cars were sold in the metropolitan area of Norfolk by plant employees.

The plan worked as follows. All sales were handled by the dealer whose place of business was nearest to the purchaser's home. The employee would recommend a potential customer and then be involved in the negotiations for the sale. For every new car or truck sale developed by the Ford employee, he received twelve dollars from the dealer making delivery of this unit, and, in addition, five gallons of gasoline. On used cars sold at a price over fifty dollars, the employee received from the dealer making delivery $7.50 plus five gallons of gasoline. This helped dealers sell cars but reduced their profit margin. Salesmen involved in the negotiation continued to receive full compensation thus assuring their cooperation in this plan.

Any employee who sold a car, such as this 1931 Town Sedan, could earn twelve dollars from the dealer. Car is in original condition today - owner Scott McGrew.

A 1931 DeLuxe Fordor for sale at the Dunkirk flea market in 1989.

Clara and Henry Ford and Ford executives received touching letters from Ford workers and families hoping desperately to be given work. Two of these letters, each signed with a worker's name and his badge number, were written in 1931 and are contained in the files of the Henry Ford Research Center. They are from a Polish worker's wife to Ernest Liebold who handled most Ford business other than that of the Ford Motor Co., and from a hospitalized worker to Clara Ford.

The worker's wife begs Liebold to "answer a very poor woman's plea." Her husband has been laid off for nine months and she entreats Liebold to have pity on them and try to do something. "If you can't reinstate him," she writes, "let me work in his place. We are in such a desperate position that God alone can see."

Writing from his hospital bed and without work for seven months, a worker asks Clara Ford to find a job at the factory for his wife until he can get back on his feet. "I know the wife would be glad to work at anything they put her to," he writes, "she has such a hard time of it now." He also complains to Mrs. Ford about one of his two boys who had obtained jobs through Raymond Dahlinger. "When Arthur drew several pays, he left home as he felt he did not want to turn in some money toward support of the house. I was very disappointed in him."

Finally, the company had to bow to the inevitable. On October 1, 1931, the seven dollar day was quietly reduced to six dollars and the hiring-in rate for common labor was set at fifty cents an hour. Ford, which had paid out $181,500,000 to Rouge wage-earners alone in 1929, paid less than half of that or $76,700,000 in 1931. That figure would shrink to $32,500,000 in 1933.

In his "Reminiscences," Theodore Mallon says that "Attempts were made to equalize the work during the Depression period, but only after the force was cut way down." For example, instead of hiring one man for a week two would be hired, one for two days and the other for three. This, of course, led to jealousy and suspicion among workers. "I remember very well," writes worker Ernest Grimshaw, "certain individuals who were friends of the foreman worked every week; other fellows wouldn't get any work at all" (Nevins and Hill).

The company's policy of giving as many men as possible at least some work is explained in a September 1932 letter from Edsel Ford, responding to an inquiry from the president of Von Platen-Fox Co. in Iron Mountain, Michigan. "If you can tell me how we can keep our men employed every day in the week," Ford wrote, "I would be very glad to know about it. We have had a larger number of employees on our payroll due to large volume in the past, and feel that the most equitable way of handling the present situation is to give the largest possible number of employees work for a limited time rather than a very few full time."

At the beginning of 1931, there were 9,450 Ford agencies of which 2,400 were new dealers authorized during 1930. This was an example of the so-called "crossroads policy" that multiplied dealerships to increase pressure on existing agencies.

Along with directing his sales force, service department and office staff, selling cars, meeting customers, attending Branch meetings, etc., the average dealer also had to devote a significant amount of time to keeping up with mundane things found daily in his mailbox, such as information, instructions and requests from the Branch.

In 1931, for example, dealers were strictly enjoined to keep the Branch informed of any accidents or fires involving the Model A in their territory, which might be attributed to defective parts. They were to investigate these claims and keep the Branch informed. Just another thing to do.

On another occasion dealers received a letter informing them of the labor charges for work done on cars damaged in transportation by railroad. Work done on Ford bodies including refinishing and repairing defective body parts, bumping out dents, inserting felt and recrimping, spot welding, tightening screws, repairing rivets, removing bolts from the wrong side and removing rust caused by water (or other damage) from leaky roofs of railroad cars was to be charged at $1.45 per hour. All of this to be duly noted, filed and the proper people informed.

Dealers were also instructed to contact bakers and meat packers, tell them that Ford was considering adding bodies specifically for their line of work, and then get from them a sketch of the body they thought would be best adapted to their needs. This information then had to be sent to the Branch.

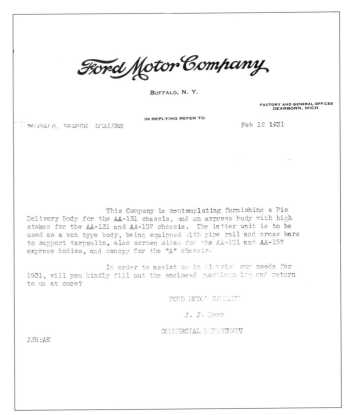

Typical letter received by a Ford dealer in 1931.

Discount Increase Hailed With Delight

The Ford Motor Company Receives Many Wires Expressing Appreciation

ONE of the most welcome messages ever received by Ford dealers was the news released on February 6 to the affect that a flat discount plan of 22 per cent had been adopted.

The wide beneficial effect was immediate. At once letters and wires began to pour into Ford branches and Dearborn in which dealers expressed their appreciation and satisfaction.

In many cases these expressions included the assurance from the dealers that the discount increase would be reflected in promptly increasing sales.

Everywhere in the dealer field was a live and optimistic reaction and a feeling that the new plan allowed more aggressive sales work but also was a more reasonable reward for work done.

The money significance of the discount increase may best be realized through considering the fact that an average dealer, selling 142 cars and trucks per year, will gross $16,401 instead of $13,794, this considering the average car to sell for $525.

In the case of the dealer selling only twenty-five units a year there still is a gross increase of over $500, while with a dealer selling as high as a thousand cars there is a margin of nearly $9000.

This pleasing differential is enough in each case to make "all the difference in the world," as one dealer said, in the administration of the dealer's business. It allows him to work with more freedom and confidence and gives him the assurance of profit, with the improved psychological result.

A large number of dealers in various parts of the country promptly wired or wrote to this magazine expressing their spirit in this welcome new Ford plan. All revealed the thought that better business would result and we share this belief.

We quote from some expressions received, the first three dealers quoted preferring to remain anonymous.

What Dealers Say

"Great! And it comes when very much needed. It would have been good judgment to let us have this 'break' earlier, but it is fully appreciated now."—*Nebraska Dealer.*

⬥——⬥

"Now that I know that I can make some real money, I feel more like going after it. I am very well satisfied."—*North Dakota Dealer.*

⬥——⬥

"After long years of experience with Ford I was confident that we would be treated right. This is my idea of right treatment. Sales will jump."—*New England Dealer.*

"Discount Increase Hailed With Delight," *Ford Dealer and Service Field,* **March 1931.**

In addition to running their own dealerships, competing with each other and scrambling for sales in a tight market, dealers also had to contend with a discount policy that continued to irritate many of them, especially those in small centers and country locations. In this case, help arrived in the form of a message from William C. Cowling, the new Ford Sales Manager, that a flat discount plan of twenty-two percent was adopted effective February 6, 1931. "This action," said Edsel Ford, "should reassure our dealers that we want all dealers both large and small to receive adequate returns from their business when conducted with sound merchandising practice" (Nevins and Hill). (Note: The twenty-two percent discount was evidently in effect at the Rouge as early as November 10, 1931.)

It was one of the most welcome messages ever received by Ford dealers. The money significance of this meant that an average dealer, selling one hundred-forty-two cars and trucks per year, would gross $16,401 instead of $13,794, considering that the average car sold for five hundred-twenty-five dollars. In the case of a dealer selling only twenty-five units a year, there was still a gross increase of over five hundred dollars, while a dealer selling 1,000 cars could expect an increase of nearly $9,000.

Letters and wires expressing appreciation and satisfaction poured into Branch offices and Dearborn from around the country. One dealer wrote that the change had come just in time. He had lost about $4,000 in 1930 in spite of having sold five hundred new cars and seven hundred used cars, and was "without hope" for 1931 (Nevins and Hill).

A large number of dealers wrote to *Ford Dealer & Service Field* expressing their pleasure with this welcome news. "Now that I know that I can make some real money, I feel more like going after it. I am very well satisfied," wrote a North Dakota dealer. "It is the writer's opinion," said a dealer from Ogden, Utah, "that the new discount. . .is the best piece of news we have received since the announcement of the new Model A car."

And, from Leominster, Massachusetts, came this testimonial: "We believe that the return to the 22 percent discount will be the means of a great many of the dealers returning to the profit column rather than stay in the red column where many of them have been for the past six months. With the Ford dealer rendering better service than any other dealership, he should be as well paid."

In October, further discounts ranging from twenty dollars for the DeLuxe Roadster to one hundred-fifty dollars for the Town Car Delivery were authorized on seven of the higher-priced types. The company also revised its discount policies on Model A and AA parts. General letter #18 from the Service Department dated October 14, 1931, instructed dealers to grant a discount to garages, insurance companies and dealers in other makes of automobiles. Items billed to the dealer at forty percent discount, were to be billed to any of the above mentioned people at twenty-five percent off list price on

purchases of fifty dollars or more, and twenty percent on smaller purchases.

This policy was made in order to create a better feeling among the garages and secure additional goodwill for Ford products. Dealers were cautioned that garages that operated with no thought of cleanliness or precision work, and did not have competent mechanics, were not eligible for the discount.

General letter #18 also noted that National, State or Limited Fleet Owners would continue with their present discount of twenty-five percent on the forty percent items, and ten percent on the twenty-five percent items, if the parts were installed in the dealer's shop or the fleet owner garages. Model T and TT parts still being sold by the company and its dealers retained their discount of twenty-five percent on the forty percent items and ten percent on the twenty-five percent items.

In addition to raising the discount, introducing DeLuxe models to diversify the body line and greatly expanding the development of truck bodies to fit a wide variety of purposes, the company also initiated a number of sales schemes during 1931 to help Branches and dealers move cars and trucks. These included: sales contests, monthly sales campaigns, ads in newspapers and magazines, larger shows in the metropolitan centers and Branch cities, smaller displays at local and regional shows, Ford Days, traveling circuses under the Ford "Big Top," commercial caravans and displays at national conventions, such as those at the Dairy Industries Exposition in Atlantic City, and the American Road Builders' Association in Detroit.

The sales drive for 1931 kicked off in January with a door-to-door canvass in every district in the United States. Dealers were to visit every home, hiring additional representatives if needed. The intent was to stimulate retail business and line up a large number of future orders. In the Buffalo region, a pre-January trial of this method showed some success. One dealer in a small community of one hundred-eighty people, secured eighteen orders over a period of three weeks from these visits.

In April, a nationwide sales campaign was initiated. Each of the three hundred-fifty sales zones throughout the country was given a definite quota. Branches were instructed to hold special sales meetings and begin a four-piece direct mail campaign to prospects through their dealers. Salesmen in larger population areas were given a quota of one family per night to bring to the showroom.

At the end of the month, the quota for April of 100,000 car and truck retail sales was exceeded by more than 9,000 units, prompting Ford to hold a similar campaign in May with a 125,000 quota. Branch standings at the end of April showed Atlanta in first place and the Pittsburgh Branch in last place (thirty-fifth). Buffalo, the parent Branch of our local dealers D.D. Norton and Nortz & Virkler, placed eighth. Interestingly, the Dearborn Branch was thirty-third.

More than 73,000 miles in a New Ford

THE substantial worth of the new Ford is reflected in its good performance, economy and reliability. Its stamina and endurance are particularly apparent in sections where bad roads and severe weather put a heavy extra burden on the automobile.

In less than a year a new Ford Tudor Sedan was driven more than seventy-three thousand miles over a difficult route. The operating cost per mile was very low and practically the only expense for repairs was for new piston rings and a new bearing for the generator.

The car carried an average load of 1200 pounds of mail and was driven 250 miles daily. "The Ford has never failed to go when I was ready," writes one of the three mail carriers operating the car. "The starter did the trick last winter even at 34 degrees below zero. The gas runs about 20 miles per gallon. At times I pull a trailer whenever I have a bulky load."

Many other Ford owners report the same satisfactory performance. Every part has been made to endure — to serve you faithfully and well for many thousands of miles.

THE NEW FORD TUDOR SEDAN

LOW PRICES OF FORD CARS

$430 to $630

Typical ad used by Ford to help dealers sell cars in 1931, "More Than 73,000 Miles in a New Ford," March 12, 1931, issue of *The Express*, Lititz, Pennsylvania.

Under the Ford Big Top

WITH the advent of Spring, the traveling circuses under the Ford "big top" have turned northward from their sojourn in the far South and with the exception of one will soon be following the robins to the states north of the Mason and Dixon line. The remaining show will stay in Mexico until late in June when it also will return to the North.

One of the circuses, after a busy itinerary in Louisiana, has crossed to the island of Cuba where it is now exhibiting.

FORD SHOW
ADMISSION FREE

Entrance to Ford Show.

Right—The enlarged photographs on the columns are a source of much interest on the part of visitors.

During the winter months, the Ford road shows have been exhibiting in the far South.

"Under the Ford Big Top," *Ford News*, **April 1931.**

When one of the Ford shows opened in Brenham, Texas, a drive of 101 hours came to an end in front of the tent. The endurance run was staged by the dealer and drew a large crowd.

"Under the Ford Big Top," *Ford News*, **April 1931.**

To stimulate local dealer shows a five-page outline of the method for conducting them was sent to all dealers in February. These shows were intended principally for small dealers in the rural sections where a tent show might not stop. Branch representatives helped dealers set up the shows, providing parts boards, sample handout and letter, literature, a sound motion picture outfit, as well as advice and support. Dealers were expected to get out invitations or hand-outs. Newspaper ads were supplied and paid for by the company.

One such show was held in Alma, Michigan, a community with a population at that time of 6,700. The dealer held a two-day show exhibiting nine Ford passenger cars, three Ford commercial units and a Lincoln automobile. Total attendance for the two days was 1,833, names of prospects secured totaled two hundred-twenty-five, and three sales were made. The dealer spent eighty-four dollars in putting on this show.

In some areas dealers of several adjoining towns combined to stage a display. In many places, showings were given of the sound motion picture presenting a trip through the Rouge plant, or that depicting "Hidden Qualities" of the Model A. A "flying squadron" of fifteen Ford cars and trucks, including a body in white, led parades in small towns, followed by a display in the showrooms of the local dealer.

The Ford tent shows inaugurated in 1930, remained an important part of Ford's promotional activities throughout much of 1931. These big traveling circuses with their complete display of the Ford line and their motion pictures averaged showings in two towns a week. By the end of February 1931, nearly two million persons had visited one of the six shows. During the year, both Cuba and Mexico were visited by a traveling road show.

"Ford Day" programs were successfully carried out in many communities throughout the country. They were organized by the local Ford dealer working in conjunction with the community newspaper and the merchant's association and its members. An eleven page instruction booklet sent to dealers by the company provided ideas for organizing the day and stressed that the purpose of the day was to help the entire community. Needless to say, since the day largely focused on the Ford line, the Ford dealer also benefited greatly.

A typical "Ford Day" began with a parade made up of new cars and trucks and commercial units owned by participating merchants. The instructions suggested that one of the DeLuxe cars, either a Phaeton or a Roadster, should lead the parade and be "preferably driven by some prominent young woman." Following that there were showings of Ford films and, when appropriate, the unveiling of a new body type not yet introduced in the

community. Prize drawings, special bargains by local merchants, a gasoline mileage contest, an essay contest for school children and demonstrations of Ford cars and trucks were also included.

A successful "Ford Day" took place in Chickasha, Oklahoma, a town of 14,099 population. An estimated 15,000 to 20,000 persons checked in at the Ford dealer's place to see the car and truck display and enjoy the motion picture. All the merchants in the town participated. They gave out 200,000 tickets on purchases of one dollar or more merchandise, entitling the holder to chances on the Tudor Sedan that was given away later in the day. This meant that the merchants sold about $200,000 worth of goods on that day. The local Ford dealer sold six cars and obtained sufficient good live prospects to keep his sales force busy for some weeks to come.

Ford Days were also run in larger communities. In Cincinnati, Ohio, twenty-four dealers participated in a day held at Coney Island, a local amusement park located on the Ohio River, about ten miles east of the heart of the city. They gave away about one hundred substantial prizes including a Model A car.

Folks living in Galveston, Texas, were treated to a two-day "Ford Frolic" at Galveston Beach, which drew throngs estimated at 75,000. Two Ford cars, one each day, were given away as attendance prizes. Ford cars representing every year since 1903, one for each year, traveled in the parade under their own power. The 1931 line of Ford cars and trucks formed another part of the parade.

So many body types were added to the Ford commercial line during 1930 and 1931, that it was virtually impossible for a single dealer to display the complete line to prospective users. During the spring of 1931, Ford Branches began to send out commercial caravans to visit small towns, rural areas and county fairs in order to show the different body types to prospective purchasers. By May, each Branch had at least one caravan on the road.

During the time spent at a location, demonstrations were made under actual operating conditions. For example, the Ambulance would be stationed at a first aid depot if there was one, Funeral Coaches were offered for demonstration to local undertakers, stock bodies were used for hauling stock, ice bodies were used to bring in loads of ice, etc. The Ford units featured the many different standard colors, which were optional for the purchaser. In some cases a single unit was painted with all the colors on it, so that people could easily compare the colors available.

On Saturday morning, May 9, 1931, Goodland, Texas (population 3,425), was abuzz with activity as more than 1,000 people gathered to see the Ford Commercial Caravan sponsored by the Thompson Motor Co. The caravan included the new DeLuxe passenger body styles as well as providing a first look at new commercial bodies. (See *The Restorer*, November/December 1991.)

A Ford Motor Co. report from all Branches on the Commercial Caravans through May 16, 1931, shows that the thirty-eight caravans then on the road had generated

Model AA Packers Express Truck was an important component in a Commercial Truck Caravan. (Photo courtesy of Henry Ford Museum and Greenfield Village)

A 1931 Model AA Panel Delivery truck for Coke.

A 1931 Model AA truck with closed cab and non-Ford body equipped for electric company work.

32,362 demonstrations and 2,234 sales. Caravan #1 from Chicago led in sales with one hundred-forty-four. The Chester Branch was highest in demonstrations with 2,673, which translated to one hundred-thirty-four retail sales.

Throughout 1931, Ford dealers struggled to find ways to compensate for their diminishing retail sales of new Model A cars and AA trucks and used vehicles and keep their employees working. Consequently, they concentrated even more than normal on selling Lincolns, tractors, accessories, parts for both the Model A and Model T, engines, batteries and miscellaneous items such as ammonium sulfate and charcoal. They also did what they could to hang on to or increase their fleet sales and service and to improve their service departments.

Nortz & Virkler in Lowville, New York, started 1931 with an inventory of eleven Model A units, including one that was shipped to the dealer in May 1930. The dealership received thirteen more by the end of January, including six Pickups and one AA-131 closed cab Stake Rack truck. Sales were slow, however, averaging six or less per month for the first four months. Concentrating on parts, service, used cars and tractors was obviously most important to the life of this small town dealer.

During the year this dealership also received a telegram from General Sales Manager, J.R. Davis, carrying congratulations upon the completion of twenty-five years as a Ford dealer. "We hope this connection with

the Ford Motor Company," Davis said, "has been pleasant and profitable to you and that you may have many more years of success selling Ford products." As it turns out, Davis' wish is a prophecy fulfilled. At the dawn of the 21st century, Nortz & Virkler is still going strong in the same location where it sold Model A Fords.

Trying to be as helpful as possible, the Ford Branches sent dealers ideas on products they could sell to supplement their income. For example, in May, dealers received an advertising folder for the Willett Spring-Scraper used in connection with Ford trucks to maintain roads. Although not endorsing the product, the Branch let dealers know it was a good item to offer for state highway work. In July, dealers received a book of suggestions to help them concentrate their sales efforts on a campaign to sell the new DeLuxe body types.

Earlier in the year dealers were advised that Model A engines were being used by many manufacturers in motor boats, agricultural implements, railway equipment, farm machinery and industrial machinery. These engines, parts and service were available through any Ford dealer who cared to promote them. The engine assembly sold for one hundred-fifty dollars with clutch and transmission and one hundred-twenty dollars without. The AA engine assembly equipped with heavy-duty truck clutch and four-speed transmission listed at one hundred-eighty dollars.

Telegram of congratulations for twenty-five years as a Ford dealer received by Nortz & Virkler, Lowville, New York, August 15, 1931.

The sale of these engines entitled both the purchaser and the dealer to a discount. Interestingly, the purchaser's discount went up as more were bought while the dealer's discount went down. For example, on a purchase of one to ten, the discount to the purchaser was ten percent and to the dealer, fifteen percent. When 1,001 to 5,000 were purchased the buyer got a twenty-five percent discount and the dealer none because the sale was handled direct by the company.

Some dealers worked on expanding their fleet sales to businesses and government units. The discount for 1931 remained the same as for 1930, depending on how many units were bought (see Chapter Four). A November 10, 1931, list of fleet owners distributed by the Buffalo Branch, lists one company with a ten percent discount (AT&T); sixty-eight with a seven percent discount; and seven hundred-fifteen with a discount of five percent.

Considering the fact that in 1931, the Fleet Owner List Co. of New York City estimated the number of fleet owners as well in excess of 270,000, there was obviously a rich potential market for the enterprising Ford dealer.

Numerous dealers were able to effect fleet sales during 1931. In New York City, a dealer sold two hundred-forty-four new Model A Roadsters to the police depart-

Model "A" Engine

(SPECIAL WHOLESALE PRICES TO MANUFACTURERS)

A Precision built Engine

for

Industrial

Agricultural or Marine

Purposes

Model A engine for industrial, agricultural or marine purposes.

ment. The biggest single Ford car deal registered in October was the sale of one hundred-thirty-seven new cars to the City of Detroit. Of this number, one hundred-three went to the police department at an average cost of two hundred-thirty-eight dollars with the trade-in.

Paul X. Johnson Inc., dealers at Shawnee, Oklahoma, sold six Model AA-131 Ford trucks with ice bodies to the Leibman Independent Ice Co. These trucks were painted white. In Canada, a coal company purchased the first of a fleet of Ford trucks with all-steel combination coal and coke bodies. The truck bodies were also painted white inside and out.

In Dallas, the Dallas Gas Co. purchased eighty Fords, including sixteen 1-1/2 ton trucks, forty-nine light delivery cars, and the balance in Coupes and Sedans. Reflecting on the decision to buy the Ford fleet, the purchasing agent for the gas company cited the delivery of new cars and trucks to the door of the company garage, the economy and service on parts offered by Ford dealers, the easy availability of parts and attractive body design, as factors in the decision.

Mindful of the importance of fleet owner sales, dealers were encouraged to have their Service Manager or a competent service representative call on all fleet owners in their locality at least every two weeks. A periodic report of the success of these calls was to be made to the Branch.

Despite the Depression, more than 8,000,000 Fords, Model A and Model T, on the road and in use, needed service and/or parts. Aware of this potential market, the company constantly worked on its dealers to maintain clean, well-equipped shops staffed by competent personnel. To help dealers, the Branches continued to run sales and service schools in 1931 as they had in the previous years. And, to make it easier, these schools were also held in Branch cities and outlying areas.

In the Philadelphia area, the Chester (Pennsylvania) Branch operated evening Service Schools in dealer's places of business. A total of six hundred-seventy-one Ford dealers' mechanics, service managers, parts men, dealers, salesmen, fleet owners and their mechanics and Ford Motor Co. employees attended these schools. The Chester Branch reported that the schools resulted in a fifty percent reduction in service complaints.

On July 31, 1931, the Chester Branch provided Ford mechanics with an updated version of a Ford Service Questionnaire for the Ford service man. The questionnaire consisted of over two hundred questions and answers on Ford service for the service man to study and learn. In the introduction to the questionnaire, the Branch Service Manager asked readers to consider whether they are better qualified to perform service work this month than last month. "Are you satisfied that you are fully capable of performing your duties?" he wrote. "The moral of it all is: If you want to get anywhere, wishing isn't enough, other qualifications and qualities are necessary, but knowledge and confidence are absolutely essential."

Lengthening the Arm of the Law

THE substantial worth of the new Ford is reflected in its alert, capable performance and economy of operation and up-keep. Men and women everywhere have found it ideally suited to their business and social needs. Its many uses make it truly The Universal Car.

An interesting use of the Ford is by police departments for the detection and apprehension of criminals. In their ceaseless vigil, these cars are driven in all kinds of weather, virtually twenty-four hours a day.

A fleet of 42 Model A Fords in Louisville covered a total of 2,620,800 miles

in twelve months, or the equivalent of 105 times around the world. Five new Fords on police duty in Niagara Falls have been driven more than 100,000 miles each. In Miami a police Ford has gone 120,000 miles.

The average for the eighteen Fords in Omaha is 35,000 miles per car for two years of police service. The superintendent of automotive equipment says the cost of repairs has been "very low."

The police departments of New York, Chicago, Philadelphia, Boston, Detroit,

San Francisco and other large cities use hundreds of Ford cars and trucks. In New York, the total exceeds four hundred and fifty.

Large industrial companies operating large fleets of Ford cars and trucks report the same reliability and good service. Long, hard usage emphasizes the value of simplicity of design, high quality of materials and unusual care in manufacturing and assembling.

The first cost of the new Ford is low, and you can purchase it on convenient, economical terms through the Authorized Ford Finance Plans of the Universal Credit Company.

Ad for a 1931 police Roadster from *Liberty* magazine, May 16, 1931.

As part of its service program, the company also supplied to dealers without charge, a quantity of small sixteen page booklets titled, "A Schedule of Standard Charges For Ford Service." These were to be used to promote service work by mailing or delivering them personally to owners. A form letter for mailing to owners was provided along with the booklets. This letter stressed to owners the importance and advantages of service for their Model A cars and Model AA trucks in a dealer maintained service facility. With this schedule the owner could determine in advance what the repair would cost for labor.

The booklet covered service on twenty-one major components from the front axle to the windshield. Following is a sampling of labor charges listed:

Overhaul the engine only, including
    rebabbitting and reboring $25.00

Overhaul the entire brake system
    (trucks $1.00 extra) $5.00

Replace front fender (1930 type - $3.00) $2.50

Align front wheels ....$.75

Overhaul carburetor $1.50

Overhaul radiator, requiring four to
    seven hours time $7.50

Zonemen or "travelers" as they were also called, were the on-the-scene link between dealers and their Branch headquarters. Ideally, each zoneman averaged about thirty dealers for whom he was responsible. His duties involved rendering dealers assistance in building a strong retail sales organization, and helping them improve the general efficiency of their sales and service departments.

Zonemen also gathered information on each dealer's operation and filed that with Branch officials. In 1931, the reporting form was changed so that each sheet reflected one dealer's activity for the entire year. This form, or sales chart as it was called, listed the dealer's prospects (Now have/Should have), salesmen (Now have/Should have), number of car, commercial and truck sales for each month and how that compared to the highest competitor. It goes almost without saying, that maintaining a good relationship with the zoneman was a matter of priority for responsible dealers.

Concerned about reports that some dealers asked owners to take replaced parts back to the dealer from whom the car was purchased for credit, the company emphatically made it known that this was not company policy. Dealers who replaced the part were to issue the credit in the same manner as they would if they had sold the car. Model A Fords did not have to be serviced only by the selling dealer. All dealers were obliged to service any Model A that came into their shops.

Ever alert to using innovative as well as tried and true ways to attract customers, dealers came up with many novel ideas in 1931. One dealer gave free driving lessons to buyers who took title to an automobile for the first time. Another, in a humanitarian mood, set out free box lunches and coffee at 5 p.m. every evening for twenty-five people, first come, first served.

There were likely as many ideas as there were Ford agencies. Dealers used free tow-ins of a disabled car, balloons suspended above the dealer's location, shadow boxes for special parts and accessory displays, kept a Coupe serviced and ready for an afternoon's shopping trip or pleasure jaunt exclusively for car-less feminine drivers, used women to solicit housewives in a door-to-door census and even parked a wrecked Model A in the showroom to demonstrate the car's ability to protect passengers from serious injury.

A woman dealer in California got her dealership operating like clockwork and doing a better job of selling, by hiring a man with a cheerful disposition as foreman of the shop, sponsoring family gatherings for employees and eliminating "Fussing and mussing, as well as cussing."

And, *Ford Dealer and Service Field* was happy to report, some Ford dealers even made money in 1931.

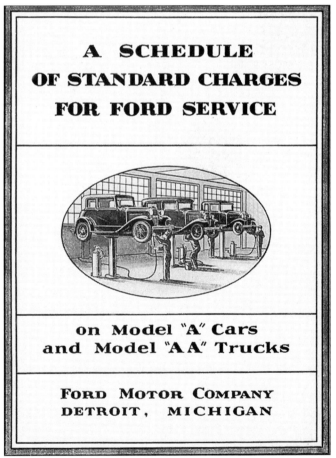

Ford booklet, dated February 16, 1931, "A Schedule of Standard Charges For Ford Service."

The Parrott Motor Co. of Oklahoma, for example, had a thirty-three percent increase in income during the first four months of 1931 over the same period in 1930. Owner/Manager Forrest Parrott said: "A great portion of the increase was from the sale of units, both new and used, but the greatest percentage of increase was shown in the service department. I believe we are servicing a far greater percentage of our cars than last year. We will not be satisfied until we reach 100 percent."

The story of the1931 Model A Ford would be incomplete without recounting some of the uses to which they were put and the stories and adventures of people from all walks of life who bought them, drove them and enjoyed them during that fateful, final model year.

One of the people who drove a Ford was the famous inventor Thomas Edison, creator of the incandescent electric light and a close friend of Henry Ford. Unfortunately, Edison got to enjoy his Model A only a few brief years, passing away on October 18, 1931, at the age of eighty-four. After his death, Henry Ford took the unprecedented step of honoring his departed friend's memory by closing all assembly and service plants on Wednesday afternoon, October 21.

Model A Fords were adapted to just about every possible job or service, sometimes even defying imagination. They were traveling grocery stores, movable stables, sprinkler trucks, hydraulic spray machines, portable oil rigs, mud pumps, armored trucks, ambulances,

Three friends: (l-to-r) Henry Ford, Thomas Edison and Harvey Firestone outside the Edison Laboratory, Fort Myers, Florida, March 15, 1931—about seven months before Edison's death.

dump trucks, funeral cars, taxis, hay trucks, shooting galleries, buses, peddler's wagons, etc. They built roads and dams, carried a vast assortment of products and served as transportation for people in every walk of life.

At Elmira, New York, Albert Hastings won the national soaring championship in a glider launched with the help of his Model A Sport Coupe. Small airships of the Goodyear lighter-than-air fleet, used a Model AA Panel job as a mobile mast or "traveling harbor" for mooring purposes. The Sparks-Withington Co. of Jackson, Michigan, manufacturers of Sparton radios and automobile horns, equipped three Model A cars and a Lincoln with everything a police car needed in order to combat crime and sent them on educational tours around the country.

The three Ford police cars were specially equipped with a high compression head and a high-speed engine, easily capable of speeds over eighty miles per hour. All four cars were equipped with shatterproof glass throughout, two police radio receiving sets, a dome light over the seat next to the driver, regulation police siren, stop lights, loudspeaker and search lights. They were heavily armed with a Thompson machine gun, rifle, sawed-off shotgun, riot gun, tear gas bombs, hand grenades, bulletproof screen and other essentials.

The Ford dealer in Santiago, Dominican Republic, sent a letter detailing the horror of a one hundred-eighty mile per hour hurricane that hit that island. A closed Model A, he wrote, stood out in the street during the whole storm with the chauffeur huddled in the back under the rear cushion. The strength of the Model A body saved his life. The car withstood the violence of the wind, as well as timber and sections of buildings flying through the air.

A special four-page supplement to the September 1931 issue of *Ford News*, featured a letter to a dealer in California from a woman owner. "The new Ford DeLuxe Roadster which I recently purchased from you," she wrote, "has given me the biggest surprise of my life! Up until now, never having owned a Ford car before, I was more or less inclined to treat them as a joke and as a target for a good many wisecracks. But I wish to say right now, that the new Ford models have everything that makes for comfort, efficiency and convenience."

Eighteen cars of various makes participated in a ladies race that started in Stockholm and covered some three

hundred miles of hills and difficult roads. In the main group, three cars completed the run without losing a single point, and of these three, two were Model A Fords. "Once again," stated *Ford Dealer and Service Field*, "the Ford car found itself in fast automotive company and gave the usual account of itself."

Speaking of the ladies, the Ford Motor Co. treated them with great respect as important influences on male decisions to buy a Ford and as buyers themselves. A 1931 survey done by the Curtis Publishing Co., says car distributors and dealers reported that in nearly two-thirds of their sales the woman and children in the family were the determining influence. Well aware of this, Ford executives aimed ads at women and tried to make dealers aware of the importance of features such as looks and ease of handling to attract women to the Model A. The *Ford News* supplement previously mentioned, "Milady and Her Car," featuring twenty-five women drivers and their Model A Fords, was sent to all Ford dealers as part of the company's efforts to make them aware of this segment of the market.

The following is a testimonial from a Winston-Salem, North Carolina, salesman, proud of his Ford: "You may be interested in the service I have received from my Business Coupe, purchased May 8, 1928, and run at this date 121,767 miles. It has never stopped on the road for repairs of any nature except punctures.

"The brakes were relined at 101,000 miles. My gas mileage has averaged twenty-one miles to the gallon, and my tires 19,000 miles per tire. My territory is both mountainous and flat country; therefore, I have all kinds of roads and road conditions. The repairs have been two sets of pistons and rings, one front spring and a few minor repairs. I consider this a wonderful record and assure you my next car will be another Ford."

And then, there is this from the October 1931 issue of *Ford News*: "A Ford car that talked, sang, answered questions, turned its lights on and off and sounded its horn mystified crowds in showrooms of Ford dealers in the Chester, Pennsylvania, territory. There are no visible wires or apparatus. The interlocutor is not a ventriloquist. And yet the 'human Ford' appears to see, to hear, to think and to speak.

"The interlocutor holds a coin before a headlight and the Ford tells its denomination and date. It reads the numbers on currency and tells the time. It even reads French—at least to the extent of identifying a ten-centime piece. The mystery car tells a small child to take her finger out of her mouth, calls individuals by name, winks a cowl light at a pretty girl and otherwise amuses its audience. How it is done is a trick the inventor declines to disclose."

Non-stop and car endurance records were shattered and a new high mark was established, when a Ford "Natural Wood" Delivery, after operating continuously since May 13, 1931, for one hundred-fifty-seven days, three hours and twenty-four minutes, was timed in on October 16 at Los Angeles. A distance of 50,091 miles was covered up and down the Pacific coast between Mexico and Canada.

Radio cruiser, *Ford News*, **May 1931.**

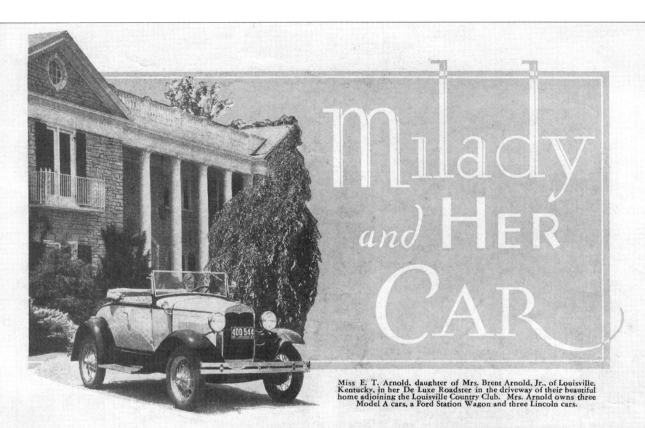

Miss E. T. Arnold, daughter of Mrs. Brent Arnold, Jr., of Louisville, Kentucky, in her De Luxe Roadster in the driveway of their beautiful home adjoining the Louisville Country Club. Mrs. Arnold owns three Model A cars, a Ford Station Wagon and three Lincoln cars.

THE Model A has always been popular among women motorists since its first appearance. They have liked its looks and its ease of handling; they have fallen in love with its responsiveness. After a few days of driving, they have learned that it can be depended upon, particularly in heavy traffic. Its quick acceleration, alert speed, effective four-wheel brakes and Triplex safety glass have added to their sense of security and their confidence in it. Its ease of steering, parking, gearshifting and turning, has delighted them and won their approval.

The attractive appointments and rich finish of the various types have been particularly appreciated by feminine owners. "Wherever I go," writes one of them, "my friends comment on its distinctive lines and beautiful colors, and the richness of its upholstery."

Herein are portrayed a few of the countless women who have made the Model A their choice. It is a marvelous compliment to the car to discover among them many daughters who have been presented with Model A's by their parents. No greater tribute could be paid to the car than this confidence reposed in it by the elders.

At the pool of the Pittsburgh Field Club—Miss Gretchen Warmcastle is at the wheel of the Convertible Cabriolet, Miss Barbara Warmcastle is standing beside the Phaeton, and Miss Rhoda Gamble is at the wheel of the Phaeton. Passengers in the Phaeton include (front) Mrs. S. C. Lewers, (rear right) Mrs. K. W. Warmcastle, (center) Mrs. L. Bingell, (left) Mrs. J. Lovett.

"Milady and her Car," *Ford News*, September 1931.

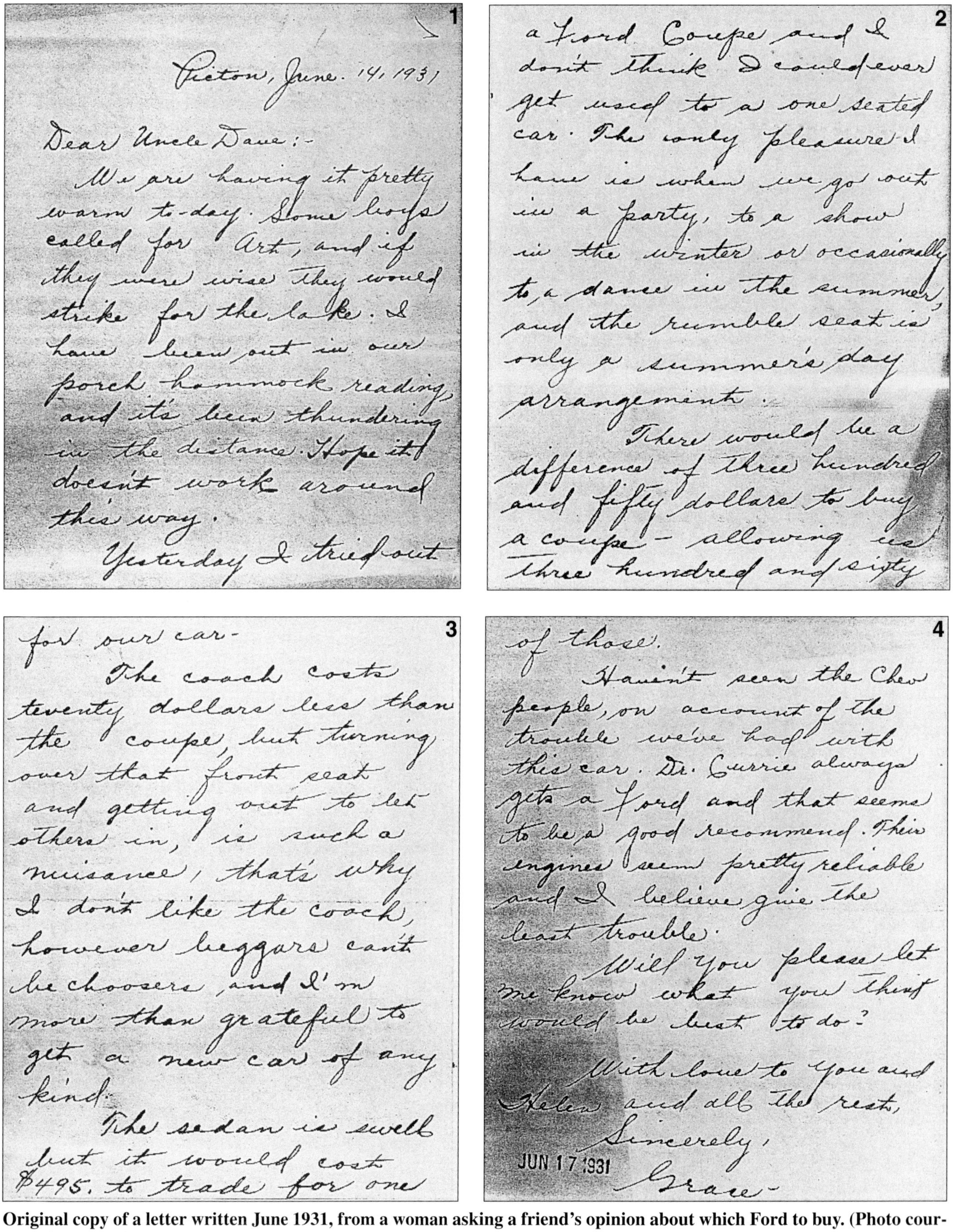

Picton, June. 14, 1931

Dear Uncle Dave:—

We are having it pretty warm to-day. Some boys called for Art, and if they were wise they would strike for the lake. I have been out in our porch hammock reading, and it's been thundering in the distance. Hope it doesn't work around this way.

Yesterday I tried out

for our car—

The coach costs twenty dollars less than the coupe, but turning over that front seat and getting out to let others in, is such a nuisance, that's why I don't like the coach, however beggars can't be choosers, and I'm more than grateful to get a new car of any kind.

The sedan is swell but it would cost $495. to trade for one

a Ford Coupe and I don't think I could ever get used to a one seated car. The only pleasure I have is when we go out in a party, to a show in the winter or occasionally to a dance in the summer, and the rumble seat is only a summer's day arrangement.

There would be a difference of three hundred and fifty dollars to buy a coupe — allowing us three hundred and sixty

of those.

Haven't seen the Chev people, on account of the trouble we've had with this car. Dr. Currie always gets a Ford and that seems to be a good recommend. Their engines seem pretty reliable and I believe give the least trouble.

Will you please let me know what you think would be best to do?

With love to you and Helen and all the rest,

Sincerely,

Grace—

JUN 17 1931

Original copy of a letter written June 1931, from a woman asking a friend's opinion about which Ford to buy. (Photo courtesy of Sal Comito)

At the conclusion of the run, this car, profiled in *Ford News*, was still using its original tires and, reportedly, averaged twenty-three miles to a gallon of gasoline on the open highways and 1,200 to 1,500 miles for each oil change. During the test, engine and wheels were not allowed to stop, making it necessary to transfer fuel and lubricants while the car was moving. Gas was added through a reserve tank on top of the car. A special petcock was installed to enable the drivers to drain the crankcase while the vehicle was moving.

The lubrication of gears, bearings and chassis always drew a crowd since the mechanic would lie on the floor and grapple with the car as it slowly shuttled back and forth over his prostrate body. The two drivers took turns sleeping on a bed placed in the rear. When halted for traffic stops, the driver had to keep shuttling back and forth between low and reverse gears until the way was clear to go forward.

To make sure that the drivers would not cheat, the ignition was sealed so that the car could not be controlled from the switch, and the starter and crank were removed so that in case the engine stopped the car could not be started again.

And finally, in a feat not to be imitated by most current Model A Ford owners, the strength of the Ford steel body was strikingly demonstrated during a parade in Detroit. Twenty-one people perched on a Ford Coupe to view the parade. Thirteen were on top of the body, one each on the right fender, hood and cowl, two on the rear deck and one each on the left running board, left rear fender and spare tire (*Ford Dealer & Service Field*).

As the months of 1931 ticked off the calendar one by one, there was a bit of *deja vu* reminiscent of 1927 in what was happening. With falling sales and pressure from the new Chevrolet and the new Plymouth hounding the company, it became increasingly clear to astute observers that Ford could not stand pat on the Model A.

As early as February 1931, *Automobile Trade Journal* mentioned "persistent rumors that major changes in the Model A were in the offing." In an article titled "Can Ford Sell 30,000,000 Model As?," the magazine quoted a dealer handling a make competing with Ford: "I doubt very much that the Model A can go for over three years more without revisions radical enough to call for a model change." The dealer, of course, was right, only his time line was off.

Two months later, *Automobile Trade Journal* featured a story that speculated about rumors that a new Ford eight to sell under $1,000 was in the works. And, in July, the magazine ran an article that posed this question about Ford's next move: "Will he cut prices or bring out a new model in battle for sales leadership?" It was the feeling of the author of this article that Ford would probably have to add a Ford eight to his line, and that he would also have to continue to sell a car in a lower price class. In August 1931, however, according to Nevins and Hill, Henry Ford "shut down production of the four-cylinder Model A 'indefinitely.'"

A July 29 Detroit newspaper report quoted in *Automotive Industries*, stated that approximately 75,000 men were out of work for an indefinite period due to the shutdown of Ford plants. "A few thousand men will be kept on the assembly line in Detroit," the story stated, "and 11 of the 36 assembly branches throughout the country will continue on curtailed schedules."

Beginning in August, newspaper articles, cited by Jim Schild (in *Selling the New Ford*), provide information but not necessarily all the answers to the questions about where Ford was headed. An August 1 statement from the company said that the Dearborn plant would be shut down for one month for vacation, but "when manufacturing is resumed, production of Model A and AA units will be continued. Schedules call for the building of more than 100,000 units during the next 60 days."

On September 12, it was reported that the Ford Motor Co. main factories in the Detroit district were reopening that week, and it was expected that 50,000 to 60,000 Model As would be turned out "without important change." The report stated that dealer stocks of Model A Fords had been reduced to less than 70,000. Two months later, on November 14, the company told dealers that the new Ford models would not be ready until close to the end of the year. At this point, there were about 50,000 to 60,000 Model As left to be sold, including some 10,000 still to be assembled at various plants.

What happened next is explained in a story written by James Sweinhart and carried in newspapers throughout the country on February 11, 1932. Sweinhart's story was the first authoritative announcement on plans of the Ford Motor Co. to offer a V-8 and an improved four-cylinder car in 1932. Sweinhart also explained what happened to the Model A at the end of 1931.

In late autumn, orders were given to put the improved Model A, as it was called, into production and soon cars started rolling down the assembly lines in a steady stream. Then came the morning of December 7.

"Suddenly, things began to happen," writes Sweinhart. "Orders went out to the plants to stop production—to stop production when 35,000 of the new improved 'Model As' were already manufactured and on their way to the west for early January showing—with 50,000 more of them 'in float'; that is coming through the plant in finished parts and bodies ready for assembly. The whole production organization was suddenly thrown back on its haunches. . . . What had happened? The Ford 'eight' had been born. Henry Ford had decided to put it into production as his chief offering for the coming year."

Although 60,611 Model A and AA Fords would be assembled after 1931 ("Ford Motor Company World Production 1903-1943"), for all practical purposes the 1931 model year was the last for the domestic Model A and AA Fords. "Discontinuation of the Model A Ford," writes James K. Wagner, "was in some ways one of the saddest events ever recorded in the history of the automobile, for it marked the demise of one of the most functionally simple yet totally reliable vehicles ever produced."

Chapter Six

1932: The End and the Beginning!

Nineteen thirty-two is a special year in the history of the Model A Ford. Domestically, it was the last year in which dealers still had new Model A and AA Fords to sell in their showrooms. More importantly, it marks the beginning of a sixty-seven year (and counting) post-production love affair for Model A enthusiasts around the globe. Four stories illustrate this point.

Jack Ruckle, of Millville, Pennsylvania, is ninety-four years old and still going strong today. In 1932, Ruckle and his high school friend, Donald Bennett, packed their gear into a special box attached to the rear of Ruckle's 1929 Model A Coupe, and set off on a cross-country tour during which they would visit seventeen states and Mexico. The box was hinged at the bottom so it could be opened as a table. It contained a small gas stove, oil, water, gas, cooking pans, food and two army cots. A tent large enough for the two cots was fastened to the side of the car.

Ruckle kept a journal of the June 7 to July 29, 1932, trip, and still remembers his adventure fondly. The two young men traveled 9,766 miles, visited 99 towns, spent $11.51 on oil and $99.97 on gas. Except for a minor carburetor problem, the car ran flawlessly. Tires were another matter. They had one blowout, five punctures and bought three tires along the way.

In 1945, *Ford Times* found the saga of a 1928 Model A Coupe "so outstanding" that it presented the story in full, as written by the car's owner, W.L. Gambill of Sistersville, West Virginia. Gambill ordered the car in February 1928, but it was not delivered until the following September, a delay of seven months. "But I have never been sorry," wrote Gambill, "I waited so long for my Ford."

After driving the car more than 287,000 miles, Gambill proudly wrote that his car still had "the original body, fenders, headlamps. wheels, wheel bearings, taillight, top, transmission, differential, universal joint, bumpers, running boards, speedometer, tailpipe, muffler and engine with original pistons as the cylinders have never been rebored."

The engine was overhauled in 1935 at 146,420 miles, and again in 1941 at 231,118 miles. "I have not put one nickel's worth of expense on the engine in the last 56,000 miles," he wrote, "and it seems to have just as much power as it had when the speedometer registered the first 10,000 miles. I have had my tenth set of tires recapped and I am now using the sixteenth set of spark plugs."

From time to time new parts had to be added to the car. These included the windshield, water pump, camshaft gear, and sector gear. A new-type clutch was added at 221,500 miles. The windshield wiper and the original wiper blade lasted for 242,404 miles. The rear wheel brakes were relined once at 142,104 miles and the front wheel brakes were untouched.

The May 1953 issue of *Ford Times* featured the following letter from A.M. Bennstrom of Stockholm, Sweden:

"Dear Sirs: When I came to the U.S. a year ago, I had decided to buy a fine, expensive car. Six months later I wound up with a Ford, 1931, but I have never regretted it. With my traveling companion, Zim, owner of this green-colored treasure with one yellow-painted reserve wheel, we started from California in June intending to see more of the world. We thought: if this jalopy can take us forth and back to Canada it would be a brave thing. It did—without even a flat tire, and we smoothed on around 40 mph all the time.

"The old aristocrat was to us what a palace is to a king. A shelf of driftwood from Lake Tahoe was fixed up in back, and by removing the back of the front seat one gets a comfortable bed for a grown person. A candlestick made from an old can is tied below the front window, and to play the guitar better, Zim removed half of the steering wheel. For long drives at night, a piece of light metal was fixed like an eyelash to one of the headlights with a string to the driver, and when we meet another car we give a salute with a halfway closed eye.

"Back in Santa Monica we decided to go to Mexico, so we washed the dust out of the front seat and took off, realizing we might have to stash the Ford along the road because even a new car would need repairs after all this. It was a silly thought. Now, down in Tapachula, where the road ends in wilderness with deep rivers, the car is better than ever. A press of the starter and it runs—and only two flat tires and a new brush to the generator."

Photos taken during Jack Ruckle's 1932 trip in a 1929 Model A Coupe.

Frank Hartmaier and his 1929 Standard Roadster. Frank is the original and only owner of the car.

Owning a Model A Ford since it was new is an experience few of us are privileged to enjoy, but that is what makes the story of Frank Hartmaier and his 1929 Model A Standard Roadster so special.

Hartmaier took delivery of the Roadster on May 16, 1929, when he was just seventeen years old. He paid five hundred-sixty dollars, including eighty-five dollars for the two options he wanted: a rumble seat and a spare tire. For the next twenty years the Model A was his only transportation.

If the old Ford could talk it would tell you about Hartmaier's dates with Elizabeth, his wife-to-be, and the trip with the minister to Audubon, New Jersey, for the wedding ceremony. In 1942, the Model A carried Elizabeth to the hospital for the birth of the couple's daughter, Judith. There were few family events for which the car was idle. "I could write a book about all our experiences with our Model A Ford," Hartmaier writes. "We did not just drive to work with it. We went on vacation all over the eastern states."

On one trip, Hartmaier recalls a frightened horse rearing up and planting its front feet directly between the car's radiator and front bumper. On another day a trolley car hooked onto the Roadster's front bumper and dragged it around a corner. Luckily, the car was not damaged either time. A collision with a 1929 Buick, the Model A's only accident, was not as fortunate. "But," says Hartmaier, "the Buick got the worst of it."

During the past seventy years, Hartmaier has painted his Model A four times, most recently only the wheels, fenders and splash aprons, put three new tops on it, replaced the interior twice and rebuilt the engine four times. He restored it for the last time in 1972, after his retirement, doing most of the work himself. Today, the car is still driven regularly even during the winter on good weather days.

The speedometer on Hartmaier's Rose Beige and Seal Brown Roadster broke in 1944 after logging 416,000

miles. "My friends tell me I've got a million miles on the car," he says with a twinkle in his eye, "but I really don't know." At eighty-eight years, Hartmaier still manages to drive the car from 2,000 to 3,000 miles a year. "It was the car I wanted when I was seventeen," he says, adding "I loved it when I got it and I love it just the same right now. I service it myself except for the engine."

These four men and their Model A Fords are a reminder of how enduring the legacy of the Model A has been. In 1932, when Ruckle took his trip, the Model A had been replaced by the V-8 and, for a short time, by the Model B. By 1944, when Gambill wrote his letter, Model A Fords were "old" cars still occasionally found on used car lots or driven by someone as wartime transportation, but they were gradually disappearing from the daily automotive scene. Only nine years later, in 1953, Bennstrom was driving his Model A on the West Coast at the time that interest in the Model A Ford as a hobby was beginning to blossom. The Model "A" Restorers Club was already one year old, and the Model A Ford Club of America would soon follow.

Today, more than seventy years after the first Model As hit the roads, thousands of them are in the hands of hobbyists around the world, who not only restore and maintain them but enjoy driving them. Frank Hartmaier's life spans those years. He started out using the car for his daily chores as we would our modern iron. After seventy years, he has a lifetime of memories of a car that served him well and continues to do so to this day.

Although Model A production "officially" ended in 1931, trucks and a scattering of passenger units continued to be produced for several more years. During 1932, a total of 46,942 Model A and AA units were assembled worldwide. An additional 13,669 were built from 1933 into 1936. U.S. Branches assembled 12,936 Model A and AA Fords in 1932. Only forty-three of these were passenger cars and they were built during the first two months. The last domestic Model A and AA production was a mix of forty-five commercial, 112-inch drop center and AA-131 truck chassis in December 1932.

Original 1929 Tudor - owner John Waltz.

George DeAngelis says that "on a very limited basis" Ford continued to produce sequentially numbered Model A engines—as well as Model T and Model B—up to World War II (*Model "A" News*). His research is based on recently discovered foreman's logbooks that list aftermarket engine production to World War II. Based on these records, more than 26,000 Model A engines were produced between the middle of March 1932 and January 31, 1944.

Outside of the United States, the last of 3,068 Canadian-built Model As, a 112-inch drop center chassis, came off the assembly line at Walkerville in July 1932. Foreign production in South America, Europe and Japan (30,938 units in 1932) leaned heavily toward light commercial and truck units. A few passenger cars were produced, but by July 1932, these were almost entirely Standard Phaetons.

Wilkins and Hill summarize the European situation in their book *American Business Abroad*. Aside from Dagenham, which employed 7,024 workers by the end of 1932, they write, "the European operation, while fairly encouraging in the northern countries, was temporarily darkening in Spain, had blacked out in Italy, was becoming a deficit operation in France and had a catastrophic performance in Germany."

Robert Scoon writes that the Russian Model AA (Gaz AA), was in production from 1932 to 1948. The last Model A engines were manufactured in Russia in 1947. The Russian plant at Gorky began turning out Gaz As, four-door Phaetons, in 1933 and continued to manufacture them until 1936, when a version of the 1934 Ford V-8 was adopted. The Gaz 1936-39 Phaeton also used the Model A engine. Scoon says that, beginning in 1943, Gorky turned to the production of jeeps—all of which were equipped with Model A engines.

Scoon claims that it is difficult to arrive at accurate totals of Gaz A and AA production. Misrepresentation of figures by the Soviets was not uncommon. We do know that from 1932 to 1938, the Gorky plant built 600,000 Model A engines, more than half of which went into cars. In 1939, the Soviets claimed that between 1932 and 1937 they built 550,000 cars, most of which were Model A Fords. It is possible that well over one million Russian Model A and AA Fords were built, but no one seems to know for certain.

All of these Model A Fords built after 1931 leads to a fascinating question. Which was the last Model A? The answer depends at least in part on what is meant by the "last Model A." Does this mean the last car built with some Model A components? If so, then possibly one of

This Model A is identified by Ford-Werke AG, Cologne as a Ford 1932 Modell A (as they spell it), although it appears to be a 1929. It is not impossible that it was actually produced at Cologne in 1932.

The SALES PICTURE	Position		Total Retail Sales for Twelve Months		Per Cent of Grand Total of Retail Sales		Gain or Loss in 1931 over 1930		Retail Sales for January	
	1931	1930	1931	1930	1931	1930	Number of units	Per Cent	*1932	1931
General Motors..	..	..	825,495	905,428	43.3	34.5	— 79,933	— 8.8	43,781	56,728
Chevrolet.....	1	2	583,387	618,901	30.6	23.6	— 35,514	— 5.7	32,403	41,073
Buick........	4	3	90,871	122,645	4.8	4.7	— 31,774	— 26.0	4,403	6,716
Pontiac.......	5	4	73,154	68,387	3.8	2.6	+ 4,767	+ 6.9	4,081	4,175
Oldsmobile....	8	12	47,080	50,503	2.5	1.9	— 3,423	— 6.7	2,280	2,458
Oakland.......	19	18	12,985	21,652	.7	.8	— 8,667	— 40.0	.....	917
Cadillac.......	20	22	11,135	12,078	.6	.5	— 943	— 7.8	388	917
LaSalle........	23	25	6,883	11,262	.4	.4	— 4,379	— 38.9	226	472
Ford...........	..	..	532,004	1,059,461	27.9	40.3	—527,457	— 49.8	12,718	37,174
Ford.........	2	1	528,539	1,055,105	27.7	40.1	—526,566	— 49.9	12,507	36,958
Lincoln........	29	28	3,465	4,356	.2	.2	— 891	— 20.5	211	216
Chrysler.........	..	..	228,435	224,635	11.9	8.5	+ 3,800	+ 1.7	8,657	9,880
Plymouth.....	3	5	94,276	64,305	4.9	2.4	+ 29,971	+ 46.6	4,170	2,376
Dodge........	6	6	53,086	64,155	2.8	2.4	— 11,069	— 17.2	2,249	3,815
Chrysler......	7	8	52,644	60,908	2.7	2.3	— 8,264	— 13.5	1,178	2,402
DeSoto.......	14	13	28,429	35,267	1.5	1.4	— 6,838	— 19.4	1,060	1,287
Hudson.........	..	..	61,731	93,854	3.2	3.6	— 32,123	— 34.2	2,988	5,231
Essex.........	11	7	42,543	63,388	2.2	2.4	— 20,845	— 32.9	2,107	3,366
Hudson.......	16	14	19,188	30,466	1.0	1.2	— 11,278	— 37.0	881	1,865
Willys-Overland..	..	..	51,341	65,766	2.7	2.4	— 14,425	— 21.9	2,315	3,328
Willys........	10	10	42,936	51,686	2.3	1.9	— 8,750	— 16.9	2,047	2,555
Willys-Knight..	21	20	8,405	14,080	.4	.5	— 5,675	— 40.3	268	773
Studebaker......	..	..	51,054	63,320	2.6	2.4	— 12,266	— 19.3	2,327	3,666
Studebaker....	9	9	46,532	56,525	2.4	2.2	— 9,993	— 17.6	2,187	3,270
Pierce-Arrow...	27	27	4,522	6,795	.2	.2	— 2,273	— 33.4	140	396
Nash..........	12	11	39,366	51,086	2.1	1.9	— 11,720	— 22.9	1,000	2,622
Auburn.........	..	..	30,951	13,149	1.6	.5	+ 17,802	+135.4	588	1,116
Auburn.......	13	24	29,535	11,270	1.5	.4	+ 18,265	+162.0	557	1,041
Cord.........	30	29	1,416	1,879	.1	.1	— 463	— 25.1	31	75
Graham........	15	15	19,207	30,137	1.0	1.1	— 10,930	— 36.2	1,038	1,097
Hupmobile......	17	17	17,425	24,307	.9	.9	— 6,882	— 28.3	648	1,069
Packard........	18	16	16,252	28,318	.8	1.1	— 12,066	— 42.6	823	1,230
Durant.........	22	19	7,229	21,439	.4	.8	— 14,210	— 66.2	175	828
Reo............	24	23	6,761	11,449	.4	.4	— 4,688	— 40.9	266	678
Marmon........	25	21	5,687	12,369	.3	.5	— 6,682	— 52.0	255	827
DeVaux........	26	..	4,808	....	.3	...	+ 4,808	....	200	......
Franklin........	28	26	3,881	7,511	.2	.3	— 3,630	— 48.3	186	316
Miscellaneous....	..	..	6,489	13,889	.3	.5	— 7,400	— 53.2	430	996
TOTAL........	..	..	1,908,016	2,626,068	...	...	—718,052	— 27.3	78,395	126,786
Total without Ford	..	..	1,379,477	1,570,963	...	...	—191,486	— 12.2	65,888	89,828

* Estimated on returns from 24 states.

"The Sales Picture," Motor, March 1932.

the Gaz Model A Fords, or the wood-bodied convertible built in 1945 on a 1931 Model A chassis by special request of Henry Ford II is the last Model A.

As described by Vic Zannis in an article in *Antique Automobile* (September-October 1991), the convertible, with a body designed by E.T. Gregorie, is a mix of Model A and other components. Fenders, running boards, splash aprons, radiator and shell are all stock 1931 Model A. The engine is a 1932 "B," the instruments are 1939, the steering wheel 1940 and the wheels and bumpers 1941. At the time, Zannis wrote that the car was unrestored with less than 19,000 miles on it and owned by a Model A collector.

For those who want their last Model A Ford to be an "authentic" car, meaning a car with all the regular Model A components, it would seem that one of the cars built in the United States or overseas in 1932 or a subsequent year was the last one. This writer is unaware which car that was or whether it still exists.

During the first three months of 1932, while the country waited for the V-8 and the Model B, retail sales of Model As plummeted to about one-third of the 1931 average. Part of the reason for this was certainly due to a "wait and see what Ford comes up with" attitude on the part of some potential buyers. Much more of it was the result of the country's preoccupation with unemployment, business failures, hunger in the cities, a revolt of farmers against foreclosure and the great debate over which political party was best suited to do something about the mess the country was in.

With sales of new cars winding down, Model A did not have a chance against Chevrolet, which sold 68,206 units in the first two months, against the Model A's 26,395. Chevrolet even outsold Ford in trucks by a small margin in the early going, but Ford was eventually able to rally and keep its first place status in truck sales for 1932, although tenuously. Keep in mind that 1932 was the low point of the Depression for the automobile industry. A total of 1,370,678 passenger cars, trucks and buses were built that year, the lowest total since 1918 and the lowest until the 1942-45 war years (Automobile Manufacturers Association, "1951 Facts and Figures").

Diminishing sales throughout the industry increased pressure on dealers to move cars. In March, *Motor* magazine stated that "Most Ford dealers are loaded and are willing to sell at a substantial discount although they have received no factory assistance." Model A factory prices remained the same in early 1932 as in 1931. In April, after the prices for the new four-cylinder commercial units were announced, dealers were informed of a price decrease ranging from fifteen to thirty dollars for their remaining stock of Model A and AA commercial units. Units that had received a substantial price decrease in November 1931, such as the Ambulance and Town Car Delivery, were not included in this change.

Examples of the actual prices paid for Model A Fords in 1932 can be found in the files of Lowville, New York, Ford dealer, Nortz & Virkler. By the middle of January 1932, the dealership had an inventory of eleven Model A and AA Fords. Interestingly, the dealer's base price was

Copy of sales data (January 21, 1932) from an original ledger at Nortz & Virkler Ford dealers in Lowville, New York.

higher than the factory list, likely reflecting, at least in part, the cost of freight. For example, a Deluxe Roadster with a factory price of four hundred-seventy-five dollars was listed by Nortz & Virkler at five hundred-twenty-three dollars. Additional charges to the buyer were seventeen dollars for the bumpers, thirteen dollars for a tire and tube and four dollars for gas and oil.

Other sales included a Pickup with closed cab listing at four hundred-fifty-five dollars at the Rouge and priced at five hundred-seven dollars by Nortz & Virkler, and a 1-1/2 ton, 157 inch closed cab chassis with dual wheels, which the dealer listed at seven hundred-twenty-eight dollars including bumper, dual wheels, one set of helper springs and gas and oil.

As the 1930s moved on and new Model A Fords were no longer available, the buying and selling of Model As focused on the used car market and, after World War II, gradually became a hobby-related activity. As anyone who owns a Model A today knows, the value of good-condition examples and, for that matter, even cars in mediocre condition, is far higher than the original prices paid in 1927-32. However, it was not always that way. Following are examples of asking prices for used Model A Fords, from 1931 to the present.

A 1937 photo of a 1929 Model A Tudor and a 1930 Chevrolet. (Photo courtesy of Bob Osborn)

The *Motor-Fax Price Bulletin* for August 1931, lists the delivered price of a 1931 Roadster with rumble seat at five hundred-seventy-seven dollars, and the retail market value as five hundred dollars. In November, the same model was appraised at three hundred-seventy-five dollars in the *Pacific Coast Red Book*. A year later, in December 1932, the *Red Book's* trade-in appraisal was down to one hundred-sixty-five dollars. This was a drop in value of more than fifty percent in one year, but still considerably better than a 1928 Roadster (factory price three hundred-eighty dollars) with a trade-in appraisal of just seventeen dollars.

By 1933, prices for used Model As seem to have leveled off. The Clark Cadillac Co. of Portland, Oregon, sold a 1931 Roadster for one hundred-seventy dollars; a 1931 Tudor Sedan in "perfect" condition was advertised at one hundred-eighty-five dollars in the *Chicago-American*; a 1931 Rumble Seat Coupe was listed at two hundred-sixty-one dollars and a 1931 Panel truck (with 15,000 miles) at three hundred-twenty-five dollars in the Syracuse (New York) *Post-Standard*.

As might be expected, the passing of years made Model A Fords less valuable. In February 1936, Clark Cadillac sold a used 1929 Coupe for $145, and in August 1937 a used 1929 Roadster was sold for only $92.08 by Highland Motors, Inc. of Portland, Oregon. An upstate New York Buick dealer appraised a 1930 Tudor at $76.80 in 1936, and later sold it for $87.50. About the same time, this dealer sold a used 1929 Tudor for $180. Condition was obviously a factor in the prices charged for these cars.

After World War II, Model As were not as commonly found on the lots of used car dealers as they once were. The September/October 1948 NADA official used car guide does not even include the Model A, going back only to 1935.

In the 1950s and early-1960s, Model A Fords were still relatively inexpensive. For example, in 1958 your

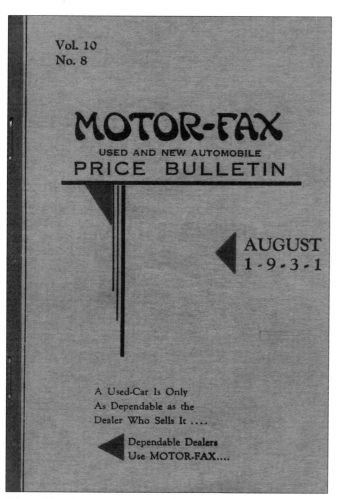

Motor-Fax, August 1931.

Early-1930s photo of a 1931 Model A Coupe with damaged rear fender. In 1933, a Coupe like this, but undamaged, was advertised for two hundred-sixty-one dollars.

A 1958 photo of a 1931 Sport Coupe. Obviously a driver in only fair condition, this car would have sold at that time for under five hundred dollars.

A 1960 photo of a 1929 Model A Station Wagon. In the early 1960s, the author recalls a Station Wagon like this in good condition that sold for less than $1,000.

In 1982, this Coupe was still in daily use by its original owner.

At Dunkirk, New York, in 1985, the owner of this "barn fresh" Model A was seeking $2,000.

author bought a 1930 Tudor for one hundred-fifty dollars and put about three hundred dollars into it for tires, paint and an engine overhaul. In 1962, he purchased a ready-to-go 1930 Fordor with new paint, original interior, rebuilt engine and only 43,275 miles for just four hundred-thirty-five dollars.

A 1957 issue of *MARC News*, the publication of the Model "A" Restorers Club at that time, advertises a restored 1931 two-door Deluxe Phaeton and a 1931 Cabriolet needing restoration for the best offer over $1,000. The owner says that his reason for selling the Phaeton is "too much draft on back of neck." The same issue offers a 1929 Sport Touring in excellent condition, and a 1930 Model A Roadster in fair condition, both for $1,000.

Antique Automobile includes several Model A Fords for sale in its November 1961 issue. A 1931 Roadster in "very good condition" was priced at eight hundred-fifty dollars and a restored 1930 Coupe with rumble seat for eight hundred dollars. For just three hundred-ninety-five dollars one could purchase a 1931 Model A, body style not mentioned, with original interior, new paint, four new tires.

Statistics for the average prices asked for one hundred-thirty-three Model As in 1965-67 and nearly two hundred in 1972-73, are listed by Phil Allin in the November/December 1973 issue of *The Restorer*. These figures show that at that time there were still Model As being offered for under three hundred dollars, but the top prices had more than doubled. Allin wrote that in the six years between the two surveys the average asking price more than doubled.

Several examples from Allin's survey are provided showing average prices for all production years: Roadsters, $1,509 in 1967 and $3,734 in 1973; Tudors, $782 and $1,868; Coupes, $708 and $1,805; AA trucks, $881 and $788 (the only units selling for less after six years).

By the 1980s, prices were up significantly. The September/October 1983 issue of *Model "A" News* contains ads for a restored 1931 Deluxe Roadster at $10,500, and a fully restored 1928 Roadster with side mount and rumble seat for $15,000. Also listed are a 1929 four-door leatherback in unrestored, excellent condition for $7,400, and a restored 1930 AA dump truck for $9,500.

Today, while asking prices might be high in some instances, selling prices are not accelerating rapidly, if at all. In August 1998, *Evergreen Echoes*, publication of the Seattle Evergreen Chapter (MAFCA), listed a 1930 Deluxe Roadster with dual side mounts, hydraulic brakes, turn signals, seal beam headlights, side curtains and rear trunk, in excellent condition and including a spare engine for $15,000. A 1930 Model A Briggs Fordor with good sheet metal, some bodywork completed, a running engine and a new top wood package uninstalled, was priced at $3,000. Also advertised was an original unrestored 1931 Tudor for $4,999 OBO (or best offer).

Ads in *The Restorer* for September/October 1998 list a 1930 Murray Fordor with 10,000 original miles for $22,000; a restored 1931 Pickup for $7,500 OBO; a

1929 Coupe, older restoration, at $9,500; a late-1931 Tudor, unrestored with lots of mechanical work done, for $5,500; and a 1931 two-door DeLuxe Phaeton, an older restoration, for $26,000 firm.

Ads in *Old Cars Weekly* for October 29, 1998, include an older restoration 1931 Victoria for $12,000; a 1930 Coupe in restorable condition and with some new parts for $4,000; a 1928 Tudor, restored nine years ago and with extra parts for $10,000; and a 1930 Model A dump truck for $4,400.

Model A enthusiast Bob Johnson compiled a database of asking prices for 1,473 Model A cars offered for sale in *The Restorer* and *Model "A" News* from 1993-97 (cited in *Evergreen Echoes*). Following are some results for cars that he designated as a "driver" (a car that runs and is either partially restored or an older restoration showing its age). In this group the average price for a Coupe was $8,770; Pickup, $7,700; Tudor, $7,590; Fordor, $9,140; Roadster, $13,070. In the restored category the highest average asking price was $24,930 for the 400-A.

The first quarter of 1932 was not an easy time for Ford dealers. They had new Model A Fords to sell but not enough to carry them for long. In addition, they were limited by the significant decline in national purchasing power, and by the reluctance of some prospective buyers to purchase a new car until they knew what Henry Ford had up his sleeve. The used car market was also hurting, especially in the two hundred-fifty dollar and up price field, because of a reluctance to invest in a second-hand automobile until it was known what the new Fords would be like, and how much they would cost.

Reviewing the situation *Motor* magazine stated, "Ford dealers who have had nothing but clean-up cars to sell for months are waiting breathlessly for the new jobs and doing their best to hold their prospects. Speaking generally, their finances are in a far worse state than when they were awaiting the Model A and their morale is so badly shaken that Branch managers are having a hard time keeping them in line. It now seems the policy of the company to reduce the number of outlets and in some places half the dealers have been invited to buy out the other half, taking over their leases and stocks of cars, truck and parts. This program has aroused no great enthusiasm."

What was the Ford dealer to do? He could either fold his tent or continue to find ways to sell the new cars he had left, move used cars and expand his parts and service

A 1931 Phaeton similar to this was advertised for $26,000 in 1998. In 1931, a DeLuxe Phaeton with five painted wheels listed for five hundred-eighty dollars.

business. Following is a sampling of what was done by Ford dealers to keep their businesses on the black side of the ledger during that trying time.

One dealer offered a radio set for the home or car or three months' worth of gasoline free with each purchase of a used car. Another targeted people who would normally buy a $2,000 car, reasoning that they could afford a Ford outright, while many people who would buy a Ford did not have the money during hard times.

An El Paso, Texas, dealer offered ninety days free parking on his downtown lot to purchasers of a used car. The Baker Motor Co. in Salt Lake City, Utah, concentrated on service and local advertising with a personal touch to get the message out. The Baker message was featured in an occasional newspaper, *The Ford Corner News*, which directly appealed to area Ford owners by carrying localized human interest stories to them.

On the other side of the world, the local Ford dealer on the island of Java, aware that most car owners on the island employed chauffeurs, conceived the idea of awarding watches to chauffeurs with excellent driving records. He also presented a watch to every person outside his organization who was instrumental in effecting the sale of a car or truck. More than three hundred watches were given out during the first three months of this campaign.

In the small town of Waverly, New York (population 5,000), the Walker brothers, owners of Walker Motor Sales, a Ford franchise since July 1929, made a reality of their slogan, "New houses for old, used cars!" Realizing that much of their used car business was practically eliminated because the working classes in the town were working only four or five days a month, the brothers conceived the idea of trading used cars for time and/or material. Over a period of months they traded eleven used cars and trucks and two new Ford trucks, a repair bill for which they could not collect cash and a tenant's rent for a vacant lot, construction material and labor. At the end they had a house worth $3,500 plus $250 in coal and $310 in cash.

In *Old Cars Weekly*, author John G. Robinson relates the story of the Jarnagin Motor Co., Ford dealer in Rutledge, Tennessee. He quotes Bill Jarnagin, one of the two original owners of the dealership, commenting on the difficult times between 1929 and 1932. "'We had to cut our overhead down,' Bill Jarnagin says with the tone of a proud survivor. 'We were selling gasoline and anything else that would make a dime or a nickel—refrigerators, radios, all kinds of electrical appliances. We'd take livestock (in trade for vehicles). We had the farm down here, and we could put the cattle on the farm to get more money out of them.'"

The sale of used cars, an important part of virtually every automotive dealer's business, was viewed both positively and negatively at this time. James Dalton, the industrial editor of *Motor* magazine characterized the market for used cars, except those selling for two hundred-fifty dollars or less, as exhibiting all the symptoms

of "locomotor ataxia." In his view this market was about to collapse because buyers had decided it was foolish to buy used cars when they could get new cars in all body styles for very little more.

Ford dealers such as O.L. Simpson, president of the Simpson Auto Co. in Oklahoma City, Oklahoma, took a much more positive approach. "At this time," he stated, in a February 1932 interview for *Ford Dealer and Service Field*, "a good used car will sell more readily than a new one." In Simpson's view, the secret was to recondition the car's body and mechanical components so that it was in first class condition.

About sixty percent of the used cars sold by Simpson's dealership went through the paint and body shop and thirty to thirty-five percent of the engines were overhauled. "In times of financial uncertainty, when motorists prefer to drive their old cars rather than buy new ones," Simpson said, "we must sell our service and push the used car trade."

In addition to selling new and used cars, Ford dealers were encouraged to pay strict attention to the operation of their service and parts departments if they wanted to stay out of the red. "Let me grease the old car and I won't have much trouble selling the new one," said an Oregon dealer.

Lubrication, the one service that cars needed at regular intervals, gave dealers frequent contact with their customers. Add to this a competent and friendly service staff and a clean, well-maintained service and parts department, and the dealer could easily generate much more business than just selling automobiles.

Thomas B. Martindale, Ford dealer in Philadelphia, was the subject of a two-reel Ford film detailing his motto that "Service: Intelligently Directed and Conscientiously Rendered Pays." His service department handled between one hundred-twenty-five and one hundred-seventy-five cars a day without any outside solicitation of service business. In his clean, and professionally equipped shop, customers received prompt, friendly and competent service. If they chose, they were allowed to watch the mechanic work on their cars. At the end, each job was checked carefully by the foreman before the car was released to the customer.

After surveying 1,219 customers and following them through 6,463,000 driven miles, the Butler County Motor Co. of Butler, Pennsylvania, came up with a plan to keep new car owners coming in for service after the three—500/1,000/1,500 mile—free inspections. The plan included a written guarantee covering key mechanical parts, as long as the customer continued to bring the car in for lubrication and inspection at five hundred to eight hundred mile intervals. For example, the water pump was guaranteed for 18,000 miles, the engine bearings for 50,000, the rear axle for 70,000 and so forth.

According to records kept by the company, the cost of backing this service guarantee was about three dollars per car, some cars costing more, the majority less. The dealer's profit came from the sale at regular intervals of

oil and lubricants. Assuming that the average Ford car was replaced at least every five years, the regular contacts with the customer gave the dealer an insight into when the owner was ready to buy another car and an obvious advantage in making that sale.

As they awaited the new Fords and tried to move out their remaining Model As, Ford dealers were also busy trying to secure advance orders for the "new" Ford. One dealer, Robert W. Ford, from Dearborn, Michigan, had a total of six hundred-twenty-four orders by the beginning of March, with deposits ranging from one dollar enrollments to full cash payment. He also had forty-four signed orders with agreements subject to appraisals at time of delivery.

The Buffalo Branch wrote to its dealers, "If your prospects could only see the parts as they come in here, they would realize that we are planning a real automobile and that there is nothing on the market at present with which it can be truly compared. Not many people would make the mistake of buying another make of car at this time if they knew what was in store for them. It is up to you to keep your salesmen enthusiastically on the job from early morning till late at night, contacting every possible prospect."

In the early months of 1932, Ford was unable or unwilling to help dealers by lowering prices or raising the discount, but the company did make some efforts to provide support. The Buffalo Branch, for example, ran a "Pinch-Hitters" contest in February that resulted in the sale of the remaining stock of Model AA trucks, except for three Funeral Coaches. The Dearborn Branch sponsored a Ford battery sales contest for its dealers.

Letters were sent to the Branches advising them to plan the work of their commercial caravan operation to secure the maximum results. Also stressed was the importance of arranging a transfer between Branches, if types requested by a fleet owner were not immediately available at the Branch of the dealer handling the sale.

Through its Branches, the company circulated a film, "The Successful Ford Dealer," which brought to Ford agencies across the country the wisdom and expertise of dealers who enjoyed outstanding success in sales and service. In addition, a list of ninety-five sales promotion films was sent to dealers with encouragement to use them to promote goodwill in their communities for Ford products.

Although new Model A types were not being introduced, the company still tried to motivate its dealers with

Referrals to a company such as the Wood Hydraulic Hoist and Body Co. helped Ford dealers sell a chassis or build goodwill in 1932.

ideas on selling special units such as the Standrive Delivery for the baking industry, and Standard Police Patrols, Ambulances and Funeral Coaches for other lines of work.

Sometimes, help came from outside suppliers. For example, the Baker-Raulang Co. of Cleveland, Ohio, designed a house-to-house delivery body mounted on the Ford standard 112-1/32-inch wheelbase Standrive chassis. Features included full height, dust-proof rear doors, which folded flush with the sides of the body, fully insulated roof, sides and rear doors, and a new-type, easier operating outside folding door. Drawers and other compartments could be furnished to suit individual requirements.

The Red Ball Transfer Co. of Indianapolis purchased nineteen Ford trucks equipped with Olson extensions, Warford transmissions and trailers from a local Ford dealer. The first one of these units delivered carried between eight and ten tons, and by March 1932, had traveled well over 20,000 miles with few problems, and an average of between eight and eleven miles per gallon of fuel.

The Portland Branch completed the sale of four Model 290-A Standard Patrols for city newspaper delivery. Pre-paring these units involved removing the seats and installing racks on either side to carry the bundles of papers. One-half of the partition back of the front seat was removed to allow access to the rear from the driver's seat.

From San Francisco came word of a new use for the Model A DeLuxe Delivery. The San Francisco Wheel Co., specializing in truck body work, filled an order from the Bank of America for a light armored car. The Ford Delivery was fitted with steel plate and mechanical improvements to take care of the extra load. When completed the job cost $1,100 including the cost of the car, the steel fittings and the mechanical improvements. The car averaged twelve miles to the gallon, and because of its size was easier to park and got around faster, thereby speeding up the pickup service.

The Des Moines Branch reported the sale of a Ford Ambulance modified to transport members of an orchestra and their instruments. The alterations on this vehicle were a woven wire partition about 3-1/2 inches ahead of the rear doors to provide a compartment for the instruments. Directly in front of the partition a Tudor rear seat was installed, and directly in front of the Tudor seat three bucket seats were placed. Branches were encour-

In 1932, The Portland (Oregon) *Journal* used a fleet of Ford trucks for the delivery of newspapers. (Photo courtesy of Henry Ford Museum and Greenfield Village)

aged to pass on these ideas to dealers in hope that a number of sales would result.

In June 1932, Henry Ford's wife, Clara, received a letter from the wife of an unemployed Ford worker with ten years seniority. It is reprinted here courtesy of the Henry Ford Research Center:

My Dear Mrs. Ford:

"Will you do what you can to get my husband back to work in your factory? He has stood in line hours at a time and is never permitted to enter the employment office to speak to anyone about work. He has worked there all the past ten years with the exception of this last when he has worked only five days. We cannot understand being forgotten when so many are hired who have never been there before. We only ask fair treatment, not expecting favors. We have three children and have tried so many times to get back there that we are about desperate. . . . Please do what you can for us, we've tried to help ourselves.

"Any help you may give us in trying to get us work will be very deeply appreciated. He worked in the rear axle housing department but can run the machines in other places too."

This poignant letter brings home the anxiety, suffering and desperation of one Ford family among hundreds of thousands in that last official year of the Model A Ford. The Great Depression reached its bottom in 1932. Across the land, in the countryside and in the cities, people were unemployed, hungry, cold and homeless. By the winter of 1932, the Michigan jobless rate had reached forty percent, and 125,000 Detroit families, one in three, were without any financial support. Four thousand children a day turned up in bread lines. Those on relief in Detroit were getting just $3.75 a week. The number of Ford unemployed reached 90,000, according to Ford figures.

Even those who found work for at least a few days in Ford factories were suffering. Nevins and Hill recount the story told by Theodore A. Mallon, of Ford's testing department. At noon one day, Mallon saw a man take his lunchbox into an obscure corner. It turned out he was lunching on boiled potato peelings, so he could send food to his wife and children who had gone to a low-rent area.

Even though in some respects, as Joyce Shaw Peterson points out, auto workers fared better than other workers, the picture for them was gloomy at best. For many the Depression meant the loss of job security, and the comfort they had struggled to attain through hard work for relatively high wages.

At Ford, the daily minimum wage rate established in October 1931 was six dollars a day. By September 1932, this was down to five dollars and then to four dollars in October. In many instances it was as low as thirty cents an hour. In February 1932, the company Branch salary and wage schedule lists seventy-five cents an hour as the hiring rate for unskilled labor for all U.S. Branches. Skilled laborers (machinists, millwrights and chief electricians) were hired at ninety or ninety-five cents depending on individual skill. By the following November, the Rouge hourly wage ranged from an average fifty cents an hour for some men in the open hearth department to $.7957 for some welders. Foremen were paid $1.0866 an hour.

By late-1932, the average hourly rate at the Rouge was $.6144; at all plants it was $.6175. An interesting aside to this pertains to women's wages. At the Ypsilanti Ford plant, men averaged $.5305 an hour while women earned an average of just $.2996 an hour.

Unemployment demonstrations in industrial cities organized by the Communist Party started in 1930. The most spectacular of these was the Ford-Hunger March that happened during the last days of the Model A and the eve of the V-8. On March 7, 1932, about 3,000 people participated in a march from Detroit to the Rouge plant to dramatize the plight of the unemployed and present their demands to the Ford Motor Co.

They were met in Dearborn by tear gas, truncheon wielding police, fire hoses and eventually bullets that killed four and wounded twenty or more. For the most part, the *Detroit Free Press* stated, "the demonstrators were ordinary men and women, out of jobs and out of the necessities of life."

Twenty thousand mourners participated in the funeral of the four men on March 11. "A funeral banner," writes Joyce Shaw Peterson, "proclaiming FORD GAVE THEM BULLETS FOR BREAD was telling evidence of the change in Henry Ford's public image in Detroit and represented for many auto workers the shattering of a final illusion."

Increasingly, it appeared that Henry Ford was out of touch with the depths of the misery experienced by his unemployed workers and millions across the nation. In February 1932, the newspapers carried the announcement that the Ford Motor Co. was going to "risk everything, if necessary, to see if we cannot make what the country needs most—work, jobs." It was a promise on which Ford could not deliver. By the end of 1932, Ford closed all but eight assembly plants.

In mid-1932, three letters from Henry Ford were published as advertisements in two hundred daily newspapers. They contained his advice to the suffering nation: cultivate family gardens; organize self-help programs; keep one foot on the land and another foot in industry— his village industries idea. "The ads appeared out of touch with reality to many readers," notes David Lewis.

Even William J. Cameron, Ford's chief press interpreter, was at a loss to explain where Henry Ford was at. According to David Lewis, Cameron was asked the following question by a journalist: "He thought he had the answer to Depression. Now how does he take it?" Cameron replied, "I don't know. He doesn't talk about it much. It's so terrible that I believe he doesn't dare let himself think about it."

In the midst of adversity, one can often find a light, and even great achievement. In a sense this happened in the Ford world in 1931, when the Mexican artist, Diego Rivera, one of the greatest muralists of the 20th century, was commissioned by Edsel Ford to paint murals with an industrial theme at the Detroit Institute of Art.

Rivera took his inspiration from the Great Rouge plant, touring and sketching there for two months in early 1932. The result was twenty-seven fresco panels or "visual books" in the museum's garden court. In her study, "diego rivera," Dorothy McMeekin says that the two large murals are representations of the automobile industry, but the majority of the other twenty-five panels deal with some aspect of theoretical and applied science.

James Cockcroft, author of *Diego Rivera*, argues that "they remain the world's most acclaimed painted vision of technology and science."

Robert Asher and Ronald Edsforth in *Autowork*, state that in focusing on people in the factory, "Rivera's murals suggest a negative side of factory life." He depicts the machines as "dominating the men around them." Rivera's Rouge they say, "is frenetic, reminding the observer of the nervous condition called Forditis suffered by workers in the early days of the assembly line." Rivera himself called his Detroit murals "the great saga of machine and steel."

As the curtain rolled down on the Model A in 1932, there were still millions of them in daily use, doing yeoman service for the transportation and haulage life of the nation. Then, slowly, as they were replaced by newer models, they became less and less of a presence in the day-to-day transportation scene. However, as we well know, there has never been an end to Model A. Since December 1927, Henry's Lady has been a survivor in numbers unmatched by any other prewar vehicle.

Today, Model A Fords exist in substantial numbers and command the loyalty and enthusiasm of a large group of hobbyists. In some cases, they are still being used for daily transportation. Henry and Edsel Ford would be pleased and, probably, more than a little surprised.

The story of the seven decades of Model A since production ended is rich in anecdotal and published material. It is also an unfinished story to which chapters are added daily. Although this writer can barely scratch the surface, here is a glimpse into the life the Model A has enjoyed since 1932.

Even as the V-8 Ford became the centerpiece of the Ford Motor Co.'s publicity efforts, *Ford News* continued to carry the experiences of Model A owners in its pages. A man from Fairfield, Ohio, for example, took delivery of a Model A Coupe in 1929, fully intending to drive it at least 100,000 miles. As it turned out, he did not quite make it, trading the Coupe with 82,836 miles on the odometer, for a new Model B in July 1932.

The record he sought, was terminated short of achievement when the Coupe was hit in the side by another car and forced into a telephone pole. "It was only the staunchness of the Ford that saved me," he wrote. "I escaped without injury. The Ford was in perfect running condition at the time and no one could have bought it from me, but after this mishap I decided to get a new one."

The man said that during the period of almost four years that he owned the Model A he bought 4,300 gallons of gasoline and managed 19.277 miles per gallon. The cost of operating the car was only $.0215 per mile, which included the cost of the car, all repairs and labor, tires, insurance, gasoline, oil and other minor expenses minus the trade-in allowance.

A 1929 Sport Coupe at a 1960 gathering of Model A enthusiasts.

A 1935 photo of an abandoned 1930 Model A used by two fugitives from the law. (Photo courtesy of ACME)

A badly damaged Model A Fordor that was involved in a roll-over accident. Note the rope visible between the fender and headlight base. The car probably rolled down an embankment and the rope was used to pull the car back onto the road. The Ford has a 1938 New Jersey license plate

A 1931 Model A slant window Fordor with minor front end damage. Note how the bumper was torn completely off its mounting brackets. The worn condition of the tires might have contributed to this wreck. The Ford had a 1933 New Jersey license plate.

A 1936 photo of a father and daughter and their Model A Tudor back from a successful fishing trip.

A 1937 photo of Don Van Slyke and the family's 1931 Model A Coupe.

In 1933, Ford notified its Branches that it was classifying parts for service into four categories: fast moving, medium moving, slow moving and inactive. Because of the demand for them, many parts for the Model A were classified as "fast moving."

As the 1930s rolled on, the saga of the Model A Ford continued. In 1934, *The Diabolical*, a book by H.H. McWilliams, was published in England. This is an account of the adventures of five people who set out in a converted Ford truck to make a journey from Palestine to England across Asia Minor and the Balkans. The "Diabolical" was a modified 1-1/2 ton Model AA truck. It inadvertently received its name from two of the Palestinian men involved in modifying it whose command of

English was quite limited. The truck lived up to its reputation for "diabolical strength," carrying the group over difficult terrain for 3,933 miles in fifty days.

A ten-year-old Model A Coupe was still doing its work for the Travis Park Methodist Church of San Antonio, Texas, in 1939. The owner of the Coupe, Mrs. Fugua, the official church visitor, drove the car 98,646 miles during those years. "Miss Special," as the car was called, and its owner made approximately 62,600 calls in homes and hospitals, took 28,213 bouquets to sick members and shut-ins, welcomed 618 babies into the world, witnessed 520 weddings and arranged for 892 funerals. By 1939, the car had its second coat of paint, second set of tires, new seat covers and was about to get new piston rings.

The prewar years would be incomplete without mentioning speed equipment for Model A Fords as well as their use in "hot rod" racing. In December 1930, Ford announced the release through service of a high compression head for Model A Fords. These heads had a compression ratio of 5.22 to 1 and were to be installed, the company warned in a follow-up notice, "on cars for police work only." Dealers were even told that they had to supply the engine number of the police car and the owner's name and address when they ordered one of these heads.

By April 1931, the demand was so strong that the company changed its policy, and dealers were permitted to sell these heads to anyone desiring them, as long as the purchaser was fully advised that the engine was not quite as smooth in its general operation with this high compression head as with the standard head. The price of a high compression cylinder head was $5.50 plus 35 cents for the gasket and $1.50 for installation or a total charge to the customer of $7.35.

MODEL A FORD

Announcement

In accordance with our usual policy, we are first to announce the new overhead valve system for the Model A Ford. We will begin deliveries October 1, 1928.

Detailed information will be ready in a few days.

If you want the first one in your territory write Morton & Brett, Indianapolis, Ind., for full particulars.

Morton & Brett announcement of the new overhead valve system for the Model A Ford (1928), *Secrets*, **January 1998.**

Speed equipment for the Model A was available as early as 1928 from aftermarket suppliers. According to *Secrets* magazine of the Secrets of Speed Society, the first overhead valve (OHV) system for the Model A Ford was announced by Morton and Brett on October 1, 1928.

Ford Dealer & Service Field carried numerous ads and articles for non-Ford high-speed equipment in the pages of its monthly publication. Companies running ads for speed equipment included R.R. Giant, Schofield, Morton and Brett, Harry A. Miller, Winfield, Green, Hal, Riley, Reus, Ruckstell and Columbus. In February 1930, Schofield offered a big discount on Miller Ford products. For example, the Schofield high-speed overhead valve head, which normally retailed for $137.50, was offered at a special introductory price of just $82.50. Miller carburetors retailing for twenty dollars were reduced to twelve dollars. For the dirt track racer with big bucks there was also the Miller double overhead cam, eight-valve racing head reduced from five hundred dollars to two hundred-ninety-nine dollars. A new head for Model A Ford engines was announced by Harry A. Miller in the June 1930 issue.

An example of the speeds attained was a test run with a Model A Roadster over a two-and-one-half mile course at Anderson, Indiana, on July 22, 1931 (*Secrets* magazine). The Model A was stock with no change in gear ratio, cams or pistons. It was equipped with R & R Cyclone overhead valve equipment that included a 1-1/2 inch downdraft Winfield Carburetor and High Duty Water Pump. The car achieved one hundred-one miles per hour with the wind, and one hundred miles per hour against.

In *Secrets* magazine, Don Radbruch writes that track roadster or "hot rod" racing was popular from its beginning in 1924 in California, until 1956 when the sport died out. The roadsters competed on hundreds of tracks in thirty-five states. Before World War II, many of the cars were "pure" Model A Fords with an A or B engine and speed equipment. "They won most of the races in Indiana and a fair share of the races in California," Radbruch says. In Texas, a 1931 Roadster driven by owner Lee Wick was "virtually unbeatable."

In *Ford Hot Rods*, author Dain Gingerelli devotes a full chapter to the Model A and what he terms its "timeless style, endless possibilities." Gingerelli argues that the Model A Ford was a solid candidate for building a hot rod or racer because of the adaptability of the Model A engine and the car's "simplicity and resounding durability." The fact that a hot rod conversion could be done relatively inexpensively also helped.

"Today," writes Gingerelli, "as was the case more than half a century ago, the legendary Ford Model A engine enjoys a widespread popularity among hot rod engine builders. . . . Simply, the Model A is considered one of the all-time beautiful Ford bodies and especially lends itself to customizing." Gingerelli also points out that a large number of original Model A hot rods that were built shortly before or after World War II, have survived and can be seen on the road or at rod runs to this day.

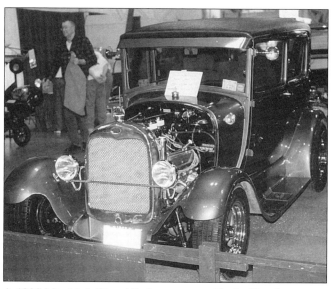

A 1929 Model A Street Sedan - owner Kevin Keating.

Although not the ordinary means of transportation for most people, Model A Fords were still seen on the roads here and there during the 1940s as the story of W.L. Gambill at the beginning of this chapter testifies. The author can still remember hitching a ride to school in 1948 from a man driving his Model A Coupe to work.

Motorin' Along! (Reminisce Books), a collection of anecdotes about people and their cars, includes several Model A adventures from the 1940s. On one occasion, two young men traveling down a highway in their Model A heard a loud bang and felt the Model A's left rear drop somewhat just as they met a late-model Oldsmobile going in the opposite direction. Thinking they had had a blowout they got out only to find the entire wheel gone.

Finding this funny, the young men began to laugh until they were confronted by the angry owner of the Oldsmobile. Turns out the wheel hit the Oldsmobile and disabled it to the point that it could not move under its own power. Luckily, no one was hurt and, in time, tempers cooled. After looking a bit, the young men found the wheel in a field where it landed after jumping a fence. It was undamaged and did not have a mark on it.

A 1930 Model A Tudor and a 1941 Ford, circa 1941.

Special Announcement
To Ford Owners!

Harry A. Miller

Production is now under way on my new Harry A. Miller Head for Model "A" Ford engines, which is the only Head for this type Ford car ever designed by me, and is a combination of the principles included in the Miller racing engines which have established world's speed records on land and water.

My new Miller Head for Ford cars has an Overhead Camshaft like all Miller racing cars and is being manufactured at the new address below.

Equip your Ford engine with this new Head, backed by my many years reputation in designing racing motors and built under my personal supervision.

I also wish to take this opportunity to announce to the motoring public that I have absolutely no connections with any other Head for Ford engines.

Further details of this new Miller product will be announced in this publication next month.

Harry A. Miller

1348 Venice Boulevard   · · · · Los Angeles, California

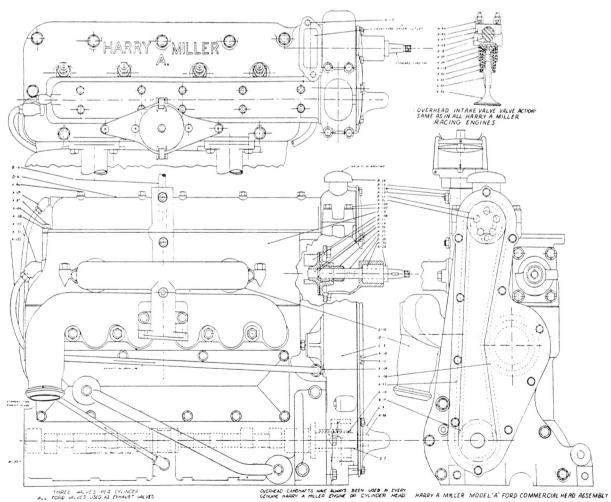

Sketch Showing Details of New Miller Head for Model "A" Fords

Harry Miller ad from *Ford Dealer & Service Field*, June 1930.

A Model A active in the 1940s and still around today, is Bob Pierce's 1930 Model A racer that ran on the Winchester (Virginia) Airport Speedway in 1946-48. Pierce and his jalopy Model A were profiled by John Haines in *Old Cars Weekly*. Put to rest due to a blown engine, the

A 1941 photo of a wrecked Model A Tudor.

jalopy languished outdoors, rusting away for forty years, until Pierce rescued it, and, with the help of his friends and a lot of hard work, returned it to its original condition. In 1996, the racer debuted at the Speedway's 50th anniversary celebration. Pierce enjoys showing the car and, for those interested, a good place to see it is at the annual fall Hershey Meet.

The tale of how Henry Ford borrowed a young Edison Institute student's Model A Ford during World War II is recounted by David Lewis in his "Ford Country" column in *Cars & Parts* magazine. The story originally appeared in the September 1992 issue of *American Heritage*. The student drove his Model A to school, parked it in the parking lot, and, when he found it missing, was told that Henry Ford had borrowed it. Ford took the car for several laps around the nearby speed oval and then returned it. In that time of rationing, the student could only think of the precious gas he would find so difficult to replace.

After returning the car, Ford asked to see the owner and told him that he had a special place in his heart for the Model A and just had to drive it when he saw it in the parking lot. He also told him that the car ran well. Ford then jotted a note on a small card, gave it to the student and told him to take it to the company gas pump. The student ended up with a full tank of gas for his Model A,

A 1930 Model A Ford jalopy - owner Bob Pierce. This car ran on the Winchester Airport Speedway in 1946-48.

George DeLaRoche returned from military service in 1946, and bought this 1930 Fordor. He recalls tipping it over on a snowy winter's day without any damage to the occupants or the car.

Harold McAdam (left) and friend with a 1928-29 Model A Fordor in a photo taken May 1, 1945, near Liepzig, Germany. Car is equipped with blackout lights.

the importance of which only those who remember gas rationing can fully appreciate.

The Doodlebug or poor man's tractor as it is sometimes called, was popular during World War II. They were used for farm work, odd jobs and recreation and can occasionally still be found in use today. Many of them were built by backyard mechanics from whatever parts they could scrounge. Others, were converted into Doodlebugs with kits available from Sears and Roebuck Co., and Montgomery Ward.

In his *Old Cars Weekly* "Questions & Answers" column, Tom Brownell says that, "Although one could be constructed from any automotive chassis, the most common starting point was a Model A Ford." The reason for that was that they were fairly common, cheap and the gas tank location in the cowl eliminated the problem of where to mount the fuel tank.

An example of a doodlebug still around, is the unit of Dick White of Oneida, New York. He has owned one for many years and uses it around his property, mostly for odd jobs and for his grandchildren to drive. In the Shelby (Michigan) *The Herald-Journal*, Carrisa White writes that a club of "doodlers" has been in existence in Mears, Michigan, for about twenty years. The only prerequisite for joining this Doodlebug Club is that the bug should be as original as possible, not repainted, and have good brakes.

The 1950s is the decade in which the Model A Ford as a hobby began to take off. Increasingly, Model As emerged from the barns and sheds where they had rested, and were put in driving condition or restored completely. In response to a common need to exchange information and parts and share the enjoyment of the car, two national clubs were formed.

The Model "A" Restorers Club, Inc. (MARC) was founded by William E. (Bill) Hall in West Hartford, Connecticut, in 1952. As this group became better known people around the country began to join. In 1955, the Model A Restorers Club of Southern California was organized as a region of MARC by Red Grow. It became a new and separate non-profit organization, the Model A Ford Club of America, Inc. (MAFCA) in 1957.

At the end of 1998, MARC, headquartered in Dearborn, Michigan, had over 10,000 families, one hundred-forty-eight U.S. chapters, nine special interest groups and eight chapters in Canada, New Zealand and Norway. MAFCA, with headquarters in LaHabra, California, had almost 13,000 families, two hundred-fifty U.S. chapters, sixteen special interest groups, five regions, and twenty-nine international chapters in Canada and thirteen foreign nations.

Six times a year, these two clubs publish quality magazines and distribute them to their members. *Model "A" News* is published by MARC and *The Restorer* by MAFCA. Both offer excellent technical and historical articles for the benefit of people who own Model A Fords, or for anyone interested in automotive history.

Model A Doodlebug - owner Dick White.

MARC News

Published Monthly by the Model "A" Restorers Club

Published by MARC

1127 Raymond Ave., Glendale, Calif.

August - September, 1957

EDITOR'S NOTE

We regret to have made you wait until this late date for your August issue of the News. To obtain the complete coverage of the Dearborn meet and in order to set up needed equipment for addressing the mail we have waited until this date and included the September issue along with that of August.

To eliminate errors and omissions in future issues it will be necessary that all info including classified ads and news items be in our hands on or before the 10th of each month. Thank you for your patience and understanding. We hope to improve and better serve you with each future issue.

BROTHER OF GOVERNOR AND CHICAGOAN WIN
TOP AWARDS AT 1957 FORD MODEL A MEET

DEARBORN, Mich.--Richard E. Williams, 290 Hillcrest Road, Grosse Pointe Farms, Mich., brother of Michigan Governor G. Mennen Williams, and Russell J. Gerrit, 5719 North Milwaukee, Chicago, Ill., shared top honors in the 1957 Ford Model A Restorers Club national meet at Greenfield Village (August 6, 7, 8).

Williams won first place in the 1928-29 division with his 1929 Touring, while a 1930 Roadster took the same honor for Gerrit in the 1930-31 group.

Second-place winners were William Abbott, 1322 Washington, Alton, Ill., 1929 Touring in the 1928-29 division and Robert J. Carini, 67 Denslow Road, Glastonbury, Conn., in 1930-31 competition.

Third places went to Wendell F. Chapelle, Route 1, Rathbone, N. Y., 1929 Roadster in the 1928-29 group and George

O. Boellert, 4112 North 39th, Omaha, Neb., 1931 Victoria, in 1930-31.

A 1930 Sport Coupe, tagged an early favorite by observers after its arrival by van from California, won for its owner, Claude Grow of Glendale, a special grand prize for the most outstanding restoration "above and beyond the original Model A standards." Grow valued his entry at $4,000.

A fellow Californian, Peter D. Pershing, 23-year-old electronics engineer from (6098 Homestead Road) Los Altos, made the 2,809-mile trip in his 1931 Deluxe coupe and thereby won a prize for the longest distance traveled. Appropriately, he was given a choice of two Model A white wall or four black wall tires.

Pershing, however, won by only 35 miles over a third Californian, John Tous-

continued on page 6

1

Early (1957) issue of *MARC NEWS*, which later became *Model "A" News*.

In the 1950s, as interest in the Model A hobby grew, there was a need for parts and for qualified people to do the restoration work. New old stock (NOS) parts were readily available and much of the restoration work was done by hobbyists, either the car owner himself or someone in his local area who devoted spare time to working on Model A Fords.

In time, as the hobby grew and NOS parts became harder to find, a reproduction industry began to fill the need and today sells parts through national and local outlets across the country. Many of these parts are made in the United States, some in foreign countries. Most are of high quality for restoration work, but are not necessarily correct for concours judging. NOS parts are still available, but in limited quantities and at rising prices.

As the 1990s wind down, cars are still being restored by individual hobbyists, although restoration shops specifically geared to doing this work do much more of it than in the early days. The cost of a restoration has accelerated rapidly and is primarily determined by how much of the work the hobbyist can do himself and the kind of a car he wants—a good-looking, dependable driver or a trailered, blue ribbon show car.

The 1950s are also noteworthy in the life of the Model A because it was during this decade that we saw the first signs of sufficient interest in the car to warrant the publication of important books and articles about it. As early as 1954, *Popular Science* featured "A Lament for the Model A" by Frank Rowsome, Jr., a nostalgic look at

what Rowsome calls "an uncommonly willing car." At the end of the article he made a prediction and proved himself somewhat of a prophet; "26 years from now, in 1980, darn few of us will recall the glistening 1954 models with the same warm affection with which we now remember the Model A." (This article is reprinted in Mary Moline's excellent book, *The Best of Ford*.)

The most significant Model A book of the decade was *Henry's Fabulous Model "A" Ford* by Leslie R. Henry, published in 1959. This groundbreaking book was unique, particularly because it contained previously unpublished material about the Model A. Another book from the 1950s, not nearly as well-known, is *Model A Mule* by Robert J. Willis, an award-winning children's novel (ages twelve to sixteen). It is about a boy and the Model A truck he built from scrap heaps and junkyards.

In 1958, longtime *New Yorker* writer E.B. White added his thoughts about the Model A to the growing literature about the car. As cited by David Lewis, White said in part, "The reason the A is going strong today is simple: The car is a triumph of honest, unfussy design and superior materials. It doesn't look like a turbojet or like an elephant's ear, it drinks gasoline in moderation, it puts on no airs, and when something gets out of adjustment the owner can usually tinker it back to health himself."

Placing the Model A into a historical perspective, John B. Rae in *American Automobile Manufacturers* (1959), acknowledges that the Model A "was good enough to arrest the decline of the Ford Motor Company,

In Germany, during military service, Norm McGowan owned this 1930 Model A Roadster with jeep wheels and headlights.

although not to restore the company to its former position." In Rae's view, the Model A was only a temporary success because the Ford Motor Co. was "now following automotive development rather than leading it."

In addition to the formation of clubs and the publishing of books and articles about the car, there was a lot of other activity in the Model A world of the 1950s. More and more people, hobbyists and not, were driving and enjoying them. Included among these drivers were the famous such as Nelson Rockefeller and Averell Harriman who in the 1958 New York gubernatorial election featured Model A Fords in their campaigns.

Rockefeller bought his 1931 Phaeton from his brother David in 1933 and, according to Leslie R. Henry, was still driving it at his summer estate at Seal Harbor, Maine, in 1958. Harriman's Model A was a 1929 Roadster. Henry says that on December 2, 1927, Harriman was the first purchaser of a Model A Ford in New York City.

Finally, let's not forget the land of television, just beginning to grow up in the 1950s. A 1931 Model A Phaeton played a prominent part in the comedy series, "The Real McCoys," featuring Walter Brennan.

On June 20, 1962, a round trip transcontinental tour left New York City for San Francisco. Forty-one adventurers and twenty-one Model A Fords set out to attend the Second National Convention of the Model A Ford Club of America. The trip covered 7,000 miles and took twenty-four days. Along the way they were joined from time to time by other cars. The caravan, broken up into groups of four or five cars, was accompanied by a 1962 Thunderbird and a new Econoline truck, both contributed by the Ford Motor Co.

In addition to minor difficulties such as a timing gear failure, flat tires and a clogged radiator, the group encountered only two major problems and one unfortunate accident. The problems were a broken fan blade,

Lineup of Model A Fords at a meet of the Mohican Model A Ford Club in 1962.

Cover of *Science and Mechanics*, December 1960.

which necessitated the replacement of an entire cooling system, and an engine breakdown in one of the cars. The only serious mishap happened to a four-door sedan that was forced off the road by a large trailer truck and rolled over 2-1/2 times. The car was totaled but saved its occupants from any serious injury. On the whole, the Model A Fords performed admirably.

The complete story and pictures of this remarkable trek, written by tour chairman Ed Rossig, can be found in the September-October 1962 *The Restorer*. Rossig concludes his report with the following comment: "It didn't need proving, but nevertheless we have proved that the Model A Ford is definitely here to stay, not only as a pampered showpiece but as a practical tour car."

Motivated, no doubt, by the growing fascination with the Model A Ford, several magazines published reports on the Model A in the 1960s. These included: *Science and Mechanics* in December 1960, *Motor Trend* in August 1962 and *Mechanix Illustrated* in November 1968.

The article in *Science and Mechanics* includes a color fold-out, suitable for framing, featuring a 1931 Deluxe Roadster, as well as several other Model A Fords. Com-

Centerfold of *Science and Mechanics*, December 1960.

parison is made to the compact cars of 1960: Falcon, Corvair and Valiant. In fuel economy the Model A's overall was 16.9 miles per gallon, which was close to Corvair and Valiant but well behind Falcon. "In other respects," the magazine stated, "Model A is no challenger to the modern breed of compacts."

In the opinion of *Science and Mechanics* the Model A should be called a "classic compact," disagreeing with those who say that a car should be both extremely rare and expensive to qualify as a classic. "We predict," the article concludes, "that in another 30 years you will see 60-year-old Model As running around, while there won't be many 30-year old compacts."

Motor Trend published the details of a fifth-wheel performance test on a 1931 Roadster. With driver and passenger, the Roadster was put through acceleration tests at Riverside Raceway in California. A pickup from zero to thirty miles per hour registered 8.4 seconds in one test, 7.9 on the second—the difference due to the headwind. Acceleration from zero to forty-five miles per hour was 19.5 seconds in the first instance, 18.7 in

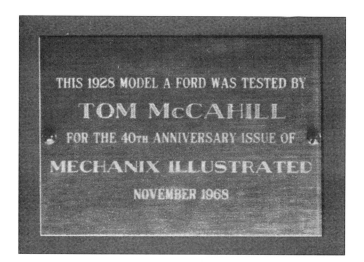

November 1968 issue of *Mechanix Illustrated*, fortieth anniversary issue, showing the plaque (top) attached to the Model A Ford after it was road tested by Tom McCahill.

the second. Top speed was fifty-eight miles per hour. Speed in gears, at 3000 revolutions per minute, was twenty-one miles per hour in first, thirty-two in second, and fifty-eight in third. The brakes were "unimpressive," the magazine stated. "Stopping distances from 30 mph were 33 feet, and from 58 mph (60 on the speedometer), 206 feet."

Tom McCahill tested a 1928 Model A Tudor for the fortieth anniversary issue of *Mechanix Illustrated*. The article included an anecdotal history of the Model A as well as a description of the test car. Tests were run by McCahill on the parkways of the state of Connecticut. The top speed was sixty-seven miles per hour, which, McCahill wrote, "is similar in noise and anxiety to doing 150 with a full-house hemi."

McCahill found the Tudor's steering "a little stiff," mentioned the need for double and even triple clutching and noted, wryly, that once when he had to stop fast to make an exit, "there was enough brake chatter to shake up the goldfish in a house eight miles away." On several occasions McCahill tried to drag with the modern traffic but, he said, "there were no red faces in the other cars."

In summing up, McCahill says that in its day the Model A Ford was "one of the greatest automotive buys of all time. It was as rugged as mother-love and as reliable as the tide." He concludes, "Today there are still thousands of Model A Fords being used as everyday transportation and I expect long after I'm gone there will still be many of them running. Though Henry would probably be the last to admit it, the four years of the Model A was Ford's finest hour."

In celebration of its birthday, *Mechanix Illustrated* ran a two-part puzzle contest with the Model A Ford tested by Tom McCahill as the prize. The car had a plaque on the dash stating that it was tested by him. The author wonders if that Model A is still around?

From a historical perspective, two books published in the 1960s bear mention. The *Ford Model 'A' Album*, compiled by Floyd Clymer and Leslie R. Henry was published in 1960. It is primarily a pictorial history of the Model A Ford, but also includes technical and other articles, reprints of ads and a truck section. *Model A Ford Construction, Operation and Repair* by Victor W. Page, is a technical book for the restorer, which includes several pages of valuable historical information.

A record for a tour with a single Model A was set in 1979 by two residents of Corrales, New Mexico, Bill Klenck and his son, Angelo. The Klenck's original goal was to travel from the north coast of Alaska to the southern tip of South America, a distance, they calculated, of about 12,000 miles. The car selected for the trip was a 1929 Model A chassis fitted with a motorhome body equipped with bunks, stove, ice box and storage. They returned home some seven months later, after actually covering 30,525 miles at an average speed of twenty-eight miles per hour. The highlights of Bill and Angelo's unforgettable adventure are chronicled in *The Restorer*, July-August 1979 and March-April 1980.

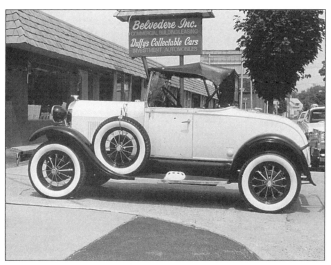

A 1929 Shay Model A replicar.

Among numerous other noteworthy Model A happenings during the 1970s were the television appearance of Model A Fords as part of a Ford Motor Co. ad campaign for the Pinto in 1972; Environmental Protection Agency tests on the Model A that, according to *The Restorer*, achieved 14.1 miles per gallon city and 19.4 highway, with a combined fuel economy of 16.1 miles per gallon; the Shay Model A replicars; and the growing number of books about the Model A available to the Model A enthusiast. Also, in 1973, a *Life* magazine panel of historians, designers, and collectors rated the Model A as the seventh best American car. And, in a special seventy-fifth anniversary Ford issue (June 1978), *Car Collector* included two Model As, the 1929 Town Car and the 1931 Deluxe Roadster in its list of "The Ten Most Collectible Fords."

As explained by Tom Brownell in his *Old Cars Weekly* "Q & A" column, the Shay Model A Fords were 1929 Model A replicas using Pinto drivetrains. Shay "As" were produced between 1979 and approximately March 1982 in Michigan. More than 2,000 of them were sold through selected Ford, Lincoln and Mercury dealers. A 1955 Ford Thunderbird replica was also built in limited numbers. Unable to sell enough cars the company went out of business. The Shay was not the only Model A replicar. For example, Lewis points out that in 1966, Glassic Industries, Inc. of West Palm Beach, Florida, began producing full-scale fiberglass, 1928-styled As.

By the end of the 1970s, there were more than twenty books about the Model A, most of them technical in nature. Three influential books were published in the early-1970s and are still popular today: *The Ford Model "A"—As Henry Built It* by George DeAngelis, Edward P. Francis and Leslie R. Henry, was first published in 1971 and is now in its fourth edition; *Henry's Lady* by Ray Miller was published in 1972; *Model A/AA Truck Owner*, compiled under the direction of A.G. McMillan, was published in 1975. These books deserve a prominent spot in the library of a true Model A Ford hobbyist.

Although not specifically Model A, the author would be remiss by not mentioning *Ford Life* magazine, which contains numerous period photos and articles about the Model A Ford. Sadly, the magazine ended after twenty-two issues (November/December 1970 through May/June 1974). Lorin Sorensen, publisher of *Ford Life*, later published *The Fordiana Series*, six lavish books about the Ford Motor Co. and its cars. Several of these have extensive sections on the Model A.

The Model A as a collector car was in full swing by the 1970s, but there were still many being used for everyday transportation or being put to other uses by innovative owners. In a 1993 letter to *Old Cars Weekly*, reader Jerry Voss, described how his uncle, "a dyed-in-the-wool Ford man who lives on a farm," found many uses for Model As and Bs.

"One with a shortened frame and no body," Voss writes, "was used to pull a rotary hoe, another a dump truck, and still another made into a winch or boom truck as he called it. All were used in the worst kind of weather with no hoods of any kind over the engines."

The experience of Voss' uncle was not unusual. Just like its ancestor, the Model T, the Model A has been readily adapted to a myriad of non-traditional uses. They have been used as lawn mowers, rollers, tractors, wood cutters, yard locomotives, railroad cars, motor tugs, stationary and portable power units, snowmobiles, to moor dirigibles and launch gliders. The Model A engine has powered boats, airplanes, a smithy, etc. Its steering wheel has been adapted for bobsleds.

Two original Model A owners, still driving and enjoying their Model A Fords in the 1970s, were profiled in an article by Hall Townsend in *The Restorer* (November-December 1977). In September 1931, Julia Roevens' husband gave her a brand new Model A Standard Fordor for a birthday present. Forty-six years later the Model A was still owned and used by Julia for regular transportation and for her outings with the New Orleans As, the local club to which she belonged.

Robert Foster, of Rutherfordton, North Carolina, paid five hundred dollars for his new 1928 Roadster. Nearly fifty years later, he still owned and drove it regularly. Offered considerable money to sell the car, Foster just shook his head and said, "It would be like one gone from the family if I sold this car."

The last two decades of the century have been busy ones in the Model A world. Both national clubs have prospered and grown in number of members and chapters. Two important developments that strengthened the hobby were the formation of the Model A Ford Foundation Inc. (MAFFI) in 1987 and the Secrets of Speed Society (SOSS) in the late-1980s.

The Model A Ford Foundation is a non-profit organization dedicated to preserving the Model A, its history and memorabilia, for future generations. *The "A" Preserver*, a quarterly newsletter, keeps members informed of projects and events. The Secrets of Speed Society is a special interest group devoted to the history of Model T,

A 1931 Model A Tractor - owner Ray Hart. Kits to make these tractors were available from Sears and Montgomery Ward.

Toro Model A lawnmower, manufactured in Minneapolis.

Model A Snowmobiles.

Cartoon booklet "A-Toons." (Photo courtesy of Stan Blinco)

Cartoon booklet "Henry 'A' sez..." (Photo courtesy of Gene Patrick)

A and B Fords as used after the assembly line in racing, hill climbs, cross country touring and all forms of performance. Membership is approximately 2,400. A quarterly journal, *Secrets*, the Ford Speed and Sport Magazine, is published by the Society.

As the century closes out, there have been several important books with a historical twist added to the ever growing amount of technical information available to the Model A hobbyist. Most important is "The Model A Judging Standards & Restoration Guidelines" published jointly by the Model "A" Restorers Club and the Model A Ford Club of America. These guidelines, first published in 1989, have gone through two revisions, most recently in 1997. Those with an interest in the Model A Ford, as a restorer, hobbyist, or just as a historian, should not be without this book. Another excellent historical reference is *Selling The New Ford*, by Jim Schild, which was updated in 1996. Schild also publishes *The Restorer's Model A Shop Manual*, updated in 1998, and an AA Truck Supplement.

Both national clubs and small local clubs, such as the Mohican Model A Ford Club (New York) have kept the Model A hobby thriving into the 1990s.

Cartoon booklet "I'm Gonna Fix It Up Someday." (Photo courtesy of Bruce McDougal and *The Restorer*)

Three other books of the 1990s for the Model A enthusiast are: *Practical Information About 1930 and 1931 Coupes - A to Z*, by Marith McCoul, the *Model A Ford Mechanics Handbook* by Les Andrews and *Ford Model T & Model A Buyer's Guide* by Paul G. McLaughlin. Also of interest, is a non-club quarterly publication, *Model A Trader*, which contains in-depth articles, product reviews, and practical information for the Model A hobbyist.

For those with an interest in drive reports, *Special Interest Autos* published a lengthy comparison of the 1928 Chevrolet Coupe and Model A Sport Coupe in its December 1987 issue. Author Arch Brown says that, given their age and the remarkably low prices at which they were first sold, both cars are impressive automobiles. "Our overall impression is," he writes, "that the Chevrolet is the more refined of the two, while the Ford appears to have the edge in sturdiness. They're cute, reliable, fun to drive, and lots of car for the money."

Not technical or historical, but definitely Model A-related, are three collections of cartoons about the Model A, which deserve a spot on any enthusiast's bookshelf. The oldest of these is "I'm Gonna Fix It Up Someday!," by Bruce McDougal, which was published by *The Restorer* in the 1960s. The other two collections are more recent: "Henry 'A' sez...," by Gene Patrick and "A-Toons," by Stan Blinco. Also of interest, in a humorous vein, is a booklet by K. Dalton titled "The Saga of the Model A Ford."

As we approach the millennium, there is one major concern shared by many Model A enthusiasts and that is the so-called "graying of the hobby." The significant lack of younger Model A owners, with some exceptions, is apparent to anyone who cares to look at the people who own and drive Model A Fords. In the latter half of the 1990s, efforts have intensified to remedy this situation. The Model A Ford Club of America, for example, began publishing *A World*, a youth newsletter in 1997. Across the country, a number of Model A chapters offer youth awards of one kind or another or make other efforts to catch the interest of the younger generations.

People who love to drive Model A Fords find it exciting, challenging and quite unlike the experience of driving a modern vehicle. Stan Guignard was sixty-four years old when he drove his Model A Ford around the world in 1983. During the trip he covered 49,000 miles (24,000 driving and 25,000 by sea) raised $300,000 for cancer research and met his new wife-to-be at an antique car rally in Hong Kong. When he returned to his Callander, Canada, home he was greeted as a hero, which he

Dolly Kester's 1930 Model A Coupe has been part of the family since 1936.

found hard to understand. "All I did was go around the world in a Model A Ford," he said. (See *Model "A" News*, May-June 1985).

Two accounts of long distance Model A travel published in the 1980s involved people who were not Model A hobbyists. A book, published in 1988, *Globe-Trotting By Vintage Car*, is the story of the trials, breakdowns and memorable experiences of Bevan Sharp and Geoff McEwan as they drove a 1929 Tudor from London to Sydney, Australia, in the London to Sydney vintage car endurance trial. Also in 1988, *Road & Track* magazine featured a two-part story, "Model A Odyssey," which was the account of a trip from Wisconsin to California in a 1930 Tudor by writer Peter Egan and friend Chris Beebe.

Neither of the trips were trouble free, but passengers and cars always managed to return to the road and eventually complete their treks successfully. Egan's evaluation of the Model A is worth repeating: "When Henry Ford built the Model A, he ignored his accountants' pleas to use lower-grade materials and make the car cheaper. He told them that if you made a high-quality product, the public would recognize the quality, buy more cars, and the profits would take care of themselves. Ford was a visionary who wanted to build something permanent, a machine with lasting worth and value. After all these years, the vision is still a good one and the Model A remains a fine car. Like a Woody Guthrie song or a good guitar, it doesn't get old, it just gets better."

In 1977, Robert Foster would not consider parting with his Model A because it was "family." Frank Hartmaier, written about earlier in this chapter, would agree. So would Dolly Kester, John Mumford and Adam Byers who today own and drive Model A Fords "still in the family."

Dolly Kester's 1930 Coupe has been an indispensable part of the family since her mother bought it in 1936 with quarters diligently saved from her job as a pastry baker. Kester was taught how to drive the car and used it for transportation as a high school student. She drove the "A" her first day of work at Ohio Bell in 1946, and last day in 1982.

Among her many memories of the car are teaching her high school friends how to drive it and double dating with one couple in the front seat and the other in the trunk. On one occasion a friend was riding in the trunk with the lid held up by a broom handle. The car hit a bump and the girl tumbled out. Grabbing the spare tire she hung on for dear life and yelled for Dolly to stop the car.

John Mumford's 1929 Model A Tudor has been in the family since 1933.

Copy of Nortz & Virkler ledger entry for John Mumford's Model A when it was originally sold in 1929.

In 1976, Dolly's mom, Tessie Jacobs, gave the Ford to her and husband, Don, who restored it. The "A" was painted its original colors, tobacco brown body, black fenders, and wheat wheels and given the name "Tessie." The engine was reconditioned, the interior reupholstered and the trunk converted to a rumble seat. Since then the couple drive it frequently around Canton, Ohio, and enjoy participating in the activities of the Canton Chapter of the Antique Automobile Club of America. Dolly Kester's 1930 Model A Coupe is a family heirloom she would never consider parting with. "I love old cars and old men," Kester writes, "the value of both grows each year."

On March 11, 1929, a new Model A Tudor was delivered to the Nortz & Virkler Agency in Lowville, New York, and subsequently sold to a man in Carthage, New York, for six hundred-twelve dollars, including bumpers, spare tire and tube. Four years later, the Coupe was sold to John Mumford's grandfather for one hundred-twenty-five dollars. "It runs like a watch," his grandfather said. In 1940, the Model A, sporting a brush paint job with a $1.50 can of black paint, was given to Mumford's parents who drove the car until they turned it over to their son in 1947.

Mumford used the car to attend college and, in 1949, after 100,000 miles and several main bearing failures, modified the Ford with a flathead V-8, hydraulic brakes and steering from a 1940 Ford. The engine was rebuilt at college where Mumford was enrolled in the Auto Tech course.

After he did the conversion, Mumford says that the Tudor, still with its 3.78 to 1 differential ratio, was a great hill climber and could beat most new cars on the hills. "One new Buick owner," Mumford recalls, "complained to his dealer that his new car couldn't catch an old Model A."

In storage from 1960 to 1988, but started annually, the Model A was restored as needed mechanically in 1989 and put on the road again. In 1992, it received new paint, upholstery, bumpers, safety glass and turn signals. Today, it has over 175,000 miles on it and is used for car shows and summer cruises. "The '29 has always been a part of my life," Mumford says, "and I surely have had a lot of fun with it. As it's been in my family for 66 years, I plan to keep it and pass it on to my daughter, Mallory."

Adam Byers of Waynesboro, Pennsylvania, bought his Rose Beige Model A Sport Coupe from Hoachlander Ford of Greencastle, Pennsylvania, on June 6, 1929. At that time, the Fords were assembled at Chester, Pennsylvania, and the dealers would frequently go down and drive their new cars the one hundred-fifty miles from Chester. Byers went down on June 5, drove the car to the dealer and had it delivered the next day. Equipped with a fender well and extra wheel, the car cost about six hundred-eighty dollars.

After being driven for forty-five years, time and miles took their toll on Byers' Model A and the engine was overhauled in 1974. In the early 1990s it was restored with the help of Byers' three sons. Approaching ninety

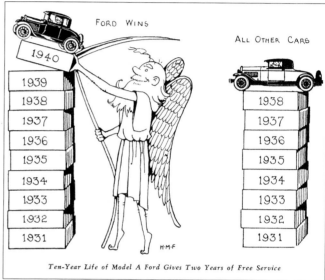

Ten-Year Life of Model A Ford Gives Two Years of Free Service

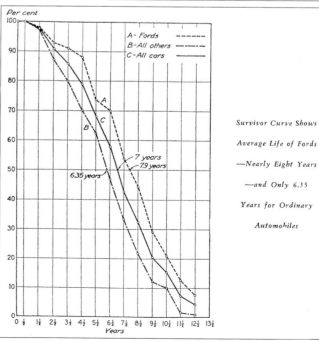

Adam Byers is the original and only owner of this 1929 Sport Coupe, still on the road today.

Envisioned as a product with at least a ten year life in 1931, many Model A Fords are still going strong after sixty years, *Ford Dealer and Service Field,* **August 1931.**

Some Model A Fords are gone forever. This one, with a tree growing through it, is on a golf course in upstate New York. (Photo courtesy of Lou Trunko)

and still driving the "A" from time to time, Byers looks upon the old Ford with great fondness. "it is an object of joy and pride for our children, grandchildren and friends," he says. "We give it the respect an elderly family member deserves. No going out in the snow, rain and ice."

As we wind down the story of the Model A Ford, one last question remains to be considered. From 1927 through 1936 there were close to 5,100,000 Model A Fords produced worldwide. (This figure does not include Russian Model As.) How many of them still exist? The answer is that no one really knows for certain. There are rough statistics, assumptions and just plain guesses, but little hard data on the basis of which a definitive answer can be given.

In 1959, Leslie Henry in *Henry's Fabulous Model "A" Ford* estimated at least 920,000 Model As and AAs were registered in all the United States. He does not give the source on which that figure is based. Murray Fahnestock, however, in *The Restorer* (July-August 1963), uses the much lower number of 300,000 in existence and about 280,000 of them still in active use.

By the 1990s, these estimates have been reduced substantially. In his "Technical Questions" column in *Model "A" News* (September-October 1990), Roger Kaufman states that "Approximately four percent is the normal survival rate for all Model A Ford body styles except for trucks, both 'A' and 'AA.' Trucks were used, overloaded, abused and then used some more. I feel the survival rate for trucks would be about one percent." Based on Kaufman's projection, there are less than 190,000 Model A and AA Fords that survive today.

"The general feeling is there are about 250,000 Model As left around the world, but I can't give you a solid foundation on which this is based," says Lyle Meek, in an e-mail to the author. Meek is the 1998 vice-president of MAFCA. "Between The Model A Ford Club of America and The Model "A" Restorers Club we have a total membership of about 25,000," he continues. "We guesstimate an average of 3.5 Model As per member. That could amount to approximately 80,000 to 100,000 As.

"We also know that there are thousands of them out there whose owners do not belong to a club or our organizations. Our membership continues to grow every year from people who don't know a national organization exists. Many Model A owners belong to the Antique Automobile Club of America and we don't know their numbers." Based on this information and the fact that Model As can still be found here and there in fields, pastures and even junkyards, Meek believes that the guess of 250,000 "may be conservative."

No matter which figures one accepts, the reality is that the survival rate of the Model A Ford is remarkable.

The fun of owning a Model A is evident in this 1970s photo showing the 1931 Pickup owned by J.B. Gentry participating in bulls-eye parking at a gymkhana. Howard Goines is the judge determining the outcome of the skill contest. (Photo courtesy of V.M. Hanks, Jr.)

The scrap metal drives of World War II took many cars of all makes, yet thousands of Model As escaped that fate to live far beyond that period's usual ten-year age limit of cars. If the Model A was only intended to be an "intermediate car," as Charles Sorensen characterized it, it was the most lasting in automotive history.

The basic honesty and simplicity of Model A, the low cost of parts, mechanical performance, attractive styling and the wide distribution and availability of Ford service dealers were all factors in the fact that, today, the Model A Ford is not an uncommon car. It was then, and still is, a car for the average man and woman.

When they see a Model A, people point and smile and, for the older generation, those smiles are usually connected with pleasant memories of an incredibly willing car once owned, now gone, but never forgotten. Today, the Model A Ford still exists in memories, old photos, printed publications, museums and in the garages and backyards of innumerable enthusiasts around the globe. Truly, it was and is a legendary car.

The Model A: Looking into the future down a Model A kind of road. A 1929 Tudor - owner Robert Oberst.

Appendix

Correspondence from the files of Cazenovia, New York, Ford dealer D.D. Norton

May 26, 1927, telegram from Edsel Ford to D.D. Norton informing him of the start of production of an entirely new Ford.

THE NEW FORD CAR

A New and Modern Car

First of all, I'd like to emphasize the fact that the new Ford car is not a refinement of the former Model T Ford, but an entirely new car from radiator cap to rear axle. It is distinctly a new and modern car designed to meet new and modern conditions. It is more than a new automobile - more than just another model. It is the advanced expression of a wholly new idea in modern, economical transportation.

I wish I had enough cars here to take everyone of you out for a ride in this new Ford. I'd like to have you behind the wheel and drive this car yourself. I tell you frankly, ladies and gentlemen, you're going to get a real thrill when you drive this car. There's nothing quite like it anywhere in quality and price.

When it comes to performance I'll match this new Ford against almost any car on the road, regardless of price. That's an enthusiastic statement I know, but you can't help but be enthusiastic about this car. I've ridden in it and I know.

It just can't help being a great car because many of its important parts are made in exactly the same way and of the same materials as those in high-price cars. The use of steel forgings is just one indication of this quality. They are used throughout, except, of course, for the engine castings. More steel forgings, in fact, are used in the new Ford than in almost any other car, regardless of price.

Why the Price Is So Low

The only reason Ford can sell it at such a low price is because he has found new ways to give you greater value without a great increase in his own costs. As Mr. Henry Ford has said, "No other automobile manufacturer could possibly give you such a fine automobile at such a low price, because no other manufacturer does business the way we do."

The Ford Motor Company owns its own ore mines, coal mines and timber lands and the source of most of its raw materials. It makes virtually every part used in the new Ford. And it has always believed in making a small profit on a large number of cars, rather than a large profit on a small number of cars.

One reason why the Ford Motor Company took so long to perfect this car was because it was constantly trying to find ways to give you more quality without extra cost. And they succeeded. Otherwise you would have to pay a great deal more for the Ford car than the price we're asking.

Yes, sir! You're going to be surprised when you see the performance of this car.

Beautiful New Body Lines

I don't need to say a great deal about the new bodies because you can see them for yourself. If you have been abroad you'll know what I mean when I say there is a bit of a European touch in the coachwork and contour of the new Ford.

The bodies are all steel and appointments and hardware are of a type seldom found in a low-price car. Upholstery is of rich, durable material and the cushions are deep and easy. The headlamps and radiator shell, as you can see, are fully nickeled. So are the door handles and window lifts. The speedometer, gasoline gauge, ammeter and theft-proof coincidental lock are all mounted on an instrument panel of satin-finish nickel, illuminated by a lamp in the center.

A six-page sample dealer presentation of the New Ford sent to dealers in December 1927.

THE NEW FORD CAR   - 2 -

Lots of Room for Every Passenger

Now a word about room, for I know you are all interested in that.

When the Ford Motor Company began designing this car it spent weeks
in finding out how much room motorists needed for comfortable riding. It didn't
start with the wheel base and says the dimensions of the car would have to follow that. It began with comfort and that's one reason why the new Ford is such
a comfortable car in which to ride.

Seat space is generous and ample even for men and women who are inclined to be a trifle overweight and there is ample leg room even for six-footers.

Clear vision is another thing you'll like about this new Ford. You can
see that the pillars are unusually narrow. Look, too, at the size of those windows in the pictures of the closed models.

Choice of Seven Colors

There's another point I'd like to emphasize about the new Ford - the
attractive colors. We are giving you the choice of seven colors - Niagara Blue,
Arabian Sand, Dawn Gray, Gun Metal Blue, Rose Beige, Andalusite Blue, and Bal-
same Green. This is an unusually good feature in a low-price car, and one I am
sure you will appreciate.

You'll like that pyroxylin lacquer finish too. That's the most enduring finish for automobile bodies. It is not affected by heat or cold, is not
easily marred or scratched, and withstands all kinds of weather. It actually im-
proves with washing.

Now a word or two about speed, for I know you're all interested in that.

An Unusually Speedy Car

This new Ford car will do 55 and 60 miles an hour with ease. That is a
conservative statement. In many road tests out at Dearborn, the new Ford has exceeded 65 miles an hour. I tell you, that's moving along!

Best of all, you can travel at this pace with a new feeling of comfort
and safety because this new Ford is a steady car. You'll be delighted with the
way it holds the road.

You're going to be surprised too when you see these new Ford cars on
the hills. I won't say it will climb them all on high, because no car will do
that. But I will say that you won't have to take anybody's dust when you drive
this new Ford. You will face the steepest grades with confidence, knowing that
you have power to climb them all without greatly reduced speed, without strain,
or unnecessary shifting of gears. And you won't have to get a long running
start to do it, either!

A Remarkable Engine

The new Ford has a four-cylinder engine which develops 40-brake horsepower at 2200 revolutions a minute. Please note that carefully, for it is an important point - the engine in the new Ford develops 40-brake horsepower at only
2200 revolutions per minute.

THE NEW FORD CAR   - 3 -

That means you can do 55 to 65 miles an hour in the new Ford and yet you do not have a high-speed engine. Such an engine is a new development - a really amazing engineering feat.

This low r.p.m., or revolution speed, is low for such power and shows that the engine is unusually efficient. It also means long life, because the lower the speed of the engine, the less wear on its parts.

Those of you who are engineers will be interested to know that the bore of the new Ford engine is 3-7/8 inches and the stroke is 4-1/4 inches.

Remarkable Acceleration, Quick on the Get-Away

The quick acceleration of the new Ford is another of its outstanding features. In tests in high gear, with a Tudor Sedan body and two passengers, it has accelerated from 5 to 25 miles an hour in 8-1/2 seconds. That's a mighty good record and we tried to be fair in making it. Please remember that it was made with a Tudor Sedan - in high gear - and with two passengers.

Some of these other acceleration tests you sometimes read about are made in a roadster without passengers.

Engine Practically Vibrationless

Another point about the Ford engine is the fact that it is practically vibrationless. This is due in part to the low r.p.m. that I spoke about a few minutes ago, the statically and dynamically-balanced crankshaft, and the aluminum pistons. To insure quiet, the timing gears are made of bakelized fabric instead of metal, and the cams on the camshaft are so designed that the valve push-rods follow them closely, preventing valve clicking.

Some of this may sound a little technical, but I'll try to keep it as simple as possible.

But I do want you to see that value has been built into the new Ford car and to know why it is such a really fine car.

This car is one of the finest mechanical jobs ever turned out by any automobile manufacturer. To me the mechanical beauty of the car - the beauty of the mechanism on the inside - is even more important than the beauty of its outside lines and colors. After all, the most beautiful car in the world isn't of much use if it won't run.

Gasoline Economy

This new Ford will break a few records when it comes to gasoline economy. It will give you 20 to 30 miles per gallon of gasoline, depending on the speed at which you drive. Feed to the carburetor is by gravity from a unique, welded one-piece steel tank, integral with the cowl.

Economy of Upkeep

The new Ford is low in price and you will find it an inexpensive car to run. We have made this car to endure - to last for thousands of miles with a minimum of upkeep cost. You will find the new Ford the most economical car you've ever driven.

Ford-Design Oiling System

The oiling system in the new Ford is a combination of pump, splash and gravity feed. I believe you will be interested in knowing just how this system works.

The pump delivers the oil to the valve chamber and from there it flows by gravity feed to the main bearings of the crankshaft. An oil dipper is provided on each connecting-rod bearing cap, so that the force of rotation of the crankshaft drives oil into the connecting-rod bearings, as well as splashing oil over all parts within the engine. This is a complete but entirely dependable system and assures proper lubrication of each bearing and each cylinder without pressure.

A Word about Cooling

It is exceedingly difficult to make the new Ford engine overheat. The only way you can do it is through abuse, such as running without oil. The radiator is unusually large, as you can see, and a centrifugal water pump is used. The fan runs on the pump shaft and is made according to the latest airplane propeller design.

Unique Ignition System

The ignition system of the new Ford is unique in mechanical design and extremely simple. It will give you exceptional performance with a minimum of trouble - something we all want.

There is only one coil and that is in a water-proof case.

The distributor is located on top of the engine where it is clean and easily accessible. I am sure you will appreciate that. Connections are made to the spark plugs by short bronze springs - another good feature.

The theft-proof coincidental lock is placed right in the ignition circuit and not only replaces the regular ignition switch, but in the "off" position grounds the circuit.

Note this too - from switch to the distributor a steel cable protects the primary current wire, this wire being grounded to the distributor casting. This makes it impossible to wire around the device.

The generator is of the new power-house type. It is really a miniature copy of the great dynamos that supply power and light to your homes.

Standard Selective Gear-Shift

Now you all want to know about the transmission. This is of the selective sliding-gear type, with standard shift. It has three speeds forward and one reverse. The main shaft runs on ball bearings, the countershaft on roller bearings, and the reverse idler on a bronze bearing.

This is the highest type of bearing mounting and is unusual on light cars. You will be delighted with the ease with which you can shift gears in the new Ford. You can go from one to another easily, silently, with the pressure of a finger. I am sure that women, in particular, will appreciate this feature.

Irreversible Steering Gear

Here's another thing you'll like about the new Ford - the irreversible steering gear. That means that road-shocks will not be transmitted to the hands of the driver. A light touch is all you need to guide the car safely.

Another thing that makes for easy steering is the large size of the steering wheel itself. It is made of steel, covered with hard rubber. The light switch and horn button are conveniently located on top of the wheel.

New 4-Wheel Brakes

Here's a surprise for you - 4-wheel brakes in the New Ford. When I say 4-wheel brakes, I mean the finest 4-wheel brakes made.

They are of the mechanical, internal-expanding shoe type and are self-centering.

Tests have proved that this is the most reliable and simplest type of four-wheel brake and the easiest to adjust.

All adjustments, you see, are made from the outside without removing any parts.

No special tools are needed and uniform adjustment on each wheel is quickly and easily obtained.

The emergency brakes operate on the rear wheels and are entirely independent of the service brakes. Thus there are actually six brakes on the car, with a total braking surface of 168 inches on the service brakes.

Imagine that - 168 square inches of braking surface. That means real brake protection.

There is no chance of these brakes getting rusty and sticking because they are plated with cadmium to make them rust-proof and are enclosed to keep out mud and dirt.

Single, Dry-Disc Clutch

The clutch on the new Ford consists of a single disc clutch with pressure plate, engaging directly on the fly wheel face. It is reliable and easy to operate because it takes hold so smoothly and gently.

The Best Springs of All

The springs on the new Ford are of the transverse, semi-elliptic type. We adopted those springs for the new Ford because we found, after making many tests, that they were unquestionably the best springs for a car of this type.

It wasn't a matter of saving money, because these springs cost as much or more than other springs. The things wanted were safety and comfort, and the Ford Motor Company adopted these springs because it was found they gave more safety and comfort than other springs. It is interesting to note how they are made. They are constructed of the finest spring steel and the leaves are wide and thin. Each different body type has a different size and number of spring leaves because the weight of each car is different.

The size and number of these spring leaves is one of the reasons why the new Ford is such a comfortable car. The construction of these transverse springs also contributes to the safety and efficiency of the four-wheel brakes.

Hydraulic Shock Absorbers

Speaking of comfort reminds me to tell you about the hydraulic shock absorbers on the new Ford. These are a very fine type of shock absorber - indeed, the very finest made. They combine with the low center of gravity, the minimum unsprung weight, and the easy-riding qualities of the transverse springs to make the new Ford one of the most comfortable cars on the market today.

Three-Quarter Floating Axle

I want to tell you about two or three more points and then I will close. Let's take the rear axle first.

It is what is technically known as a three-quarter floating axle, and is exceptionally strong. The housing is made entirely of steel forgings and steel tubing welded into a solid piece of metal. Rolled channel steel is used for the differential housing to which the axle housings are bolted. The axle shafts carry none of the weight of the car, the wheels running on roller bearings on the housing. All rear-axle bearings are rollers. Drive is by a spiral bevel gear.

Steel-Spoke Wheels

Steel-spoke wheels, as you can see, are used in the new Ford. These wheels were designed by Ford and are of great strength because each wheel is assembled by welding and becomes one piece of metal. Each spoke has a tensile strength of 4000 pounds. There are only 30 spokes in each wheel and they do not cross. Hence the ease with which the wheels are cleaned.

A Quiet Car

Perhaps I should have mentioned this point among the first because it is certainly an important one.

I want you to know that in designing the new Ford, every precaution was taken to prevent squeaks, rattles and drumming sounds. Body panels and frame sections are welded and riveted together wherever there is a possibility of the body weaving. In all structural details, the new Ford cars are built to afford the utmost quiet and comfort.

Grease-Gun Lubrication

The chassis of the new Ford is lubricated by the pressure grease-gun system, the simplest and most effective method of lubrication.

Standard Equipment

We are giving a great deal of standard equipment with the new Ford. For instance:

Starter	Five Steel-Spoke Wheels
Windshield Wiper	Speedometer
Gasoline Gauge	Door Lock
Dash Light	Rear-view Mirror
Rear and Stop-Light	Oil Gauge
Theft-Proof Ignition Lock	Complete Tool Set

SALES   Subject: No. 41

GENERAL LETTER   THE NEW FORD TRUCK   P. 1
TO ALL DEALERS
                        December 7, 1927

The new Ford Truck is designed and built to meet all general hauling requirements. It is rated as a 1½ ton truck, but with dual rear wheels will carry above two tons.

It has the quanlty, the sturdiness and the strength to withstand hard service for a long period of time, and at low cost in upkeep.

It is powered by the new Ford Model A 40 horsepower engine, which gives it the speed necessary for quick delivery and the power needed for moving large loads of heavy materials.

It has the torque tube drive, and a three-quarter floating rear axle with the dependable worm gear.

The front springs are the transverse semi-elliptic type, specially constructed for the truck. Rear springs are of the full cantilever type, one on each side, and are an innovation in truck spring construction.

All trucks are equipped with the Ford steel-spoke wheels, a new truck wheel of unusual strength and good appearance, and have four-wheel mechanical brakes of the internal expanding shoe type.

The transmission is of the standard selective sliding gear type with three speeds forward and one reverse. A dual high transmission, which reduces the standard transmission gear approximately one-third, is offered as optional equipment at extra cost for those desiring a truck for heavy work where additional pulling power is required. The dual transmission also is provided with a power take off gear for use with dump bodies.

This dual transmission is of the planetary type and is installed between the front and rear cross members of the frame by removal of a coupling shaft which connects the transmission drive shaft with the universal joint on the standard truck.

Standard Ford body equipment for the truck includes closed cab, express body and stake body.

The cab is all steel, with wide doors and a seat 44 inches wide. The express body is all steel except the floor and sills which are of seasoned wood. Inside dimensions are 4 feet wide by 7 feet, 2 inches long. The stake body is 5 feet, 8 inches wide, and 8 feet 1½ inches long. Racks rise to 26 inches above the floor. Truck bodies and cab are in dark green Pyroxylin, a most durable finish.

December 7, 1927, three-page letter to dealers from the manager of the Green Island (New York) Branch with information about the New Ford truck.

SALES   Subject:
                                                         No. 41
GENERAL LETTER   THE NEW FORD TRUCK
TO ALL DEALERS   P. 2
                         Dec 7, 1927

SPECIFICATIONS

Engine - Four cylinder, "L" head, cylinders cast on bloc. Bore 3 7/8 in; Stroke $4\frac{1}{4}$ in. Piston displacement 200.5 cu in. Horsepower rating S.A.E., 24.03. Horsepower brake, 40 at 2200 r.p.m.

Transmission - Standard selective gear type, three speeds forward, one reverse. Gears and shafts chrome alloy steel, heat treated for hardness. Main shafts in ball bearings, countershaft in roller bearings and reverse in bronze bushings, insures exceptional wear and quietness. Dual high, reducing ratio of standard transmission one-third, optional at extra cost.

Clutch - Multiple dry plate discs. Four driving discs, five driven discs. Long wearing asbestos composition facing. Completely enclosed and protected. Smooth and easy in action.

Brakes - Four-wheel mechanical, expanding shoe type operated by both service pedal and hand brake. Front brake drums 11 in in dia., rear brake drums 14 in in dia. Total braking surface 262 sq in.

Camshaft Bearings - Five, all 1 9/16 in in dia. Length No. 1, $1\frac{3}{4}$ in; No. 2, 7/8 in; No. 3, 2 in; No 4, 7/8 in; No 5, 1 in.

Valves - on side; carbon chrome nickel alloy.

Crankshaft Bearings - Three main, all 1 5/8 in dia. Length, front and center, 2 in; rear 3 1/8 in. Bearings babbitt, lower half backed in stel, upper half in iron.

Connecting Rod - Steel forging, "X" section design. Lower bearing babbitt, $1\frac{1}{2}$ in in dia. by 1 5/8 in long. Piston pin machined seamless steel tubing, full floating type.

Carburetor - 1 in vertical. Choke and needle adjustment rod on dash. Hotspot intake manifold.

Steering Gear - Irreversible, worm and sector type with roller thrust bearings on worm shaft. Ratio $11\frac{1}{4}$ to 1.

Oiling System - Pump, splash system and gravity flow from valve chamber reservoir to crankshaft main bearings. Oil level indicator and filler on left side of motor. Capacity 5 quarts.

Ignition - Battery, coil and distributor. New Ford mechanical design.

Cooling - Centrifugal water pump in top of cylinder head on shaft which also operates fan. Tubular radiator. Two-blade airplane propeller type fan, 16 in in diameter; adjustable V belt, Capacity 3 gals.

SALES   Subject: No. 41

GENERAL LETTER   THE NEW FORD TRUCK   P. 3
TO ALL DEALERS

              Dec 7, 1927

Starter and Generator - New Ford generator of power house design; new starting motor.

Fuel - Gravity feed from welded steel tank built integral with cowl. Capacity 10 gals.

Rear Axle - Three quarter floating, worm gear. Gear ratio 5 to 1.

Front Axle - Chrome alloy steel forging, "I" beam construction. Adjustable taper roller bearings for wheels.

Drive - Torque tube.

Springs - Front transverse semi-elliptic, 12 leaves. Rear, cantilever, 17 leaves.

Wheels and Tires - Ford wire wheels. Tires, front standard 30 x 5. Rear, standard 30 x 5. Optional, rear 32 x 6.

Equipment - Hydraulic shock absorbers on front springs, gasoline gauge, ammeter, ignition lock, dash lamp, windshield wiper, rear view mirror, combination tail and stop light, grease gun for high pressure lubrication of chassis, tool equipment, tire pump, jack, oil indicator rod on engine, horn, spare wire wheel.

Wheelbase - 131 1/2 in.

Tread - 56 in.

Turning Radius - 21 ft.

Turning circle - 42 ft.

Frame - Length, 171 5/16 in. Depth, 6 in. Width, 2 3/4 in.

Road Clearance - 9 13/16 in.

                  FORD MOTOR COMPANY

                     G E WALRATH

GEW C   Manager

C O P Y

R C ALLEN
NORWICH, NY

(To be sent to visitors to our showrooms)

You were sufficiently interested in our New Ford car to visit our showrooms. We appreciate your interest.

You will be surprised to know that you have learned of but 35% of the merit of this truly wonderful car. You will learn the remaining 65% when you demonstrate the car to yourself—to drive our demonstrator under any condition of road surface, of speed, of pick up and hill climbing.

Before the first of the year we will have cars of various types for display and demonstration and it is our desire to have everyone drive or ride in this car whether they are interested in a purchase or not. Will you kindly fill in the enclosed card and mail it to us? It is addressed and stamped.

We again thank you for your call and will appreciate your further courtesy of mailing us the card of information as it will allow us to properly list your name for demonstration if desired and for literature.

Very truly yours,

R C ALLEN

RCA/B

Suggested letter to be sent to visitors of Ford showrooms after the December 1927 showings.

DEALERS   DAILY   REMINDERS

Does your sales organization consist of a sufficient number of quality men?

Are they properly directed by you as their leader?

How do you encourage them?

Do you assist them in their problems?

Do you make them feel that you consider each and every one as an integral part of your organization?

Do you assign each salesman a quota on cars, trucks and tractors?

Do you furnish new car demonstrators cheerfully?

Do you pay them 5% on service work and parts on new service customers they bring in?

Is your prospect file up to standard and are you going to check in this matter personally?

Have you supplied your salesmen with Fordex Survey Data book and Hildes Manual?

Are you going to insist on 12 calls per day being made and so reported on sales daily report forms?

Are you going to insist on actual demonstrations to each and every prospect?

Have you an up-to-date service file that contains the names of all customers?

Have you a complete line of Ford Service equipment?

Have your men been properly trained at the Branch on the use of this equipment?

Do you use the Ford flat rate repair schedule?

How do you pay your shop men?

Is your shop showing a profit?

Have you given any thought to our profit sharing plan in shop? 60-40 basis.

Does your Shop Foreman check your service customers file?

Does he solicit service work for the shop through personal calls on owners?

Do you make 20 % gross profit on your used cars?

Do you guarantee all used cars of $100 or over in value?

A two-page list of daily reminders sent to dealers in early-1928.

-2-

Are you equipped to apply pyroxylin paint to your customers' cars?

Do you keep your display models clean and presentable.

Do you prominently display all Ford accessories?

Does your shop, showroom or building need cleaning or painting?

Do you employ a tractor service man?

Do you employ a commercial salesman.

Have at least one truck equipped with Ruckstell axle, closed cab and stake body for <u>actual demonstrations only</u> and then demonstrate.

Who are the people in your community that have available means and should own a Lincoln automobile?

Have you used Mr Ryan's letter of Feb 25th as the basis of a newspaper advertisement?

What is there that you have not done but that you can and will do to further the sale of Ford products?

How many persons in your organization subscribe for the Dearborn Independent?

How soon will you secure your quota of Dearborn subscriptions?

What can the Green Island Branch do to assist you?

```
SALES                        Subject:                        No. 3

General Letter       GREEN ISLAND "DRIVE OUT" PRICES          P. 1
to All Dealers           MODEL "A" AND "AA"
                          CARS AND TRUCKS

                        Revised May 7, 1928.
```

This letter cancels and supersedes the following letters relative to prices to dealers under the Green Island Branch on New Ford Cars and Trucks obtained as driveaways from the Green Island Branch:

> (On all cars and trucks obtained as driveaways from the Kearny and Buffalo Branches, freight rates, taxes, gas, oil, etc., shown on their invoices will apply.)

LETTER - "DRIVE OUT PRICES", dated December 20, 1927.

GENERAL LETTER - SALES - "GREEN ISLAND DRIVEOUT PRICES" - No. 3
Pages 1 and 2, dated Jan 19 and Feb 16, and pages 1, 2 and 4, dated Feb 29 and Apr 17, 1928.

LETTER - "CONTRACT FREIGHT RATES", undated, from our Traffic Dept.

- - - - - - - -

Effective immediately and until further notice, the following wholesale prices to dealers apply on all New Cars and Trucks driven out of the Green Island Branch:

MODEL	LIST FOB DETROIT	NET DEALER PRICE	FREIGHT	ADV FRT ON BODY EQUIPT	TAX	GAS & OIL	TOTAL COST TO DEALER
Phaeton	395	316	43.68		10.79	2.72	373.19
Roadster	385	308	"		10.55	"	364.95
Roadster with Rumble Seat	420	336	"		11.39	"	393.79
Coupe	495	396	"		13.19	"	455.59
Coupe with Rumble Seat	530	424	"		14.03	"	484.43
Sport Coupe (Rumble Seat Standard)	550	440	"		14.51	"	500.91
Tudor Sedan	495	396	"		13.19	"	455.59
Fordor Sedan	625	500	"		16.31	"	562.71
Chassis	325	260	"		9.11	"	315.51
Pickup	395	316	"		9.11	"	371.51
Business Coupe	495	396	"		13.19	"	455.59

Note: The Excise Tax on the Pickup is the same as on the Model "A" Chassis, due to the fact that the seat, top and pickup box are non-taxable.
The above prices do not include bumpers and rear guards.
Price of Bumpers is $15.00 less 20% = $12.00.
When cars are sold with bumpers and rear guards, the cost of same will be included in the cost of the car and Excise Tax of 36¢ added.
Each car contains 11 gals of gasoline @ .19 per gal and 5 qts of oil @ .50 per gal.

Green Island "Drive Out" two-page price list, prices effective May 7, 1928.

SALES

General Letter
to All Dealers

Subject:

GREEN ISLAND "DRIVE OUT" PRICES
MODEL "A" AND "AA"
CARS AND TRUCKS

No. 3

P. 2

Revised May 7, 1928

MODEL	LIST FOB DETROIT	NET DEALER PRICE	FREIGHT	ADV FRT ON BODY EQUIPT	GAS & TAX OIL	TOTAL COST TO DEALER
Tractor	495	395	27.00			423.00
Tractor with Fenders	530	422.25	27.00			449.25
1½ Ton Truck						
Chassis	460	358.80	65.29		2.72	426.81
Chassis with Cab	545	425.10	"		"	493.11
Chassis with Cab and Express Body	600	468.00	"		"	536.01
Chassis with Cab and Stake Body	610	475.80	"		"	543.81
Chassis with Cab and Platform Body	595	464.10	"		"	532.11
1½ Ton Truck - Dual High Transmission						
Chassis	510	397.80	"		"	465.81
Chassis with Cab	595	464.10	"		"	532.11
Chassis with Cab and Express Body	650	507.00	"		"	575.01
Chassis with Cab and Stake Body	660	514.80	"		"	582.81
Chassis with Cab and Platform Body	645	503.10	"		"	571.11

NOTE: Spare Tire and Tube (32 x 6) when furnished with truck, will be
$42.05 extra.

SERVICE   Subject: No 80
                                                P 1
                SALE OF MODEL "A" ACCESSORIES
General Letter
To All Dealers   July 5, 1928

To insure owners obtaining accessories in keeping with the high standard of the Model "A" Ford, it is our recommendation that Dealers handle only accessories that are approved by our Engineering Department inasmuch as we have tested and approved a number of accessories which will soon be available for distribution to our dealers. We are giving below a list of accessories which we have approved and will soon be available, the list prices, subject to dealers' usual discount of 40%, together with some of the outstanding features of each item.

When talking to prospective purchasers of cars regarding the Ford accessories, dealers must not create the impression that the Ford car is not complete without them. These approved accessories are offered not as necessities, but to meet the demand of owners desiring additional equipment.

TIRE COVER - $2.00   Made of heavy rubber coated drill. Fits snugly around the tire and against the wheel rim. Construction permits the spare tire to be regularly checked for air pressure, and inflated when necessary, without removing the cover. Is easily installed and removed without damage. Ease of installation is due to the use of a special springless ring instead of the springs or elastic usually used in tire covers.

TIRE LOCK - $3.00   A lock of the band type which locks the spare wheel, tire and tire cover to the car. Finished in nickel and black enamel harmonizing with the attractive appearance of the car. Lock cylinder protected by an escutcheon plate. The lock permits removal of spare wheel and tire without removing lock from car. Heavy construction insures protection.

SPARE WHEEL LOCK - FOR USE WITH WELL FENDERS - $2.50   When spare wheel and tire are carried in fender well it is only necessary to lock the wheel. When wheel is locked to carrier, tire fits into well so it can not be removed from wheel. This lock is finished in black. Lock cylinder is protected by escutcheon plate. Spring plunger provides tension against wheel preventing rattling. Heavy construction insures against theft.

WINDSHIELD WINGS FOR OPEN CARS - $8.50 per set. The glass used in these wings is the Ford nonshatterable safety glass now being used in all Model "A" windshields. Brackets permit wings to be placed in any desired position and hold rigidly without loosening or tightening nuts. No interference with side curtains. Of attractive appearance and an added comfort to the open car driver.

July 5, 1928, three-page letter to dealers regarding the sale of accessories.

SERVICE   Subject: No 80
                                                                  P   2

SALE OF MODEL "A" ACCESSORIES

General Letter
To All Dealers   July 5, 1928

TOP BOOT - $7.00   Essential to drivers who like to drive with the top down. Well tailored of heavy non-shrinkable material. Fits the top snugly and affords complete protection. Adds to the neat appearance of the car.

AUTOMATIC WINDSHIELD WIPER FOR OPEN CARS - $4.50 including fittings. Electrically operated. Operates at constant speed regardless of engine speed. Eight inch blade and long sweep insure full vision. Furnished in cartons with all attachments.

RADIATOR CAP WITH ORNAMENT - $3.00   Cap locks to filler neck of radiator. Ornament represents quail in flight, symbolizing the quick acceleration of the Ford car. Ornament rigidly fastened to the lid of the cap to prevent theft. Cap is easily opened to permit filling the radiator, and seals tightly to prevent leakage.

RADIATOR CAP WITH MOTO-METER - $5.00   Same radiator cap is used with Moto-motor as is used with ornament. A standard Boyce Junior Model Moto-motor is used, with lock for securely locking it to the radiator cap.

TIRE GAUGE - $1.50   Standard tire gauge manufactured especially for the Ford Motor Company. Easily read. Guaranteed for accuracy. Ford emblem and recommended tire pressure for Ford tires shown on gauge.

SPRING COVERS - $4.25   Easily installed. Protect springs from dirt and moisture. Reduce possibility of spring breakage. Newly developed oil filled hair felt pad constantly keeps springs correctly lubricated, preventing spring squeaks and insuring continued easy riding.

FENDERS WITH WELLS FOR TIRES. (See May Service Bulletin for prices) Right and left front fenders with well for spare wheel and tire. Available through Service Department for passenger car owners who desire to carry spare tires in the front fenders.

       The Fender with well, open car Automatic Windshield Wiper and Windshield Wings are illustrated and described in the May issue of the Service Bulletin.

       The tire cover was illustrated in the February Bulletin on Page 228. The other accessories will be covered in subsequent issues of the Bulletin.

       Other accessories, including heaters, radiator shutters, are under consideration awaiting suggestions from our dealers, as well as other accessories not included in the above. If our dealers feel there is an immediate demand in their territory for any particular item, please

advise us immediately, giving percentage of cars on which you believe
this equipment is required, and we will secure samples for our Engineering Dept for approval.

        The above approved accessories present an opportunity for
increased profits which no dealer can afford to neglect.

        This accessory program calls for certain very definite
action from our dealer organization, as for example:

        Accessories must be attractively displayed in Parts
        Stockroom and Car Salesroom.
        An adequate supply of accessories must be carried
        in stock.
        Accessories must be shown and their advantages
        explained to prospective purchasers, with the
        suggestion that desired accessories be installed
        on new car before delivery.
        Time payment plan should be extended to cover
        accessories as well as car.
        Sales quotas should be established for salesmen
        and other employes and commission allowed them
        on accessory sales.

        As soon as we receive these accessories, we will sample all
of our dealers with a few of each. In sampling our dealers we wish
you to bear in mind that we will ship only a small quantity of each
available item. Inasmuch as this is exclusively a Ford item, we can
see no objections on our dealer's part for our making this arbitrary
shipment inasmuch as we are advising you in advance.

        On receipt of these accessories, we solicit your comments
and criticisms. Please call this letter to the attention of your
entire organization.

                              FORD MOTOR COMPANY

                              E A DILLON

EAD:C   Service Division Manager

REVISED PRICES   November 8 1928

	LIST	DISC	NET TO DEALER	BUMPERS	FREIGHT	GAS & OIL	NET COST TO DEALER
Phaeton	395 00	20%	316 00	12 00	28 25	2 90	359 15
Roadster	385 00	20%	308 00	12 00	28 25	2 90	351 15
Sport Roadster	420 00	20%	336 00	12 00	28 25	2 90	379 15
Standard Coupe	550 00	20%	440 00	12 00	36 25	2 90	491 15
Sport Coupe	550 00	20%	440 00	12 00	36 25	2 90	491 15
Business Coupe	495 00	20%	396 00	12 00	36 25	2 90	447 15
Tudor	495 00	20%	396 00	12 00	36 25	2 90	447 15
Fordor	625 00	20%	500 00	12 00	36 25	2 90	551 15
A Chassis	365 00	20%	292 00	5 60	28 25	2 90	328 75
Pickup Open	445 00	20%	356 00	5 60	30 80	2 90	395 30
Pickup Closed	495 00	20%	396 00	5 60	30 80	2 90	435 30
A Panel	615 00	20%	492 00	5 60	36 25	2 90	536 75
AA Panel	850 00	20%	680 00	5 60	38 80	2 90	727 30
AA Panel Dual	900 00	20%	720 00	5 60	38 80	2 90	767 30
AA Chassis	540 00	20%	432 00	5 60	30 80	2 90	471 30
AA Chassis Dual	590 00	20%	472 00	5 60	30 80	2 90	511 30
Closed Cab	90 00	20%	72 00		1 65		
Stake Body	65 00	20%	52 00		3 05		
Express Body	55 00	20%	44 00		1 40		
Platform Body	50 00	20%	40 00		2 40		
A Panel Delivery	250 00	20%	200 00				
AA Panel Delivery	310 00	20%	248 00				
Bumpers	15 00	20%	12 00	When installed on car			
Front Bumpers	7 00	20%	5 60	" " on trucks			

November 8, 1928, revised price list sent to Green Island Branch dealers.

Bibliography

In addition to the books and periodicals listed, the author made use of hundreds of letters from the Ford Motor Co. to the Buffalo, Green Island, Dearborn, Chicago and Indianapolis Branches, and from those Branches to their dealers. The Buffalo and Green Island letters are from the author's personal collection. Letters from the Dearborn Branch are courtesy the Henry Ford Research Center. The Indianapolis letters are from the Jerry Wilhelm collection, The Chicago letters are from the Irv Bishko collection. Sales manuals, leaflets, folders, sales brochures, magazines and photographs from the Model A era are from the author's collection. Other photographs are from Krause Publications or as noted in the text.

A ModEl newS,
  February 1984

A-Toons,
  by Stan Blinco

American Automobile Manufacturers,
  by John B. Rae, Chilton Co., 1959

American Automobile Workers 1900-1933,
  by Joyce Shaw Peterson, State University of
  New York Press, 1987

American Business Abroad,
  by Mira Wilkins & Frank Ernest Hill, Wayne
  State University Press, 1964

American Heritage,
  September 1992

And Then Came Ford,
  by Charles Merz, Doubleday, 1929

Antique Automobile,
  November 1961, September-October 1991

Automobile Facts & Figures, 1951,
  Automobile Manufacturers Association

Automobile Topics,
  December 1929, March 12, 1932

Automobile Trade Journal,
  selected issues from 1930, 1931 and 1932

Automotive Daily News,
  March 18, 1927

Automotive History Review,
  winter 1979

Automotive Industries,
  August 1, 1931, September 12 and 26, 1931

Automotive Production The Ford Model A,
  by Jim Schild, The Auto Review, 1982

Autowork,
  edited by Robert Asher and Ronald Edsforth,
  State University of New York Press, 1995

BAF
  (Books About Ford), January 1965

Brother Bill McKie,
  by Phillip Bonosky, International Publishers, 1953

Cars & Parts,
  November 1980, June 1991, March 1994

Car Collector,
  June 1978

Car Collector and Car Classics,
  September 1981

Chicago American,
  September 18, 1933

Detroit in Perspective,
  Fall 1982

diego rivera,
  by Dorothy McMeekin, Michigan State University
  Press, 1985

Diego Rivera,
  by James Cockcroft, Chelsea House Publishers, 1991

End of The Ford Myth,
  by Robert Cruden, International House Publishers,
  1932

Evergreen Echoes,
  August 1998

Ford Country,
  By David Lewis, Amos Press, 1987

Ford Dealer & Service Field,
  1928, 1930, 1931, 1932 issues

Ford: Expansion & Challenge: 1915 - 1933,
  by Allan Nevins and Frank Ernest Hill, Charles
  Scribner's Sons, 1957

Ford Facts,
  Ford Motor Co., May 15, 1931

Ford Fax,
  Sales Equipment Co., February 1931

Ford Hot Rods,
  by Dain Gingerelli, MBI Publishing Co., 1998

Ford Illustrated News,
  Ford Motor Co., undated 1931 copy

Ford In The Thirties,
   by Paul R. Woudenberg, Peterson Publishing Co., 1976

Ford Industries,
   1929 and 1931

Ford Life,
   1971 - 1974 issues

Ford Men & Methods,
   by Edwin P. Norwood, 1931

Ford Model "A" Album,
   by Floyd Clymer and Leslie R. Henry, Clymer Publications, 1960

Ford Model A Restoration Manual,
   Polyprints, Ford Motor Co., 1955

Ford Model T & Model A Buyer's Guide,
   by Paul G. McLaughlin, Motorbooks Int.,1994

Ford News,
   1927 - 1939 issues

Ford Pickup Buyer's Guide,
   by Paul G. McLaughlin, Motorbooks Int., 1991

Ford: The Men And the Machine,
   by Robert Lacey, Little Brown & Co., 1986

Ford Times,
   January 1945, May 1947, May 1953, May 1954, July 1963

Ford Trucks Since 1905,
   by James K. Wagner, Crestline Publishing, 1978

Giant Enterprise,
   by Alfred D. Chandler, Jr., Harcourt, Brace & World, Inc., 1964

GM Passes Ford 1918 - 1938,
   by Arthur J. Kuhn, Pennsylvania State University Press, 1986

Globe-Trotting By Vintage Car,
   by Bevan Sharp, Providence Press, 1988

Grease Rag,
   January 1998

Henry "A" sez...,
   by Gene Patrick

Henry Ford,
   by William Simonds, Bobbs-Merrill Co., 1943

Henry Ford The Wayward Capitalist,
   by Carol Gelderman, St. Martin's Press, 1981

Henry's Fabulous Model "A" Ford,
   by Leslie R. Henry, Clymer Publications, 1959

Henry's Lady,
   by Ray Miller, The Evergreen Press, 1972

Henry's Lieutenants,
   by Ford R. Bryan, Wayne State University Press, 1993

History of Negro Employment at Ford Motor Co. 1914 - 1941,
   unpublished Master's thesis by David L. Lewis, 1954

How To Restore The Model A Ford, published by Floyd Clymer, 1961

I'm Gonna Fix It Up Someday!,
   by Bruce McDougal, The Restorer

Journal of Negro History,
   1947

Know The Ford,
   by Murray Fahnestock, Ford Dealer & Service Field, 1929

Matchless Model A,
   1929 Ford Motor Co. publication, reprint by Dan R. Post, 1961

Mechanix Illustrated,
   November 1968

Michigan History Magazine,
   January-February 1993

Model A/AA Ford Truck Owner,
   by A.G. McMillan, Post Books, 1975

Model A Ford,
   by Floyd Clymer, Clymer Publications, reprint of a 1928 book, undated

Model A Ford Construction Operation Repair,
   by Victor W. Page, Post Books, 1961

Model A Ford Mechanics Handbook,
   by Les Andrews, Cottage Hill Publishing, 1997

Model "A" Ford Restoration & Maintenance Handbook,
   by Paul Moller, SK Publications, 1981

Model A Ford Restoration Handbook,
   by Floyd Clymer, Clymer Publications, undated

Model A Ford Service Bulletins Complete,
   Post Publications, 1957

Model A Ford the Gem from the River Rouge,
   by Murray Fahnestock, Post Books, 1958, revised and retitled in 1975

Model A Judging Standards and Restoration Guidelines,
   jointly published by The Model "A" Restorers Club and the Model A Ford Club of America, 1989, revised 1997

Model "A" Miseries and Cures,
   by Mary Moline, Rumbleseat Press, 1972

Model A Mule,
   by Robert J. Willis, Follett Publishing Co., 1959

Model "A" News,
    published by the Model A Restorers Club, 24800
    Michigan Ave., Dearborn, MI 48124-1713, selected
    issues

Model A Trader,
    1247 Argonne Rd., South Euclid, OH 44121

Motor,
    February 1928; March, April, June 1930; March,
    April, May 1932

Motor Fax Price Bulletin,
    August 1931

Motor Trend,
    August 1962

Moving Forward,
    by Henry Ford in collaboration with Samuel
    Crowther, Doubleday, Doran & Co., 1930

My Forty Years With Ford,
    by Charles E. Sorensen, W.W. Norton & Co., 1956

My Life and Work,
    by Henry Ford in collaboration with Samuel
    Crowther, Garden City Publishing Co., 1922

NADA,
    September/October 1948

New York Times,
    selected issues from 1927, 1928, 1929, 1931

Old Cars Weekly,
    selected issues

Pacific Coast Red Book,
    National Used Car Market Report, Inc., September to
    November 1931

Parade,
    October 10, 1982

Popular Science,
    September 1954

Post Standard,
    Syracuse, New York, September 23, 1933

Practical Information About 1930 and 1931 Coupes - A to Z,
    by Marith McCoul, 1997

Reader's Digest,
    August 1927

Reminisce,
    July-August 1994

Reminiscences,
    Black, Crimmins, Doss, Eagal, Farkas, Hicks, Sheld-
    rick, courtesy Henry Ford Research Center

Restorer's Model A Shop Manual and Supplement
    (published by Motorbooks International) and The AA
    Truck Supplement, by Jim Schild, The Auto Review,
    1998

Road & Track,
    March and April 1988

SAH Journal,
    March-April 1990

Science and Mechanics,
    December 1960

Secrets,
    Secrets of Speed Society, P.O. Box 957436, Hoffman
    Estates, IL 60195-7436, October 1994 and January
    1998

Selling The New Ford,
    by Jim Schild, Second Edition, 1996, The Auto
    Review

Special Interest Autos,
    December 1987

Springfield Daily News,
    December 1, 1927

Station Wagon,
    by Ron Kowalke, Krause Publications, 1998

The "A" Preserver,
    Model A Ford Foundation Inc., P.O. Box 310293,
    New Braunfels, TX 78131-0293

The American Ford,
    by Lorin Sorensen, Silverado Publishing Co., 1975

The American Magazine,
    December 1929

The Automobile Industry,
    by E.D. Kennedy, 1941, Augustus M. Kelley
    Publishers, reprinted 1972

The Best of Ford,
    by Mary Moline, Rumbleseat Press, 1973

The Cars That Henry Ford Built,
    by Beverly Rae Kimes, Princeton Publishing, Inc.
    1978

The Changing U.S. Auto Industry,
    by James M. Rubenstein, Routledge, 1992

The Commercial Fords,
    by Lorin Sorensen, Silverado Publishing Co., 1984

The Country Gentleman,
    September 1929

The Cowtown A,
    March 1987

The Diabolical,
    by H.H. McWilliams, Duckworth, 1934

The European Automobile Industry,
    by James Laux, Twayne Publishers, 1992

The Farmer's Wife,
    August 1929

The Ford Agency,
    by Henry L. Dominguez, Motorbooks International,
    1981

The Ford Dealer News,
    June 4, September 10, October 8, 1927

The Ford Dealer Story,
    50th Anniversary Issue of The Ford Dealer Magazine,
    May-June 1953

The Ford Factory,
    by Lorin Sorensen, Silverado Publications, 1980

The Ford Legend,
    Henry Ford Heritage Association, Spring 1998

The Ford Model "A" As Henry Built It,
    by George DeAngelis, Edward P. Francis, Leslie R.
    Henry, Motor Cities Publishing Co., fourth edition,
    1991

The Ford Shows,
    by Lorin Sorensen, Silverado Publications, 1976

The Fords,
    by Peter Collier and David Horowitz, Summit Books,
    1987

The Gravity Feed,
    July-August 1998

The Herald Journal,
    Shelby, Michigan, August 13, 1998

The Legend of Henry Ford,
    by Keith Sward, Rinehart & Co., 1948

The Most Dangerous Man in Detroit,
    Nelson Lichtenstein, Basic Books, 1995

The New Republic,
    December 14, 1927; March 25, 1931; March 16, 1932

The Open Fords,
    by Lorin Sorensen, Silverado Publications, 1977

The Passenger Car Industry,
    Report of a Survey, The Curtis Publishing Co., 1932

The Public Image of Henry Ford,
    by David L. Lewis, Wayne State University Press,
    1976

The Reckoning,
    by David Halberstam, William Morrow and Co., 1986

The Restorer,
    Model A Ford Club of America, 250 South Cypress
    St., LaHabra, CA 90631-5586 (selected issues)

The Saturday Evening Post,
    July 19, 1930; January 24, 1931

The Tragedy of Henry Ford,
    by Jonathan Norton Leonard, G.P. Putnam's Sons,
    1932

The Triumph Of An Idea,
    by Ralph H. Graves, Doubleday, Doran & Co., 1934

Time,
    August 22, 1927 and December 12, 1927

Tin Lizzie: The Story of the Fabulous Model T Ford,
    by Philip Van Doren Stern, Simon and Schuster, 1955

True's Automobile Yearbook,
    1958 issue

Twenty Years Progress in Commercial Motor Vehicles,
    by Athel F. Denham, Automotive Council For War
    Production, 1942

We Work At Fords,
    UAW-CIO Ford Department, 1955

Index